TWO MEDIEVAL OCCITAN TOLL REGISTERS FROM TARASCON

Medieval Academy Books, No. 115

1. The Royal Castle at Tarascon

Two Medieval Occitan Toll Registers from Tarascon

WILLIAM D. PADEN

Published for the Medieval Academy of America by
UNIVERSITY OF TORONTO PRESS 2016

University of Toronto Press
Toronto Buffalo London
www.utppublishing.com

ISBN 978-1-4426-2934-9

Library and Archives Canada Cataloguing in Publication

Paden, William D. (William Doremus), 1941–, author
Two medieval Occitan toll registers from Tarascon / William D. Paden.

(Medieval Academy books ; no. 115)
Includes bibliographical references and index.
Text in English; includes Occitan texts with English translations.
ISBN 978-1-4426-2934-9 (cloth)

1. Tolls – France – Tarascon (Bouches-du-Rhône) – Registers – Early works to 1800. 2. Transportation – France – Tarascon (Bouches-du-Rhône) – History – To 1500 – Sources. 3. Occitan language – Dialects – France – Tarascon (Bouches-du-Rhône) – History – To 1500 – Sources. 4. Nobility – France – Provence – Economic conditions – Sources. 5. Tarascon (Bouches-du-Rhône, France) – Commerce – History – To 1500 – Sources. 6. Tarascon (Bouches-du-Rhône, France) – Economic conditions – Sources. 7. Tarascon (Bouches-du-Rhône, France) – History – To 1500 – Sources. 8. Provence (France) – Economic policy – History – To 1500 – Sources. I. Title. II. Series: Medieval Academy books ; no. 115

DC801.T18P33 2016 944.9′1 C2015-908365-6

University of Toronto Press acknowledges the financial assistance to its publishing program of the Canada Council for the Arts and the Ontario Arts Council, an agency of the Government of Ontario.

Canada Council for the Arts | Conseil des Arts du Canada

Funded by the Government of Canada | Financé par le gouvernement du Canada

Contents

Illustrations

Figures

Maps

Acknowledgments

My thanks go to Paul Saenger of the Newberry Library and Jeffrey B. Garrett of the Northwestern University Library for arranging the collaboration between their institutions that brought the Newberry-Northwestern manuscript to the Chicago area. Sarah Pritchard of Northwestern and David Spadafora of the Newberry approved the acquisition.

Aldo Bastié, director of the archives of the city of Tarascon, and his assistant Stéphanie Arnaud have been most helpful. Representatives of other libraries and archives in France have been supportive and generous, including Michel Chazottes of the Bibliothèque municipale d'Avignon, Annie Prunet of the Archives de Marseille, Lydie Brailleur of the Archives départementales de Vaucluse (Avignon), and Sophie Barelier of the Archives départementales des Bouches-du-Rhône (Aix).

Michel Hébert of the Université du Québec à Montréal and Richard Kieckhefer of Northwestern provided useful references. The staff of the Interlibrary Loan Service of Northwestern University Library, especially Victoria Zahrobsky, have been tireless and unfailingly good-natured. Raashi Rastogi was an excellent research assistant. Matt Taylor, of the Multimedia Learning Center at Northwestern, provided invaluable help with the visuals, as did Ann Aler, of the Northwestern University Library, with the maps. Lesa Dowd, of conservation services at the Newberry Library, gave me the benefit of her expertise.

The two anonymous readers for Medieval Academy Books made excellent suggestions. Lisa Fagin Davis, executive director of the Medieval Academy of America, and Suzanne Rancourt, executive editor of the University of Toronto Press, have eased the process of publication.

Last and greatest is my gratitude to my wife, Frances Freeman Paden.

Abbreviations

A_1	Latin MS A_1, Aix-en-Provence, A.D. B.d.R., B 169; quoted from Baratier
A_2	Latin MS A_2, Aix-en-Provence, A.D. B.d.R., B 1019; quoted from Martin-Portier 2:41–8 or Delebecque 3:47–59
abl.	ablative
acc.	accusative
A.D.	Archives départementales
adj.	adjective
adv.	adverb
Alcover	Alcover 1968–9, *Diccionari català-valencià-balear*
Alibert	Alibert 1966, *Dictionnaire occitan-français selon les parlers languedociens*
Baratier	Baratier 1969, *Enquêtes sur les droits et revenus de Charles Ier d'Anjou*
Battaglia	Battaglia 1961–2002, *Grande dizionario della lingua italiana*
B.d.R.	Bouches-du-Rhône
B.n.F.	Bibliothèque nationale de France
Bondurand	Bondurand 1890, "Les Péages de Tarascon"
Cat.	Catalan
Corominas	Corominas and Pascual 1980–91, *Diccionário crítico eti mológico castellano e hispánico*
DAO	Baldinger and Popelar 1975–, *Dictionnaire onomasiologique de l'ancien occitan*
DAOS	*DAO Supplément*, 1980–
Delebecque	Delebecque 1929a, "Histoire de la ville de Tarascon depuis les origines jusqu'à l'avènement de la reine Jeanne (1343)" (dissertation)

Du Cange	Du Cange 1883–7, *Glossarium mediæ et infimæ latinitatis*
Edler	Edler 1934, *Glossary of Mediaeval Terms of Business, Italian Series, 1200–1600*
Eng.	English
Faraudo	Faraudo de Saint-Germain, under construction, *Vocabulari de la llengua catalana medieval*
fem.	feminine
Fennis	Fennis 1995, *Trésor du langage des galères*
FEW	Wartburg 1928–, *Französisches etymologisches Wörterbuch*
Fr.	French
fut.	future
Ger.	German
Godefroy	Godefroy 1881–1969, *Dictionnaire de l'ancienne langue française*
Guérard	Guérard, Wailly, and Delisle 1857, *Cartulaire de l'abbaye de Saint-Victor de Marseille*
hhd	hogshead
Honnorat	Honnorat 1846–7, *Dictionnaire provençal-français*
imperf.	imperfect
indic.	indicative
It.	Italian
Jal	Jal 1848, *Glossaire nautique*
Lat.	Latin
Littré	Littré 2010, *Dictionnaire de la langue française*
LR	Raynouard 1844, *Lexique roman*
Martin-Portier	Martin-Portier 2006, "Les enquêtes domaniales des comtes de Provence"
masc.	masculine
Med.	Medieval
Mistral	Mistral 1879–87, *Lou trésor dóu Felibrige*
Mod.	Modern
MS, MSS	manuscript(s)
N	Occitan MS N, Newberry Library (Chicago)/Northwestern University (Evanston) MS 1; Newberry Library, Vault Case MS 220
n.	noun
n.f.	noun, feminine
Niermeyer	Niermeyer and van de Kieft 2002, *Mediae Latinitatis lexicon minus*

n.m. noun, masculine
nom. nominative
OCat. Old Catalan
Occ. Occitan
OED *Oxford English Dictionary*, 1992
OFr. Old French
OLD *Oxford Latin Dictionary*, 2012
om. omitted
P Latin MS P, Paris, B.n.F., lat. 10125; quoted from Guérard 1:lxxiii–c
Pansier Pansier 1924–32, *Histoire de la langue provençale à Avignon*
part. participle
PC Pillet and Carstens 1933, *Bibliographie der Troubadours*
PD Levy 1909, *Petit dictionnaire provençal-français*
pers. person of a verb (1st, 2nd, 3rd)
pl. plural
pres. present
pret. preterite
sg. singular
Sp. Spanish
subj. subjunctive
SW Levy 1894–1924, *Provenzalisches Supplement-Wörterbuch*
T Occitan MS T, Tarascon, Archives municipales, AA9, f. 3r–17r; edited by Bondurand and here, consulted directly and in digital images
TL Tobler and Lommatzsch 1925–, *Tobler-Lommatzsch Altfranzösisches Wörterbuch*
TLFi *Trésor de la langue française informatisé*
vb. verb

TWO MEDIEVAL OCCITAN TOLL REGISTERS FROM TARASCON

Introduction

The *Livre rouge* of Tarascon, the municipal cartulary preserved in the town's archive, contains among many other things a toll register written in Occitan. This register was published in 1890 by Édouard Bondurand, the archivist of the neighbouring department of the Gard. Although his edition has been found useful for studies of history and language, it has shortcomings: some of the readings and glosses are inaccurate; the transcription is incomplete, lacking two tables that Bondurand omitted because, as he said, he found them uninteresting; the edition does not communicate the layout of the manuscript.[1] Most importantly, faced with a source lacking any direct indication of its own chronology, Bondurand provided no cogent analysis of its date other than that of the *Livre rouge*, which he said was written in the fifteenth century. He assigned the composition of the register to the thirteenth or fourteenth century, and most later scholars have followed him.[2] One put it as early as the twelfth.[3] Another dated the *Livre rouge* to the sixteenth century, which is when the latest entries (not including the register) were made.[4] No reliable consensus on the date of the register has emerged.

A second, later Occitan register became accessible in 2011, when it was purchased jointly by the Newberry Library and Northwestern University. Formerly in private hands, this manuscript has not been published before. It is not merely another version of the text contained in the register still in Tarascon, but an independent source that sheds valuable light on its predecessor.

The contrast between the earlier and later versions, between before and after, makes it possible to perceive both these documents in terms of historical change. By relating them to their Latin predecessors, we can study the history of tolls at Tarascon over three centuries. Sometimes regarded as static, this history turns out to be marked by constant change that reflects larger issues in economic history and history in general. The vernacular registers themselves provide new linguistic information on a host of words. They can help us understand the language and history of medieval Tarascon and Provence.

1. Manuscripts

The register in Tarascon (here MS T) is contained in the *Livre rouge* in the Archives municipales. The volume has the call number AA9, and the register occupies folios 3–17. In an inventory published anonymously and without date, but which must have appeared in 1865–7, Paul Meyer described the *Livre rouge* and gave the dates of the earliest and latest documents in it, ranging from 1168 to 1535.[5] The young philologist had submitted a more expansive text of the inventory; when he realized that the Ministère de l'intérieur had mutilated his work in the version it published, he wrote an angry article in which he summarized his demonstration that the older part of AA9, containing the register of tolls, was written about 1438, and the rest at the end of the fifteenth century and in the sixteenth.[6] These conclusions were repeated in a new inventory completed by the Archives municipales in 2009.[7]

The register at the Newberry Library was acquired as a joint purchase with Northwestern University in 2011. It is Newberry Library/Northwestern University MS 1 (here MS N), and its call number at the Newberry is Vault Case MS 220. The Newberry catalogue dates the manuscript between 1385 and 1400, following a suggestion by the dealer that sold it.[8] We shall revise this conclusion below.

A third register of tolls from Tarascon, also written in Occitan, was described by Meyer in 1864 and mentioned by him in a review of Bondurand's edition of MS T.[9] It had the call number CC9 in the Archives municipales; Meyer dated it to the fifteenth century.[10] Unfortunately this manuscript has been lost. Its incipit was *Sec s'en lo registre du peage de Tharascon translatat de ebrayc en romans per Ferrer Vidas Jusieu, loqual avia de sos predecessors anciens exactors du dit péage*,[11] "Here follows the register of the tollhouse of Tarascon, translated from Hebrew into Occitan by Ferrer Vidas, a Jew, which he got from his predecessors, the former collectors of the said toll." In the review Meyer pointed out that Bondurand had overlooked this resource, which could have provided "les éléments nécessaires pour corriger et interpréter le texte souvent obscur qu'il a publié."[12] However, Kahn reported in 1899 that he had been unable to find manuscript CC9 in the Archives.[13] The inventory of 2009 does not mention it, and I have been informed by the administration of the Archives in 2013 that it cannot be found today.[14] According to Meyer's description, register CC9 differed from MS N in respect to several details, so any thought that they were one and the same can be dismissed.[15] The usefulness that CC9 could have had in helping us to understand tolls at Tarascon falls to the Newberry-Northwestern manuscript.

Latin sources provide a mass of additional information about tolls charged at Tarascon. Several have been published, including two that derive from an investigation of the revenues of the county of Provence made for the count, Charles I, in 1252. One of these is Aix, A.D. B.d.R., B 169 (here MS A_1); its editor, Baratier, dated the hand to the second half of the thirteenth century.[16] The other is Paris, B.n.F., lat. 10125 (here MS P), titled the *Terrier du comté de Provence*, or "Register of landed property of the county of Provence." Its editor, Guérard, dated it to the mid-thirteenth century, but according to Baratier the hand is rather from the end of the century.[17] A second investigation was made for Charles II in 1298. It is contained in Aix, A.D., B.d.R., B 1021 (here MS A_2). The passage concerning Tarascon was edited by Martin-Portier (2006).[18] A third investigation, made for Robert I in 1332 and contained in Aix, A.D., B.d.R., B 1060 and B 1061, has been studied and edited by Martin-Portier (2006) and by Pécout and Portier-Martin (2010). These thirteenth- and fourteenth-century Latin sources will provide context for the present study of the registers in Occitan.

In his edition of MS A_1, Baratier introduced other documents bearing upon tolls at Tarascon. In a monumental survey of medieval sources of economic and social history of Provence, Bautier and Sornay listed yet more witnesses.[19] Additional documents from before the sixteenth century that bear in some way upon my subject include the following nine.

- 1246 and fourteenth century. Aix, A.D., B.d.R., B 2 (*reg. Pergamenorum*), ff. 49r (fourteenth-century copy of a passage from an investigation concerning Orgon and its toll, dated 1246), 57v (toll at Saint-Gabriel), 59r–61r (investigation of the *viguerie* of Tarascon).[20]
- 1250 circa (mid-thirteenth century). Aix, A.D., B.d.R., B 143 (*reg. Pedis*), ff. 86v–90r. Fragment concerning tolls at Saint-Gabriel and elsewhere.[21]
- 1308–66. Aix, A.D., B.d.R., B 1152, ff. 20r–25v. Investigation of tolls at Tarascon, Orgon, Saint-Gabriel, and elsewhere.[22]
- 1334. Aix, A.D., B.d.R., B 1469 (3), ff. 85r–91r. Investigation of tolls at Tarascon.[23]
- 1349 circa (?). Aix, A.D., B.d.R., B 1477 (16), ff. 1r–2r. Evaluation of royal revenues, including tolls at Tarascon and elsewhere.[24]
- 1350 circa (mid-fourteenth century). Aix, A.D., B.d.R., B 170. Baratier's MS N, which he describes as a poor copy of A.D., B.d.R., B 169 (here MS A_1), the subject of his edition.[25]

- 1366–81. Aix, A.D., B.d.R., B 1153, ff. 67r–70r. Investigation of abuses committed in collecting tolls in Provence and elsewhere.[26]
- 1400–99 (fifteenth century). Avignon, A.D., Vaucluse, 1 J 163, ff. 46r–54v. Investigation of tolls along the Rhône; declaration of tolls paid to the king upstream and downstream from Pont-Saint-Esprit.[27]
- 1490 circa (end of fifteenth century). Avignon, Bibliothèque municipale, 1755, ff. 1r–17v. Register (*tarif*) of the toll at Tarascon and headings of this toll.[28]

All of these documents are written in Latin.[29] They make clear that the Occitan registers did not exist in a vacuum but in a context in which numerous manuscripts were drawn up concerning tolls at Tarascon, most of them in Latin, at least one in Hebrew, and some in the vernacular, including an Occitan translation from Hebrew (the lost register CC9). Pending the labour of scholars who will make all this material more accessible, this book will examine the known sources in Occitan.

2. Chronology

MS T was copied into the *Livre rouge* about 1438, as we know from Meyer. The palaeographic evidence suggests that MS N is contemporary: its body and headings were written in the second quarter of the fifteenth century using Gothic *textualis media*. The mirror image of a pastedown in the inside front cover was written a little earlier, in the first quarter of the century, using Gothic *cursiva formata*.[30]

The composition of the texts transmitted in the MSS can be dated by more indirect means. They must have been written after 1252, when Charles I commissioned the first investigation of comital revenues. That investigation said nothing about quicksilver or verdigris, according to the Latin sources (MSS A_1P); the investigation of 1298 (MS A_2) mentioned neither; but MS T brings up quicksilver, and both T and N refer to verdigris.[31] So we may conjecture that they were written after 1298, which puts them both roughly in the fourteenth century or the first half of the fifteenth.

Both vernacular registers refer to the ruler of Sicily and Provence as *rey*, "king," which would have been contrary to decorum when the monarch was a queen. This was the case from 1343 to 1382, the reign of Joan I.[32] From 1343 to 1349 Joan ruled alone as queen of Naples and countess of Provence and Forcalquier, and claimed the crowns of Jerusalem and Sicily; from 1349 to 1362 she ruled jointly with her husband, Louis I; from 1362 to 1382 she ruled alone once more as a widow. Her coins are inscribed in her own name in the first and third of these periods; in the second they bear the names of Louis and Joan.[33] Some coins from the last period portray the queen's head and shoulders, or depict her standing or sitting.[34] At some time between 1366 and 1381 she was referred to in public debate as *domine nostre regine*, "our lady queen."[35] Joan's subjects were well aware that she was not a king. It follows that the texts of the Occitan registers must have been originally composed either before Joan's reign or after it.

MS N contains a historical anecdote from 1325 about a ship that posed a problem for the tollkeepers since it was carrying ashes, and no toll on ashes was specified in the register; the king decided that the ship must pay as though it were carrying lime or gypsum (N12v24). The king at this time was Robert d'Anjou (ruled 1309–43), the son of Charles II. Although the point may have been the principle of analogy as much as this specific toll, it seems unlikely that a register could have been drawn up after Robert's decision that did not mention ashes. Therefore, since ashes (*cendres*, *sendres*) are not mentioned in MS T, we may narrow the range for the composition of its text to 1298–1325, the first quarter of the fourteenth century, well before the reign of Joan I.

The text in MS N was evidently written after 1325. Unlike MS T, MS N refers to the coin called the *coronat*, first minted in 1330,[36] and the *patac*, introduced in 1339.[37] Since the period 1339–43 is a narrow window, it seems likely that the text in MS N was written after the reign of Joan. We can push its composition a few years further forward in view of the tangled affairs of Tarascon and Provence in the years after Joan died. Childless, she had named her cousin Charles de Duras (or Durazzo; the title refers to Durrës in Albania) as her successor in 1370, but replaced him in 1380 by adopting Louis of Anjou, a son of Jean le Bon, the king of France. In 1381 the disinherited Charles took Joan prisoner in Naples, which he controlled even though Louis had the title of king. In 1382 Joan was assassinated in Charles's prison. A confederation of cities in Provence including Tarascon formed the Union of Aix (1382–7) in support of Charles and defiance of Louis.[38] In 1384 Louis I died, leaving his son Louis II, who was proclaimed king of Sicily. Tarascon swore homage to Charles de Duras in 1385,[39] but after he died the next year, a prisoner in Hungary, and after prolonged hesitation, the town submitted to Louis II in December 1387; it was among the last cities in the Union to do so.[40] It seems unlikely that MS N could have referred imperturbably, as it does, to the major share of the king in revenues from tolls during the tumultuous years when Tarascon was in open rebellion against Louis I and then Louis II.[41] By this argument the text in MS N must have been composed after the Union of Aix, that is, after 1387, and before the manuscript was written circa 1425–50. It was, then, more likely written in the early fifteenth century than the late fourteenth.

The proposals made here are not categorical; they involve inferences, arguments from silence, approximations, and speculation. Nevertheless they seem plausible. They lead to coherent conclusions that place the composition of the text transmitted by MS T in the first quarter of the fourteenth century, and that of MS N at the end of that century or the first half of the next. Study of the Italianisms in MS T (§3) will be consistent with the view that the first text was written in the early fourteenth century. Study of the tolls (§5) will support the view that the two vernacular registers were composed quite a few years apart, and quite a few years after the ones in Latin. It is a fact that the three Latin sources date from the thirteenth century; MS T dates in all probability from the early fourteenth century; although it is not so certain, MS N may well date from the early fifteenth.

The tradition worked by accretion and reduction of specific elements. Already in 1252, Sir Pons de Prato was invoked for his authority as a former tollkeeper.[42] His name did not appear in the investigation from 1298, but reappeared in MS T (T14r3) only to disappear again in MS N. Quicksilver and verdigris were overlooked in 1252 and 1298, but quicksilver was picked up in MS T, and both were mentioned in MS N. The decision regarding ashes in 1325 is recorded in MS N. Members of the Alba family are mentioned as shareholders in 1298 (*domina Elys*, MS A_2), early in the following century (*Johan Alba*, MS T), and in the one after that (both *ma dama Elis* and *Johan Alba*, MS N). The discontinuities in the tradition – Pons de Prato omitted in MS A_2, Lady Elys and the bridge omitted in MS T, all three to reappear at the following stage – reveal the complexity of its intertwined strands.[43]

3. Language

The two Occitan registers exhibit linguistic features that set them apart, some involving languages or dialects that influenced their composition and others that imply a chronological difference within the development of Occitan. The latter features are delicate to judge because they could be dialectal; two dialects, like two languages (such as French and Italian), may be more or less innovative, and so appear to be later or earlier, although they are actually contemporary. It appears, though, that the language of MS T is earlier than that of MS N. Analysis of their language supports the conclusions reached above concerning their relative chronology.

MS T is marked by Italianisms of various kinds that accumulate into a strong effect, although each one of them is scattered. Certain final vowels remain, as in Italian but not in Occitan: final *-o* in Italian *argento vivo*, *cento*, and *uno* (Occitan *argent viu*, *cent*, *un*), final *-e* in *avalle* (Occitan *aval*), *parte*

(Occitan *part*), *vernice* (Occitan *vernis*).[44] An unstressed vowel in the penult remains in *vendere* (Occitan *vendre*). Intervocalic *t* remains in *partita* and *travata* but was voiced to *d* in Occitan *partida, travada.* In conjugation, a persistent trait is use of Italian *prende*, the third-person singular, present, of *prendre*, "to take," beside Occitan *pren*; *prende* occurs nine times and *pren* twice. The third-person singular present of *eser*, Occitan *es*, turns up as Italian *e* (modern *è*). Imperfect *faccia* (stressed *faccía*) shows the Italian root, as in modern *faceva*, but with a different ending. Lexical items are *çafarame*, "saffron" (Occitan *safran*), *ma*, "but" (Occitan *mais*), and *piatta*, "plate" (Occitan *plat*). Orthographic items are *che* (Occitan *que*) and *qualche* (Occitan *qualque, calque*). MS N, in contrast, has no certain Italianisms; the only possibility is the noun *ful*, perhaps meaning "purse," like Italian *folle*. The occasional form of the numeral 4 with *-o* (*iiij*°, *.iiij.*°) may represent Italian *quattro*. (Roman numerals such as *xvij*, "seventeen," *xiiij*, "fourteen," and so on, usually occur without the final vowel.) In the margin of MS N we find *monede*, an Italian plural of *moneda*, "currency" (Occitan plural *monedas*).[45] The material support of MS N, its parchment, is of a fine quality that suggests it may have been made in Italy.[46]

Taken together, the Italianisms in MS T occur on eleven of its sixteen folios. The strong Italian influence in this manuscript, containing a text that, as we have argued, was in all probability composed after 1298 and before 1325, corresponds to the first years when the pope moved from Rome to Avignon, as Clement V did in 1309, followed after his death in 1314 by John XXII (1316–34). The Curia had begun to arrive in 1308, soon followed by a colony of merchants who crossed the Alps and made Avignon the capital of European banking; among them was the father of Petrarch, who came in 1311.[47] After Gregory XI returned the papacy to Rome in 1377, Italian merchants must have begun to return home. The municipal archives of Avignon contain documents in Italian from the fourteenth century but none from the fifteenth.[48] With its telling Italianisms, MS T reflects the influx of Italian merchants in Avignon and nearby cities early in the fourteenth century. Early in the fifteenth, the waning Italian presence left MS N nearly untouched.

Another contrast with chronological implications is the simplification of the final cluster *-tz* in the plural of past participles, nouns, and so on, by reduction of the *t*, producing the ending *-s*. The most common type, which is *-átz*, continued to be stressed as it had been before the simplification (*-ás*), in contrast to unstressed *-as* in the plural of feminine nouns. The earlier form, *-átz*, occurs only in T; the later form, *-ás*, occurs only in N. Examples of *-átz*, all in T, are *adobatz, brocatz, prelatz, privatz, quairatz*, and *tiratz*. Examples of *-ás* as the plural of *-át*, all in N, are *adobas* (plural of *adobat*), *blas* (plural of *blat*), *cairas* (plural of *cairat*), *coronas* (plural of *coronat*, a coin, in the phrase *los coronás*), and *salas* (plural of *salat*, used in *porcs salás*, salted pigs; that is, salt pork). Less frequently we find the same development after other vowels.[49]

An Occitan dialectal feature in MS T is the definite article in the form *lu*, which occurs thirteen times as the masculine plural, all in Table T1 (f. 10r–10v), and three times as the singular (f. 12r–12v). These forms occur in various dialects of Modern Occitan, the singular less widely than the plural; the most likely source of the forms in the registers is perhaps Nice, which was linked commercially to Genoa and Corsica.[50] This evidence suggests two things. It implies that the composition of the text in MS T included a distinct dialectal source, at least for certain passages. And it suggests, since there is no trace of *lu* in MS N, either that such traces in the tradition were corrected in successive versions, or, as seems more likely, that there was no direct transmission from MS T to MS N, rather that N sprang from a different node in the transmission than the one that produced T. The latter implication may also be drawn, all the more strongly, from the more widespread evidence of the Italianisms in T. The broad flow of traditional discourse about these tolls certainly included both T and N, but more specific textual continuities within that broad flow must have been independent, braided strands. The strand that produced T did not continue in the form of N. The two documents represent distinct strands in the tradition.[51]

MS N shows two forms of dialect influence pointing towards the modern department of the Hautes-Alpes. Feminine nouns ending in *-a* in the singular, and normally *-as* in the plural, sometimes show plurals in *-es* in MS N: *avelanes*, *canes*, *cordes*, *faves*, *persegues/pesseges*, *totas vegades*, whereas T has *avellanas*, *cannas*, *cordas*, and *perseguas*. Ronjat found this ending in modern speech around Briançon and Embrun.[52] The masculine plural personal pronoun, normally *els*, "them," sometimes has *elos*, and the demonstrative adjective, normally *aquels*, "those," occasionally has *aquellos*. Ronjat found such forms in the Hautes-Alpes.[53] Although these phenomena are not frequent (seven cases of feminine plural *-es*, two of *elos*, four of *aquelos/aquellos*), they suggest a possible role of speech from the Hautes-Alpes in the tradition that produced N, in contrast to the possible influence of dialect from Nice in T.

The word *pezage*, "toll, tollhouse," which is central to the purpose of the registers, occurs eighty-five times in MSS TN. Its manifestations in the two manuscripts involve both chronological and dialectal factors. It occurs in forms that illustrate two phases in lenition, which is the gradual reduction and eventual effacement of a single consonant between vowels.[54] The intervocalic [d] in the etymon, Latin *pedaticum*, has become [z][55] in twenty-eight occurrences, all in T; the sound is spelled *z* or *s* (*pezage*, *pezag*, *pesage*). These forms predominate in T, but there is another type, represented seven times in T, showing the subsequent stage of lenition in which the [z] is effaced (*peage*, *piage*, *piag*). MS N has no occurrence of the form with [z]; all fifty cases in N show disappearance of this consonant (*peage*, *peages*). For the word *pezagier*, "tollkeeper," too, MS T has both types (*pezagier*, *peagier*), while MS N has only the form showing effacement (*peagier*, *peagiers*). Ronjat found the change to [z] widespread, but reduction to zero in modern Alpine dialects including the departments of Alpes-Maritimes and Hautes-Alpes, which recalls the possible origin in these same areas of the feminine plurals in *-es* and the pronoun *elos*.[56] *Pezage* and *pezagier* provide strong evidence that MS N, compared to MS T, shows effects of either a later phase or a different dialect – or a later, different dialect – in the evolution of the language.

Corresponding to the frequent Italianisms in T, a handful of French and Catalan or Spanish forms occur in N. French influence appears in the vowel of *jour* (normal Occitan *jor*) and *tout* (normal *tot*), the consonant *f* in *totas fes* (cf. French *fois*, Occitan *vetz*), and the suffix of *montaison*, in contrast to the normal Occitan suffix in *montazon* (MS T). Catalan or Spanish provides the plural *tornesos*, "tournois" (a coin), in contrast to singular *tornes*, the normal Occitan plural *tornes*, and the variant plural *torneses*, made perceptible by insertion of the support vowel.

Bondurand suggested another linguistic argument, alleging that a "grand nombre de mots" in T shows "archaïsme."[57] He adduced seven words: *albire*, "judgment"; *linh*, "rowing ship"; *pertegua*, "pole"; *razis*, "root"; *romieu*, "pilgrim"; *Sant Jacme*, "Santiago"; and *solpre*, "sulfur." He provided no evidence that these words are archaic. Four of them – *razis*, *romieu*, *Sant Jacme*, and *solpre* – occur in N as well as T. Convenient information about the dates of words in the Occitan of Avignon is available from Pansier, who provided the year of attestations in his lexicon.[58] That lexicon includes five of Bondurand's seven words; four are attested in the fourteenth century and one in the late thirteenth.[59] This is not strong evidence – the single year of each attestation does not limit usage of the term to that year – but it seems to confirm, for what it is worth, that MS T was written in the fourteenth century. If we consider all the words in the glossary of this book that are also included by Pansier, we find the bulk of them attested in the fourteenth century. Focusing on the words in each register that do not occur in the other one, we find that Pansier's attestations place fourteen words that occur only in T in the fifteenth century, but forty-one words that occur only in N in that period.[60] This observation supports the view that N was written later than T.

We have distinguished the language of the two registers in terms of influence from Italian (T) or other languages (N); dialectal features, perhaps from Nice (T) or the Alps (N); and their position in the evolution of Occitan, earlier (T) or later (N).[61] Together with the arguments we made before, they suggest that the texts contained in these manuscripts were composed, perhaps, about a century apart, one in the early fourteenth century (T) and the other in the early fifteenth (N).

4. Description of Manuscripts T and N

4.1. Appearance

The Tarascon manuscript of the register is one part of a large book called the *Livre rouge*, a compendium of texts from the history of the town that contains materials written from the twelfth century to the sixteenth, and runs to 411 folios in 18 quires. The first quire is 18 folios long. The register occupies 15 of these folios, from 3r to 17v.[62] The page measures 29.6 × 21 centimetres. In the register the written rectangle measures 23 by 14 centimetres,[63] so its area is 322 square centimetres.

The Newberry/Northwestern manuscript is a freestanding codex that comprises two quires of eight folios apiece. The page measures 19 by 13.5 centimetres; each dimension is about two-thirds as large as the corresponding one in MS T. The written rectangle is 11.5 by 8.3 centimetres, so its area is 95.45 square centimetres, less than one third the written area on each page in MS T.

Both manuscripts use black or brown ink for the body of the text and red for the rubrics. In the tabular format of MS T, major sections are marked by initial capital letters in red, decorated with black fine-line ornaments extending up and down the margin. Minor sections are often marked by red pilcrows (¶). Within minor sections, individual items are written flush left; when the toll is added flush right, the space between item and toll may be filled with a leader in red.[64] Occasionally the initials of items are ticked in red (ff. 3v, 10r1–11v21). The text is sometimes displayed in multiple columns.[65] The first page of MS T (f. 3r) is decorated with an extensive mat of black fine-line curlicues that covers the margins on all four sides. On f. 15r, the ornaments around an initial letter produce caricatures of a face and a bird.

MS N adds a third ink that is blue. In MS N's paragraph format, the initial capitals of the first two paragraphs use both red and blue; after that, the initials alternate colour, first blue, then red, with occasional exceptions.[66] Tolls are written within the prose paragraph; they are not positioned flush right, and there are no leaders.

4.2. Content

The contents of the two manuscripts differ, as may be seen in this outline of their rubrics (the numbering of which is editorial):

Rubrics

MS T	**MS N**
I. Tolls at Tarascon and Lubières Commodities	I. John 1:1–14
II. Tolls at Tarascon and Lubières Salt	II. Tolls at Tarascon and Lubières Salt: Tolls, Shares (Tables N1, N2)
III. Tolls at Tarascon and Lubières Salt: Tolls, Shares (Table T1)	III. Tolls at Tarascon and Lubières Commodities
IV. Tolls at Lubières: Commodities	IV. Exempt Items
V. Tolls at the Gates of Tarascon Commodities	V. Currencies
VI. Tolls at Saint-Gabriel Commodities	VI. Tolls at the Gate of Tarascon Commodities, including Salt
VII. *Montazon* at Tarascon, First Version Salt (Table T2)	VII. Tolls at Saint-Gabriel Commodities
VIII. *Montazon* at Tarascon, Second Version Salt (Table T3)	

The two manuscripts have much in common and much that sets them apart. Rubrics common to both are the toll on commodities at Tarascon (T I, N III), the toll on salt (T II, N II), the shares in the toll on salt (T III, N II), the toll at the Gates or Gate of Tarascon (T V, N VI), and the toll at Saint-Gabriel (T VI, N VII). But three of the rubrics in T (IV, VII, VIII) are absent from N, and three rubrics in N (I, IV, V) are lacking in T. Some of these absent materials are contained less conspicuously within the texts.[67] Lubières is bundled with Tarascon in both manuscripts (T I–III, N II–III), but also appears in a separate rubric in T.[68] Nothing in T corresponds to the biblical text from John that begins MS N. The items that were exempt from toll, with a rubric in N (IV: *causas ... francas*), are grouped with commodities in T (I), using different words (*non donan peage*). The sections on currencies in N (all of V, the last part of VII, brief mention in II at the start of Table N2) correspond to nothing in T.

Under each rubric commodities tend to be grouped primarily by toll, but also by type. The dominant pattern, subject to exceptions, proceeds by toll in descending amounts:

Commodities

Tarascon and Lubières

MS T, Rubric I	**MS N, Rubric III**
29.5d (cloth, etc.)	30.5d (cloth, etc.)
21d (wool, etc.)	19d (wool, etc.)
16d (woad)	fabrics, leather
fabrics, leather	14d (woad)
11d (tartar, etc.)	9d (grease, tiles, etc.)
9d (tiles)	9.5d (grain)
9.5d, etc. (grain)	6d (lead, alum, wine; also payment in kind)
6d (wine; also payment in kind)	77d (sumach)
77d (sumach)	18d (materials: rocks, lime, etc.)
6d (lead)	live cargo (horses, large animals, travellers)
wood and wood products	wood and wood products
4d or 3d (domestic objects: tiles, etc.)	4d, etc. (domestic objects, foods)
4.5d to 0.5d (foods: almonds, etc.)	
18d or payment in kind (materials: glass, lime, etc.)	
exemptions	
live cargo (horses, travellers, large animals)	
arribage, a fee for unloading	

Contrariwise, for salt the toll is given going up from one to 40 hogsheads in T. N goes up from one to 40 small hogsheads, then up from one large hogshead to 14:

Salt

Tarascon, Lubières, and the *Peage dels Mujolans* (T) or *dels Violans* (N)[69]

MS T, Rubrics II, III	**MS N, Rubric II**
29.75d per hogshead (II)	29.75d per small hogshead
29.25d for one hogshead (III)	29.75d for one small hogshead

up to £4 13s 10d for forty hogsheads	up to £4 13s 10d for forty small hogsheads
salt loaded at Beaucaire	salt loaded at Beaucaire
salt unloaded at Beaucaire	salt unloaded at Beaucaire
	6s 8d (152d) for one large hogshead
	up to £4 13s 4d for fourteen large hhds
	salt loaded in large hhds at Beaucaire
	salt unloaded in large hhds at Beaucaire
	salt unloaded in large hhds at Tarascon
	salt loaded in large hhds at Beaucaire or Tarascon

The registers for the Gates or Gate of Tarascon and for Saint-Gabriel mention salt carried by animals, not shipped, since these tollhouses were not located on the Rhône. Their schedules for commodities are briefer:

Commodities

Gates (T) or Gate (N) of Tarascon

MS T, Rubric V	**MS N, Rubric VI**
26d (cloth, etc.)	26.5d (cloth, etc.)
19d (oil, etc.)	18d (wool, etc.)
6d (lead)	8d (tartar, alum, etc.)
2d (salt carried by animals)	4d (grain)
4d to 0.5d (food, domestic objects)	6d (lead)
exemption	2d (salt carried by animals)
	4d to 0.5d (food)
	exemptions

Saint-Gabriel

MS T, Rubric VI	**MS N, Rubric VII**
13d (oil, etc.)	13d (oil, etc.)
26d (cloth, etc.)	26d (cloth, etc.)
	as at Gate of Tarascon (other small things)

Looking over these summaries, one observes extensive unanimity between the two manuscripts. In many cases the amounts in the two registers are the

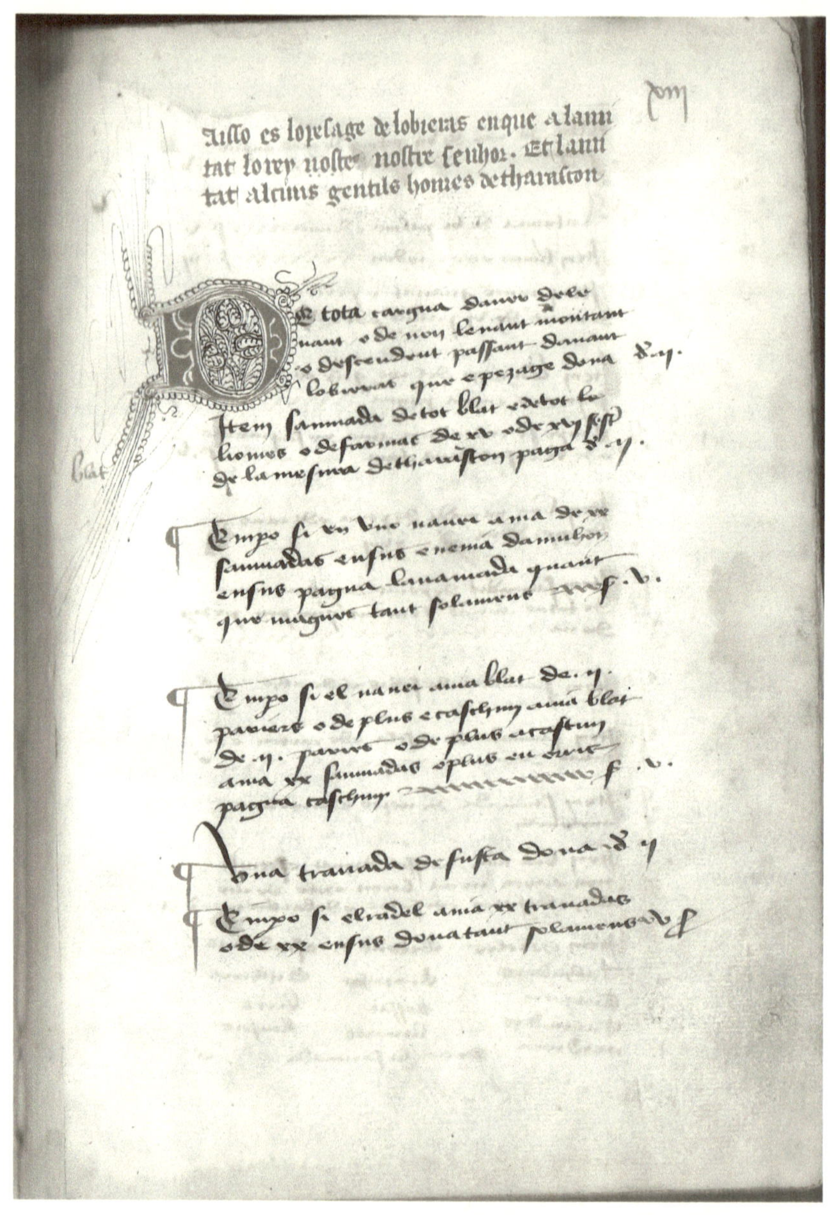

2. MS T, folio 13r. Tarascon, Archives municipales, AA9

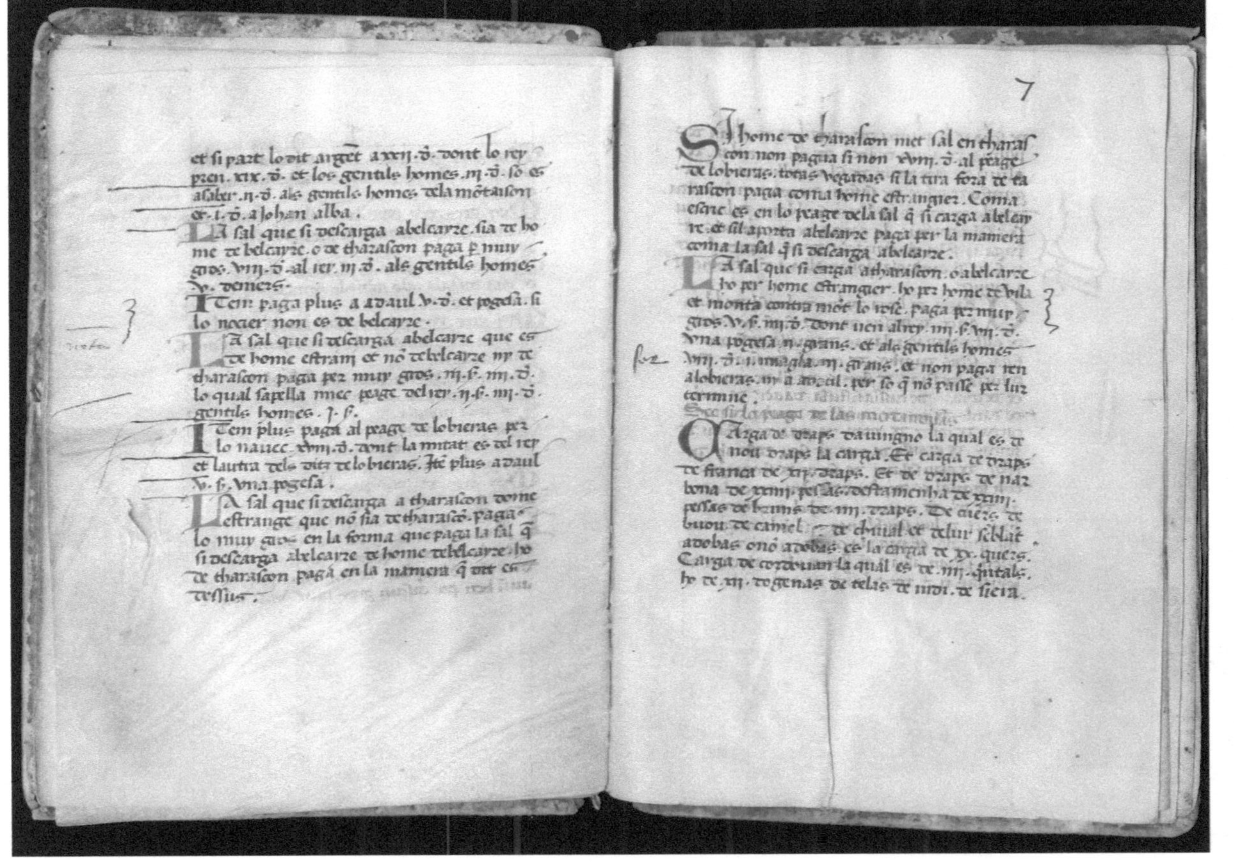

3. MS N, folio 7r. The Newberry Library, Chicago. Vault Case MS 220

same, most conspicuously in regard to salt, with its steady rate of 29.75d per hogshead or small hogshead; the second statement in T, 29.25d, looks suspiciously like a scribal error. Some tolls went up: for commodities at Tarascon and Lubières, the highest toll (for cloth and so on) went up by one denier from 29.5d to 30.5d, and at the Gates or Gate of Tarascon, by one obole from 26d to 26.5d. Among the following tolls on commodities, several went down, for example at Tarascon from 21d on wool, etc., to 19d, and at the Gates or Gate of Tarascon, from 19d to 18d. For the few tolls on commodities at Saint-Gabriel there was no change. We shall investigate changes in the registers further in §6 below.

4.3. Layout

The layouts in the two registers differ. T is tabular, while N is written in paragraphs. T shows a strong, though not constant, tendency to give each item a line, with the text on the left, the toll justified right, and a leader between them consisting of ornamental red strokes or a red line. The result is highly accessible: the eye easily picks out each item on the left and scans the tolls down the right. T is not ruled, and its use of vertical space is irregular; the number of lines on a page, including blank spaces roughly equivalent to one line or more, varies from 22 (f. 9r) to 42 (f. 5r). N is ruled with 25 lines on each page.

T looks like a register or a schedule, while N looks like prose. The layout of T is more pragmatic, that of N more aesthetic. T might have been conceived to be useful to a tollkeeper; N, to be pleasing to a shareholder.[70]

4.4. Purposes

4.4.1. INSTRUCTION

Although both registers are generally couched in indicative language that simply states, for the benefit of anyone concerned, that a certain commodity pays a certain toll, occasional variations make clear that all such statements are directed in part specifically to the tollkeeper, instructing him in his duty. The tollkeeper is told, "You must understand" (*deves entendre*, T15r2) how to apply the rules. He is told that the register for the Gate of Tarascon must be considered (*sia esgardada*, T15v2) in relation to tolls at Saint-Gabriel – that is, he must consider it in that light. The corresponding passage in MS N uses imperative forms directed to the tollkeeper: "Look at" (*regarda*, N16r4) the register for the Gate, and "Levy" (*leva*, N16r6) the toll at Saint-Gabriel accordingly. To determine the toll on a round tree, the keeper is instructed to measure it one-third of the way up from the root: *Tout arbre redon si deu mesurar al ters sotterran de la rais*, "Any round tree must be measured one-third up from the root" (N10v1–2). The same thought is expressed more simply in MS T, and the effect of instruction is minimized but still implicit: *Albre de nau que es de vij palms o de plus de gros, a la tersa part de l'abre dos la razis ...*, "A ship's mast that is seven palms or more around, [measured] one-third [of the way] up the tree from the root ..." (T5r[33]). Both registers explain carefully how many pieces of various woods make a *travada*, here translated as "stack" (T5v33–6r9, N11r17–11v4), information that was of interest to all concerned but essential to the tollkeeper's competence. In fact every toll, on every commodity, was equally important to the tollkeeper. The registers may be regarded, among other things, as memoranda of the manifold duties that constituted his office.

4.4.2. REVISION

We have already touched on one purpose of MS N: to update the tolls that had changed, and, by contrast, to restate those that had not. The all-important toll on salt remained stable, with identical tolls for one hogshead in T and one small hogshead in N, as for 40 units in both MSS; but MS N introduced a new measurement, the large hogshead, which must have reflected a change in shipping.[71] The lead-off toll in MS T, the highest toll for commodities (cloth, etc.), rose by 1d in MS N, while the second category (wool, etc.) fell by 2d, as did the following toll for woad. At the Gate of Tarascon, the first of these categories rose 0.5d and the second fell 1d, half the changes at Tarascon proper. At Saint-Gabriel all tolls remained stable.

Tables T2 and T3 give the *montazon*, a fee paid by a ship going upriver according to its cargo, from one to 40 hogsheads of salt. The figures in the two versions do not match in five cases out of 40, or 12.5% of the lines.[72] The discrepancies are small, one denier up or down, or 0.75d, or (once) two deniers; the sum of all 40 figures is almost identical for the two tables (up 0.25d in Table T3). As a percentage of the total, the discrepancies are insignificant.[73] The two versions may represent two stages, a first schedule of rates for the *montazon* and a subsequent revision incorporating a series of small changes in policy. Alternatively, one version may represent an attempt to revise errors in the other, or the two versions may have been intended to control each other for accuracy (see §4.4.4).[74]

4.4.3. PUBLICATION

It is not enough to state current rates; they must be made known, and made known with authority. Another purpose of the registers is implied in the anecdote from 1325 (N12v24–13r10). When a ship carrying ashes came up to Tarascon, the captain disputed the toll that was asked of him by pointing out that no toll for ashes was mentioned in the register. The tollkeepers responded that no exemption for ashes was mentioned either. Since the king of Naples and count of Provence, Robert of Anjou (*nostre senhor lo rey*), happened to be in Tarascon at the time, the dilemma was taken to him. Robert resolved it by declaring that the ship must pay as though it were carrying a listed commodity similar to ashes, such as lime or gypsum. Clearly, the register could be invoked as an expression of royal authority for the determination of a toll. Such authority was motivated by the king's major share in the tolls. In turn it motivated the decoration of the registers, the use of ink in two or three colours, the coloured and decorated initials, the ornamental design of the first page of MS T, and the putative illustration that may have been intended for the blank space on the first page of MS N. These manuscripts are not merely pragmatic, like a train schedule, though pragmatic they certainly are. They are both documentary and monumental. They concern the business of a king, and this king was a businessman.[75]

Publication of the king's business was continual and industrious. One of the authorities cited in the *terrier* attests that he learned about tolls from oral testimony by witnesses and from a "public instrument" written in the hand of a notary.[76] Such written instruments must have continued down to and including the vernacular registers. From time to time their content was subsumed into the investigations of comital revenues made for Charles I in 1252 (MSS A_1 and P) and for Charles II in 1298 (MS A_2).[77] When a third investigation was made for Robert I in 1332, however, the *ritus et consuetudines*, "procedures and customs," for collecting tolls were spun off into separate documents to be kept in the royal archive at Aix:

> *Item redditus pedagii riparie Rodani qui per pedagerios deputatos levantur et percipiuntur secundum certos ritus et consuetudines qui et que in archivio regio Aquensis seriosius esse dicuntur.*[78]

> Item, revenues from the tollhouse on the bank of the Rhône, which are levied and collected by the appointed tollkeepers according to certain procedures and customs that are said to be [given] in fuller detail in the royal archive at Aix.

The words *ritus et consuetudines* denote formalized actions but extend to denote, as here, the documents that describe those actions.[79] In both senses they correspond to *forma et modus* in MSS A_1P, and, in Occitan, to *la forma et la maniera* in MSS TN, "proper and customary procedure." Such formalized activity and/or documents may have included the *publicum instrumentum* mentioned in MS P (above) and the *registre* (N13r3) in which a ship's captain verified what commodities were subject to toll in 1325. All these terms could have been applied also to MSS TN, called *registre* in their own texts (T3r1, N1v17). The registers edited here could have been copied by notaries from documents in the royal archive at Aix. Information about tolls that was crucial to shippers, captains, tollkeepers, and shareholders circulated in various forms, both oral and written, through investigations and registers in Latin, Hebrew, and Occitan.

4.4.4. ACCURACY

The effectiveness of the registers was limited, though, by their lack of precision. As we have noticed, MS T contradicts itself by stating the base rate on salt as two different amounts, first as 29.75d per hogshead from one to six, and then, turning the page, as 29.25d for the first hogshead in Table T1.[80] An obole (half a denier) has been left out the second time.[81] The difference is small, but an obole was the toll for many commodities. If a captain were to challenge the toll asked for his hogshead of salt, he could point to the lower statement and save an obole – assuming that the register was made available for him to read, as it evidently was in 1325.

Such unreliability is not an isolated problem, as may be seen in the tables. MS N contains a table on salt in small hogsheads from one to 40 (Table N1) and another on salt in large hogsheads from one to 14 (Table N2). In both an inattentive scribe has omitted the crucial number of hogsheads, small or large, from every entry – from one to 40 and then from one to 14, that is 54 times – and provided only the escalating series of tolls, which is incomprehensible without the matching, escalating number of hogsheads that generates the tolls. The entries begin, one after the other, “Hogsheads pay ...,” and continue with a rising number of deniers, but fail to provide a rising number of hogsheads; they must have been intended to read, “One hogshead pays ..., Two hogsheads pay ..., Three hogsheads pay ...,” and so on. This flaw highlights the interest in the toll, rather than the item subject to toll, that we have noted in analysing the ordering of commodities in the registers, often beginning with a high toll for the most varied goods and proceeding down. It suggests a greater interest in the sum of tolls collected than in the collecting of them. It makes it impossible to observe the number of hogsheads in a ship and then look up the toll in the table, which was the tollkeeper’s presumed duty. It must be a massive scribal error.

Other scribal errors, while less extensive than these, must nevertheless have introduced a certain haphazard quality into the collection of tolls. Table T1, on salt in hogsheads from one to 40, skips over the line for 27 hogsheads, omitting information at that level for Toll, King, and Knights. Table N1, on salt in small hogsheads, skips the nobles’ share three times.[82] Like an earlier multiplication table which states that five times five is 15,[83] indeed like all manuscripts, these registers are subject to the shortcomings of scribal practice. Unlike most manuscripts, however, the registers speak with royal authority even when giving erroneous figures.

Reading the tables as escalating series of tolls, we find another kind of irregularity. If they were simple and straightforward, the series could be predicted by multiplying a certain toll per unit times the rising number of units, but they are not. Nor are they predictable if we add an adjustment by some regular, recurring algorithm. We can detect regular sequences in the ascending multiplication of base rate times units, and we can detect regular adjustments, but anomalies remain. Thus in Table T1, assuming a scribal error in the second statement of the base rate, the first statement (29.75d) holds true from one small hogshead of salt up to six.[84] The increment falls to 26.75d per hogshead from seven to eight, leaps to 52d for nine, falls back to 26d for ten and eleven. Thereafter it varies but returns to 26d for thirteen to seventeen, nineteen to twenty-four, twenty-six to thirty-six, and thirty-eight to thirty-nine hogsheads. At the remaining levels it is higher: 32d per hogshead for twelve hogsheads, 31d for eighteen, 38d for twenty-five, 36d for thirty-seven, 29d for forty. This bewildering array may be seen as roughly coherent, running around 29d per hogshead with a slight advantage for larger loads, but it is interrupted by punitive raises at irregular intervals (for nine hogsheads, twelve, eighteen, twenty-five, thirty-seven, and forty). The canny shipper must have taken care to avoid consigning a load at those levels. If we calculate the effective rate per hogshead at each level (in contrast to the increment), we find that the beginning rate (29.75d), good from one hogshead to six, rises to its high of 31.56d at nine and then declines slowly, ending at 28.15d for forty hogsheads.

Tables T2 and T3, the two versions of the *montazon*, invite similar observations.[85] In Table T2 the base fee of 4.5d per hogshead works for one to eight and most following units, but is repeatedly interrupted by higher increments or occasional lower ones.[86] In Table T3 the anomalies occur at many of the same entries but some different ones.[87] If we calculate the effective rate per hogshead at each level (in contrast to the increment), we find that the *montazon* favoured small loads of one to eight hogsheads at the expense of middling loads from nine to eighteen, with some slight advantage for loads in the middle-thirties.

Table N1, on salt in small hogsheads, resembles T1: it establishes a base rate (29.75d) that holds from one unit to seven, but then, with some reversals, declines slowly, reaching a rate of 21.25d for forty hogsheads.[88] The reversals aside (sharp fall at eight, sharp rise at nine, back up at twenty-three, down sharply at twenty-five), this is a mostly regular progression. Table N2, on salt in large hogsheads, is the simplest of the five tables: it maintains a rate of 80d per large hogshead from one to fourteen, with the only exceptions at ten and eleven, which are more advantageous to the shipper (at the rates of 72d and 69d, respectively).[89]

If we think of the tables as cascades, they are characterized by the presence of barriers at irregular intervals that produce anomalies, departures from the ongoing progression, which takes up again after each barrier. The anomalies tend to penalize the shipper with a higher toll, although some reward him with a lower one. The tolls in Tables T1 and N1 are regressive, somewhat lower per unit for large loads than for small ones, but the *montazon* (Tables T2, T3) is first progressive, then regressive, with its highest rates from nine to 18 hogsheads. The toll on large hogsheads, introduced in Table N2, approximates a flat rate.

4.4.5. BALANCE

Table T1, like Tables N1 and N2, gives the toll on each number of hogsheads and the division of that toll between the king and the knights.[90] It would appear that the toll should be equal to the sum of the shares – the fundamental principle of double-entry bookkeeping – and this is often the case, but sometimes not. Of the 40 lines in Table T1, nine do not balance, which is an error rate of 22.5%.[91] It is possible to devise corrections on the assumption that the toll should equal the shares to king and nobles, and by consulting Table N1. These corrections are the presumed errors in the table; they are all small, either an obole or a denier, and in one case 5.5d (at twenty-six hogsheads, the knights' share).[92] As a percentage of the total tolls, these nine errors come to 0.02%; they are, in effect, negligible.[93] We may conclude that although these nine figures are not precise, Table T1 is quite usable aside from the omission of the line for 27 hogsheads.

The figures in Table N1, on salt by the small hogshead, fail to balance on 17 lines out of 40, or 42.5%.[94] If we assumed they should balance and devised corrections drawing on Table T1, we would arrive at a mere reproduction of that other table. We may speculate that this was the intention of Table N1, since the tolls and shares for one unit and 40 units (hogsheads in T, small hogsheads in N) are identical; the differing figures occur between these extremes. By such a conjecture, the tolls on salt were entirely stable from one version to the other. But while this may have been the intention, it remains the fact that the manuscript reads as it reads, and was apparently put forth as an expression of royal authority including its errors. As in Table T1, however, the scale of the errors is small: they come to about 1% of the total.[95] Again, the figures are not mathematically precise, but they are pragmatically adequate. Their irregularity is marginal.

In Table N2, on salt by the large hogshead, income (the toll) fails to match outgo (the shares of the king and the nobles) in seven items of 14, or 50% of the entries.[96] The toll goes up by a regular increment of 80d per large hogshead except for ten, eleven, and twelve, where the exceptional increments add up to 240d, as they would if they were corrected to 80d for each one. In contrast to the relative regularity of increments in the tolls, the shares for the king and the nobles go up by irregular amounts: for the king no two increments are the same, except two for nothing; for the nobles the increments tend towards repeated numbers (17d, 23d), but irregularly. Table N2 does little to support an assumption that income and outgo were intended to balance.

This table also contains something else, a listing of the equivalence of large hogsheads, from one to fourteen, to small hogsheads, from one to forty. It begins with a fractional statement (one large hogshead equals 2 and 20/21 small ones), and continues with the nearest integer at each step. It is accurate except once, when the value for nine large hogsheads is repeated for ten. This scribal error may account for the irregularity in the increments for the toll and the king's share at ten to twelve large hogsheads. Reading down the tolls, we notice what may have been an attempt to compensate for the zero increment at ten units, first inadequately at eleven and then fully at twelve. We could correct these three tolls by substituting a uniform increment of 80d, but that would be to override the apparent attempt to re-establish regularity after it had been lost. Table N2 may well contain rates that arose as errors – a captain or shipper was perhaps delighted to learn that there was no increment in the toll from nine to ten large hogsheads – but any such errors have been institutionalized in the table as transmitted, and subsequently put forward with royal authority. This observation suggests an explanation for the approximate sense of a balance of income and outgo: since the registers were universally manuscript, and since manuscripts are inherently subject to scribal error, no exact sense of balance was possible. The scribal medium imposed a degree of tolerance for unavoidable error.

Three of these tables (T1, N1, N2) provide the toll and the shares into which it was divided, which, it is tempting to believe, may have been intended to balance. But the tables provide no evidence of an attempt to attain a balance that was mathematically precise; the figures fail to balance in 22.5% of the lines (T1), or 42.5% (N1), or 50% (N2). However, the overall result of the discrepancies is so small that they may be considered not to undermine the importance of balance understood in an approximate sense. In Table N2, we glimpse a process in which an original scribal error, enunciated with authority, appears to have been recuperated by introducing compensating adjustments. It appears that a balance of income and outgo was one purpose of the tables among others, although the sense of that balance was inexact in these documents as elsewhere at the time.[97]

5. The World around the Registers

5.1. Tarascon, Its King, and Its Tolls

Tarascon is a city in Provence, situated between Avignon upstream on the Rhône and Arles downstream. It is on the left bank as one sails downstream, that is, to port, which was called the side of the *empire*, holy and Roman, because the emperor was consecrated by the pope, and not to starboard, on the side of the *royaume*, the kingdom of France.[98] The count of Provence was not subject to the king of France; in principle he was subject to the Roman Emperor.[99] From the thirteenth to the fifteenth century the count of Provence was a king himself, the king of Sicily, known in his county of Provence by his greater title as *nostre rey*, "our king." Tarascon was the site of a royal court.[100] The imposing castle, with its foundation in the Rhône, stood sentinel as it does today at the northwest corner of the town. A castle has existed in this place since the eleventh century; in its present form it was founded by Louis II in 1400 and completed by René d'Anjou in 1449.[101] It defied the castle of Beaucaire that it confronted across the Rhône, a stronghold of the king of France. In 1481, when the childless Count Charles III bequeathed Provence to his cousin, King Louis XI of France, the castle of Tarascon lost its purpose.[102]

The counts of Provence and kings of Sicily were originally counts of Anjou, with its capital at Angers in northwest France. In 1246 Charles I of Anjou, the brother of King Louis IX of France, married Beatrice, the heiress of the House of Barcelona, which held Provence, and became count of Provence by his wife's title. When he became king of Sicily in 1266,[103] he founded the line of count-kings who would receive the largest share in the tolls described by the two registers edited here. He was succeeded as king of Naples and count of Provence by his son, Charles II (1285–1309), and Charles II by his son Robert (1309–43). In 1325 Robert must have adjudicated the dispute over the toll on a ship carrying ashes that is mentioned in MS N (12v24–13r10). Robert was followed by his granddaughter Joan I, queen of Naples (1343–82). Joan left her titles to her adopted heir, Louis I, who was nominal king of Naples (1382–4). Louis I was soon followed by his son Louis II (1389–1417), also king in title only, and he in turn by his son Louis III (1417–34), who was succeeded by his brother René d'Anjou, *le Bon Roi René* (1434–80). When MS N mentions two kings who commissioned work at the mint of Tarascon, those of Sicily and France, *lo rey de Sicilia* may refer to Louis III or René.[104] René was followed by his nephew Charles III (1480–1), who bequeathed Provence to the king of France.

Local government in Tarascon combined administration by the *viguier*, who was a representative (Latin *vicarius*, Occitan *veguier*, English "vicar") appointed by the king, and an oligarchic council divided evenly between nobles, defined not as a legal class but, essentially, as those recognized by others as noble, and bourgeois, who aspired to become noble.[105] The *viguier* governed a territory, the *viguerie*, that was bordered by the Rhône on the west, the Durance on the north and east, and the Alpilles to the south; this roughly triangular area was supplemented by a separate zone to the south, beyond territory governed from Arles, that was bordered by the Mediterranean and included L'Albaron and Saintes-Maries-de-la-Mer.[106] Tolls were administered by the royal court (the *curia regia Tharasconis*) and the *viguier*.[107] Revenue from the tolls was shared by the king and the lords, the *senhors* or *gentils homes*. The king took about three-quarters of the sum, and the lords got the rest.

Tarascon was one node in a network of toll points that provided income for her count and king.[108] Charles I had a *terrier*, or register of landed property, drawn up in 1252, listing the sources of his income from tolls.[109] The Paris manuscript lists twelve places, both great and small, where tolls were collected; one was Avignon, which became the capital of Christianity when a series of French popes resided there from 1309 to 1377. The listing traces a zigzag pattern across Provence from east to south to north to west. Starting on the Mediterranean coast at Nice, it moves inland to Séranon (Alpes-Maritimes), goes west overland to Brignoles (Var) and west again, returning south to the coast at Les Pennes-Mirabeau (Bouches-du-Rhône); then north to Aix and north again to Digne, doubling south to Valensole (Basses-Alpes); then west to the Rhône valley, to Saint-Gabriel on the outskirts of Tarascon and to Tarascon itself; then upstream to Avignon, east to Orgon on the Durance, and, returning to the Rhône, downstream to Arles.[110] A document from about 1349 lists Tarascon as one of four principal sources of the count's revenue, after Arles/Marseille and Aix/Les Pennes, slightly before Berre/Istres.[111] In the registers edited here we find mention only of Avignon and Arles, upstream and down, among the other major cities of Provence.

The tollhouses seem to have changed with time.[112] In 1298 the tolls of Tarascon were collected on the island of Jarnègues, just north of the castle.[113] MS T indicates tollhouses on the Rhône at Jarnègues, Lubières, and *Los Mujolans*, and on roads at the Gates of the town and Saint-Gabriel. In 1332 a report on the *viguerie* of Tarascon mentioned tolls at the castle, Lubières, and in the neighbourhoods of Pin (on the west between the castle and the quarter of Lubières), Saint-Nicolas, and Vigne.[114] MS N may refer to the castle as the tollhouse *de l'aigua*, "of the water," again as the tollhouse *del rey*, "of the king," and yet again simply as the tollhouse of Tarascon. It also mentions tolls at Jarnègues, Lubières, *Los Violans* (a corruption of *Los Mujolans* in MS T), the Gate of

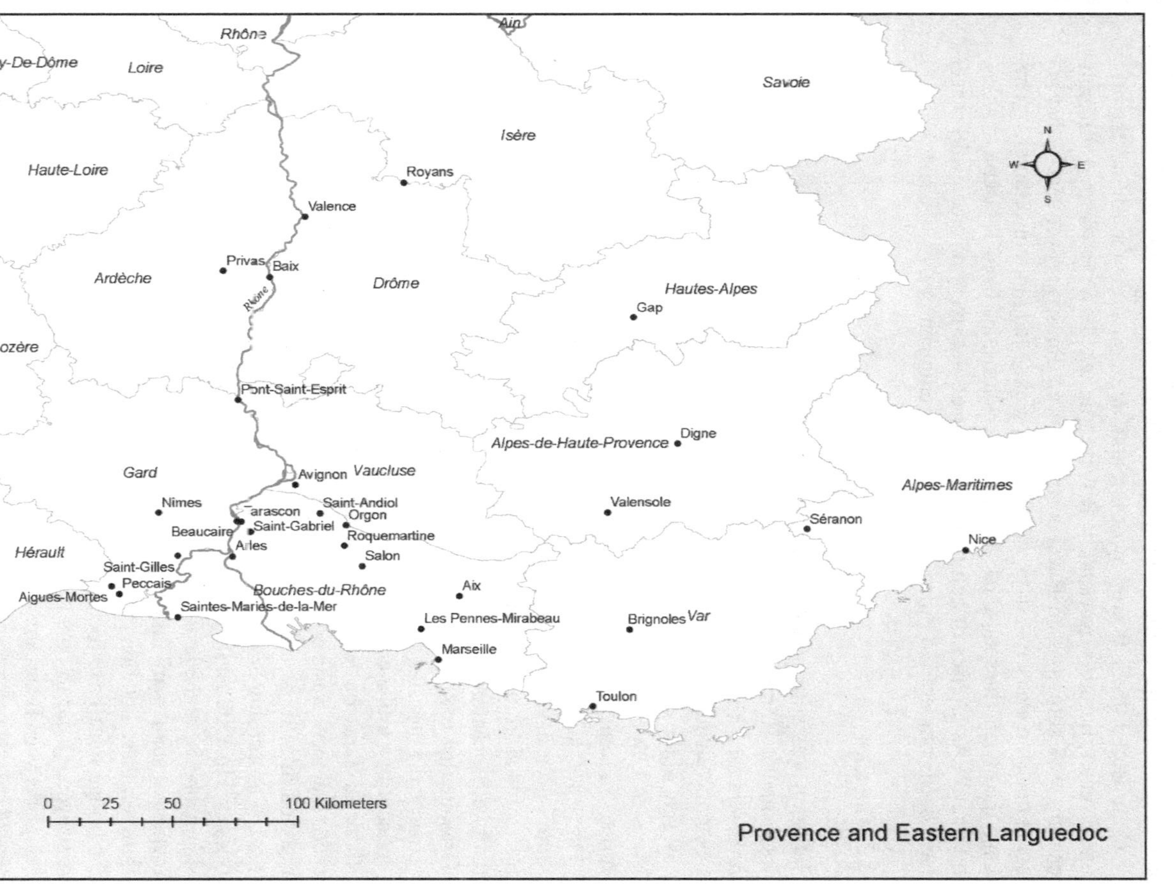

Map 1. Provence

Tarascon, Saint-Gabriel, and *Adaul*, which may be identified as Saint-Andiol, some 27 kilometres to the east but within the *viguerie* of Tarascon.

Commercial traffic flowed by or through Tarascon along the Rhône, the primary vector, but also overland.[115] River traffic was busy: in the mid-fifteenth century, 187 ships passed Baix, upstream from Tarascon, in a year – that is, about one ship every two days, but fewer in winter and more in summer.[116] The king, the queen, the seneschal, and the princes travelled from Tarascon to Arles by river.[117] As arteries of commerce and travel, the rivers of medieval France have been compared to railroads in the nineteenth century.[118]

5.2. The City

Tarascon was surrounded by water, and its environs were marshy.[119] On its west side the Rhône ran north and south; to the north lay an arm of the river, a *brassière du Rhône* (Occitan *brassiero*), with a port at the island of Jarnègues where merchandise was unloaded.[120] Another arm flowed into a ditch down the east side of the city, across the south side, and back into the main channel. The island of Lubières, downstream from the castle, marked the town's southwest corner. At some time after 1332 the Rhône shifted, and the island became part of the town; after each flood, which is to say every few years, the Rhône would settle into a new bed, obliterating old islands, creating new ones, or moving plots of land from one bank to the other.[121] According to a legend known since the twelfth century, the river was home to an amphibious dragon called the Tarasque that would emerge to capsize ships and drown travellers.[122] We may consider the monster a metaphor for the dangers of the torrent.

According to the consensus among historians there was no bridge across the Rhône at Tarascon before the seventeenth century, although some have conceded that there was a boat bridge in the thirteenth.[123] However, the investigation reported in MSS A_1 and P attested that a bridge, a *pons*, was built, *factum*, in 1251.[124] According to one of them, taxes were paid on houses, *domibus*, on this bridge.[125] In 1332 an inquiry into the *viguerie* of Tarascon mentioned taxes levied on a house at the head of the bridge.[126] About 1348, Queen Joan's text of the municipal statutes of Tarascon mentions upkeep of bridges as well as roads.[127] Between these notations in the early fourteenth century and the early fifteenth, the bridge must have been washed away.[128] MS N recalls a time before it was destroyed: *Quant lo pont d'entre Belcayre et Tharascon era entier*, "when the bridge between Beaucaire and Tarascon was whole" (N9v16–17). In 1426 a bark ferried passengers across the Rhône.[129] The *pons* that was *de novo facto* in 1251 and remained *entier* for years, supporting houses and contributing to the king's revenue, must have been a more solid construction than a boat bridge or a ferry.[130]

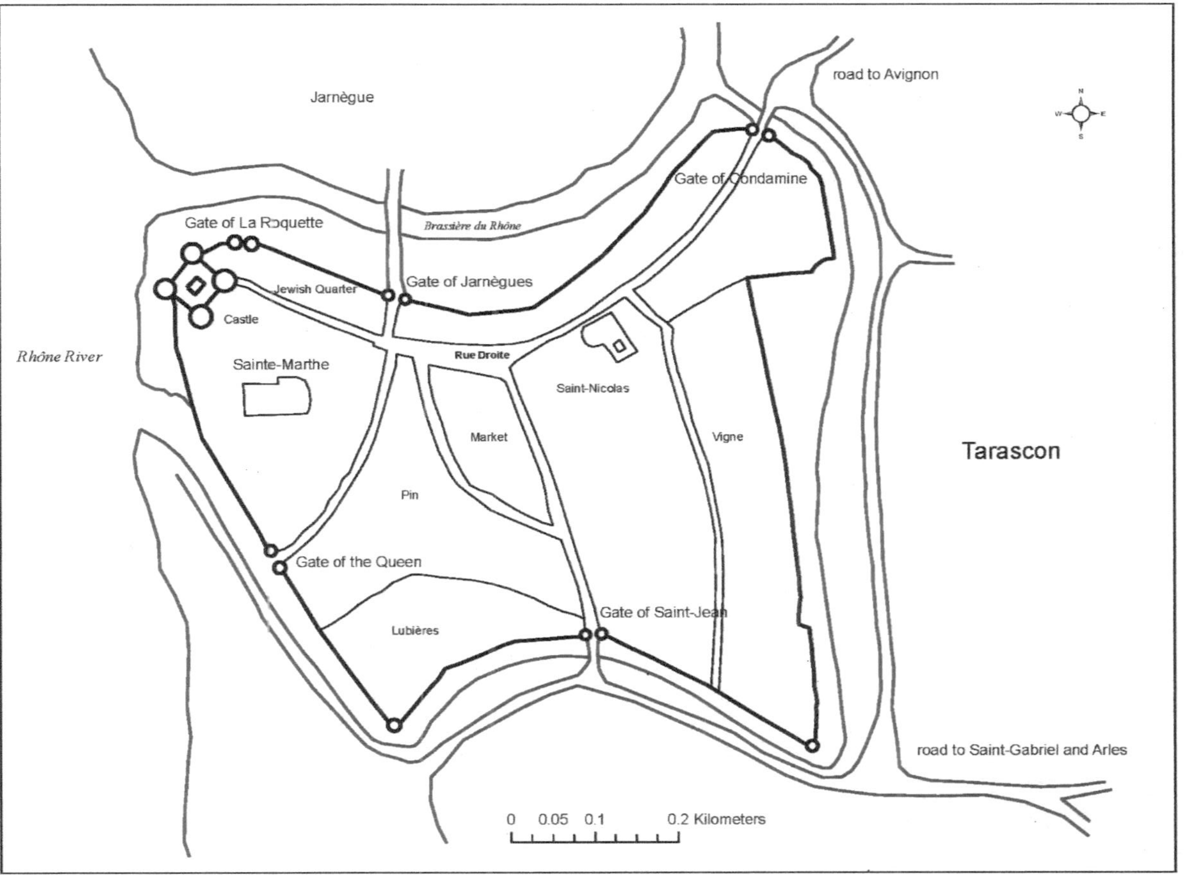

Map 2. Tarascon

By the end of the fourteenth century the wall around Tarascon had five gates.[131] Near the castle were the *maison commune*, where the city council met; the public slaughterhouse; the public fish market; and the Jewish quarter, with its synagogue and its school.[132] The mint, created in 1249, was originally housed in the castle but later moved to a separate building not far away.[133] A nearby salt shed did a lively business.[134] From the castle the *rue droite*, or "straight street," ran east parallel to the *brassiero*, past the gate of Jarnègues, which opened onto a bridge leading to the island of that name, and up to the Condamine gate leading north to Avignon. South of the *rue droite* and near the castle stood the church of Sainte-Marthe, which is still there today. Towards the middle of town was the market; the eastern quarter called *La Vigne* contained vineyards, tanneries, and a municipal brothel.[135] At the southwest corner was Lubières, first an island, then a quarter. Between Lubières and another quarter to the east called Saint-Nicolas, the Saint-Jean gate opened to the road going south past Saint-Gabriel and onward to Arles.[136] Every quarter had its inn and its well. The town counted more than 700 houses and a hundred stables.[137]

Tarascon was not a *civitas*, the seat of a bishop; when the church of Sainte-Marthe was consecrated in 1197, the ceremony was performed by the archbishop of Arles assisted by the bishop of Avignon. It was called a *villa* (a city) in the investigation for Charles I in 1252; a *castrum* (a fortified place) or a *villa* in the one for Charles II in 1298; a *castrum* in the one for Robert I in 1332; and a *vila* in MS N.[138] The uncertain terminology may reflect a loss of population. Tarascon had fewer than 5,000 people at the end of the fourteenth century.[139] By the mid-fifteenth it had about 4,000, but remained one of four municipalities in Provence – after Aix, Arles, and Marseille – with more than five hundred hearths.[140] By 2008 the population had grown to almost 15,000 people, but other cities had grown faster, leaving Tarascon in our century a relatively small town.

5.3. Ships and Shipping

Tarascon was a seaport, but an inland seaport.[141] Ships from the Mediterranean sailed up the Rhône as far as Arles, Tarascon, and even Avignon, but the largest ones did not go beyond Arles.[142] There, in the fourteenth century, grain imported from Tarquinia in central Italy was reloaded onto riverboats before continuing upstream.[143] Most of the seagoing ships seen at Tarascon were barks or small galleys, which is why MS T assigns tolls for a *barca* or a *linh* (T6r14–15). A bark on the river might carry up to 37 tons, a galley up to 78 tons.[144] MS N gives the same toll for a *barca* but omits the *linh* (N11v8), perhaps reflecting the smaller size of ships on the Rhône in the fifteenth century.[145] MS T also mentions a round ship (*nau*), but says only, "We are in doubt" about the toll it paid (*duptam*, T6r16); MS N gives the word *nau* without a word about its toll (N11v9). Evidently the *nau* was rarely seen.

Ships at this time were of two basic types: the round ship, high and wide, and the long ship or galley, low and narrow. The round ship (Latin *navis*, Occitan *nau*) was mainly driven by sails, though it carried oars as well. It had two or three decks, measured up to 37 metres long and 12 metres wide, and carried as much as 860 tons.[146] In contrast, the galley (Medieval Latin *galea*, Occitan *galea*) was mainly driven by oars, though it also carried sails; it had one deck, measured about 43 metres long but only 5 metres wide, and carried up to 170 tons.[147] The ratio of length to width for a round ship was about 3:1, for a long ship 8:1. Round ships were economical but slow; long ships were faster and more independent of wind and weather, but also more expensive because of the larger crew.[148] About 1318 the city of Marseille proposed to charter a squadron of ships, both round and long, for a crusade that was planned by the duke of Clermont. The round ships would take a large cargo of grain, a hundred and twenty horses, four hundred passengers, and a crew of fifty. The galleys would carry a hundred and twenty oarsmen and ten sailors, that is, 130 fighting men.[149] Oarsmen at this time were not slaves, as in late antiquity and the early modern period; labour was scarce, and oarsmen were free.[150]

A small round ship was called a *navec* in Occitan, in Latin a *navigium*. According to the account books of Francesco di Marco Datini, the great merchant from Prato (Tuscany) who died in 1410, a *navegio* carried 20 to 33 large hogsheads of salt by the measure of Peccais, that is, 110 to 180 tons.[151] The smallest and most numerous type of sailing ship was the *barca* or bark, although the word *barca*, like *navec*, could also be used more generally.[152] A typical *barca* has been estimated to carry 33 to 40 tons of salt.[153]

A small galley was called a *linh*, in Latin a *lignum*. MS T mentions a *linh de Roda*, which seems to have been a small galley from Rhodes in the Levant. The *caupol* was a flat-bottomed barge with one mast and from four to fourteen oars. A *caupol* evenly laden carried 8.5 hogsheads of salt, but filled to heaping it could carry 12 hogsheads (T12v26–8), perhaps about half the cargo of a *navec*.

In the castle of Tarascon today, a fifteenth- or sixteenth-century graffito represents a splendid round ship, scratched on the wall of one of the rooms that served as a prison.[154] It carries three masts, a design that appeared in the first quarter of the fifteenth century.[155] The foremast and mainmast are square-rigged, the mizzenmast lateen-rigged (its triangular sail is supported by a yard at an angle to the mast). There are railed platforms, or tops, at the head of the mainmast and the foremast, and fighting platforms at the bow and stern (forecastle and sterncastle). The rudder is affixed to the sternpost, unlike the older stern quarter rudders or steering oars, which were suspended over the side.[156] The prisoner who drew this graffito must have seen such a ship somewhere, but perhaps not in Tarascon.

Going upstream from the Mediterranean, ships sailed, rowed, or were towed as far as Beaucaire and Tarascon. From there on they were towed by teams of horses, oxen, donkeys, and men.[157] A team of five or six men could tow a ship carrying one hogshead of salt; if it carried more, as it usually did, more were required.[158] Convoys included up to seventeen ships.[159] Salt was carried in flat-bottomed barges from the salt pans at Peccais on the Mediterranean, up the Rhône and past Tarascon, to be unloaded at ports in the kingdom (of France) such as Tournon and Lyon, or in the empire at Avignon, Orange, or Vienne.[160] For the return trip downstream, hogsheads of salt were replaced with commodities such as cereals, wood, and cloths, in packs of similar weight and bulk, or other heavy products such as tiles, barrels, skins, ropes, charcoal, and pitch.[161] The trip upstream, covering the 141 kilometres from Peccais past Tarascon to Pont-Saint-Esprit, took fourteen to forty-two days depending on the hazards encountered and time spent loading, unloading, and measuring salt. The return downstream, riding the rapid current, took four days or as few as two.[162]

The power of the river was also used for shipping timber in the form of rafts, which were assembled on the upper Rhône in places like Seyssel and Saint-Nazaire-en-Royans. The mention of timber from these places in the registers (see Glossary: *saisel*, *roans*) evokes scenes in which hundreds or thousands of logs, bound into rafts sometimes longer than a hundred metres,[163] came floating past the castle at Tarascon.

5.4. Commerce, Bookkeeping, Currencies

The city participated in the economic revival and commercial revolution of its age.[164] A man of Tarascon could form a company (*companhia*, T5r8, N8v25) with a man from another town to import wine. Such companies had developed in Tuscany beginning in the twelfth century; in them, "for a determined period of time a circle of investors joined in common enterprises with stable capital investment."[165]

> With few exceptions, each partner made some contribution to the capital. Originally the *compagnia* was a family partnership, but by the first quarter of the thirteenth century, outsiders were occasionally taken in, especially factors [agents] who were made junior partners. Partnership in one form or another is characteristic of mediaeval business, especially of commerce. The individual merchant trading on his own behalf is the exception.[166]

These companies depended, as for their life's blood, on bookkeeping.

The "earliest known example of commercial double entry" is the Farolfi ledger from 1299 to 1300, maintained by the branch at Salon, in Provence, of a company of Florentine merchants who had established their head office in Nîmes. This ledger shows "a debit and credit for every item and a serious attempt at annual balancing." However, "owing to the bookkeeper's propensity for making one-sided adjustments, and to human error ... there was almost always a difference between total debits and total credits; if it was not too large the bookkeeper was satisfied, and adjusted the profit total to fit."[167] This characteristic sheds light on the imperfect reckoning in our registers and the tolerance for small degrees of error, but not large ones, which we have discussed (§4.5). Accounting also helps us understand the difference in layout between our two registers (§4.3). The tabular Farolfi ledger, like MS T, has "entries in lines, close to the left-hand edge but leaving a wide right-hand margin into which are extended the sums of money in Roman numerals, neatly ranged in a column."[168] It illustrates the "Venetian-Genoese two-sided presentation" in contrast to "the traditional Tuscan paragraph format of accounts."[169] MS N shows the older paragraph format despite its more recent execution, while MS T, older in substance but newer in form, follows the tabular layout as in the Farolfi ledger.[170]

Bookkeeping in turn depended on currency, or rather the multiple currencies that the tollkeepers encountered, which are the subject of Rubric V in MS N (N13r10–13v24). Payment was required in *tornes d'argent fin* (N13r15–16), "tournois of pure silver," that is, the Provençal imitation of the original tournois, a coin minted in Tours since the twelfth century.[171] The counts of Provence from Charles I to Joan minted tournois in denominations of a denier, an obole (half a denier), and a *gros* (12 deniers), with their type representing Tours as a *tor*, or castle.[172] The register defines the value of the *tornes* in terms of the *florin de Florensa* (N13r18–19), the "florin of Florence," a gold coin struck in Florence from 1252 to 1533 that represented John the Baptist, patron saint of that city.[173] The florin of Florence was accepted as standard currency in Provence and throughout Europe, even though the counts of Provence, like the lords of many other places, minted imitations of it themselves.[174] The register adds the *blanc*, a silver coin of sufficient purity to remain white (unlike coins made of alloy that turned black),[175] and the *patac*, defined here as one fifth of a *blanc* (N13v6), that is 1.67d (N13v7). The calculations implicit in our registers must have been performed on counting tables by placing counters, or jetons, in columns for pounds, sous, deniers, oboles, *pogezas*, and grams.[176] The format of the counting table underlies the tabular format of accounting books and MS T.

The rate of exchange from tournois to florins of Florence is stated three times in MS N as 10:1.[177] This rate varied historically, like other rates of exchange then and now. According to Spufford on medieval exchange, the rate of 10:1 was true in Tarascon in 1293 and in Aix-en-Provence in 1311, but later, from 1317 to 1343 in Avignon and Arles, it rose to 15:1 or 20:1.[178] In France more generally the rate was around 10:1 at the beginning of the fourteenth century, but rose by the early fifteenth to around 30:1.[179] It appears that MS N repeatedly states a rate that had been accurate at the time of MS A_2 but must have become obsolete long before the composition of MS N. The fossilization of this exchange rate in the textual tradition provides a marked contrast with the more sensitive variations in tolls that we will study below (§6.5).

5.5. Networks, Commodities, Slaves

The Rhône valley was part of one circuit in a worldwide commercial system that stretched from England to Italy, Cairo, Calcutta, Peking, and Palembang in modern Indonesia.[180]

> In the eleventh and twelfth centuries, with the political, military and economic expansion of western Europe (stimulated by the dynamism of Latin merchants from Italy, Provence, the Iberian Peninsula, and the rest of Europe as well), the Mediterranean became the center of complex networks connecting very remote economic spaces. This activity permitted an intensification of the commercial relations between different ports, but also led to a permanent state of war and competition between regional powers over control of the shores and maritime routes.[181]

The registers record that Tarascon was linked to Alap, in Syria, and to Vulcano, an island off Sicily, both important sources of alum, and perhaps to Cologne in Germany for thread. It was connected directly to Rhodes in the eastern Aegean, if the galley we have mentioned came from there. The toll-house at Lubières distinguished between goods from the Levant and those from anywhere else, the *non-Levant* (T13r6–7). At closer range, the lower Rhône valley and Tarascon linked the fairs of Champagne to the ports of Arles, Aigues-Mortes, and Marseille.[182]

Exotic goods subject to toll included Barbary apes (*isime*), which were favoured as attractions by street entertainers and as pets by bourgeois and ladies.[183] Skins of camels (*camel*) and lions (*leons*) came from Africa, which was also the source of the gold used to mint florins.[184] From the East Indies came Brazil wood (*bresilh*) and zedoary (*citeal*); from India, indigo (*indi*);

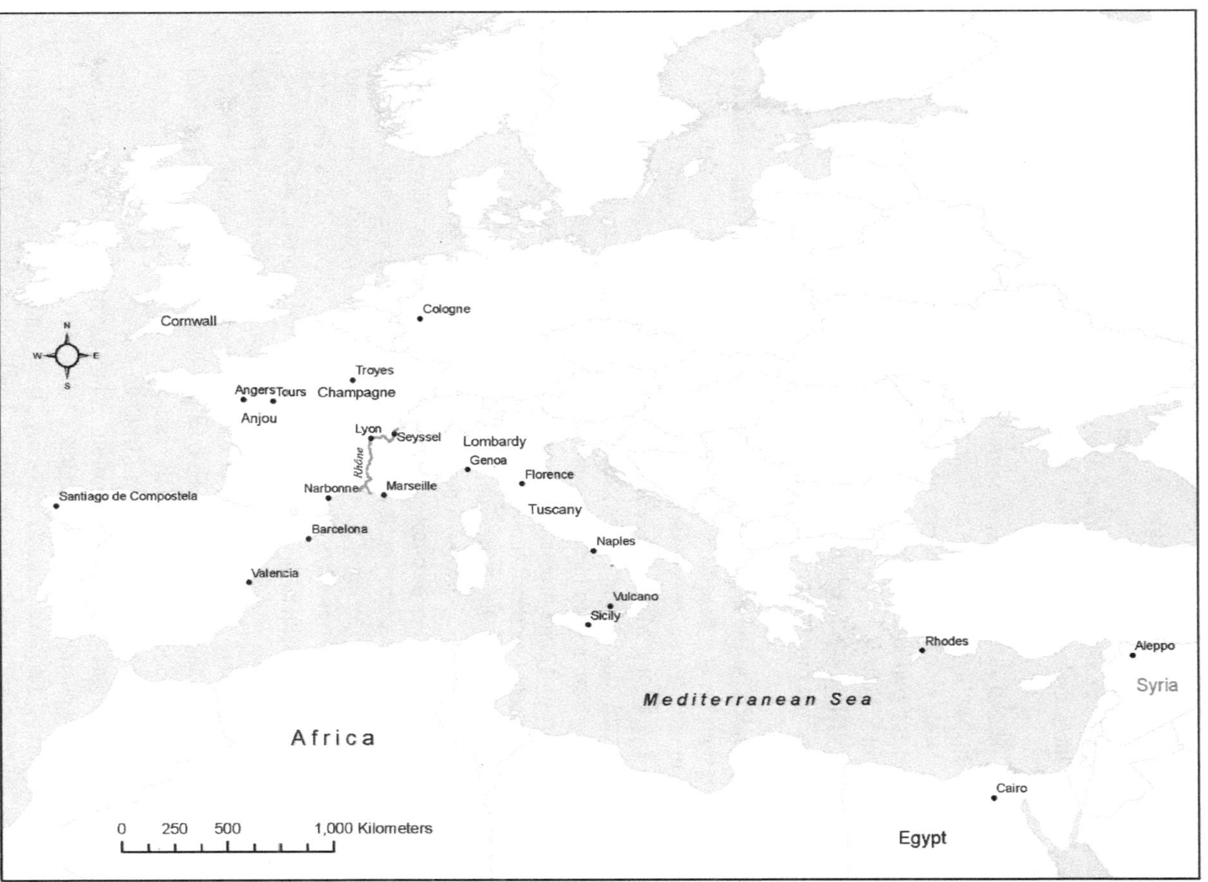

Map 3. The Mediterranean

from India or Egypt, *cassia fistula*; from the Levant, cumin (*comin*); ginger (*gingibre*) came from the tropics.[185] East Asia sent spices like saffron, cinnamon, pepper, cloves, and sugar, and textiles such as cotton, linen, and silk.[186] Tin came to Provence from Cornwall.[187] The horizon of direct maritime commerce at Arles extended in an arc from Latium and Tuscany to southern Catalonia, including major ports from Genoa and Marseille to Barcelona and Valencia.[188]

Pilgrims passed through Tarascon coming from northern Italy (Lombardy) and going to Santiago in northwest Spain (T9r1, N10r16). They came from Spain, England, Germany, and France (i.e., *de Lihon en amon*, "from Lyon up"), bound for Santiago or Saint-Gilles in Provence (T9r8, N10r20).[189] Pilgrims to Sainte-Marthe in Tarascon were allowed to cross the Rhône without paying toll (N10r22–4). Like other medieval people, the Tarasconnais travelled for many reasons; pilgrimage was one motive for travel that has become less common now.[190]

Tolls depended on the nature and quantity of the cargo. Salt was measured by the hogshead (Latin *modius*, Occitan *mog*, French *muid*), a unit that varied locally from the basic large hogshead of Peccais, 60 quintals or about 6 metric tons, up to 7 or 8 tons. MS N introduced the large hogshead, equivalent to just under three small ones. Other commodities subject to toll ranged from animal products and live animals to building materials, cloth and clothing, dyes, foods, furniture, plants and plant products, spices and medicines, and wood and wood products. Live cargo included horses, other large animals, and travellers from prelates and nobles to ordinary people.

Among large animals, between a horse and an ape, MS T mentions a Saracen (T8v1). MS N makes explicit the reference to a Saracen slave, male or female – *un sarrazin, esclau o esclava* (N9r22) – between horses and mastiffs. The Latin investigation from 1252 mentioned Saracens for sale at Nice and near Aix.[191] The one from 1298, MS A_2, treats slaves after animals, large or small, and before pilgrims: *Pro quolibet Saraceno vel Saracena, vel Surio seu Suria, qui traducuntur per Rodonum ad vendendum, recipiuntur pro pedagio Tharasconis solidi duo denarii sex*, "For each Saracen man or woman, or Syrian man or woman, that is taken across the Rhône to be sold, 2s 6d are received for the toll of Tarascon."[192] The toll is the same in the three sources. There can be no doubt that the registers refer to full-blown slavery.[193] Slaves were listed among commodities by Francesco Pegolotti, a Florentine merchant who wrote a description of business practices around 1340.[194] From the thirteenth to the fifteenth century the slave trade in Provence, Italy, and elsewhere in southern Europe was growing, to burst into its fullest development in the sixteenth century, when Africans would be enslaved and carried to the Americas.[195]

A female slave was sold at Tarascon in 1457–8 by Guy d'Albe, son of Johan Alba, who was a shareholder in the toll.[196] But slavery did not mean there were no free Muslims in Provence: paradoxical though it may seem, Christians, Jews, and Muslims collaborated in business affairs.[197]

5.6. *Shareholders and Tollkeepers*

Most of the revenues from the tolls at Tarascon went to the king, who took about 75% of the total, and the knights of the city, who got the rest. But the registers provide two more names of individual shareholders: Johan Alba in MSS T and N, and Lady Elis in MS A_2, where she is called *domina Elys* in Latin, and MS N, where she is called *ma dama Elis* in Occitan. The intervals in time between the sources, at least half a century between MSS T and N, about a century between MSS A_2 and N, make it unlikely or impossible that either of these names concerned the same individual in the two sources.

The Alba family had two branches, one in Tarascon and the other in Roquemartine, about 40 kilometres to the east, where the ruins of their castle may be visited today at Castelas-de-Roquemartine, near Eyguières (Bouches-du-Rhône). The Tarascon branch is known from the thirteenth century to the fifteenth, when their holdings were absorbed by their cousins in Roquemartine.[198] The Albas of Roquemartine included men named Johan from the mid-thirteenth century to the sixteenth.[199] In the early fifteenth century a Johan Alba of Roquemartine, perhaps the man of MS N, was part-lord of Saint-Andiol; his interest there may account for the several mentions of that town in the register.[200] Bertran Alba, the husband of the first Lady Elis (below), was also from Roquemartine.

Johan Alba appears as a partner in the tolls at Tarascon seventeen times in MS T and twenty-five times in MS N. We seem to be dealing with an original shareholder in MS T and his heir or eventual heir in MS N. The shares in the name of Johan Alba remained constant for twelve items.[201] From MS T to MS N, someone (the heir, the original owner, or an intermediary) sold three holdings in salt and modified another, increased the share on large masts, and added eleven items, including six listed in MS N as merchandise (old ropes, masts from six and a half to five palms around, wood) and five listed under the Gate of Tarascon (cloth, wool, grease, more old ropes, tiles).[202] These changes suggest aggressive management of a portfolio. The aggregate value of the shares held by Johan Alba in MS T was 3s 0.5d (36.5d); in MS N, his namesake's holdings were worth 7s 11.5d (95.5d), more than twice as much.

Domina Elys is identified in MS A_2 as *uxor quondam domini Bertrandi Albe*, "the wife of the late Lord Bertran of Alba."[203] We know of at least five men named Bertran d'Alba; the first of these, lord of Roquemartine, son of Alba d'Alba of Tarascon, did homage to the archbishop of Arles for a fief called the Bois Comtal in 1267. He had four sons, the eldest of whom (another Bertran) did homage for the same fief in 1303.[204] The information in MS A_2 enables us to add that the wife of the first Bertran d'Alba was *domina Elys*, and that she was widowed by 1298. This manuscript goes on to say that *ex regia concessione*, "by royal grant," she received one denier of the toll on each hogshead of salt carried up the Rhône beyond Beaucaire.

Ma dama Elis appears seven times in MS N, perhaps a century later than MS A_2, as a shareholder in tolls on salt.[205] She enjoyed four rights: 1d for each small hogshead coming upstream, from one hogshead to forty (N1v25, N2r8, N2r16); 1d for each one over forty (N4r20); 1d for each one loaded at Beaucaire and going upstream (N4v1, N4v15); and 1d for each one unloaded at Beaucaire and belonging to a foreigner, an *home estrany*, that is, a man who was not from Beaucaire or Tarascon (N4v20).[206] The third of these four is the same right *Domina Elys* had in MS A_2; the other three are new. Perhaps the expression *Ma dama Elis* in MS N refers to an eventual heiress of the woman with the same name who was alive in 1298; the name Elis may have continued through the family, as the masculine names Johan, Bertran, and Albe did.[207] The holdings had evolved from one, producing an income of 1d, to four with combined income of 4d.

The Alba family seems to have been loyal to their Angevin monarchs. *Domina Elys* was the beneficiary of a royal grant. The Johan Alba of MS T appears to have been a loyal subject, as he took 1d on each ship's yard subject to toll at Lobieras *de la part del rey nostre senhors*, "on the part of the king our lord" (T5v9). During the tumultuous years of the Union of Aix most of the Alba family supported the Angevins, as did many other nobles.[208] But their towns did not. Tarascon and Roquemartine joined the Union of Aix and resisted the ascent of Louis II of Anjou; the lord of Roquemartine, named Albe Albe, finally submitted to the king on 27 October 1387.[209] The struggle between the cities and the Angevins was also a war between townspeople and nobility.[210]

Most of the shareholders in tolls at Tarascon and elsewhere were men, but some others were women like Lady Elis. In 1252 the *terrier* of Charles I recorded women shareholders at Arles and Orgon (Bouches-du-Rhône), 34 kilometres east of Tarascon.[211] In the mid-fifteenth century, one of the proprietors of the toll at Baix (Ardèche), upstream from Tarascon, was a widow.[212]

Among other people involved in these tolls, we know a little about the tollkeepers. There was Pons del Prat, identified as a former tollkeeper in the *terrier* and in MS T, whose authority lingered in memory for half a century.[213] In 1252 a Pons de Prat, perhaps the same man, owed the count taxes for a *terra de Prato* and a house in *Condamina*, the quarter in the northeast part of Tarascon.[214] The *terrier* mentioned another tollkeeper in Tarascon, *Rainaldus francigena* ("born in France"), and a former tollkeeper at Aix, Bernardus Raimundus.[215] Other witnesses regarding tolls were Jews; they were probably tollkeepers, since they possessed the knowledge needed to provide testimony.[216] The lost register from Tarascon, Archives municipales CC9, was translated from Hebrew by the Jew Ferrer Vidas (*Ferrer Vidas Jusieu*), another tollkeeper. Of these ten known tollkeepers or sworn witnesses regarding tolls, seven, if not more, were Jews. Collecting taxes, including tolls, was regarded as a "malodorous but lucrative task," and often committed to Jews, especially in Provence, "where they were especially numerous"[217] after the expulsion of Jews from France in 1306.

These men are all mentioned as providing sworn testimony for the registers; the citations of former keepers, in particular, contribute to the effect of cumulative, traditional authority. It was local authority: the toll was farmed out by the *viguier* with preference for men of Tarascon.[218] Although the authority was traditional, practices changed. We shall now turn to change and awareness of change in these registers more generally.

6. Historical Change in the Toll Registers

In the description of MSS T and N (§4), we studied those registers in themselves. Now, in order to understand their position in the larger historical process, we shall consider them as extending the series of Latin investigations into the count's revenues, MSS A_1, P, and A_2. The two types of document are different: the investigations consider all the sources of comital revenue, the toll registers just one; the investigations became a major political instrument, one means among others to construct a coherent and stable state, whereas the registers served more narrowly to review the tolls, to regularize them, and make them produce more income.[219] Nevertheless the two types overlap because both provide detailed lists of commodities subject to toll with the amount required for each one, and both publish those lists with royal authority. The fact that tolls rise from the investigations to the registers, as we shall see, may reveal the reason for the shift from one type of document to the other: the felt need to make the tolls go up. The register, more focused on tolls than the investigation, may have been adopted as one of the means to produce that effect.

It has sometimes been assumed that toll registers from Tarascon and elsewhere did not change with time. In her thesis on the early history of Tarascon, Delebecque studied the count's sources of revenue, including tolls, and edited the Latin investigation of tolls drawn up for Charles II in 1298 (MS A_2). She said that it does not differ significantly from the investigation made for Charles I half a century earlier, in 1252:

> On ne constate pour ainsi dire pas de différence entre l'enquête de Charles Ier et celle de Charles II à ce sujet. Les tarifs sont les mêmes dans les deux enquêtes, et il y a peu de différences dans la façon dont sont disposés les paragraphes. Les mêmes marchandises sont groupés ensemble.[220]

In her following discussion, Delebecque describes tolls as they are stated in the later investigation but does not compare those in the earlier one. Rossiaud declared that the investigation of 1298 (MS A_2) was still in use as late as 1644, only updated in regard to the amounts of tolls.[221]

A similar attitude was expressed by Stouff regarding the four *tarifs*, or registers, that we have from Arles, compiled from 1252 to the fifteenth century:

> Tous sont identiques. Deux siècles durant, les scribes ont recopié le même texte ... Pour le XVe s., une interminable liste de produits inchangée depuis des générations.[222]

On closer inspection, however, it turns out that the toll documents from Tarascon – compiled in 1252, 1298, the early fourteenth century and probably the early fifteenth – contain overt recognition of change, a recognition that provides evidence of historical consciousness. Furthermore the manner of organizing the lists of tolls changed, and so did the tolls themselves.

6.1. Awareness of Change

The language of these documents, Latin or vernacular, is mostly timeless. Their purpose is pragmatic, not historical: to state that a given commodity pays a certain toll, meaning that it has done so since time out of mind and, more pointedly, that it will do so again the next time a ship arrives carrying such a cargo. Occasionally, however, the registers take note of a change that has occurred in a toll. Thus in MSS A_1 and P, we are informed that sheepskins used for making parchment have paid 9d for the past ten years although they paid nothing before, and that a range of commodities, including oil, hemp, and others, have paid 18d for five years, although they formerly paid 13d.[223] These manuscripts also note that earlier documents omitted any mention of quicksilver and verdigris.[224] In introducing the section on tolls at the bridge between Tarascon and Beaucaire, they mention the recent completion of that bridge:

Forma et modus percipiendi pedagium constitutum apud Bellicadrum et Tarasconem in ponte de novo facto anno Domini M° CC° LI°.[225]

The proper and customary procedure for collecting tolls established at Beaucaire and Tarascon on the bridge newly built in the year of the Lord 1251.

These Latin manuscripts recall changes small and large over the past year, half decade, or decade, changes that involved raising tolls by 5d or 9d, or that introduced a new tollhouse.

MSS TN do not include remarks about changes in tolls, but they both observe historical change in other ways. When MS T mentions individuals by name or title it makes a clear distinction between the present and the past, which it describes with verbs in the preterite tense. It mentions the oath by a former tollkeeper, Sir Pons del Prat, who witnessed (preterite *manifestet*, T14r3) a certain procedure; indeed, this oath, by this tollkeeper, had already been mentioned in the Latin registers in 1252, perhaps 70 years earlier.[226] When MS T says the king bought the toll at *Los Mujolans*, it uses the preterite again (*compret*, T9v21).[227] Since he bought those rights, *son aras del rei nostre senhor* (T12r12), "they now belong to the king our lord"; *son del rei* (T5v22), "they belong to the king."

MS N shows more extensive consciousness of past time. An episode from 1325 is the occasion for an extended past narrative, the only one in any of these registers:

Nota que l'an mil ccc. xxv. et lo ix. jour del mes d'octubre, passet par dessus lo Rose un navech cargat de sendres, et li fon demandat lo peage; lo qual respondet que non devie ren per so car non era trobat al registre que degessa. Et en aquel temps nostre senhor lo rey era aisi, et la question venc davant el. Et fon covegut que, vesent que las cendres non [s]ont ambe las autras causas francas, que deguessan pagar segons la mercadaria que fora plus propia et plus senblant a las cendres, et que pagessa coma caus ho gip. (N12v24–13r10)

Note that in the year 1325 and the ninth day of the month of October, a boat loaded with ashes passed over the Rhône, and the toll was asked of it; which [the ship, viz. the ship's captain] answered that it owed nothing, because it was not found in the register that it owed [anything]. And at that time our lord the king was here, and the question came before him. And it was agreed, seeing that ashes are not with the other exempt things, that it must pay according to the commodity that was closest and most like ashes, and that it would pay like lime or gypsum.

These events may have occurred as much as a century before the composition of MS N. The passage focuses sharply on the year, the month, and the day. It uses the preterite as the primary tense of past narration (*passet ... fon demandat ... respondet ... venc ... fon covengut*), with imperfects subordinate to the preterite (*devie ... era*) or interspersed with it (*lo rey era aisi*), and, subordinate to the imperfects, past subjunctives (*degessa ... deguessan ... pagessa*) and a second conditional (*fora*). To refer to the text of the register as it stood in 1325, MS N rather surprisingly uses a present, perhaps by attraction to the strong effect of the present tense throughout the registers (*dona, paga*, etc.): *vesent que las cendres non [s]ont ambe las autras causas francas*, "seeing that ashes are not with the other exempt things."[228] This tense should be regarded as an instance of indirect discourse, paraphrasing the present tense that was appropriate during the discussion that took place in 1325.

Elsewhere MS N uses the preterite for the minting of coins:

> *Per egalar los coronas a la moneda dels tornes que foren fach davant los coronas, fon mes l'argent que si levava a [x]ij. s/ viij d'. lo florin de Florensa ... Totas vegadas los peagiers ordeneron que lo peage de la sal si levessa a xiij. s/ iiij. d'.* (N13v8–15)

> To compare *coronats* to currency in the tournois that were made before the *coronats*, the money that was levied was put at [1]2s 8d per florin of Florence ... However, the tollkeepers ordered that the toll on salt be levied at 13s 4d.

Since the *coronat* was introduced in 1330, this passage appears to recall exchange rates from at least half a century earlier, possibly a century.[229] Again the preterite carries the past narrative (*foren fach ... fon mes ... ordeneron*), with an imperfect (*levava*) and a past subjunctive (*levessa*) in subordinate positions.

MS N also uses the imperfect to describe the bridge between Beaucaire and Tarascon before it was destroyed:

> *Et quant lo pont d'entre Belcayre et Tharascon era entier, pagavan los procans .ij. d'., et los luehn .iiij. d'. et los peagiers devian lo pont .j. miagla.* (N9v16–19)

> And when the bridge beteween Beaucaire and Tarascon was whole, those from nearby paid 2d, and those from far away 4d, and the tollkeepers owed the bridge 0.5d.

Here the imperfect conveys the narrative of past state or situation (not events): *era ... pagavan ... devian*.

6.2. The Organization of the Registers: Tollhouses

Each register is organized according to an implicit logic. The two reporting the investigation made for Charles I (MSS A_1P) list the tolls charged in five sections: at Saint-Gabriel (in the original sequence), then Tarascon, the Gate of Tarascon, Saint-Gabriel again (in a revised sequence), and the bridge between Tarascon and Beaucaire. The reasons why Saint-Gabriel comes first are obscure, but the order is largely historical: it proceeds from the first three toll points to a recent revision of Saint-Gabriel and the more recent innovation of tolls on the bridge, newly constructed in 1251, one year before the investigation was made.

The register for Charles II (MS A_2) lists tolls on commodities shipped on the Rhône, that is at Tarascon; tolls collected at the Gates of Tarascon, on commodities that are not shipped on the Rhône; those collected at Saint-Gabriel, said to be the same as those at the Gates except as noted; and those at Lubières. Here the order is hierarchical, beginning with the central tollhouse on the river, continuing with the houses that are not on the river but part of the town (the Gates), then farther afield at Saint-Gabriel, which is treated in a manner subordinate to the Gates. Lubières had not been included under Charles I, although tolls had been collected there since before 1200;[230] it is not clear why they were excluded from MSS A_1P but included in MS A_2. Tolls on the bridge do not reappear after the investigation for Charles I, perhaps because the bridge had been destroyed.

MS T combines listings for Tarascon and Lubières, which had been separate in MS A_2. Rubric I concerns commodities in general at both places, rubric II salt in particular, and III salt again, giving both tolls and shares in the tolls; IV lists distinct, generally smaller tolls on commodities at Lubières.[231] Then come tolls at the Gates (V) and Saint-Gabriel (VI). The general order goes from centre to periphery, as in the investigation for Charles II. But then MS T adds a different tax entirely, the *montazon* on salt at Tarascon, and provides two versions of it running from one hogshead to 40. The repetition of the *montazon* in rubrics VII and VIII echoes the repetition of tolls on commodities at Lubières, first with Tarascon in rubric I, then separately in IV. The two versions of the table on *montazon* differ at several points, but perhaps only because they involve different scribal errors. Whereas the register for Charles II is governed by a sense of logic, MS T is developmental; it almost allows us to see it grow.

MS N begins with a biblical text, John 1:1–14, which was widely copied as a semi-magical gesture to invoke success when beginning a new enterprise.[232] There follow rubrics on salt and then commodities, combining Tarascon and Lubières as in MS T; a separate rubric for exempt items; one on currencies, perhaps a more complicated subject than it had been earlier; and finally tolls at the Gate of Tarascon and Saint-Gabriel, as before.

6.3. The Organization of the Registers: Tolls

The sources mix two principles for ordering tolls, from high to low and by the nature of the commodity. But they depart from any such principle to insert some tolls seemingly at random. Each source shows independence of the others.

MSS A_1 and P. These two reports on the same investigation of the county's income differ in organization at one important point. In their sections on Tarascon proper, both proceed from high tolls to low (27.5d, 19d, under 10d), then back up and down again. Both depart from the descending sequence to intersperse higher tolls among lower ones. But after the second sequence of tolls at 27.5d, MS A_1 inserts a major section of very high ones on ships, parts of ships, and lumber, beginning at 70s (840d) and ending at 50s (600d). MS P moves this section to the beginning. MS P appears to have put the ships and lumber at the beginning in order to regularize the sequence in terms of descending tolls.

For the Gates of Tarascon, both MSS A_1 and P list tolls of 27d, then 18d, then under 5d. In the original sequence on Saint-Gabriel, MS A_1 lists tolls at 26d, then 12d (with some at 6d), then under 5d, and MS P does the same; the revised sequence in both manuscripts raises the tolls of both 12d and 6d to 13d. Tolls at the bridge are given in MSS A_1P from 1.5d to 1d, 0.5d, and 0.25d, with exceptions. MSS A_1 and P organize the tolls in terms of descending value, with the constant possibility of irregularity.

MS A_2. The investigation for Charles II imitates MS A_1 in deferring the high tolls for ships and lumber until midway through the tolls for Tarascon. Then A_2 innovates with a long passage on salt, including a scale that proceeds from one toll for up to eight hogsheads to single increments from nine hogsheads up to forty (24s 11d, that is 299d). Last come tolls under 10d (skins of parchment quality) and under 5d: animals, animal products; travellers, pilgrims (slaves are more costly at 30d); foodstuffs and domestic objects.

The shorter listing for the Gate of Tarascon begins with high tolls of 26.5d, then 18d, then falls to 4d or less for a range of commodities. At Saint-Gabriel and Lubières, however, there is no apparent effort to go from high to low. At Saint-Gabriel the tolls go from 3d to 6d to 9d, continue at 9d for foods, materials, and cloth, and then decline to 3d and 1d. Lubières begins and ends at 2d, goes down to 0.5d and 1d, but intersperses these with higher tolls on sumach, salt, and lumber for ships or other purposes. The lists for outlying tollhouses seem to follow no order; they are miscellaneous.

MSS T and N. The Occitan registers proceed from large tolls to small within their combined sections on commodities at Tarascon and Lubières, from 29.5d (MS T) or 30.5d (MS N) down to 4d, except that they insert the highest toll in the section arbitrarily (77d for sumach), and do so again with the tolls on building materials (18d). The items clustered within one toll are sometimes quite diverse; it seems to be implied that the tollkeeper will remember all these things by the toll charged, not by any property in the commodities themselves. The following sections on salt proceed, contrariwise, from one hogshead up to forty, which makes sense because the list is a progressive series of multiplications, with constant modifications, based on the toll for one hogshead. Tolls at the Gates or Gate of Tarascon are listed going down from large to small, those at Saint-Gabriel going up from small to large (there are only two, 13d and 26d), as they seem to have done historically, beginning at the lower level (see §6.4). The common element in this array of seemingly contradictory organizations may be experiential: the tollkeeper remembers lucrative high tolls especially well, but works his way down to the more ordinary ones; he figures the toll on salt by loosely multiplying the base; he already knew the low tolls at Saint-Gabriel before the high ones were added.

6.4. Economic Background

Historians since Marc Bloch have subscribed to a view that in the fourteenth and fifteenth centuries, the landed nobility throughout Europe suffered a severe loss of revenue.[233] This crisis resulted from factors that converged in Provence as they did elsewhere: plague, which struck in 1347 and frequently thereafter, recurrent famine, and unremitting warfare. All of these disasters struck Tarascon, causing reversals in population, prosperity, and public order, between the dates of MSS T and N. The kingdom of Naples was the scene of a fifty-years war that lasted from 1348 to the end of the century, including the episode of the Union of Aix that we have described.[234] Famine struck Tarascon in 1374–6, and plague in 1384.[235] Furthermore, the commercial revolution of the thirteenth century was followed by a long depression throughout Europe in the late fourteenth and early fifteenth centuries.[236] In Provence the first two decades of the fifteenth century were a period of relative quiet.[237]

To compensate for their loss of income nobles adopted vigorous measures, among them higher taxation.[238] The counts of Provence were no exception.[239] The registers from Tarascon offer vivid illustration of the means by which one noble house strove to increase its revenue. Tolls declined in the thirteenth century from MSS A_1P to MS A_2, but rose in the early fourteenth (MS T) and rose again in the late fourteenth or early fifteenth century (MS N). The registers enable us to grasp specific decisions that produced this result: to raise the levels of some higher tolls, but occasionally to lower some others; above all, to introduce tolls on new items, and to do so in such numbers as to increase the aggregate value of tolls listed in the registers. As an unavoidable result, the revenues of the king, the knights, and the other shareholders rose.

6.5. The Evolution of Tolls at Tarascon

These fundamental changes are not immediately apparent to the reader of the registers. Because the documents differ in organization by tollhouses and by tolls, the changes do not leap out. Only by tabulating the tolls, comparing them from one register to another, and calculating and comparing their aggregates, do we come to realize the long-term movement that was afoot. The appearance of business as usual persists, and has lulled modern readers into a belief that business was indeed as usual. It may have had the same effect on those who paid the tolls, who perhaps did not realize the gradual but continual increase from 1298 onward. The occasional reductions in tolls on particular items may have been motivated by an intention to mitigate the effect of the overall increases, or to mollify or deceive those who paid them.

In general, the level of tolls, as seen in the number of commodities taxed and the aggregate of tolls listed, declined slightly from 1252 to 1298 and then rose. The initial decline was about the same for the tollhouses of Tarascon, the Gate of Tarascon, and Saint-Gabriel. The following rise was vigorous at Tarascon, where the number of items listed rose by nearly half from MS A_1 to MS T, and by more than half from MS A_1 to MS N, although the aggregates rose more slowly. It was even more vigorous at the Gate, where the number of items and the aggregate both doubled in MS N what they had been in MS A_1. It was more modest at Saint-Gabriel, where the increase in items from T to N did not regain the level of A_1, but the increase in the aggregate more than did. At Lubières, which does not figure in the thirteenth-century registers for Tarascon, the number of items tripled from MS A_2 to N, and the aggregate rose by half. For the Bridge we have only A_1 and P, which are identical; the aggregate was very small.

The royal court at Tarascon, charged with administering the tolls, made decisions that produced these results. The rates set for a few individual commodities varied from one register to another as though randomly, without participating in significant patterns, but many changes must have been implemented as a matter of deliberate policy. At each iteration after MSS A_1P, the court decided to delete certain commodities from the list and added others. In A_2 deletions outnumbered additions, as they did in T for Saint-Gabriel, so the lists grew shorter; but in T for the more numerous tolls at Tarascon and the Gate, and in N for all the tollhouses, there were more additions than deletions, so the lists grew longer. Moreover the additions favoured higher tolls.

The court took an aggressive attitude towards managing toll levels at each house:[240]

- For Tarascon, MS A_2 made no systematic changes relative to MSS A_1P. But MS T raised several rates 2d from what they had been in MS A_2 (27.5d to 29.5d, 19d to 21d, 9.5d to 11.5d, and 9d to 11d), and added numerous items at the top two levels, 29.5d and 21d. Then in MS N the highest former rate, 29.5d, went up by another denier to 30.5d, while the others that T had raised went back down by the same amount, returning to their level in MS A_2 (21d to 19d, 11.5d to 9.5d, 11d to 9d). As a result of all these modifications, the number of items, after subsiding slowly in MSS P and A_2 from the original level in MS A_1, rose to 147% of that original in MS T and 164% of it in MS N. The aggregate, after subsiding similarly, rose to 116% in MS T, then went down to 107% in MS N.
- For the Gate of Tarascon, MSS A_1 and P are identical. MS A_2 reduced one rate by a half denier (27d to 26.5d) and another by three-quarters of a denier (4.75d to 4d). MS T took another half denier off the 26.5d, to 26d, but raised 18d to 19d, added many new items at 26d, and more at 19d. MS N reversed both these decisions, returning to 26.5d and 18d as in MS A_2, while adding many new items at both these rates. Overall, the number of items rose from MS A_1 to 139% of that number in MS T and 202% of it in MS N. The aggregate rose to 164% of the original level in MS T and 224% in MS N.
- For Saint-Gabriel the manipulation of toll rates was the most active. Even the first two sources, MSS A_1 and P, which report on the same investigation made in 1252 but were written at slightly different times (A_1 in the second half of the century, P at the end), differ on Saint-Gabriel: the rate of 13d that was charged on 16 items in MS A_1 was diversified in MS P to 13d for one item, 12d for ten, and 6d for five. MS A_2 raised the top rate from 26d to 26.5d, changed the rate of 12d either up to 18d or down to 9d, raised 6d on some items to 9d, and raised 2d on some items to 4d. MS T changed the rates on all the items that continued from A_2: down a half denier on the highest (26.5d to 26d), down 5d on one item (18d to 13d), up 4d on a dozen others (9d to 13d). MS T also discontinued a large number of items (forty-one of them) at rates ranging from high to low, and replaced them with a smaller number of items (fifteen), all at 13d. As a result all the tolls charged at Saint-Gabriel were either 26d or half as much, 13d;

there appears to have been an intention to simplify the system. In MS N these two levels continued; items discontinued were all at the lower rate, while those added, which were more numerous, were mostly at the higher one. Overall the number of items fell to 46% of the original in MS T, then rebounded to 62% in MS N. The aggregate fell to 67% of the original in MS T, and then nearly doubled, to 129%, in MS N.

- For the Bridge, which appears only in MSS A_1 and P and appears identically in these two sources, we have no information about any change other than the termination of this revenue.
- For Lubières the Tarascon registers begin with MS A_2. From that source to MS T the rates remain stable, but MS T adds many new items at tolls of 2d (from six old items to thirteen new ones) and 1d (from one old item to sixty-three new ones). MS N raises many of the 1d tolls to 2d (twenty-eight of them), while lowering some to 0.5d (six items). The number of items tripled from MS A_2 to MS T (to 316%), then rose slightly in MS N (to 321%). The aggregate rose to 144% of MS A_2 in MS T, then to 159% in MS N.

Tables for the tolls on salt, running from one to forty hogsheads, occur in MSS A_2, T, and N. I have set these scales aside in my discussion so far; I have not included their tolls in the numbers of items or in the aggregates for these manuscripts because they represent a refinement on a single commodity rather than forty separate commodities, and because they mount up to large figures that would distort the comparisons among the five sources. (They would distort them in the direction of further enhancing the increase in the number of items and the aggregates.) Nevertheless, the tables can be compared among themselves.

The *pezage*, or toll, on salt is set forth in Tables T1 and N1. Both appear to be rife with scribal errors (see the discussion of their accuracy, §4.4.4). They are nevertheless identical for thirty of the forty quantities listed, not including the first (one hogshead pays 29.25d in T, 29.75d in N), but including the last (forty hogsheads pay £4 13s 10d, or 1126d, in both manuscripts). The discrepancies regarding the other ten quantities may have been produced by mere scribal error, in which case there was no policy decision to change the *pezage* on salt. But if these ten quantities represent authoritative pronouncements of tolls that were expected to be paid, then the variant rates may have been deliberately set. Although some of the variant tolls went up in MS N and others went down, the aggregate for the two tables rose by 4%.

Table N2 gives the *pezage* on salt in large hogsheads, which were equivalent to just under three small hogsheads (three minus 1/21, or 2.95). The invention or codification of the large hogshead was a major commercial innovation, but the single table allows no comparative analysis. Its irregularities have been discussed elsewhere (§4.4.4).

The *montazon*, a distinct fee paid on merchandise (in this case salt) going upriver, appears in MS A_2 and in MS T, where it occurs twice in succession (Tables T2 and T3). The base rate in MS A_2 is 6d per hogshead; in MS T it is 4.5d in both tables, so there appears to have been a deliberate reduction. However, the tables show frequent irregularities: in MS A_2 thirteen quantities diverge from the 6d model; in Table T1 fifteen diverge from the usual 4.5d, and in Table T2 twelve. The aggregate fell to 75% of MS A_2 in both the tables in MS T.

As a result of all these decisions, the number of items for all the tollhouses considered together, after declining slowly from MS A_1 in MSS P and A_2, went up by half from A_1 to T, and by four-fifths from A_1 to N. The aggregate for them all similarly declined, then rose, first to 116% in T, then in N to 122% of the point of departure. It follows that the king's income from the tolls at Tarascon must have risen as well. We can confirm that it did. It was estimated about 1349 at 1,030 florins per year; in 1366 and 1369, two documents agree that it was about 2,000 florins.[241] These estimates are imperfect; it seems too much to believe that the revenue nearly doubled in about 17 years. Perhaps the first figure is a low estimate, or the second a high one, but the direction is clearly upward. The second, high figure may represent a target. In any case, it appears that the king increased his revenue from these tolls. No doubt he did so to compensate for loss of income from other sources, as nobles across Europe were striving to do however they could.

7. This Edition

The editions and translations imitate the format of the manuscripts. MS T and the edition are tabular, with frequent use of columns, leaders from one column to another, and pilcrows (¶). Leaders between the item and its toll (which is flush right), ornamental red strokes or a red line in the manuscript, are represented in the edition by strings of periods (.....). When a leader is suppressed in the manuscript because there happens to be no space between item and toll, but leaders are present in the preceding and following items, a leader is represented in the edition within square brackets [.....]. MS N and the edition are set in paragraphs; in the manuscript rubrics appear as run-ons in distinctive red ink, while in the edition rubrics are set as new paragraphs.

Line numbers are indicated in parentheses () for every line in the editions, with folio number and line (3r1) for the first line on a folio, thereafter only the line (2). Sometimes the line number falls within a word in the editions, as it does in the manuscripts. Blank lines in MS T are numbered in the editions and the translations. In the translations, for the sake of legibility only the first lines of sections or paragraphs are numbered; when a new folio begins inside a paragraph, its number is provided at the start of the following paragraph (2v2). Editorial headings indicating rubrics and subsections are inserted in the editions and translations. All editorial insertions are enclosed in square brackets [].

In the verbal text of the editions, punctuation and capitalization conform to modern usage. Consonantal *j* and *v* are distinguished from vocalic *i* and *u*. The cedilla is provided as needed.[242] In general the impulse to emend the text has been resisted, since the registers had the status of official pronouncements bearing authority even in their flaws. On apparent scribal errors, see the discussion of accuracy (§4.4.4). Emendations that seem unavoidable are enclosed in square brackets and listed in the Textual Notes.

Currency is noted in the editions as in the manuscripts (*libr'*, *s/*, *d'*, *o'*), but in the translations in modern format (£ s d). Fractions of deniers are converted to deniers: one obole (*o.* for *obol*, or the synonym *mealha*) = 0.5d, one *pogeza* = 0.25d. In the editions, numerals are given as in the MSS, often ending with *j* instead of *i* and setting the numeral off with a period before and after it *(d' .xviij.* = 18d).

The translations aim at literal accuracy within the constraints of the English language.[243] At the same time they strive to be receptive to subtleties in Occitan expression.[244]

8. Afterword: Toll Registers and Troubadours

For the reader who approaches these toll registers from the point of view of troubadour poetry, as I did, they represent a world apart. The troubadours were concerned with erotic desire in a context of idealized humane value, while the registers designated the toll to be charged on specific and concrete commodities. But there are overlaps. For example, the poets use the word *pretz* (Latin *pretium*, French *prix*, English "price") to express the worth or merit of a person and the reputation that such merit should assure.[245] The unstable quality of *pretz* as reputation[246] is analogous to the instability of prices, tolls, or exchange rates on currencies. Though the early register, MS T, avoids *pretz*, the late one, MS N, uses it occasionally, literally pricing an item in pounds, sous, and deniers, as a means of determining its all-important toll.[247] The poets sing of love, the registers ring with business and commerce, and yet these voices come to us from the same place at almost the same time.

We know four troubadours from Tarascon. They were all active in the early thirteenth century. Ricau de Tarascon, documented circa 1200–40, wrote a *canso*, or love song; he was joined by Cabrit in a *tenso*, or debate poem, in 1215–16. Tomier and Palaizi, perhaps brothers, collaborated in writing three *sirventes*, or political satires, concerning events that occurred from 1216 to 1226.[248] All four were knights, *cavaliers*, privileged members of the urban knighthood that the registers would later describe as receiving about a quarter of the income from tolls, the rest going to the king. These troubadour knights were on a par with Johan Alba in the registers. They served Raimon Berengar V (1209–45), the last count of Provence from the House of Barcelona. Raimon Berengar's son-in-law, Charles I, became count of Provence in 1246, and commissioned the first investigation of comital revenues in 1252.

In the *tenso*, Ricau and Cabrit bring the themes of love and merchandise together. Ricau challenges Cabrit to a mock judicial duel over an offence that becomes clear at the end, when Cabrit acknowledges that he may indeed have undressed with Ricau's *dona*, his lady – who, in view of the mock duel, must have been his wife.[249] The exchange of aggressive stanzas, rhetorically lunging and parrying, takes a humorous tone typical of the *tenso* and opposed to the more elevated style of the *canso*; accordingly the poets invoke elements of reality that correspond to the language of the toll registers. Cabrit says he will prove his innocence by eating a capon in company if Ricau makes him a good dish, a *bon'escudela* (line 17). The farcical logic of the defence seems to be that if Cabrit has the appetite to eat Ricau's *escudela*, he cannot have consumed his *dona*. *Escudelas*, "dishes," are among the domestic objects that were subject to certain tolls in the registers.[250] When Ricau dares Cabrit to mount a *destrier*, a warhorse, to do battle, Cabrit answers that if Ricau brings him two horses, a *bel caval bag*, "a fine bay horse," and a *ros doloiros mal fag*, "a wretched misshapen nag,"[251] and he fails to pick the better one, then his guilt will be established. These two classes of horse appear in the later register, MS N (9r18), where a horse worth £12 10s or more pays a toll of 2s 6d (as also in T8r22), while another one that is worth less – much less, to judge by the toll – pays only 4d, a little more than one-eighth as much. The difference is between a warhorse and a plough horse, a stallion and a jade. Cabrit says that his guilt will be proved if it is shown that he cannot tell a good horse from a bad one; the implied analogy is not complimentary to Ricau's lady. Ricau accuses Cabrit of treating him worse than Reynard the Fox, of the animal epic *Roman de Renard*, treated Isengrin the Wolf, whose wife, Hersent, Reynard seduced.[252] The whole comedy casts Ricau in the role of cuckold and Cabrit in that of his wife's lover.

In the *canso* Ricau takes a very different attitude towards love and marriage, idealistic rather than materialistic, and yet this attitude too is hedged about by real experience. He praises obedience to the commands of love, by which he means, as he explains, good faith in love, fidelity to one's beloved, not deception; he rejoices in his own happiness in love and the perfection of his lady.[253] He states his theme as *la fe d'amor*, "the (good) faith of love," according to one source (line 2 in MS C), which is consistent with the development of the theme throughout the song, but in other sources it becomes *l'afan d'amor*, "the torment of love" (MSS AB) or, more generically, *l'afar d'amor*, "the business of love" (MSS DIK). Although *afan*, "torment," is contrary to the happiness of which Ricau sings, it recurs frequently as word and theme in other troubadours,[254] which explains its appearance here; it is a more usual, hence more expected expression, a *lectio facilior*. Ricau goes on to say that the flower of true joy, *de fin joi la flor*, falls to two hearts that agree on *amistat*, love and friendship, through loyal love, *leial amor*, as he claims to show in the words of his songs (lines 25–32).

The claim to love faithfully is heard in many *cansos* but is not limited to them. It echoes in the words of the marriage ritual, in which the Church enjoined fidelity upon husband and wife, *ut castitatem inter se custodiant*, "that they keep fidelity between them."[255] In the nuptial mass that followed the exchange of vows, two readings warned the new husband against fornication and repudiation, both of which were commonplace.[256] Customary law forbade fornication by a wife but allowed it by a husband;[257] recall that Tarascon maintained a municipal brothel. Lady Audiart, called by Ricau to be judge of the *tenso* (line 49), had been repudiated by one husband in 1211 but married another after 1213.[258] *Amistat* and *leial amor* in Ricaut's song correspond to the doctrine of mutual consent. This doctrine was fundamental to the Church's view of marriage but controversial in civil law, which interpreted consent to marry as including the consent of the spouses' families as well as their own.[259]

In the three *sirventes*, Tomier and Palaizi hew so close to the political events of the day that the editor, István Frank, judged that their witness can be considered real.[260] Martín de Riquer spoke of their *candente actualidad*, their "red-hot topicality."[261] They too employ realistic vocabulary, such as *bus*, a regionalism synonymous with *barca*, "small boat," and *palus*, "marsh," referring to a characteristic of the riverine landscape around Tarascon.[262] They mention the *emperi*, the empire of Frederick II, which included Avignon, as we have learned, in the shipping language that distinguished the left bank, *empire*, from the right bank, the *royaume*.[263] And they express concern for the *prez*, the failing merit of their erstwhile allies the Catalans.[264] Their driving concern is to relate the fortunes of Tarascon to the just cause of resistance to the Albigensian Crusade.

Raimon Berengar, the count of Provence served by Ricau de Tarascon and the beneficiary of tolls from the town, was an occasional poet himself.[265] Among other, dubious attributions, a bawdy *tenso* surely belongs to him, along with his interlocutor, a certain Arnaut. Raimon Berengar provokes Arnaut to say that he will produce such a mighty fart that it will propel a hundred "ladies of high nobility" home from across the sea.[266] It is a parody of an earlier, more genteel *tenso* that praises a "lady of high nobility."[267] Raimon Berengar's son-in-law and successor, Charles I, wrote poetry too, and acted as a patron of troubadours.[268] His son, Charles II, was welcomed to Provence in 1288 by Jacme Motet, a minor troubadour and member of a knightly family in Arles.[269] Jacme hails the new prince, trusting that he will be good and courtly, *bons e cortes*, and that he will surround himself with courtly followers, *jent corteza*. He reminds Charles that his grandfather, Raimon Berengar, did everything that was fitting for *fin pres*, "true merit," and praises the Angevin counts, *aquist seinhors franses*, "these French lords," for maintaining justice.

The troubadours have gained an undeserved reputation for conventionality and artificiality in their love poetry, as though they had expressed no actual feeling in a real context. By recalling that Ricau de Tarascon and these other poets lived and sang in the same world that produced the toll registers, we return them to the reality that surrounded their lives and imbued their work. I see no reason to switch, as many do, from a literal reading of the supposed "realism" of the satires and bawdy songs to a fictive reading of the so-called courtly ones.[270] I take it as a working hypothesis that the troubadours' *amor*, their love, was as real as their anger and their laughter.[271] Juxtaposing troubadours and toll registers also helps us read the registers in a spirit that does not reduce them to records of tolls alone but sees them as factors in a busy world that included commerce, trade, shipping, slavery, large animals and small ones, money, pilgrimage ... and knights, counts, and kings, among them poets who sang about love in tones of mockery or sincerity. Love songs were more real than some readers of the troubadours have assumed; reality was more poetic, more amorous, than a reader of the registers might think. The world around them had room for both.

NOTES

1 Bondurand 1890, "Les Péages de Tarascon," republished as an extract (1891b); see the reviews by Meyer 1891 and Thomas 1891. Bondurand also published "Les coutumes de Tarascon" (1891a). He made a transcription of the rubrics in the *Livre rouge* which was not published; see Meyer 1893.

2 "Vers le XIIIe ou le XIVe siècle, époque de sa rédaction ... Le *Livre rouge* a été écrit au XVe siècle, mais il est bien évident que le texte provençal des péages de Tarascon existait déjà depuis longtemps à cette époque" (Bondurand 3). Thomas

agreed: "ce document est certainement beaucoup plus ancien" than the fifteenth century (1891, 420). Rossiaud seems to refer to MS T among "des copies tardives (XIVe–1446) de très anciennes pancartes" (2002, 2:334). Fourquin and Rigaud date MS T either as "milieu XVe," perhaps thinking of the date of the manuscript itself, or as "ca. 1329" or "1329," perhaps thinking of the composition of the text (1994, s.v. *antenna, navada, timon*, "milieu XVe"; s.v. *montazon*, "ca. 1329"; s.v. *radel, travata*, "1329"). Pansier refers to MS T as "XIVe" (1924, 3:1–178, s.v. *travada*, etc.). Pfister dates it "ca. 1300" (1980, 126). Bautier and Sornay give the title of Bondurand's edition as "*Les péages de Tarascon, texte provençal, XIIIe siècle (Mém. Acad. Nîmes*, 1890)" (1968–74, 1:44n2), although the expression "XIIIe siècle" is not present on the title page of Bondurand 1890 or 1891b.

3 Rossiaud gives the title of Bondurand 1890 as "Les péages de Tarascon. Texte provençal (XIIe siècle)" (2002, 1:235).

4 "Ms. du XVIe siècle" (Stein 1907, 520).

5 Meyer 1865–7, Série AA, 2. Meyer was named as author in fascicles concerning Series AA and BB that were published in 1864, but this publication provoked him to disassociate his name from the eventual volume (Meyer 1865). Wailly (1865) confirmed that the complete inventory would appear without Meyer's name. The volume as a whole appeared anonymously and without date, but bore the signature of Charles de La Valette as Ministre de l'Intérieur ("Deuxième rapport à sa Majesté l'Empereur," [12]), so it must have appeared during his tenure of the office in 1865–7. I refer to the copy in the B.n.F., Tolbiac - Rez-de-jardin - magasin FOL- L43- 13.

6 Meyer 1865, 68, states his conclusion but not his evidence, which we do not have. For background see Monfrin 1996, 9–10.

7 Roucaute 2009.

8 The title of the manuscript in the Newberry online catalogue is *Lo registre del peage de Tarascon* (quoted from N1v17). The catalogue provides a link to the description by the dealer, Les Enluminures.

9 [Meyer 1865–7], Série CC, 2–3. Meyer 1891.

10 [Meyer 1865–7], Série CC, 2.

11 Perhaps Meyer substituted Fr. *du dit péage* for Occ. *del dit peage*.

12 Meyer 1891, 482.

13 "Nous n'avons pas pu trouver aux archives le document qui relate ce fait" (Kahn 1899, 104n1).

14 Stéphanie Arnaud, *Assistante du directeur des archives*, Ville de Tarascon, email to the author, 7 August 2013.

15 The title of CC9, provided above, does not occur in N. CC9 had fifteen folios according to Meyer ([1865–7], Série CC, 2; 1891), whereas MS N has sixteen. A paragraph on currencies was on the last folio of CC9 (Meyer 1891), but begins in

N at f. 13r10, four folios from the end. On the other hand, pilgrims from Provence paid no toll according to both CC9 ([Meyer 1865–7], Série CC, 3) and N (10r11–12); pilgrims to Santiago or Saint-Gilles paid 5d if riding, 1d on foot, according to both CC9 ([Meyer 1865–7], Série CC, 3) and N (10r13–15).

16 Baratier 1969, 19.

17 Guérard 1:lxxiii–c, Appendice à la Préface, Tarif des péages du comte de Provence. Mid-century for Guérard (1:lxxiii). Baratier 1969, 20. "XIIIe siècle" in the B.n.F. catalogue.

18 And by Delebecque 1929a, which I have used in digital images very kindly provided by Annie Prunet, *bibliothécaire* of the Archives de Marseille.

19 Bautier and Sornay 1968–74.

20 Baratier 1969, 20.

21 Baratier 1969, 20.

22 Bautier and Sornay 1968–74, 1:44.

23 Bautier and Sornay 1968–74, 1:44n2.

24 Bautier and Sornay 1968–74, 1:38.

25 Baratier 1969, 20.

26 Bautier and Sornay 1968–74, 1:43.

27 Bautier and Sornay 1968–74, 1:275.

28 Bautier and Sornay 1968–74, 1:44n2. Labande 1894–5, 2:126.

29 I have consulted Aix, B.d.R., B 2, B 1152, B 1153, B 1469, and B 1477 directly, and B 143 in microfilm, at the Centre aixois des archives départementales. I have examined Avignon, A.D., Vaucluse, 1 J 163, and Avignon, Bibliothèque municipale, 1755 in digital images kindly provided, respectively, by Lydie Brailleur of the archive and by Michel Chazottes of the library.

30 I owe this palaeographic analysis to Paul Saenger, Curator Emeritus of Rare Books at the Newberry Library (e-mail to the author, 15 August 2014). As for the scripts of MS T, Saenger describes them as Gothic *textualis formata* and Gothic *textualis media* in the headings, and Gothic *cursiva media* in the body. On these terms, see Lieftinck 1954.

31 *Nihil dixerunt de argent vivo, verdent* (Baratier 385, Guérard lxxxiii). Cf. *argento vivo*, T4r15; *verdet*, T8r4, N12v9.

32 The dealer that sold MS N, Les Enluminures ([2011], 1–2), made this argument regarding N. Less persuasively, Les Enluminures also claimed that the church of Sainte-Marthe (N10r24–5) "was erected c. 1330," whereas the church was consecrated in 1197 and underwent continual construction throughout the thirteenth and fourteenth centuries according to Esquieu 1979.

33 Duplessy 2004–10, 2:12–20.

34 Duplessy 2004–10, item 1671, head and shoulders; items 1675, 1676, 1678, 1679, 1680, standing; item 1683, sitting.

35 In an argument against a proposal to relocate the port of Arles (MS Aix, A.D., B.d.R., 1153, f. 67r, line 19).

36 "La monnaie de coronats ... apparaît en 1330 avec les nouvelles espèces de coronats réforciats" (Venturini 2008, clxvi). The word was used to describe several types of coin made of alloy: the *royal coronat, provençal coronat, double coronat,* and *coronat reforciat* (Rolland 1956, 85). The counts of Provence minted the *denier coronat*; the *double denier coronat*, worth two deniers; the *gros coronat*, worth twelve deniers; the *obole coronat*, worth half a denier; and the *pite coronat*, worth a quarter denier (Duplessy 2004–10, 2:7–8). Neither the *coronat* nor the *patac* is mentioned in MS T, which rarely mentions specific coins (but see Glossary s.v. *rial)*; for other coins as money of account in MS T, see Glossary s.v. *denier, mealha, moneda* [2], *obol, pogeza.*

37 The *patac*, made of billon (debased silver), was produced from 1339 to 1480 (Rolland 1956, 85). Against the assertion that it first became current in Provence in the early fifteenth century (Fauris de Saint-Vincens 1778–80, 143), we have evidence for 1361 in Avignon (Pansier 1924–32, 3:127, s.v. *patat*) and for 1362 in Nîmes (*pataquus*, Du Cange 1883–7, 6:207, s.v. *patacus*).

38 Xhayet 1990, 417–18.

39 Xhayet 1990, 419.

40 Xhayet 1990, 408n33.

41 On the constant violence in Tarascon during the years 1368–1400, see Hébert 1979, 210–22. Coulet speaks of a fifty-years' war that began in 1348 (1988, 1:59) and provides a narrative of those years (1:60–90).

42 Guérard lxxxvi, Baratier 388.

43 The fact that MS T does not mention the bridge constructed at Tarascon in 1251, according to MSS A_1P, is apparently without meaning. N mentions that a bridge between Beaucaire and Tarascon was once whole, implying that it had since been washed away (9v16–17). See §5.2.

44 See Glossary for these and the following words.

45 Another marginal note in N, *ben(que)* [?], may relate to a variant form of Italian *banca.*

46 Lesa Dowd, Director of Conservation Services at the Newberry Library, conversation with the author, 2 August 2013.

47 Renouard 1941. "Dès la première moitié du XIVe siècle, lorsque les marchands italiens affluent à Avignon et prennent une part considérable au trafic fluvial" (Rossiaud 2002, 1:188). The influx occurred against a background of Italian omnipresence on the Mediterranean (Dufourcq 1975, 83).

48 Pansier 1924–32, 1:36. Italians began arriving at Orange in 1311, and did so in large numbers in the second half of the century (Gasparri 1979, 48–9). At Arles, the Tuscan colony left traces from around 1360 to 1420 (Stouff 1986, 229, 251).

49 After *i*: *cabris*, "kids," for *cabritz*; *petis*, "small," for *petitz*. After *e*: *caules* (stressed *caulés*), "cabbages," for *cauletz*. After *u*: *mantegus*, "mentioned," for *mantegutz*. All of these reduced forms occur in MS N. MS T has *dis*, singular (T5r6, T5r23, T11v25), as a form of the past participle of *dire*; the *-s* is a graphyfor the affricate, not a reduction of *–tz*. Compare *dig* (T12v23).

50 Plural *lu(s)* occurs in the regions of Provence-Alpes-Côte d'Azur (Nice, Alpes-Maritimes), Auvergne (Vinzelles, Puy-de-Dôme), Midi-Pyrénées (Quercy; Lombez, Gers), Aquitaine (Sarlat and Nontron, Dordogne), and the Limousin; *lu*, singular, occurs in Nice, Sarlat, and the Périgord (Ronjat 1930–41, 3:109, §533; *FEW* 4:551b). On the commercial links of Nice, see Dufourcq 1975, 19.

51 This claim is supported by orthographic or lexical practices that distinguish one manuscript from the other (see Glossary for the following words). Spellings that vary include *mog* (etc.), "hogshead," in T, but *moy* (etc.) in N; *saquiera* (a measure of weight, about a ton) in T, but *sequiera* in N; *Tharascon* in both manuscripts, but *Tarascon* only in N. Word choices that vary include *caval*, "horse," in T, but *chival* in N; *peis*, "fish," in T, but *peisson* in N; *pom*, "apple," in T, but *poma* in N; *sap*, "fir," in T, but *sapin* in N. Expressions: *de gros*, "around," in T, but *de redon* in N; *a l'albire del peager*, "at the tollkeeper's judgment," in T, but *al plaser del peagier*, "at the tollkeeper's discretion," in N. *Los Mujolans*, the name of a tollhouse in T, has become *Los Violans* in N.

52 Ronjat 1930–41, 1:212, §119 delta. Compare the adjective *grandes*, feminine plural, in MS N.

53 On the masc. pl. *aquélous* in modern Occitan dialects in the department of Hautes-Alpes (Embrun, Gap, Serres, Orpierre), see Ronjat 1930–41, 3:89, §521. On *élous*, also in Hautes-Alpes (Embrun, Champsaur, Valgaudemar), see Ronjat 1930–41, 3:55, §502.

54 Lenition is a general phenomenon in Old Occitan; see Paden 1998, 130–4.

55 I use square brackets here for symbols from the International Phonetic Alphabet.

56 Ronjat 1930–41, 2:121, §289; 2:123, §289 gamma.

57 Bondurand 1890, 135.

58 Pansier 1924–32, 3:1–178, 5:159–96.

59 1285: *romieu*. 1366: *pertega*. 1397: *solpre*. Fourteenth century: *albire, linh.* Pansier does not include two terms mentioned by Bondurand: *razis* and *San Jacme*.

60 Attested in the fifteenth century (as well as other centuries, in many cases) by Pansier, and occurring in T but not in N: *cavalcadura, dela, duptar, egua, feda, frut, grazalet, leon, mainage, manifestar, mula, quiti, sarja, visitar*. In N but not in T: *agive, aigual, armari, avelana, avis, blanquet, carn, cavalcador, costuma, diaque, egalar, ensemble, ensens, esclau, gran, jamais, jor, lentilha, lentiscle, liga, liome, mercandisa, mesurar, milh, nerta, ors, paniera, partison, plaser, polvera,*

pres (1), *privilegiat, rauba, ribiera, roge, sapin, segla, sotterran, terratori, tractar, vair* (1).

61 Like most modern Occitan dialects, MSS TN observe prosthesis in words that began in Latin with *s* + stop (see Glossary: *esc-*, *esp-*, *est-*). Aphetic forms (*sc-*, *sp-*, *st-*) occur occasionally, however, in both MSS, as in modern dialects in the Alpes-Maritimes and northwestern Italy (Ronjat 1930–41, 2:191, §321).

62 The first two folios contain obituaries of counts of Provence and Calabria; f. 18r contains the beginning of a transaction between the nobles and bourgeois of Tarascon settling points of municipal administration (Meyer 1865–7, Série AA, 2; Roucaute 2009).

63 I am grateful to Stéphanie Arnaud, assistant to the director of the Archive, for these dimensions.

64 The red leaders begin on f. 4r and continue to f. 14v, but not constantly, as the space between item and toll may be left blank or the toll may be deferred to the end of a list of items.

65 Two columns (ff. 10r1–11v2, 14r10–18, 14r24–35, 15r14–27, 15v17–16r6), three (f. 13v33–6), or five (ff. 16r19–17r6).

66 Initials in MS N with both red and blue occur in the words *In* (1r17) and *Lo* (1v21). The subsequent alternation of blue and red breaks down five times: on ff. 10r–v (the last initial on f. 10r, at 10r22, is red, and so is the first one on f. 10v, at 10v1); f. 11v9–10 (both red); ff. 11v–12r (the last initial on 11v, at 11v25, is blue, and so is the first one on 12r, at 12r3); f. 15r7–9 (both blue); ff. 15r–v (the last initial on f. 15r, at 15r16, is blue, and so is the first one on f. 15v, at 15v1).

67 The association of nobles who held the *montazon*, which has two rubrics in T (VI, VII), is mentioned in N under the toll on salt (II), but no rates for this fee are given.

68 Most of the commodities listed separately for Lubières (T IV) also occur with Tarascon (T I). The tolls on most of the items listed twice are smaller for Lubières, around 10% to 25% in T IV of what they are in T I, though some of them are the same (18d for lime, gypsum, and rock).

69 *Los Violans*, corruption of *Los Mujolans* (see Glossary).

70 On the historical origins of the two layouts in accounting practices, see §5.4.

71 See Appendices 1 (Table T1, salt in hogsheads), 3 (Table N1, salt in small hogsheads), and 4 (Table N2, salt in large hogsheads).

72 See Appendix 2 at 12, 18, 27, 30, and 32 hogsheads. The increments are irregular, and so perhaps wrong, in T2 at 20 and 27, and in T3 at 12, 18, and 30; but the increments are irregular in both T2 and T3 for 35 and 40 hogsheads.

73 Figuring the discrepancies as absolute values, they total 5.75d, which is one-thousandth of one per cent (0.0012%) of the sum of the *montazon* from one to forty hogsheads.

74 Tolls differ in MSS TN because of scribal errors in N at units 11, 19, and 35; the correct tolls are those given in T, as is confirmed by the figures in N for King, Nobles, and Balance. At unit 34 in N, Toll is up 2d, King down 0.25d, Nobles down 0.50d, and Balance is off by 2.75d; if all three figures (Toll, King, Knights) were corrected with those from T, they would balance.

75 Compare the anecdote about Theophilus, the emperor of Constantinople in the year 829, who, upon seeing a beautiful ship that, as he learned, belonged to his wife, exclaimed to her with indignation, "God made me an emperor, you would make me a ship captain!" and ordered that the ship and all its cargo be burnt (Lopez 1976, 66).

76 *Et hec omnia de pedagiis habui tam ex dictis Salvis, Crescas de Profecto, Comprati, Crescas de Les et Belli Hominis, judeorum, juratorum, quam ex tenore cujusdam publici instrumenti confecti [per manum] Poncii de Salves, publici notarii, super pedagiis et lesdis.* "And all these things about tolls I got from both the words of Salves, Crescas de Profecto, Compratus, Crescas de Les, and Bellus Homo, Jews, witnesses, and from the tenor of a certain public instrument drawn up in the hand of Poncius de Salves, public notary, about tolls and market fees" (Fr. *droit de leude*) (Guérard 1:c).

77 We shall study the evolution of tolls from the investigations and into the registers in §6.

78 Aix, A.D., B.d.R., B 1060, f. 6; Martin-Portier 2006, 2:243.

79 A marginal note (ibid.) refers to *ritus* as documents, then (not altogether clearly) as procedures: *Videantur dicti ritus in archivio Aquensis et inserantur in hoc regestro pedagii habebant ritus ipsorum remansis provinciali superius de archivio predicto*, "The said *ritus* [documents] may be seen in the archive at Aix, and may be inserted in this register of toll; they had their *ritus* [procedures] from those left in the archive of Provence mentioned above." On *habere*, "to have knowledge of, be in possession of (facts, information)," see *OLD* s.v. *habeo*, §11; here with the dative for the source of information (*remansis*).

80 The first time the register reads *s ii, d v, o., po. j*, "2s 5d 1 obol 1 pogeza," that is, 2s 5.75d or 29.75d (T9v25). The second time, in Table T1, it reads *s ii, d v, po*, "2s 5d pogeza," that is, 2s 5.25d or 29.25d (T10r4).

81 As is confirmed when Table T1 proceeds with the base rate of 29.75d from two to six hogsheads, and in Table N1. See Appendix 1.

82 At seven, ten, and thirteen hogsheads.

83 A later hand corrected this table from *xv* to *xxv* (Smith and Hawthorne 1974, 73).

84 See Appendix 1.

85 See Appendix 2.

86 For nine hogsheads (24d!), twelve (9d), eighteen (8.25d), twenty-five (13.5d), twenty-seven (5.5d), twenty-eight (3.5d), thirty-two (5.5d), thirty-three (3.5d), thirty-five (5d), thirty-six (4d), thirty-seven (12d), and forty (7.25d).

87 At nine, twelve, thirteen, eighteen, nineteen, twenty-five, thirty, thirty-one, thirty-five, thirty-six, thirty-seven, and forty hogsheads.

88 See Appendix 3.

89 See Appendix 4.

90 No allowance is made for the cost of the tollkeeping operation itself, which was presumably underwritten by the king.

91 See Appendix 1 and the notes provided there for explanation of these corrections.

92 At one hogshead, the toll should be 0.5d more. At fourteen hhd, it should be 1d less. At seventeen hhd, the king's share should be 0.5d more. At twenty-four hhd, the knights' share should be 1d less. At twenty-six hhd, the king's share should be 1d more and the knights' share should be 5.5d less. The entire entry for twenty-seven hhd (Toll, King, Knights) has been skipped. At thirty hhd, the knights' share should be 0.5d more. At thirty-seven hhd, the knights' share should be 1d more. At thirty-eight hhd, the knights' share should be 0.5d less.

93 To calculate this percentage, the discrepancies have been considered as absolute values.

94 See Appendix 3.

95 The corrections (that is, presumed errors) in the figures for Tolls come to 0.15% of the total of the figures provided in the MS; in those for the King, to 1.55%; in those for the Nobles, to 4.03%; in all figures combined, both income (Toll) and outgo (King and Nobles), to 1.14%. For this calculation, corrections have been treated as absolute numbers rather than positive or negative.

96 See Appendix 4.

97 Lee (1977, 94) argues that the Farolfi ledger shows greater interest in other operations such as segregating accounts, maintaining an inventory, and recording withdrawals by the partners, than in calculating the balance. In certain administrative functions of the Avignonese papacy, regular calculation of balances became the norm under Benedict XII, who ruled from 1334 to 1342 (Weiß 2002, 35–6). "Even in the fifteenth century, most of the 'balance' sheets of the Medici did not balance, and there is no evidence of efforts to find and correct the mistakes" (Arlinghaus 2004, 1:149).

98 Rossiaud 2002, 2:120–1.

99 "En 1033, le roi d'Arles, Rodolphe III, céda ses droits à l'empereur d'Allemagne Conrad III. La Provence devint alors terre d'Empire" (Bondurand 1891a, 118n1). The city attracted immigration mostly from Provence, relatively little from across the Rhône (Hébert 1979, 82). Tarascon remained theoretically dependent on the Roman Empire until 1481, when the county of Provence passed to the king of France (Roux 2004, 1:4).

100 Delebecque 1929b, 62. The statutes of Queen Joan, promulgated about 1348, identified Tarascon as a *villa regia* and the seat of a *curia regia* (Bondurand

1891a, 27, 41), as did those of Marie de Blois in 1390 (*curia regia*, ibid., 124). In 1325 the king was present in Tarascon to settle a dispute over tolls (N12v24–13r5). "Siège d'une viguerie qui s'étend vers les Saintes-Maries-de-la-Mer, Fos, Orgon et Châteaurenard, lieu de résidence d'un juge et d'un clavaire royaux, elle [Tarascon] fait pratiquement figure, au XVème siècle, de deuxième capitale comtale après Aix, tant les déplacements et séjours princiers y sont nombreux" (Roux 2004, 1:238).

101 Hébert 1979, 39–40. The original castle was built between 994 and 1010 (Delebecque 1929b, 58) or 1033 and 1036 (Hébert 1979, 8–9).

102 Pressouyre 1963, 221.

103 The title Charles used on his coins was king of Sicily (Duplessy 2004–10, 2:5–6). This title continued to be used after 1282, when Sicily seceded from Charles's kingdom in the aftermath of the Sicilian Vespers. The remainder of the Kingdom of Sicily became the Kingdom of Naples; Joan, Charles's eventual successor as king of Sicily, was styled queen of Naples. The two dominions merged in 1816, forming the Kingdom of the Two Sicilies.

104 N10r5, parallel to the *rey nostre senhor*, T9r20.

105 Hébert 1979, 62, 96, 125, 146–7.

106 Pécout and Portier-Martin 2010, pp. xcix–c (Figs. 28, 29); Martin-Portier 2006, 1:173, 345 (carte C1).

107 Bondurand 1891a, 124, item XXXVIII, issued in 1390.

108 For a map that indicates toll points all over Provence as well as ports, roads, and fairs, see Baratier, Duby, and Hildesheimer [1969], carte 86. For discussion of the toll points, see Baratier 1969, 39–44 (map, 42). In principle any toll was considered payment for services such as maintenance of port facilities or protection against piracy (Lalou 1993).

109 The tolls were one source of income among others including *albergue*, that is, income from *emphytéoses* or long leases; *chevauchées*, the obligation of a vassal to accompany his lord on military expeditions; *quêtes*, the collection of fees on certain lands by the occupants; *droit de poids et mesures*, the right over weights and measures; and *salnaria*, the sale and concession of salt (Delebecque 1929b, 61).

110 In MS P (Guérard): *Nicia, Saranonum, Brinonia, Castrum de Pennis, Aquae, Digna, Castrum de Valansola, Sancto Gabriele, Tarasco, Avinio, Orgo, Arelates.* The list is extended, but follows the same overall pattern, in MS A_1 (Baratier): *Episcopatus Nicie, Episcopatus Vencie* (Vence, Alpes-Maritimes), *Episcopatus Grasse* (Alpes-Maritimes), *Episcopatus Forjuliensis* (Fréjus, Var), *Bajulia Sancti Maximini* (Saint-Maximin, Gard), *Episcopatus Massilie* (Marseille, Bouches-du-Rhône), *Archiepiscopatus Aquensis* (Aix, Bouches-du-Rhône), *Bajulia Dignensis generalis* (Digne), *Episcopatus Glandantensis* (Glandèves, Alpes-de-

Haute-Provence), *Episcopatus Senescensis* (Senez, Alpes-de-Haute-Provence), *Episcopatus Avinionensis (in villa Tarasconi, in civitate Avinioni), Civitas Aralatenis.*

111 Income from Arles/Marseille was estimated as £2500, from Aix/Les Pennes as £1050, from Tarascon as £1030, and from Berre/Istres as £1025. No other source among the sixteen provided more than £600. MS Aix, A.D., B.d.R., B 1477 (16), ff. 1r-2r.

112 On the tollhouses, see Glossary s.v. *pezage*.

113 *Item habet dominus rex in insula Gernete quemdam locum plantatum arboribus juxta quod percipitur pedagium Tharasconis*, "Item: The lord king has on the island of Jarnègues a certain place planted with trees, beside which the toll of Tarascon is collected," according to MS A_2 (Martin-Portier 2006, 2:46). The toll for the Gate was collected at Jarnègues (ibid., 2:51). The tollhouse on Jarnègues may have been the same as the *pedagium riparie Rodani*, the "tollhouse on the bank of the Rhône," in the investigation made for Robert I in 1332 (ibid., 2:243). Roux (2004, 1:250) avers that tolls on merchandise were paid at Jarnègues and those on passengers at Lubières, with what evidence I do not know.

114 Pécout and Portier-Martin 2010, 288, Index locorum, s.v. Tharasco.

115 Baratier and Reynaud 1951, 2:254, 563. Land transport cost three times as much as shipping (Villain-Gandossi 1968, 180).

116 Denel 1970, 293. Baix (Ardèche) is 123 kilometres north of Tarascon. On the Mediterranean, ships stayed in port from the end of October to the beginning of March (Pryor 1994, 74).

117 Stouff 1986, 215.

118 Bautier 1989, 33.

119 On marshy terrain near Tarascon in the thirteenth and fourteenth centuries, see Pécout and Portier-Martin 2010, lxxiii–lxxv. For a map of the *viguerie* of Tarascon marked with high places and marshes, see Martin-Portier 2006, 1:345 (carte C1). Between the Rhône to the west, the hills of La Montagnette to the north, and the small mountain range of Les Alpilles to the south, Tarascon's alluvial soil naturally produces marshy conditions (Roux 2004, 1:103).

120 Roux 2004, 1:114n43. *Brassiero*, "bras de rivière" (Mistral 1:363).

121 Hébert 1979, 26; Roux 2004, 1:114, 117. Lubières was still an island in 1332: *ad insulas Luperiarum et Luciani* (Pécout 2010, 8).

122 The Tarasque was said to have descended from Leviathan in the Book of Job and the Bonachum in Solinus, a monster with the head of a bull and the body of a horse; in the late fifteenth century it became a more ordinary terrestrial dragon (Coulet 1991, 575), on its way toward becoming the folkloric icon that it is today.

123 "Le premier pont entre Tarascon et Beaucaire ne fut construit qu'au XVIIe siècle" (Hébert 1979, 39), echoed by Roux (2004, 1:8). Weiß states that in the

fourteenth century the bridge at Avignon was the only stable passage over the Rhône between the sea and Pont-Saint-Esprit, some 58 kilometres upstream from Tarascon (2002, 98). The exception is Février, who quoted the passage from Guérard referring to a *ponte de novo facto* (see following note) and concluded, "Ce texte paraît donc fixer la date de l'achèvement de l'oeuvre en 1251" (1964, 200). Hébert (1979, 51n50) quotes Février but rejects his claim, arguing that the phrase *ponte de novo facto* "semble s'appliquer en fait à un pont de bateaux rapidement démantelé par la suite," with reference to Delebecque (1929a) but no page number. Having no direct access to Delebecque's handwritten thesis, which is preserved in the Bibliothèque des Archives municipales, Marseille, I have been unable to find the evidence cited there for this claim. In her published summary, Delebecque (1929b) does not refer to the question of this bridge. "La construction d'un pont de bateaux – d'ailleurs éphémère – à la fin du XIIIe siècle ne change rien à l'affaire" (Vignal 1989, 386).

124 *Apud Bellicadrum et Tarasconum in ponte de novo facto anno Domini M° CC° L° I*, "at Beaucaire and Tarascon, on the bridge newly made in the year 1251" (Baratier 388, Guérard lxxxvii). *Si tranceunt per pontem*, "if they cross by bridge" (Baratier 389). The word *pons* meant exactly "bridge"; Du Cange (6:406) rebuts a claim that it once meant "ferry."

125 *Guillelmus Porcel et ejus gener pro domibus de ponte .xviii. d. tur.* (MS A_1, f. 78r, line 26), "Guillelmus Porcel and his son-in-law [owe], for houses on the bridge, 18d tournois." I see no reason to capitalize *ponte* here as Baratier does (384), indicating that he interprets this word as the name of a quarter of the town, a *lieu-dit* – but why call a quarter by this name, if there was no bridge? His index (527) provides no other reference to such a quarter, nor does one appear on the maps of the city by Hébert (1979, 40, including the names of quarters), Pécout and Portier-Martin (2010, p. ci, including the names of streets), or Baratier, Duby, and Hildesheimer ([1969], carte 293, Tarascon in 1757).

126 *Pro quodam hospicio sito ad Caput Pontis*, "for a certain house situated at the head of the bridge" (Pécout and Portier-Martin 2010, 35, f. 21); *pro I hospicio sito ad caput pontis Rodani* (ibid., 35, f. 21v). *Hospitium* was used in 1332 to mean "house" (Martin-Portier 2006, 1:301, tableau T22; cf. Niermeyer 1:658). Plural *domibus*, "houses," in MS A_1 (see preceding note) confirms this interpretation. It was common for a bridge to have an associated *hospitium*, "hospital": "Plus souvent encore, l'hôpital s'implante à la tête de l'ouvrage ... ; c'est le cas de ces *domus pontis*, maisons du pont souvent signalées" (Mesqui 1986, 112). On chapels, houses, and shops on bridges, see also Spufford 2002, 176–80; Spufford agrees that there was no bridge at Tarascon.

127 *Statuimus quod officiales curie faciant aptari vias et pontes ad requisitionem hominum Tharasconis* (Bondurand 1891a, 96). Other bridges at Tarascon

included one linking the city to the island of Jarnègues, mentioned in 1332: "Jardica, pons de (*Jarnègues*); Ponte de Gervica (*île de Jarnègues, au nord de Tarascon*)" (Pécout and Portier-Martin 2010, 288, s.v. Tharasco; see map, Hébert 1979, 40). Boyer (1976, 193) mentions a "bridge to château of counts of Anjou" in Tarascon, documented in 1448, which appears to have been an entryway into the castle, not a bridge across the Rhône: *pontis lignei introitûs ejusdem castri nostri* (Lecoy 1875, 138, item 368).

128 If not earlier; MS A_2, compiled in 1298, fails to mention tolls collected at the bridge (Martin-Portier 2006, 2:40–51).

129 *Quamdam meam barcam cum qua transio gentes per flumen Rodani*, "a certain bark of mine with which I ferry people over the Rhône" (Roux 2004, 1:251n116).

130 On ferries, see Stouff, who declares, "D'Avignon à la mer [including Tarascon] n'existe aucun véritable pont" (1986, 1:210).

131 They were *la porte Roqueta, de Jarnègues, Condamine, Saint-Jean*, and *de la reine* (Hébert 1979, 40, map). Perhaps Hébert's *porte Condamine* was the *Portal de Tarascon* of MSS TN, seen from the point of view of Avignon (see Glossary, s.v. *portal*). The inquiry of 1332 also mentioned a *portale Monete*, "gate of the Mint" (Pécout and Portier-Martin 2010, 288, Index locorum s.v. Tharasco). For the fifteenth century Roux considers *la Roquette*, beween the castle and the Jewish quarter, a smaller gate (Occ. *portalet*, Fr. *portail*), and adds the gate of *la Fracha* (2004, 241–2).

132 Roux 2004, 1:253–4, 258.

133 Roux 2004, 1:254. The mint at Tarascon was established by Charles I in 1249, reopened by Joan in 1353–68 and 1371–9, and maintained by a succession of rulers in 1387–1481 (Roux, ibid.). Queen Joan struck the first Provençal gold florins there (Charlet 1976, [2]; Charlet 2004, 28). According to Baratier, Duby, and Hildesheimer [1969], carte 105: Ateliers monétaires, the mint at Tarascon was the longest-lived in Provence (1249–1481: 232 years in operation) after Avignon (1239–1481: 242 years).

Both registers mention tolls for coiners working for either the king of Sicily or the king of France (T9r20–1, N10r5–6), presumably in Tarascon, but I do not know when, if ever, the mint at Tarascon produced coins for the king of France. However, the idea should not seem surprising. Charles I, who founded the mint in Tarascon, was the brother of Louis IX of France. I have found evidence for coinage by the French king elsewhere in the Midi: in 1356 and 1359–60 the Dauphin had coins struck in Languedoc (Duplessy 1988-9, 1:127); in the late fourteenth and early fifteenth centuries, kings of France minted coins at Saint-André de Villeneuve-lès-Avignon (1391–1418, 1422–3) and in Languedoc at Beaucaire (1422–3), just across the Rhône (Duplessy 1988-9, 1:165, 208–9). Coins minted by the king of France were current in Provence since at least 1330, and became common by the 1380s (Fauris de Saint-Vincens 1778–80, 115, 138; see also 121, 143, 151).

134 "Un grenier à sel est établi sur le port de Tarascon, successeur de la saunerie qui y existait depuis 1150. En 1450, le grenier à sel de Tarascon rapporte près de 5500 livres" (Roux 2004, 1:240).

135 The brothel (*prostibulum*): Roux 2004, 1:241, 254.

136 Map: Hébert 1979, 44. Cf. Roux 2004, 1:240–7; a fourth gate, the *Porte de la Reine* or *de Madame*, at the southwest corner of the town, was closed at the end of the fourteenth century (ibid., 1:241).

137 Roux 2004, 1:261–2, 279.

138 Martin-Portier 2006, 1:311 (tableau T31); cf. 1:208. *Castrum*, "village groupé et fortifié"; *civitas*, "cité épiscopale"; *villa*, "agglomération sans fortifications ... soit un hameau dépourvu de remparts ... soit une ville neuve ... soit une ville importante qui n'est pas une ancienne cité épiscopale" (Baratier 30–1). On MS N, see Glossary.

139 Hébert 1979, 60.

140 Roux 2004, 1:239, 2:439.

141 Roux 2004, 1:250. Martin-Portier (2006, 1:234) suggests that the various supplies for naval construction subject to toll, such as rudders, masts, and yards, were intended for shipbuilding in the port of Tarascon.

142 Stouff 1986, 224–6.

143 Weiß 2002, 350.

144 Stouff 1986, 224–5. Scholars who write in English measure a ship's displacement in long tons, while those who write in French use metric tons. But since a long ton equals 1.016 metric tons and the figures quoted here and elsewhere are both general and approximate, the difference is immaterial.

145 Villain-Gandossi observes that at the beginning of the fourteenth century enormous flat-bottomed barges (*chalands*) carried up to 412 metric tons, but later in the century ships were capable of no more than 80 to 100 metric tons (1969, 55).

146 Fourquin 1990, 182, 192. Somewhat different dimensions (up to 38 metres long, capacity up to 600 tons) according to Unger 2000, 555. Further on sailed ships, Baratier and Reynaud 1951, 749–52. Here and throughout this section, further documentation on Occitan words cited may be found in the Glossary.

147 Lane 1964, 231. The word "galley" has been said to mean "swordfish" or "galeoid shark," *galaia* or *galea* in Byzantine Greek (Lopez 1976, 82), although the etymon is unknown according to the *OED*. "D'origine byzantine; son étymon exact et sa migration ne sont pas encore définitivement établis" (Fennis 1995, 2:993).

148 Lopez 1976, 81.

149 B[oislisle] 1872, 254, with provision for 120 oars and helmets, cuirasses, and shields for a crew of 130. Fourquin 1990, 191. Pryor estimates the crew of an 800-ton round ship in the thirteenth century as "around 80 officers and sailors plus some servants and ship's boys," and its passenger complement as about 560 (1994, 63–4).

150 "The popular image of the galley slave fits both late antiquity and the early modern period but not the Middle Ages, when labor was scarce and oarsmen were proud, free citizens and tough fighters" (Lopez 1976, 81). "Tous les marins sont des hommes libres"; impressment was forbidden, but in the sixteenth century slaves came to be used as oarsmen (Dufourcq 1975, 65–6). In the fifteenth century, the Genoese "supplemented the convicts that they used to row their war galleys with slaves" (Spufford 2002, 339). Slaves were included among *forçats*, "prisoners," as manpower of galleys in citations dated 1529–1723 (Fourquin and Rigaud 1994, 153).

151 Villain-Gandossi 1969, 55.

152 "Parmi ces bateaux intermédiaires, figurent les 'barques'; ce sont des bâtiments à un seul pont, munis en général d'un seul mât et pourvus de rames; on les désigne aussi sous le nom de lignes" (Dufourcq 1975, 61).

153 Stouff 1986, 215.

154 The graffito is in a room on the ground floor of the round tower facing the bank, to the left as one enters the castle from the town. For Labande the oldest of the drawings in this room date from the sixteenth century (1909, 276), but Baratier ascribes the graffito to the fifteenth (1951, facing 577). Lacroix pointed out that the prisoner who made the graffito might have seen the ship on the Mediterranean (1864, 332).

155 McGowan 1981, 10. Called in Spanish and Portuguese the *nao*, in Italian the *nave* (according to McGowan), terms corresponding to Occitan *nau*.

156 For a ship resembling the graffito in all these respects that was depicted on a Hispano-Moorish bowl *circa* 1425, see McGowan 1981, 11–12.

157 Villain-Gandossi 1969, 56.

158 Rossiaud 2002, 2:353.

159 Rossiaud 2002, 1:189, 2:347–56. A *barca* went first, facing the current, carrying the heaviest load, and supporting the principal effort of hauling; ibid., 2:37.

160 Barges: Denel 1970, 294. "Péniches à fond plat": Villain-Gandossi 1969, 55. Unladings: Villain-Gandossi 1969, 54.

161 Denel 1970, 290. "On pourrait se demander si les bâtiments étaient affrétés pour un voyage aller et retour, ou bien s'ils descendaient à vide" (Villain-Gandossi 1968, 178).

162 Villain-Gandossi 1969, 56; slightly different figures in Villain-Gandossi 1968, 177–8. Denel 1970, 291.

163 Rossiaud 2002, 2:287–9. For an image of a small raft of four logs chained together, see J. M. W. Turner, *The Harbour of Dieppe* (ca. 1826), in the Frick Collection, New York City.
164 Lopez 1976; Elbl 2000; Spufford 2002.
165 Melville and Staub 2008, 2:155–6.
166 Edler 1934, 335. See also Lopez 1976, 74–5.
167 Lee 1977, 79, 88.
168 Lee 1977, 80. For a facsimile of the Farolfi ledger, see Castellani 1952, facing 2:720.
169 Lee 1977, 94. Further on the two formats in account books, De Roover 1956, passim.
170 In what may be the oldest extant record of tolls at Tarascon (Aix, A.D., B.d.R., B 2), we see both formats: tabular form on f. 49r (with the date of the original, 1246, in a fourteenth-century copy) and f. 57v; paragraph form on ff. 60v–61r.
171 The *provençal*, or *tournois provençal*, made of alloy, was created before 1249 as the equivalent of the French tournois, and continued to be produced until the reign of Charles II, who died in 1309 (Rolland 1956, 85). For a catalogue of coins struck by the counts of Provence, including deniers, oboles, and *gros tournois*, see Duplessy (2004–10, 2:2–14).
172 Duplessy 2004–10, 2:2–14; the "châtel tournois" appears on items 1616–20, 1628–29B, 1633–33A, 1663. Counts of Provence who minted deniers included Robert (1309–43), Joan with her husband, Louis I (1349–62), and Joan as a widow (1362–82); see Duplessy 2004–10, 2:12, 15, 20. Rolland (1956, 86) says that the *denier provençal* was minted from circa 1355 to 1370.
173 For a catalogue of florins struck by the counts of Provence from the mid-fourteenth century to the early fifteenth, see Duplessy–10 (2004, 2:13–23, items 1659–60, 1668–69A, 1672–4, 1695–6). The Baptist is replaced with a bust of Queen Joan on item 1671, the "florin d'or à la tête."
174 The Provençal florin was minted at Tarascon (Charlet 1976, [2]). In Marseille, the florin of Florence was "la base de la monnaie de compte et l'étalon constant de référence de la plupart des transactions de 1299 à 1481" (Baratier and Reynaud 1951, 907). "En 1365, le 23 juin, le Conseil de la ville [de Marseille] avait demandé à Jeanne, reine de Jérusalem, de frapper de la monnaie à Marseille; ce même jour le même Conseil déclarait que nul ne pourrait accepter de force d'autres monnaies que les bons et justes florins de Florence, de la Chambre, du Pape, de Lucques et de Gênes" (ibid., 908).
175 Spufford 1986, xx. The counts of Provence minted *blancs à la couronne* in the mid-fourteenth century (Duplessy 2004–10, 2:12–13).
176 "The arithmetic, performed on the abacus or with counters, is in general very accurate" (Lee 1977, 80). Counters were essential for calculation using Roman

numerals; Arabic numerals came into general use in the later fifteenth century. "Un jeu ordinaire de jetons ne se composait que de cent pièces. L'appareil de compte était complété par une tablette rayée dans les deux sens, horizontal et vertical, de manière à former des lignes et des colonnes, et sur laquelle on faisait manoeuvrer les jetons. Cette tablette, connue des anciens et des modernes sous le nom d'abaque, ne l'était guère au moyen âge que sous celui de *comptoir*" (Rouyer and Hucher 1858, 12).

177 N5v7–8, N13r18, N16r17–18.

178 Spufford 1986, 172–9 ("The Florentine florin in sous and deniers tournois of France"). Tarascon is mentioned only once, for 1293 (ibid., 174), with an erroneous reference to Davidsohn 1896–1908, vol. 2, item 182, whereas the item concerned occurs in vol. 3. I cannot construe that item (Davidsohn 1896–1908, 3:46, item 182) to produce an exchange rate of 10:1. Nevertheless, Spufford's data for all of France from 1265 to 1498 make clear that the rate given in MS N was obsolete.

179 See the graph in Spufford 1986, 173.

180 Abu-Lughod 1989, 34. "In the south [of Europe], the Levant and Black Sea trades supplied not only 'spices' (a term that included dyestuffs and medicinal substances, as well as condiments) and luxuries, but also Black Sea grain and vital raw materials (hides, alum, cotton). Trade with North Africa brought to European markets hides, wax, wool, dyestuffs, ostrich feathers, gold, and sharp condiments ... The outermost boundary of Europe's commercial contacts, or at least commercial intelligence, now stretched from Iceland in the west to the Sahara in the south and China in the east" (Elbl 2000, 167).

181 Valérian 2014, 88.

182 Baratier 43.

183 "The ape (Latin *simia*) of medieval Western European literature is most likely the tailless Barbary ape of the African coast, or in some cases, the tailed ape of tropical Africa" (Kelly 2000, 23–4). "Apes had by [the twelfth century] become available in Western Europe in sufficient quantity, so that a good many people, at least in the towns, were given an opportunity to observe them in the flesh. They were being imported across the western Mediterranean ... The offerings of these *jongleurs* included the display of performing animals, among which the bear and the ape were the most popular. As early as the first half of the twelfth century, apes could even be kept as expensive pets" (Janson 1952, 30). Ladies kept them too (Dufourcq 1975, 102).

184 On florins: Spufford 1986, xix.

185 Crusader ships returned from the Holy Land "with the ceramics, drugs, spices, precious cloths, glassware, and perfumes of the East which were so much in demand in the West" (Pryor 1994, 70).

186 Dufourcq 1975, 101–2.
187 Spufford 2002, 326.
188 Stouff 1986, 231–2.
189 "Le pèlerinage de Saint-Gilles, en aval de Tarascon, n'était guère moins célèbre que celui de Saint-Jacques-en-Galice. On voit par cet article qu'il y venait des Espagnols, des Anglais et des Allemands" (Bondurand 150n11). "The Benedictine abbey of Saint-Gilles was founded during the seventh century traditionally by the hermit Saint Giles ... The abbey ... was the first stopping point for pilgrims bound for Santiago de Compostela in Spain, who were following the *via Tolosana* that led from Arles to Toulouse and crossed the Pyrenees to join other routes at Puente La Reina, thence to Santiago" (Wikipedia s.v. "Saint-Gilles, Gard," consulted 6 April 2015).
190 "The modern perception that medieval people seldom ventured very far from home is uninformed" (Langdon 2000, 607). On the other hand, Hébert pointed out that most of the cities to which Tarascon sent messengers and ambassadors lay within 20 kilometres of its ramparts (1979, 86; maps, 84).
191 *Sarrasceno vendito*, "a Saracen sold" (Baratier 259). *Sarrasin vel sarracena per vendre*, "A Saracen man or woman for sale" at Les Pennes, near Aix-en-Provence (Guérard 1:lxxvii).
192 Martin-Portier 2006, 2:45. I do not find Syrians among slaves in southern France from the thirteenth to the fifteenth century in Verlinden 1955, 1:748–833. Not *Surio seu Suria*, but *Sirino vel Sirina* according to Delebecque 1929a, 3:53–4, possibly referring to Bulgarians or Balkans. The Sirina River flows in Romania, and a slave *de partibus Borgarie sive Chirtarie* (possibly related to *Sirina*?) was sold at Marseille in 1414 (Verlinden 1955–77, 1:785).
193 "Over three millennia slavery was an inextricable part of Mediterranean social and economic life" (Rotman 2014, 275). "Throughout the fourteenth and fifteenth centuries, slavery was fairly common in the Mediterranean world" (De Roover 1956, 145). "Tout le monde ou presque possède des esclaves, aussi bien des religieux comme les Templiers ou les Bénédictins, que des meuniers, des apothicaires, des tailleurs de pierre ou des rois et des comtes" (Dufourcq 1975, 139). However, "slaves are not heard of in late medieval Europe north of Languedoc and Provence" (Spufford 2002, 338). On sexual services by female slaves, see Origo 1955 and McKee 2013.
194 Italian *schiavi* (Pegolotti 1936, 429).
195 On the slave trade in Mediterranean France from the thirteenth to the fifteenth century, see Verlinden 1955–77, 1:748–833. On the thirteenth century in Provence, Baratier, index des noms de matières, 541 (s.v. affranchissement), 549 (s.v. homo), 550 (s.v liber); in the fourteenth century at Marseille, Baratier and Reynaud 1951, 250–3; in Florence, Origo 1955; in the fifteenth century at

Naples, Leone 2003; in Muslim society, Feniello 2011, 154–61. In the early Middle Ages slaves were treated unambiguously as animals (Bonnassie 1999, 595–6); the slave trade grew from the thirteenth to the fifteenth century (ibid., 608).

196 Du Roure 1906, 12.

197 Dufourcq 1975, 50, citing a document from Montpellier dated 1162. Elsewhere Dufourcq (1980, 223) discusses "bateaux mixtes," ships owned in partnership by Spanish Christians and Muslims. "Il était très fréquent et pour ainsi dire normal d'être tout en même temps en état de guerre et de paix" (1980, 208).

198 Courcelles 1820–2, 3:37–8. Two women bearing the family name, Saura Alba and Gileta Alba, were among the most wealthy citizens of Tarascon at the end of the fourteenth century (Hébert 1979, 152n31).

199 Du Roure 1906, 8–18.

200 Jean d'Albe, joint lord of Saint-Andiol and Aiglun, is attested 1402–21; born about 1380, he died between 1421 and 1426. He was active in Arles and left a trace in Tarascon (Du Roure 1906, 10–11). He jointly ruled Saint-Andiol, now in Bouches-du-Rhône, canton Orgon, mentioned in the *Enquête dans la viguerie de Tarascon* in 1332 (Pécout and Portier-Martin 2010), and which we have identified for other reasons with the town called Adaul in MS N (see Glossary). He also had part ownership of Aiglun, perhaps the town of that name near Digne (Alpes-de-Haute-Provence). He was not a member of the *montaizon* (N6v4).

201 *Draps*, "cloths," T3v8, N7v8. *Lana*, "wool," T4r19, N7v24. *Gaida*, "woad," T4r23 = *caida*, N8r11. *Greza*, "tartar," T4v6, N8r16. *Teules*, "tiles," T4v10, N8r20. *Blat*, "grain," T4v15, N8v4. *Plomb*, "lead," T5r26, N8v11. *Ros*, "sumach," T5r17, N9r8. *Arbre de nau*, "ship's tree, mast," T5v8 = *entena*, N10v24. *Timon de nau*, "tiller" or "rudder," T5v13, N11r2. *Roure quairat*, "squared oak log," T5v16, N11r4. *Fusta*, "timber," T5v19, N11r16.

202 *Sal*, "salt," T9v6, T12v8, T12v18; from 1d per hogshead over forty, T12r4, to 1d per large hogshead over fourteen, N6v4. Merchandise: *arbre de nau*, "ship's tree, mast," T5r[34] (15d); N10v4 (24d); *cordas viellas*, "old ropes," N8r23; *entenas*, "yards," of four sizes, N10v9, N10v13, N10v16, N10v18; *fusta*, "timber," N11r8. At the *Portal de Tarascon*: *draps*, "cloths," N14r12; *lana*, "wool," N14v1; *gresa*, "tartar," N14v6; *sarcia vielha*, "old ropes," N14v8; *teules*, "tiles," N14v9.

203 *Domina Elys uxor quondam domini Bertrandi Albe ex regia concessione recipit pro quolibet modio salis quod defertur supra Bellicadrum per Rodonum, denarius unus* (Martin-Portier 2006, 2:44).

204 Du Roure 1906, 8–9.

205 Since the term *gentils homens* in Table N1 (N2r21, etc.) includes her, it necessarily means "nobles," not "noble men."

206 The measure of the small hogshead was equivalent to about one-third of a large one (that is, around 2 metric tons). Among these sources, the large hogshead occurs as a measurement first and only in MS N (see Glossary s.v. *mog*).

207 No woman named Elis appears in the study of the Alba family by Du Roure (1906). The name is not unusual; another possible identification for the woman in MS N is Alix, baroness of Les Baux (halfway between Tarascon and Roquemartine) and countess of Avellino in the kingdom of Naples (1367–1426). This lady did reverence to Louis II at Arles in 1410 according to Bertran Boysset, who calls her *Madama Helys* (Bertran Boysset 1893, 387).

208 Coulet 1988, 1:85, 2:644. On the collaboration between Charles I and Provençal knights who served in his expeditions, see Aurell, Boyer, and Coulet 2005, 224.

209 Xhayet 1990, 408n33. It was a widespread practice to bear identical Christian and family names, as did Alba d'Alba, the father of Bertran d'Alba, and Albe Albe, lord of Roquemartine in 1387 (Courcelles 1820–2, 3:37–8).

210 Coulet 1988, 1:85. "Les nobles et les prélats reconnaissent en Louis d'Anjou l'héritier de la reine. Parmi les communautés, seules Marseille et Apt font de même" (Aurell, Boyer, and Coulet 2005, 285).

211 At Arles, *domina Alasaxis Porcelleta*, the *abbatissa de Moleges*, and *domina Sacrestana* (Guérard 1:xcvii; Baratier 400), that is, Sagrestana Porcelleta, the founder of the abbey of Mollégès (Baratier 381n4). The Porcelets of Arles were among the most illustrious families of Provence (Aurell 1986; on Sacristane, 162–5). At Orgon, *domina Aiselena et domina Bertranda* (Guérard 1:xc).

212 Antoinette du Bois (Denel 1970, 288).

213 Baratier 388; T14r3.

214 Baratier 383.

215 *Bernardus Raimundus antiquus pedegerius* at Aix (Baratier 325) = *B.R., antiqus pedegerius* (Guérard 1:lxxix). *Rainaldus francigena pedegerius* at Tarascon (Baratier 389, Guérard 1:lxxxvii).

216 *Mosse Judeus* (Baratier 385, 387, 389, Guérard 1:lxxxv, 1:lxxxvii); *Salvis, Crescas de Profecto, Compratus, Crescas de Les, Bellus Homo,* Jews and witnesses (Guérard 1:c); again *Crescas* (Baratier 389, Guérard 1:lxxxvii).

217 Lopez 1976, 62. On the Jews of Tarascon, see Kahn 1899; Drouard 1973; Roux 2004, 2:399–420, 551–9.

218 Bondurand 1891a, 124, item XXXVIII.

219 On the investigations (*enquêtes*), see Aurell, Boyer, and Coulet 2005, 204; Martin-Portier 2006, 1:168–9, 273.

220 Delebecque 1929a, 2:309.

221 "La pancarte tarasconnaise de 1298 était encore en usage trois siècles plus tard ... En 1644 pour le péage de Tarascon on se réfère toujours au tarif de 1298 en

mettant la monnaie à jour" (Rossiaud 2002, 1:49), with reference to Archives nationales H4 3010/1.

222 Stouff 1986, 1:237.

223 *De aludis et de scodadis de quibus fiunt pergamena, de carga IX d.; et istud percipitur a X annis citra, ante vero non percipiebatur* (Baratier 386, Guérard 1:lxxxii). "*Aluda*: cuir léger; *escoudat*, en provençal, peau d'un mouton tué après la tonte (sans laine)" (Baratier 386n20). *De omnibus aliis, ut de oleo,* [etc.], *donat li carga, a V annis citra, XVIII d.; tamen consuevit dare tantummodo XIII d.* (Baratier 388, Guérard 1:lxxxvi).

224 *Nihil dixerunt de argent vivo, verdent* (Baratier 385, Guérard 1:lxxxiii).

225 Baratier 388, Guérard 1:lxxxvii.

226 *Manifestavit* (Baratier 388, Guérard 1:lxxxvi).

227 We do not know when this happened.

228 The manuscript writes *pont*, here emended. The sense of the present could also be vicarious, representing a continuation of the past, in which case one would translate "ashes were not with the other exempt things." On the vicarious present, see Paden 1998, 245, 249–51.

229 Another anachronism is the exchange rate of 10s tournois to one Florentine florin, given repeatedly in MS N; see §5.4.

230 Benoit 1925, 2:131–6, act 51 (1221), reports that the commune of Tarascon had a toll at Lubières until the death of Alfons II of Aragon, which occurred in 1196.

231 The tolls at Lubières under Rubric IV average about one third those at Tarascon and Lubières under Rubric I. Rubric IV adds some commodities not included under Rubric I.

232 The opening lines from the Gospel of John, with their beginning *In principio*, were often used as prologue to a manuscript and became an apotropaic formula (Bloomfield 1955). I am grateful to Richard Kieckhefer for this reference. The passage in MS T follows a blank space that may have been intended for a pious illustration. As Les Enluminures (2011, 1) noted: "Space left empty above beginning of text, likely for a rubric, drawing or miniature, never executed (fol. 1)."

233 Bloch 1931, 107; Miskimin 1969, 54–5; Blois 1976; Aurell, Boyer, and Coulet 2005, 246. Doubts have been expressed by Lewis 1968, 213–14, and by Heers 1973, 138–9 (but see Heers below, note 238).

234 Coulet 1988, 1:59. "Durant un demi-siècle, la Provence vit dans la crainte des gens de guerre" (Aurell, Boyer, and Coulet 2005, 292).

235 Stouff 1986, 1:117, 121. Between 1346 and 1351, towns throughout Provence lost at least half their populations (Baratier 1961, 82). The plague struck Arles and Avignon in 1348 (Biraben 1975–6, 1:74). Between 1345 and 1375, it carried off two-thirds of the population of Aix (Coulet 1988, 1:579); from 1338 to 1354,

three-quarters of that of Orange (Gasparri 1980, 218). On the "persistance des troubles et des calamités" into the fifteenth century, including famine, plague, and war, see Roux 2004, 1:18–104.

236 Spufford 2002, 16–19, 408.

237 Stouff 1986, 1:108.

238 "De nombreux seigneurs, en Angleterre, en Allemagne surtout, mais aussi en France, font, à nouveau et d'une façon plus sévère, valoir leurs droits de justice, accablent les paysans d'amendes, de tailles et de taxes arbitraires" (Heers 1973, 146). "Les revenus de l'aristocratie terrienne ont diminué au fil des ans. Pour compenser cette diminution, les nobles et tous ceux qui vivaient des rentes de la terre se tournent vers d'autres sources de revenus ... L'impôt, prélèvement complémentaire, permet de compenser la chute de la rente seigneuriale" (Balard, Genet, and Rouche 2003, 231–2).

239 "La conjoncture économique, à la fin du XIIIe et au début du XIVe siècle, tend à défavoriser et à dévaloriser les revenues issues des domaines. Dans ce contexte plus difficile, les comtes de Provence cherchent à faire confirmer leurs droits, à étendre ceux-ci si possible, et à récupérer ceux qui leur paraissent oubliés ou mal respectés ... Ces ressources pouvaient pallier dans une certaine mesure la baisse des profits provenant des domaines" (Martin-Portier 2006, 1:140, 275). During the reign of Joan, "la cour de Naples semble s'intéresser surtout aux ressources qu'elle tirait des domaines provençaux" (Aurell, Boyer, and Coulet 2005, 279).

240 See Appendix 5.

241 About 1349: MS Aix, A.D., B.d.R., B 1477 (16), ff. 1r-2r. In 1366 and 1369: Hébert 1979, 85, 92 (n. 96).

242 For the words *çafarame, Florença, França,* and *Provença*, and *diç, escriç, faç, mieç*, all of which occur in the manuscripts without it, but also with *s* (*safran, Florensa, Fransa, Provensa*) or *ch* (*dich, escrichas, fach, miech).*

243 Subject-verb agreement in Occitan is usually determined by the closer of two nouns in a compound subject, so if that noun in singular, the verb is too; the translations use the plural, as in English. Examples at T5v33–T6r9, T8v3, Table T1 (1–12).

244 Thus the word *e*, usually "and," is translated "but" at N10r11, N10r15, N10r17, N10r21; it is translated "or" at N11r1, N12r18, etc. The definite article *lo, la* is sometimes translated as indefinite "a" (N9r11, N9r15), "per" (N7v20, N12v5, N12v6), or "each" (T6r19, T6r21, T13v9). *De* is translated "as for" at N11v21. *Es de*, literally "is of," is rendered frequently as "contains": a load of cloth *es de*, contains, nine cloths. *Es de* can also mean "belongs to": a toll *es de*, belongs to, the king.

245 *Pretz* is glossed as "merit; good reputation, name; a person of merit; price, value," in Paden 1998, 461.

246 Cropp 1975, 426–32.

247 In the late form *pres:* N11v13, N12r6, N12v23.

248 On Ricau de Tarascon, see the *vida* in Boutière and Schutz 1973, 513; Guida 1979, 81–90; Guida and Larghi 2014, 479–80. On Cabrit, see Aurell 1989, 76–7; Meliga 2008; Guida 2009; Guida and Larghi 2014, 138–9. On Tomier and Palaizi, see the *vida* in Boutière and Schutz 1973, 512; Frank 1957; Guida 1979, 90–2; and Guida and Larghi 2014, 371–2, 503–4.

249 For the text, see Harvey and Paterson 2010, 3:1129–37.

250 *Escudelas* paid two deniers at Tarascon, an obole at Lubières, and 4d per mule load, according to MS T (6r25, 13v33, 14v15). They paid four pieces per hundred at Tarascon and Lubières, according to MS N (11v17).

251 Trans. Harvey and Paterson as "a wretched misshapen ginger one," surely with the intention that "ginger" mean "a light, sandy colour," and not "a showy, fast horse" (both in the *OED*). The logic of Cabrit's defense and the words *doloiros mal fag* imply that *ros* is here a masculine noun meaning "nag," otherwise unattested, but corresponding to feminine *rossa* (*PD* 330; T8v25, T14r16), Fr. *rosse*, and not the adjective meaning "reddish, sorrel, chestnut" or possibly "ginger," especially since this adjective is synonymous or nearly synonymous with *bag*, "bay," "a reddish brown colour" (*OED*), with which Cabrit describes the other horse. Cf. Lat. *badius*, "a colour applied esp. to horses, either bay or chestnut"; *russus* "red (sts. implying a warm or brownish shade)" (*OLD*); Occ. *bai, bag*, "bai; blond," and *ros*, "roux" (*PD*, 38, 330); OFr. *ros*, "horse" (*FEW* 16:735–6).

252 Harvey and Paterson 2010, 3:1137.

253 For the text, see Ricketts 2003.

254 Ricketts 2003 (66n2) accepts *l'afan d'amor* in his edition, with reference to Cropp 1975, 292–3, on *afan*; he does not discuss *la fe d'amor*. The word *afan* is glossed "grief, hardship, effort," from the verb *afanar*, "to suffer," in Paden 1998, 356; "travail pénible, peine; tourment, chagrin" (*PD* 8).

255 From the ritual of Cahors, ca. 1130–50, in Molin and Mutembe 1974, 291. *Castitas* here means having sex exclusively with one's spouse in order to produce legitimate children, which was the purpose of marriage according to the Church; it does not mean abstaining from sex altogether. "Purity from unlawful sexual intercourse; continence," not "abstinence from all sexual intercourse; virginity, celibacy" (both senses in the *OED*). The same meaning recurs in the troubadour Guilhem de Montanhagol: *D'amor mou castitatz*, "Fidelity begins in love," in Riquer 1975, 3:1438–40 (line 18). "The first degree of chastitie, is pure virginitie: y[e] second faithful matrimony" (*OED*, citation dated 1567).

256 Paden 2009, 28–31.

257 For the Church adultery applied equally to both sexes, but in civil law it applied only to the infidelity of the married woman and the cuckoldry of the deceived

husband (Carbasse 1987, 84). "A married man who had sex with an unmarried woman was not considered to have committed adultery" (Akehurst 2005, 5).

258 Harvey and Paterson 2010, 3:1137, note to line 49. Further on Audiart: Guida 1987, 200–3; Pulsoni 1994, 108–13.

259 On consent in the doctrine of the Church, see Gaudemet 1987, 174–5, 177–8, 189, 232. According to *Lo Codi*, a version of Roman law produced in the mid-twelfth century, perhaps at Arles, a minor male (under 25) could not be compelled to marry but must have his father's consent, whereas a minor female must accept a husband that her father or grandfather gave her; see §5.1 in the Occitan original (Derrer 1974, 110) and the Latin translation (Fitting 1906, 150). At Montpellier a woman could not be married without her own consent and that of her friends, her *amics*; a virgin could not marry without the consent of her parents, relatives, or guardian (Widmayer 2004, 60).

260 "Le témoignage de ce sirventés peut donc être considéré comme réel" (Frank 1957, 54).

261 Riquer 1975, 2:1154.

262 In their poem beginning *A tornar m'er enquer al primer us*, lines 11 and 27, in Frank 1957, 71; see his note on *bus*, 76. Cf. *barca* and *palun* in the Glossary of this book.

263 *De chantar farai / una esdemessa,* line 36, in Frank 1957, 75.

264 *A tornar m'er al primer us*, line 42, in Frank 1957, 72.

265 On poems by and about Raimon Berengar, see Aurell 1989, 98–9; on the troubadours active in Provence during his rule, ibid., 95–150.

266 *Amics n'Arnaut, cent donas d'aut paratge,* in Riquer 1975, 3:1353, and Bec 1984, 154–6.

267 Guionet and Raimbaut, *En Raÿmbaut, pros domna d'aut linhatge* (variant *paratge*), in Harvey and Paterson 2010, 2:671–81.

268 Charles was the author of at least two love songs in French; several anonymous Occitan poems have sometimes been attributed to him (Hasenohr and Zink 1992, 251). Aurell emphasizes the hostility toward Charles, a Guelph who was offered the crown of Sicily by the pope, among troubadours motivated by Ghibelline ideology, and minimizes his praise by Guelph poets such as Peire de Chastelnau and Guiraut d'Espanha (1989, 151–233, esp. 174–5n81). One may add Jacme Motet (following) to his professed admirers. Asperti argues that Charles's importance has been underestimated by modern historians, but that his age was a cardinal transition between the classical troubadours of the twelfth century and poets of the fourteenth century who wrote in Italian and French (1995, 12, 213–20). Charles was mentioned for good or ill by more than a dozen troubadours, according to Chambers 1971, 48 (s.v. Anjou, comte de), 92 (s.v. Carle).

269 *Non es razos qu'eu dej'aver pereza*, in Meyer 1871, 53–6. Guida and Larghi 2014, 309–10.

270 For example: "La *libido vivendi* s'extériorisait ... dans la *libido amandi*, qui menait à l'invention, à la projection dans une dimension *ficta*" (Guida 2009, 35).

271 A realistic reading of troubadour love poetry is a project that I have underway.

Text of MS T: Tarascon, Archives municipales, AA9 (*Le livre rouge*), f. 3r–17r.

[Rubric I]

[Tolls on commodities at Tarascon and Lubières]

(3r1) Aisso es la form[a] e la maniera del registre (2) del pesage de Tharascon dellas causas mon-(3)tant o descendent per Roze.
(4–6)

[2s 5.5d (= 29.5d) per load]

(7) Cargua de drapps d'Avigno, (8) que es de ix draps;
(9) Cargua de draps de Fransa, que (10) es de xij draps;
(11) Cargua de draps de Narbona, (12) que es de xxijij draps o de .iiij. quintals;
(13) Cargua de bruns, que es de .iiij. o de .v. draps;
(14) Cargua d'estamenhas, que es de xlviij pessas (15) o de quatre quintals;
(16) Cargua de telas, que es de quatre quintals;
(17) Cargua de cuors, adobatz o non adobatz, que (18) es de xx cuers;
(19) Cargua de cordoan, que es de xij dotzenas (20) o de quatre quintals;
(21) Cargua de cera;
(22) Cargua de pibre;
(23) Cargua de gingibre;
(24) Cargua de girofle;
(25) Cargua de seda;
(26) Cargua de sendat;
(27) Cargua de citeal;
(28) Cargua de çafarame;
(29) Cargua de indi;

(3v1) Cargua de pennas vayras o de conils, o del semblant;
(2) Carga d'alum d'Alap;
(3) Cargua d'alum de pluma et d'alum sicrum, que (4) es de quatre quintals:
(5)
(6) Cascuna de las causas sobredichas pagua, (7) la cargua, .s/ .ij. d' .v. o'.
(8) En que prende Johan Alba d' .i.
(9) E [lo]s senhors del peage de Lubieras, d' .i.
(10–11)

[21d per load]

(12) Cargua de lana;
(13) Cargua de canape;
(14) Carga de stopas;
(15) Cargua de cordas;
(16) Cargua de fil de cordas;
(17) Cargua de comin;
(18) Cargua d'anis;
(19) Cargua de canella;
(20) Cargua de sucre;
(21) Cargua de pols de sucre;
(22) Cargua de figua;
(23) Cargua de datils;
(24) Cargua de mel;
(25) Cargua de ris;
(26) Car[gu]a de formages;
(27) [Cargu]a de saim;
(28) [Cargu]a de seu;
(29) [Cargua] de pegua;
(30) [Car]gua de brecilh;
(31) Cargua de pels de moutons;
(32) Cargua de pels de cabret;
(33) Cargua de pels d'aninas;
(4r1) Cargua de coton;
(2) Cargua de fustanis;
(3) Cargua de borrassas;
(4) Cargua de melas frachas;
(5) Cargua de castanhas peladas;
(6) Cargua de coure;
(7) Cargua de stanhg;

(8) Cargua de ferre que (9) es de iiij quintals o de iiij costas;
(10) Cargua de oli que es de (11) xviij cannas;
(12) Cargua de piatta stagnat;
(13) Cargua de mattafellon;
(14) Cargua de vernice;
(15) Cargua d'argento vivo;
(16) Cargua de peis de mar, salat ho non salat:
(17) Cascuna de las causas sobredichas pagua, (18) la cargua de quatre quintals .... d' xxi
(19) En que prende Johan Alba .... d' .i.
(20) E lo senhors del pesage de Lubieras .... d' .i.

[Woad: 16d per load]

(21) ¶ Cargua de gaida, que es de quatre quin-(22)tals, pagua la cargua ..... d' xvi
(23) En que prende Johan Alba .... d' .i.
(24) E los senhors del pesage de Lobieras .... d' .i.
(25–6)

[Cloth and leather: from 3d to 0.5d]

(27) Una sarja pagua .... d' i
(28) Item, .i. stameha .... .o'.
(29) Item, .i. corda de tela .... .o'.
(30) Item, .i. dozena de cordoans .... d' ij
(31) Item, .i. dozena de moutoninas .... d' iij
(32) Item, .i. cuer de buou .... o' iij
(33) Item, .i. dos .... d' i
(34) Item, .i. cota .... o'
(35) Item, .i. faissa .... o'

[11d per load]

(4v1) Cargua de greza;
(2) Cargua de sarsia vielha;
(3) Cargua d'alum de Volcan;
(4) Cargua d'aludas, de que se fa pergamin;
(5) pagua, la cargua que es de .iiij. quintals .... d' xi
(6) En que prende Johan Alba .... d' i

(7) E los senors de Lubieras .... d' i
(8)

[Tiles: 9d per load]

(9) Teules: pagua lo melher .... d' ix
(10) En que prende Johan Alba .... d' i
(11)

[Grain: 11.5d per load, etc.]

(12) Carga de tot blat e de tot liome et tota (13) farina que es de xv. o xvi sestiers de la me-(14)sura de Tharascon pagua, la cargua .... d' xi. o'
(15) En que prende Johan Alba .... d' i
(16) E los senhors de Lubieras .... d' i
(17) Empero si lo blat era carguat d'Avinhon in (18) sus, et en lo navey avia de xx saumadas (19) in sus, pagua cascuna saumada, per lo pezage (20) gros d' .ix. o'.
(21) E per Lubieras, tota la navada .... s/ .v.
(22) entre lo rey e los senhors del pezage de Lubie-(23)ras. E se en lo navei avia blat de .ij. pariers (24) o de plus senhors, e cascun avia de xx saumadas (25) in sus, e.l blat seria carguat d'Avignon en sus, (26) pagaria cascum, per Lubieras .... s/ v
(27) Empero si blat o farina venia en sacs, de (28) von que venga, paga la saumada de (29) cascun .... d' xi. o'.
(30)

[Wine: 6d per butt plus payment in kind]

(31) De vin montant o deissendent per Roze, (32) de cascuna botta, pauca o granda, paga .... d' .vj.
(33) Item, de .j. bota, mieg baral de vin.
(5r1) Item, de ii botas, .i. baral de vin.
(2) E de iij. botas e d'aqui en sus, tota la navada (3) paga .j. saumada de vin.
(4) E si ven lo vin en barals, es contat .i. (5) m[ie]g aissi quant una bota, e paga aissi (6) con dis desobre.
(7)
(8) E si hom de Tharascon faccia companhia de (9) vin am homes stranis mesclament, pagaria (10) tot per entier; mais si cascun avia son vin a (11) part en vaisels sauputament, paga lo strani (12) tant solament.
(13–14)

[Dye: 6s 5d (= 77d) per hogshead]

(15) Lo mueg del ros, que es de lxxij quintals o de (16) iij saquieras e mieia, dona........ s/ .vj. d' v,
(17) En que prende Johan Alba en saquiera .... d' .i.
(18) Item, deu mais, al pezage de Lubieras, entre (19) lo rei e los senhors de Lubieras .... d' .vij.
(20) E si en lo navei avia de xx saquieras en sus, (21) per rason del peage de Lubieras paga tota (22) la navaida .... s/ .v.
(23) El peage gros, aissi quant dis desobre.
(24)

[Lead: 6d per load]

(25) Carga de plum, que es·de .iiij. quintals, paga [........] d' .vj.
(26) En que prende Johan Alba .... o'
(27) et en c[ent]° quintals dona .... d' xv
(28) Item, dona a Lobieras, per carga .... d' .ij.
(29) en que a la mitat lo rei, e la mitat los sen-(30)hors del pezage de Lubieras.
(31)

[Masts and yards]

(See Textual Notes, T5r30, on the order of lines T5r[32–42].)

[32] Albre de nau que es de vij palms o de plus de gros, [33] a la tersa part de l'abre dos la razis, paga libr. [........] iij s/ x.
[34] En que prende Johan Alba .... d' xv
[35] Item, pagua a Lubieras .... s/ v
[36] en que a la mitat lo rey, e l'autre mitat lo senhors [37] de Lobieras.
[38] Antenna de nau de vi palms e de-[39]miei de gros pagua .... s/ xxx
[40] Item, a Lobieras, entre lo rei e los senhors, paga [41] mais .... s/ v
[42] Antenna de vi palms .... s/ xx
(5v1) Et de .v. palms e demiei .... s/ xi
(2) E de v palms .... s/ x
(3) E de .iiij. palms e demiei .... s/ v
(4) E de iiij palms .... s/ iiij
(5) E d'aqui en avalle, dona a l'albire del (6) peagier.
(7) E donan mais a Lubieras, cascun .... d' .ij.

(8) Et en Johan Alba pren en cascun, de la (9) part del rey nostre senhors .... d' i
(10–11)

[Wood and wood products]

(12) Timon de nau e roure rodon dona .... s/ .xv.
(13) en que a Johan Alba .... d' v.
(14) ¶ Item, a Lubieras, entre lo re e los senhors [...............................] s/ .iij.
(15) Roure quairat paga .... s/ .v.
(16) en que a Johan Alba .... d' .iij.
(17) ¶ Item, dona a Lubieras entre lo rei e los (18) senhors, per .j. travada de fusta .... d. xij. o'.
(19) En que a Johan Alba en cascuna .... d' i
(20) ¶ Item, dona, per rason del pezage dels Mu-(21)julans, cascuna travada tro .viij. travadas [...] p° .iij.
(22) que son del rei; e de .viij. travadas en sus, (23) pagua tot lo radel per lo pezage dels (24) Mujolans tant solamens .... d' vj
(25)
(26) ¶ Item, dona la travada de la fusta (27) tro xx travadas a Lobieras, entre lo rei (28) e los senhors de Lubieras .... d' ij
(30) ¶ E de xx travadas en sus, dona a Lobie-(31)ras tot lo radel .... s/ v
(32)
(33) De .i. quairat de saisel o de meleze es (34) faita travada.
(35) De .ij. quairatz de roans es travada.
(36) De xij perteguas redonas menudas es facha (37) travada.
(6r1) De xij jainas colladieras es travada.
(2) De .iiij. o de vj. jainas bastardas es travada.
(3) De iiij grans taulas de roure e de .x. petitas (4) es facha travata.
(5) De .iiij. quairatz tiratz per buous es travada.
(6) De xx. taulas de sap es travada.
(7) De vij. taulas de meleze es travada.
(8) De vj. taulas de noguier es travada.
(9) De orsas o de corbas grans de .viij. o de .ix. (10) es facha travada.
(11)
(12) ¶ Un molin d'aigua dona de pesage .... s/ x.
(13) Un molin d'aura dona .... s/ v.
(14) Un linh de Roda dona de pesage libr' .... ij. s/ x.
(15) Una barcha dona .... s/ v
(16) De nau duptam.

(17)
(18) ¶ De navei comprat novellamens o que (19) se mene per vendre dona lo fil .... d' ij. e .j. rema.
(20) ¶ Item, a Lubieras, entre lo rey e los senhors, (21) dona lo fil .... ij d'
(22) et lo navei tot, .i. rema.
(23)

[Domestic objects: 4d to 0.5d]

(24) ¶ Lausas,
(25) scudelas,
(26) Talhador[s],
(27) Grasalos,
(6v1) Selcles,
(2) Madiera,
(3) Barals,
(4) Setons,
(5) Qulhers,
(6) brocs,
(7) Cornudas,
(8) Dona, de c[ent], iiij.
(9) ¶ Item, dona a Lubieras, lo c[ent] .... d' .ij.
(10) o la saumada .... o'.
(11)
(12) Arca,
(13) Escrinh nou am pecols,
(14) Tina,
(15) Vaissel,
(16) Dogat nou,
(17) Mola de molin,
(18) Mola de barbier,
(19) Bacon,
(20) Per quascuna d'aquestas, dona .... d' iiij
(21) Item, a Lobieras, entre lo rey e lo senhors, (22) dona .... d' .i.
(23)
(24) ¶ Saumada d'ollas,
(25) De brocatz,
(26) De pechiers,
(27) De crucols,
(28) Et de totas aizinas de terra dona, (29) per saumada .... d' iiij

[Foods, etc.]

(7r1) ¶ Saumada d'amellas am clovel,
(2) Nozes,
(3) Avellanas, que es de .viij. minas:
(4) la saumada dona .... d' iiij. o'.
(5) ¶ Item, a Lobieras, entre lo rey e lo sen-(6)hors .... o'
(7)
(8) ¶ Saumada de poms,
(9) De perseguas,
(10) De sorbas,
(11) De agriotas,
(12) De nozes fresquas,
(13) De peras,
(14) De codons,
(15) De nesplas,
(16) De sereyras,
(17) De castanhas am escorsa:
(18) Dona, per saumada .... d' .ij
(19) ¶ Item, a Lubieras, entre lo rey e lo senhors .... o'
(20)
(21) ¶ Saumada de ruscla que es de (22) ix eminas dona .... d' .i.
(23) A Lubieras .... .o'.
(24) ¶ Saumada de carbon dona .... d' .j.
(25) Item, a Lobieras, entre lo rey e lo senhors [........................] .o'.
(7v1) ¶ Saumada de rabas .... o'.
(2) Dona a Lobieyras .... .o'.
(4) ¶ Saumada de sebas grossas que es (5) de .ij. dozinas, e sebas menudas que (6) es de .iij. dozinas;
(7)
(8) ¶ Saumada d'alhs, que es de .viij. (9) o de x. dozinas, dona de pesage, per (10) saumada, rest .... .j.
(12) ¶ Item, a Lubieras, entre lo rey e lo sen-(13)hors .... o'
(14)

[Materials: payment in kind or 18d]

(15) ¶ La copiera del veire dona de pesage, (16) pesas .... ij
(17) Et de collier, dona .j. pesa.
(18)

(19) ¶ Una navaida de caus o de gip o de (20) peira, de xxv cairons en sus, paga (21) a Lobieras .... d' xviij
(22) De que a lo rey la mitat,
(23) E lo senhors del piag de Lubieras, la mitat.
(24–6)

[Exemptions]

(27) ¶ Aquestas causas non donan peage, (28) so es assaber:
(29) Sabon,
(30) peis de Roze o palun,
(8r1) Sipias,
(2) Regalisia,
(3) Gallas,
(4) Verdet,
(5) Mersaria,
(6) pellaria,
(7) argent,
(8) Solpre,
(9) Buire,
(10) Arzica,
(11) Uleta,
(12) Obra facha de ferre o de coure (13) o de loton o d'estanh,
(14) Aur,
(15) Moneda,
(16) Eisseptada la fiera de Belcayre (17) de may, que dona pelharia, lo fais (18) de una bestia .... d' vj
(19) E d'ome .... d' iij
(20–1)

[Live cargo: horses, travellers, large animals]

(22) ¶ De caval comprat o vendut on que si (23) mene per vendere, se valia de (24) xij libr' e .x. s/ en sus, e passa Roze, dona .... s/ ij d' vj
(8v1) ¶ Item, sarazin o isime dona .... s/ ij d' vj
(2)
(3) Totz homs cavalcans passant Roze, (4) eiseptat homes de Tharascon e de Bel-(5)caire, et eisseptat gen-(6)tils homes e lur mainage,
(7) Et eisseptat prelatz – so es assaber (8) de sotzdiaque en sus – si es denfra viij (9) legas, pagua .... o'. iij

(10) Et si es de viij leguas en sus, pagua d' iij. o'.
(11)
(12) ¶ De bestias grossas venent de las (13) partidas de Proensa, passant Rose, (14) si son rossins o eguas o muls o mulas, (15) pagan aissi quant desobre es dich. (16) E si son buos o azes, pagan .... d'.j.
(17) ¶ Item, fedas, cabras, porcs, e lur mensas: (18) pagua cascuna bestia .... pogeza.
(19–20)
(21) Aisso es arribage.
(22) De bestias venens de las par-(23)tidas dela Roze, compradas (24) o vendudas o menant per (25) vendre, si son rossas o mulas pagan .... .o'.
(26) ¶ Item, buous, azes, fedas, cabras, porcs, (27) pagan .... p°
(9r1) ¶ Totz Lombartz o Lombardas romieus (2) visitant Sant Jacme cavalcant do-(3)na de pesage .... d' viij
(4) E si va ad autra partz, pagua d' iij o'
(5) E si va a pe o ven per Roze, pagua d' .i. o'
(6–7)
(8) ¶ Totz Spanhol, Engles, Alaman, e totz (9) romieus de Lihon en amon visitant (10) Sant Jacme o Sant Gile ad caval, (11) pagua .... d' .v.
(12)
(13) ¶ Et si va a pe o ven per Roze, pagua d' .j.
(14)
(15) ¶ Totz romieus de qualche partita (16) que sia, eisseptat Proensals: si va (17) a pe, dona .... d' .i.
(18)
(19) ¶ Monediers, tant quant obran in (20) moneda del rey nostre senhor o del (21) rey de Fransa, son francs de lur cavalcaduras (22).

[Rubric II]

[Tolls and *montazon* on salt]

(9v1) Aisso es lo pesage de la sal.
(2) Uno mueg de sal montant per (3) Roze de Tharascon en sus, de (4) qualque part que vengua, (5) pagua per piage gros .... d' xx
(6) En que a Johan Alba .... d' .i.
(7) E lo rey nostre senhor .... d' xviij
(8) ¶ Item, dona mais per montazon, tro (9) viij mueg .... d' .vj. per mueg,
(10) En que a lo rey nostre senhor .... d' .iij.
(11) Et alcuns gentils homes de Tharascon [...................................] d' iiij. o'

(12) De viii muetz en sus, pagua plus gros (13) montazon, e part si per lo semblant.
(14) ¶ Item, dona mais per lo pezage de Lubieras, (15) tro vj muetz, deniers .iij. per muetz. (16) Et de vj muetz en sus, de tot navei [........................] d' xviij
(17) En que a la mitat lo rei nostre senhor,
(18) Et la mitat alcun gentils homes de (19) Tharascon.
(20) ¶ Item, dona mais per rason del pezage (21) que compret lo rey nostre senhor del (22) Mujolans: tro viij muetz dona per m°. [.....................] p° .iij.
(23) Et d'aquei en sus, de tot lo navey .... d' .vj.
(24)
(25) ¶ Somma que pagua per totas causas lo (26) muetz de la sal tro vj muetz: [...] s/ ij d' v. o' p° .j.

[Rubric III]

[Shares in the toll on salt]

[Table T1]

(10r1) Aiso son las partitas del pesage de la sal.
(2–3)
(4) Un mueg de sal dona s/ ij. d' .v. p°:
(5) lo rei d' xxij p°. iij, lu cavaliers d' .vij.

(6) ij muetz de sal dona	s/ iiij d' xi. o':
(7) lo rei s/ iij. (8) d' ix. o',	lu cavaliers d'. xiiij.
(9) ¶ iij m° de sal dona	s/ vii d' .v. p° .i.:
(10) lo rei s/ v d' viij. p°,	lu cavaliers s/ i. d' ix.
(11) ¶ iiij m° de sal dona	s/ ix d' xi:
(12) lo rei s/ vij d' vij,	lu cavaliers s/ ij. d' iiij.
(13) ¶ v m° de sal dona	s/ xij d' iiij p°. iij:
(14) lo rei s/ ix d' v. o' p°,	lu cavaliers s/ .ij. d' xi.
(15) ¶ vj m° de sal dona	s/ xiiij d' .x. o':
(16) lo rei s/ xi d' iiij .o'.,	lu cavaliers s/ .iij. d' .vj.
(17) ¶ vij m° de sal dona	s/ xvij d'. i p° .i:
(18) lo rei s/ xiij d' .i. o'. p°.,	lu cavaliers s/ .iij. d' xi .o'.
(19) ¶ viij m° de sal dona	s/ xix. d'. iiij:
(20) lo rei s/ xiiij d' xi,	lu cavaliers s/ .iiij. d' .v.
(21) ¶ ix m° de sal dona	s/ xxiij. d' .viij.:
(22) lo rei s/ xvij d' .ij.,	lu cavaliers s/ vj. d' .vj.
(23) ¶ x m° de sal dona	s/ xxv. d' x.:

(24) lo rei s/ xviij d' x. o'., lu cavaliers s/ vj. d' xi. o'.
(25) ¶ xi mº de sal dona s/ xxviij d':
(26) lo rei libr' .i. d' vij, lu cavaliers s/ vij d' v.
(27) ¶ xij mº de sal dona s/ xxx d' viij.:
(28) lo rei libr' .i. s/ .ij. d' .v., lu cavaliers s/ viij. d' iij.
(10v1) ¶ xiij mº, s/ xxxij d' x.:
(2) lo rei libr' .j. s/ iiij. d' i. o',
(3) lu cavaliers s/ viij d' .viij .o'.
(4) ¶ xiiij mº, s/ xxxv d'.:
(5) lo rei lib' .i. s/ v d' .x.,
(6) cavaliers s/ ix d' .ij.
(7) ¶ xv mº, s/ xxxvij d' .ij.:
(8) lo rei libr' .j. s/ vij d' .vi. o',
(9) cavaliers s/ ix d' .vij .o'.
(10) ¶ xvi mº, s/ xxxix d' iiij:
(11) lo rei libr' .i. s/ ix d' .iij.,
(12) cavaliers s/ x d' .i.
(13) ¶ xvij mº, s/ xli d' vi:
(14) lo rei libr' .j. s/ x d' xi,
(15) cavaliers s/ x d' vj o'.
(16) ¶ xviij mº, s/ xliiij d' .i.:
(17) lo rei s/ xij d' ix pº .i. libr' .i.,
(18) cavaliers s/ xi d' iij o' pº.
(19) ¶ xix mº, s/ xlvj d' iij:
(20) lo rei libr' .i. s/ xiiij d' v o'. pº,
(21) cavaliers s/ xi d' ix pº .i.
(22) ¶ xx mº, s/ xlviij d' v:
(23) lo rei libr' .i. s/ xvi d' ij. pº,
(24) cavaliers s/ xij d' ij o' pº.
(25) ¶ xxi mº, s/ .l. d' vij:
(26) lo rei libr' .i. s/ xvij d' x. o' .pº., cavaliers s/ xij d' viij pº .i.
(11r1) ¶ xxij mº, s/ lij d' ix: lo rei libr' .i
(2) s/ xix d' vij pº, cavaliers s/ xiij d' .i. o'. pº.
(3) ¶ xxiij mº, s/ liiij d' xi: lo rei libr' .ij
(4) s/ .j. d' iij o' .pº., cavaliers s/ xiij d' vij. pº.
(5) ¶ xxiiij mº, s/ lvij d' i.: lo rei libr' .ij
(6) s/ iij pº i, cavaliers s/ xiiij d'. o' pº.
(7) ¶ xxv mº, s/ lx d' iij: lo rei libr' .ij.
(8) s/ iiij d' xi o' pº, cavaliers s/ xv d' iij pº.

(9) ¶ xxvj mº, s/ lxij d' v: lo rei libr' .ij
(10) s/ vj d' vij pº, cavaliers s/ xvj. d' ij pº.
(11) ¶ xxviij mº, s/ lxvi d' ix: lo rei libr' .ij
(12) s/ x d' j pº .i., cavaliers s/ xvi d' vij. o'. pº.
(13) ¶ xxix mº, s/ lxviij d' xi: lo rei libr' ij
(14) s/ xi d' ix o' pº., cavaliers s/ xvij. d' .i. pº.
(15) ¶ xxx mº, s/ lxxi d' .i.: lo rei libr' .ij.
(16) s/ xiij d' vj pº, cavaliers s/ xvij d' vj .pº.
(17) ¶ xxxi mº, s/ lxxiij d' iij: lo rei libr' ij
(18) s/ xv d' ij o' pº, cavaliers s/ xviij. pº.
(19) ¶ xxxij mº, s/ lxxv d' v: lo rei libr' .ij.
(20) s/ xvj d' xi pº, cavaliers s/ xviij d' .v. o'. pº.
(21) ¶ xxxiij mº, s/ lxxvij d' vij: lo rei libr' .ij.
(11v1) s/ xviij d' vij o'. pº., cavaliers s/ xviij d' xi pº.
(2) ¶ xxxiiij mº, s/ lxxix d' ix: lo rei libr' iij
(3) d' iiij pº, cavaliers s/ xix d' iiij o'. pº.

(4) ¶ xxxv	mº,	libr'	iiij	s/ i	d' xi:
(5) lo rei		libr'	iij	s/ ij	o' pº .j.,
(6) cavaliers		s/ xix		d' x	pº.
(7) ¶ xxxvj	mo,	libr'	iiij	s/ iiij	d' .i.:
(8) lo rei		libr'	iij	s/ iij	d' ix po .i.,
(9) cavaliers		s/ xx		d' iij	o' po.i.
(10) ¶ xxxvij	mº,	libr'	iiij	s/ vij	d' .i.:
(11) lo rei		libr'	iij	s/ v	d' viij po .i,
(12) cavaliers		libr'	i.	s/ i	d' iiij pº j.
(13) ¶ xxxviij	mº,	libr'	iiij	s/ ix	d' iij:
(14) lo rei		libr'	iij	s/ vij	d' iiij o' po .j.,
(15) cavaliers		libr'	j	s/ i	d' x o' pº j.
(16) ¶ [x]xxix	mº,	libr'	iiij	s/ xi	d' v:
(17) lo rei		libr'	iij	s/ ix	d' i po .i.,
(18) cavaliers		libr'	.i.	s/ ij	d' iij o' pº i.
(19) ¶ xl	mº,	libr'	iiij	s/ xiij	d' x:
(20) lo rey		libr'	iij	s/ x	d' x,
(21) cavaliers		libr'	j	s/ iij.	

(22)
(23) ¶ E si en lo navei avia de xl muetz (24) en amont, pagant los xl mueg aissi (25) quant e dis desobre, e lo sobreplus (12r1) dona, lo muetz, d' xxij tant sola-(2)mens;
(3) en que a lo rei d' xix;

(4) et Johan Alba, d' i;
(5) e los senhors, d' ij de la montason.
(6)
(7) ¶ Tot home que cargua sal a Belcayre (8) pagua del muegz d' xxij, que si (9) parton aissi quant los xxij d' desobre (10) digz.
(11) ¶ Item, dona .iij. p° per muegz tro viij (12) muetz per los Mujolans, que son aras (13) del rei nostre senhor.
(14)
(15) ¶ Et de viij muetz en amont, dona, (16) per rason de las .iij. pogezas, d' vj (17) tot lo navei et non plus.
(18)
(19) ¶ Tot home de Belcaire o de Tharascon (20) que descargue sal a Bellcayre dona (21) per uzage d' .iiij. per muetz, en que (22) a lo rei nostre senhor iij meallas (23) per m°, et lo senhors, per la montazon, (24) d' ij. o'.
(26) ¶ Item, dona a Lubiera tro vi m°. (27) d' .iij. per muetz, en que a lu rei la mitat.
(28) ¶ E lo senhors de Lubieras, la mitat. Et (29) de vj muetz en sus, dona a Lubieras (30) d' xviij tot lo navei, et d'uzage d' iiij. (31) per m°, quant que n'i aia.
(12v1) ¶ Item, tot home strani que meta sal (2) in Tharascon pagua per lu semblant (3) meteis.
(4)
(5) ¶ Tot home strani che descarca sal (6) a Belcayre pagua per m° d' xiiij. o'., en que (7) a lo rei, per totas causas, d' ix. o'; e los (8) gentils homes, de. v., en que a Johan (9) Alba j d., e los senhors de Lubieras (10) iij o', e los senhors de la montazon d' ij. o'.
(11)
(12) ¶ E de vj m° en sus, dona d' xi. o' per (13) muetz, e xviij d' tot lo navei per lu pe-(14)zage de Lubieras, en que a lo rei d' viij (15) per muetz et .ix. d' per tot lo navei. Et (16) los senhors de la montazon, d' .ij. o'. (17) per m°; e los senhors de Lubieras, (18) de[.] ix en tot lo navei; e Johan Alba, (19) d' .i. per muetz.
(20)
(21) ¶ Item, totz homes que vendan sal (22) els portz de Belcayre o de Tharascon (23) pagan aissi quant es dig desobre dels (24) descarguans privatz o estranis.
(25)
(26) ¶ La caupolada de la sal que ven dels (27) estanhs, si es raza, fau viij muetz (28) e demiei; e si es comol, fau xij muetz.

[Rubric IV]

[Tolls at Lubières]

(13r1) Aisso es lo pesage de Lobieras, en que a la mi-(2)tat lo rey nostre senhor, et la mi-(3)tat alcuns gentils homes de Tharascon.
(4–5)

[Goods, grain]

(6) De tota cargua d'aver de Le-(7)vant o de non-Levant, montant (8) o descendent, passant davant (9) Lobieras, que e pezage, dona .... d' .ij.
(10) Item, saumada de tot blat e de tot (11) liomes o de farinas, de xv o de xvj sestiers (12) de la mesura de Tharascon, paga .... d' .ij.
(13)
(14) ¶ Empero si en uno navei avia de xx (15) saumadas en sus, e venia d'Avinhon (16) en sus, pagua la naviada, quant (17) que n'i agues, tant solament .... s/ .v.
(18)
(19) ¶ Empero si e.l navei avia blat de .ij. (20) pariers o de plus, e caschun avia (22) xx saumadas o plus en orris, (23) pagua caschun .... s/ .v.
(24)

[Wood]

(25) ¶ Una travada de fusta dona .... d' ij
(26) ¶ Empero si e.l radel avia xx travadas, (27) o de xx en sus, dona tant solamens .... v s/
(13v1) ¶ Albre de nau de vij palms de gros en sus (2) pagua .... [s/] .v.
(3)
(4) ¶ Antenna de vi palms e demiei .... s/ v
(5) Item, timon o roure rodon .... s/ iij
(6) ¶ Item, roure quairat e pertegua (7) de mens de vj palms e demiei .... d' .ij.
(8)

[Dye]

(9) ¶ Item, lo muegz del ros, que es de .iij. (10) saquieras e meia, pagua .... d' vij

(11) ¶ Empero si en lo navei avia xx saquieras, (12) o de xx en sus, dona tant [solament] .... s/ .v.
(13)

[Materials]

(14) ¶ Item, una naviada de peira o de caus o (15) de gip dona .d'. xviij.
(16)

[Food]

(17) ¶ Item, saumada de poms, de peras, et (18) de totas autras fruchas que pezag (19) dona .... o'
(20)
(21) ¶ Item, saumada de sebas et de alhs .... o'.
(22)
(23) ¶ Item, saumada de ruscla e de carbon e de (24) rabas dona .... o'
(25)
(26) ¶ Item, saumada de nozes e d'amellas (27) an clovelh.
(28)

[Domestic objects]

(29) ¶ Item, una tina, vaissel, doguat, escrinh (30) nou o arca nova, bacon, mol[a] de mo-(31)lin o de fabre o de barbier .... d' .i.
(32)

(33) ¶ Item, selcles,	setons,	escudellas,
(34) talhadors,	grazallet,	qulhiers,
(35) grazalis,	cossas,	brocs,
(36) cornudas,	barrals,	lausas,
(37) madiera,	dona la saumada	o'

[Rubric V]

[Tolls at the Gates of Tarascon]

(14r1) Aisso es la forma del pezage dels portals (2) de Tharascon, la qual forma per sagrament (3) manifestet en Pons del Prat, antic pezagier.
(4–6)

[2s 2d (= 26d) per load]

(7) Cargua de draps de Fransa,
(8) de draps de Narbona,
(9) de draps d'Avinhon, de telas,
(10) de stamenhas, de tot autres draps;
(11) de corduan, de indi,
(12) de pebre, de gingibre,
(13) de girofle, de sera,
(14) de seda, de sendat,
(15) de alum, de cuors de luons o
(16) de camels o de rossas
(17) o del semblans;
(18) de fil de cohanha:
(19) de totas questas causas sobredichas (20) es facha la cargua de iiij quintals, e dona, (21) de rials .... s/ ij d' ij.
(22)

[19d]

(23) Cargua d'oli que es de xviij cannas;
(24) cargua de canape, de cordas,
(25) de fil de cordas, de lana,
(26) d'anhis, de pels de moutons,
(27) de pels d'anels, de cabritz,
(28) de comin, d'anise,
(29) de castanhas peladas, d'amellas frachas,
(30) de figua, de formages,
(31) de ris, de sucre, de pols de sucre,
(32) de mel, de seu, de saim,
(33) de ferre, de assier, de stanh,
(34) de bresilh, de peys fresc,
(35) de salat, de coton,
(14v1) de fustanis, e dels semblans: es la carga (2) de quatre quintals, que dona .... d' xviiij.

[Lead: 6d]

(3) ¶ Cargua de plump es de iiij quintals; dona .... d' .vj.

[Salt carried by animals: 2d]

(4) ¶ De bestia carguada de sal, dona .... d' ij.

[Food, domestic objects]

(5) ¶ De bestia carguada de frutz, dona .... d' ij
(6) ¶ De lausas, de pechers, de enaps,
(7) ¶ de cercles, dona de c[ent], .iiij.
(8) ¶ De bestia carguada de sebas o d'alhs: (9) prendon .j. rest.
(10) ¶ De bestia carguada de brocs o de cornu-(11)das o de barals, dona .... d' iiij
(12) ¶ De bestia carguada de tot blat, o de (13) tot liomes, o de farina: es facha la sau-(14)mada de .viij. sestiers, e donan .... d' iiij
(15) ¶ De bestia cargada de scudellas, de (16) talhadors, de grazaletz, de grazals, (17) de qulhiers, dona .... d' iiij
(18)
(19) ¶ De vaissel, de tina, d'arca, d'escrin-(20)h nou, de dogan – so es assaber de xxv (21) dogas an los buetz – dona .... d' iiij
(23) ¶ Item, d'una mola o d'un bacon, dona [...] d' iiij
(25) De bestia carguada de veire, dona pessas [..] ij
(27) ¶ Item, d'olas de terras, dona de c[ent]° .... iiij
(28) ¶ de bestias menuda[s] vendudas, dona, (29) de quatre .... d' i
(30) ¶ de bestias grossas .... .o'.
(31) ¶ Saumada de sebas es de las grossas (32) de ij dozenas, e de las menudas de .iiij. (33) dozenas.
(15r1) ¶ Saumada d'alhs e de viij o de x dotzenas.

[Exemption]

(2) ¶ Empero deves entendre de totas las (3) causas sobredichas, en lo piage dels por-(4)tals es entendement si non an pagat (5) al peage de Gernegua; ma si paguat (6) avien en Gernegua, serian quitis als (7) portals.
(8)

[Rubric VI]

[Tolls at Saint-Gabriel]

(9) La forma e la maniera del pesage de Sant (10) Guabriel, que es pres sotz la forma del (11) pezage del Portal de Tharascon per la maior parte (12) de totas las causas denfra scrichas.

(13)

[13d per load]

(14) Cargua d'oli, de comin,
(15) de canela, de mel,
(16) de ris, de formages,
(17) d'amellas, de castanhas,
(18) de sucre, de cordas,
(19) de fustanis,
(20) de pol de sucre, de pegua,
(21) de saim, de stanh,
(22) de seu, de ferre,
(23) de canabe, d'assier,
(24) de stopas, de stang,
(25) de filh de cordas, de brezilh,
(26) de coton, d'anhnis,
(27) de pels de moutons, d'anhels,
(28) de pels de cabritz, e de las causas (29) semblans: es facha la cargua (30) de .iiij. quintals, de que si pren a Tharascon (31) miegz pezage, e donan totas a Sant (32) Gabriel xiij d' tant solament.

(15v1) ¶ En tota[s] las autras causas e las autras (2) mercadarias, sia esgardada la forma (3) e la maniera del pesage del Portal de (4) Tharascon en aquest pezage de Sant (5) Gabriel.

(6)

[Cloths, etc.: 2s 2d (= 26d)]

(7) ¶ Cargua de totz draps e de telas (8) e de stamenhas, de cordoan, e de las (9) autras causas semblans donan s/ .ij. d' .ij. (10) Es facha la cargua de iiij. quintals.

(11)

[Rubric VII]

[The *Montazon* at Tarascon: first version]

[Table T2]

(12) Aisso es la montazon dels cavalliers (13) de Tharascon, que prenon de .i. muetz de (14) sal entro xl. que non remangua a Tharascon (15) ne a Belcari.
(16)

(17a) ¶ J	mº	d' iiij o'	(17b) xxiij	mº	s/ x d' xi pº
(18a) ¶ ij	mº	d' ix	(18b) xxiiij	mº	s/ xi d' iij. o' pº
(19a) ¶ iij	mº	d' xiij o'	(19b) xxv	mº	s/ xij d' v. pº
(20a) ¶ iiij	mº	d' xviij	(20b) xxvj	mº	s/ xij d' ix o' pº
(21a) ¶ v	mº	d' xxij o'	(21b) xxvij	mº	s/ xiij d' iij. pº
(22a) ¶ vj	mº	s/ ij d' iij	(22b) xxviij	mº	s/ xiij d' vi o' pº
(23a) ¶ vij	mº	s/ ij d' vij o'	(23b) xxix	mº	s/ xiij d' xi pº
(24a) ¶ viij	mº	s/ iij	(24b) xxx	mº	s/ xiiij d' iij o' pº
(25a) ¶ ix	mº	s/ .v	(25b) xxxi	mº	s/ xiiij d' viij pº
(26a) ¶ x	mº	s/ .v. d' iiij o'	(26b) xxxij	mº	s/ xv d' o' pº
(27a) ¶ xi	mº	s/ v d' ix	(27b) xxxiij	mº	s/ xv d' v pº
(28a) ¶ xij	mº	s/ vj d' vj	(28b) xxxiiij	mº	s/ xv d' ix o' pº
(16r1a) ¶ xiij	mº	s/ vj d' x .o'.	(16r1b) xxxv	mº	s/ xvj d' ij. o' pº
(2a) ¶ xiiij	mº	s/ vij d' iij	(2b) xxxvj	mº	s/ xvj d' vj o' pº
(3a) ¶ xv	mº	s/ vij d' vij o'	(3b) xxxvij	mº	s/ xvij. d' vj o' pº
(4a) ¶ xvj	mº	s/ viij	(4b) xxxviij	mº	s/ xvij d' xi pº
(5a) ¶ xvij	mº	s/ viij d' iiij o'	(5b) xxxix	mº	s/ xviij d' iij o' pº
(6a) ¶ xviij	mº	s/ ix o' pº.	(6b) xl	mº	s/ xviij d' xi
(7) ¶ xix	mº	s/ ix d' v. pº			
(8) ¶ xx	mº	s/ viij d' x o' pº			
(9) ¶ xxj	mº	s/ x d' ij. pº.			
(10) ¶ xxij	mº	s/ x d' vj o' pº			

[Rubric VIII]

[The *Montazon* at Tarascon: second version]

[Table T3]

(16r11) Aisso es la montazon dels cavalhers de (12) Tharascon, que prenon de .i. mog de sal entro (13) xl que non remangua a Tharascon ni a Bel-(14) care.

(15–18)					
(19) ¶	Uno	m^{o}	d' iiij	o'	
(20) ¶	ij	m^{o}	d' viiij		
(21) ¶	iij	m^{o}	d' xiij	o'	
(22) ¶	iiij	m^{o}	d' xviij		
(23) ¶	v	m^{o}	d' xxij	o'	
(24) ¶	v[j]	m^{o}	s/ ij	d' iij	
(25) ¶	vij	m^{o}	s/ ij	d' vij	o'
(26) ¶	viij	m^{o}	s/ iij		
(16v1) ¶	ix	m^{o}	s/ v		
(2) ¶	x	m^{o}	s/ v	d' iiij.	o'
(3) ¶	xi	m^{o}	s/ v	d' ix	
(4) ¶	xij	m^{o}	s/ vj	d' viij	
(5) ¶	xiij	m^{o}	s/ vj	d' x	o'
(6) ¶	xiiij	m^{o}	s/ vij	d' iij	
(7) ¶	xv	m^{o}	s/ vij	d' vij	o'
(8) ¶	xvj	m^{o}	s/ viij		
(9) ¶	xvij	m^{o}	s/ viij	d' iiij	o'
(10) ¶	xvijj	m^{o}	s/ viijj		
(11) ¶	xix	m^{o}	s/ ix	d' v	p^{o}
(12) ¶	xx	m^{o}	s/ ix	d' ix	.o'. p^{o}
(13) ¶	xxi	m^{o}	s/ x	d' ij	p^{o}
(14) ¶	xxij	m^{o}	s/ x	d' vj	o' p^{o}.
(15) ¶	xxiij	m^{o}	s/ x	d' xi	p^{o}
(16) ¶	xxiiij	m^{o}	s/ xi	d' iij	o' p^{o}
(17) ¶	xxv	m^{o}	s/ xij	d' v	p^{o}
(18) ¶	xxvj	m^{o}	s/ xij	d' ix	o' p^{o}.
(19) ¶	xxvij	m^{o}	s/ xiij	d' ij	p^{o}
(20) ¶	xxviij	m^{o}	s/ xiij	d' vj	o' p^{o}
(21) ¶	xxix	m^{o}	s/ xiij	d' xj	p^{o}
(22) ¶	xxx	m^{o}	s/ xiiij	d' iiij	o' p^{o}
(23) ¶	xxxj	m^{o}	s/ xiiij	d' viij	p^{o}
(24) ¶	xxxij	m^{o}	s/ xv	o'	p^{o}
(25) ¶	xxxiij	m^{o}	s/ xv	d' v	p^{o}
(26) ¶	xxxiiij	m^{o}	s/ [xv]	d' ix	o' p^{o}
(17r1) ¶	xxxv	m^{o}	s/ xvj	d' ij	o' p^{o}
(2) ¶	xxxvj	m^{o}	s/ xvj	d' vj	o' p^{o}
(3) ¶	xxxvij	m^{o}	s/ xvij	d' vj	o' p^{o}
(4) ¶	xxxviij	m^{o}	s/ xvij	d' xi	p^{o}
(5) ¶	xxxix	m^{o}	s/ xviij	d' iij	o' p^{o}
(6) ¶	xl	m^{o}	s/ xviij	d' xi	

Translation of MS T

[Rubric I]

[Tolls on commodities at Tarascon and Lubières]

(3r1) This is the proper and customary procedure of the register of the toll at Tarascon for things going up or coming down the Rhône.
(4–6)

[2s 5.5d (= 29.5d) per load]

(7) A load of cloths from Avignon, which contains nine cloths;
(9) A load of cloths from France, which contains twelve cloths;
(11) A load of cloths from Narbonne, which contains twenty-four cloths or four quintals;
(13) A load of brown cloth, which contains four or five cloths;
(14) A load of coarse muslins, which contains forty-eight pieces or four quintals;
(16) A load of linen cloths, which contains four quintals;
(17) A load of hides, tanned or not tanned, which contains twenty hides;
(19) A load of cordovan leather, which contains twelve dozen [pieces] or four quintals;
(21) A load of wax;
(22) A load of pepper;
(23) A load of ginger;
(24) A load of cloves;
(25) A load of silk;
(26) A load of sendal;
(27) A load of zedoary;

(28) A load of saffron;
(29) A load of indigo;
(3v1) A load of varicoloured fur linings or rabbit [furs], or the like;
(2) A load of alum from Aleppo;
(3) A load of feather alum or sugar alum, which contains four quintals:
(5)
(6) Each of the abovesaid things pays 2s 5.5d per load,
(8) Of which Johan Alba takes 1d,
(9) And the lords of the toll at Lubières, 1d.
(10–11)

[21d per load]

(12) A load of wool;
(13) A load of hemp;
(14) A load of tow;
(15) A load of ropes;
(16) A load of thread for ropes;
(17) A load of cumin;
(18) A load of anise;
(19) A load of cinnamon;
(20) A load of sugar;
(21) A load of powdered sugar;
(22) A load of figs;
(23) A load of dates;
(24) A load of honey;
(25) A load of rice;
(26) A load of cheeses;
(27) A load of lard;
(28) A load of tallow;
(29) A load of pitch;
(30) A load of Brazil wood;
(31) A load of sheepskins;
(32) A load of kidskins;
(33) A load of lambskins;
(4r1) A load of cotton;
(2) A load of fustian;
(3) A load of coarse cloths;
(4) A load of shelled almonds;
(5) A load of peeled chestnuts;

(6) A load of copper;
(7) A load of tin;
(8) A load of iron that contains four quintals or four bars;
(10) A load of oil that contains eighteen canes;
(12) A load of pewter plates;
(13) A load of reefpoints;
(14) A load of varnish;
(15) A load of quicksilver;
(16) A load of fish from the sea, salted or not salted:
(17) Each of the things abovesaid pays, per load of four quintals 21d
(19) Of which Johan Alba takes 1d
(20) And the lords of the toll of Lubières 1d

[Woad: 16d per load]

(21) ¶ A load of woad, which contains four quintals, pays per load 16d
(23) Of which Johan Alba takes 1d
(24) And the lords of the toll of Lubières 1d
(25–6)

[Cloth and leather: from 3d to 0.5d]

(27) A serge pays 1d
(28) Item, a coarse muslin 0.5d
(29) Item, a cord of linen 0.5d
(30) Item, a dozen cordovan hides 2d
(31) Item, a dozen sheepskins 3d
(32) Item, an oxhide 1.5d
(33) Item, a fleece 1d
(34) Item, a tunic 0.5d
(35) Item, a strap 0.5d

[11d per load]

(4v1) A load of tartar;
(2) A load of old ropes;
(3) A load of alum from Vulcano;
(4) A load of sheepskins, which are used for making parchment;
(5) pays per load, which contains four quintals 11d
(6) Of which Johan Alba takes 1d

(7) And the lords of Lubières 1d
(8)

[Tiles: 9d per load]

(9) [A load of] tiles pays, per thousand 9d
(10) Of which Johan Alba takes 1d
(11)

[Grain: 11.5d per load, etc.]

(12) A load of any grain or any legume or any flour that contains fifteen or sixteen setiers by the measure of Tarascon pays, per load 11.5d
(15) Of which Johan Alba takes 1d
(16) And the lords of Lubières 1d
(17) However, if the grain was loaded from Avignon upstream, and in the boat there was from twenty bundles upward, it pays for each bundle, for the main tollhouse 9.5d
(21) And for Lubières, for the whole shipload 5s
(22) between the king and the lords of the toll of Lubières. And if in the boat there was grain belonging to two partners or more owners, and each one had from twenty bundles up, and the grain was loaded from Avignon upstream, each [partner] would pay, for Lubières 5s
(27) However, if grain or flour came in sacks, wherever it comes from, the bundle of each [owner] pays 11.5d
(30)

[Wine: 6d per butt plus payment in kind]

(31) Wine going up or coming down the Rhône: for each butt, small or large, it pays 6d
(33) Item, for one butt, half a keg of wine.
(5r1) Item, for two butts, one keg of wine.
(2) And for three butts and from there up, the whole shipload pays one bundle of wine.
(4) And if the wine comes in kegs, one half-[keg] is counted as a butt, and it pays as said above.
(7)
(8) And if a man of Tarascon made a partnership in wine with foreign men with the wine mixed together, he would pay for it all; but if each one kept his

wine separately in casks and it was common knowledge, only the foreigner pays.[1]
(13–14)

[Dye: 6s 5d (= 77d) per hogshead]

(15) The hogshead of sumach, which contains seventy-two quintals or three and a half *saquieras*, gives 6s 5d,
(17) Of which Johan Alba takes, per *saquiera* 1d
(18) Item, it also owes, at the toll of Lubières, between the king and the lords of Lubières 7d
(20) And if in the boat there were from twenty *saquieras* up, at the rate of the toll of Lubières the whole shipload pays 5s
(23) for the main tollhouse, as said above.
(24)

[Lead: 6d per load]

(25) A load of lead, which contains four quintals, pays [............] 6d
(26) In which Johan Alba takes 0.5d
(27) and on one hundred quintals it gives [him] .... 15d[2]
(28) Item, at Lubières it gives, per load 2d
(29) in which the king has half, and half the lords of the toll of Lubières.
(31)

[Masts and yards]

(See Textual Notes, T5r30, on the order of lines T5r[32–42].)

[32] A ship's mast that is seven palms or more around, [measured] one-third [of the way] up the tree from the root, pays [............] £3 10s
[34] In which Johan Alba takes 15d

---

1 "Si un habitant de Tarascon fait tansport de vins avec des étrangers, de façon que son vin soit confondu avec le leur, le péage sera levé sur la totalité du vin. Mais si chacun a son vin dans des tonneaux distincts, le vin des étrangers paie seul" (Bondurand 142nn2–3).

2 If a load of four quintals pays a toll of 6d, one of a hundred quintals cannot pay merely 15d. The reference must be to the share for Johan Alba; hence I have inserted "[him]." Johan Alba gets 0.5d on four quintals and 15d on a hundred quintals. Left unexplained by Bondurand 142 ("Et en C° quintals dona d. XV").

[35] Item, it pays at Lubières 5s
[36] in which the king has half, and the other half the lords of Lubières.
[38] A ship's yard six palms and a half around pays 30s
[40] Item, at Lubières, between the king and the lords, it pays in addition 5s
[42] A yard of six palms 20s
(5v1) And [one] of five palms and a half 11s
(2) And of five palms 10s
(3) And of four palms and a half 5s
(4) And of four palms 4s
(5) And from there down, it gives according to the judgment of the tollkeeper.
(7) And they also give at Lubières, each one 2d
(8) And Sir Johan Alba takes on each one, on the part of the king our lord 1d
(10–11)

[Wood and wood products]

(12) A ship's tiller or a round oak log gives 15s
(13) in which Johan Alba gets 5d
(14) ¶ Item, at Lubières, between the king and the lords 3s
(15) A squared oak log pays 5s
(16) of which Johan Alba gets 3d
(17) ¶ Item, [at Lubières[3]] between the king and the lords, for one wooden log, it gives 12.5d
(19) in which Johan Alba gets for each one 1d
(20) ¶ Item, it gives, at the rate of the toll of Los Mujulans (which belong to the king), for each log up to eight logs [...] 0.75d
(22) and from eight logs upward, the whole raft pays for the toll of Los Mujolans only 6d
(25)
(26) ¶ Item, a wooden log up to twenty logs gives at Lubières, between the king and the lords of Lubières 2d

3 The words *a Lubieras*, "at Lubières," seem to have been inserted in error (see Textual Notes). The passage should be read without them, so that this sentence applies to Tarascon. The passage states the toll for a ship's tiller or a round oak log at Tarascon (T5v12) and Lubières (T5v14); for a squared oak log at Tarascon (T5v15); for one stack (*travada*) of timber at Tarascon (T5v17), Los Mujulans (T5v20), and Lubières (T5v26); and then explains what one stack means in relation to various wood products (T5v33, etc.).

(30) ¶ And from twenty logs up, at Lubières the whole raft gives 5s
(32)
(33) A squared log of timber from Seyssel or of larch wood makes a stack.
(35) Two squared logs of timber from Le Royans are a stack.
(36) Twelve small, round poles make a stack.
(6r1) Twelve small, portable logs are a stack.
(2) Four or six small, irregular logs are a stack.
(3) Four large oak boards and ten small ones make a stack.
(5) Four squared timbers [that can be] hauled by oxen are a stack.
(6) Twenty fir boards are a stack.
(7) Seven larch-wood boards are a stack.
(8) Six walnut boards are a stack.
(9) Eight or nine *ourses*[4] or large curved planks make a stack.
(11)
(12) ¶ A watermill[5] gives in toll 10s
(13) A windmill gives 5s
(14) An oared ship from Rhodes gives as toll £2 10s
(15) A bark gives 5s
(16) About a sailed ship we are in doubt.
(17)
(18) ¶ Each strake [in the hull] of a boat bought recently or that is being taken to sell gives .... 2d and one oar.
(20) ¶ Item, at Lubières, between the king and the lords, each strake gives 2d
(22) and the whole boat, one oar.
(23)

[Domestic objects: 4d to 0.5d]

(24) ¶ Roof tiles,
(25) bowls,
(26) Trenchers,
(27) Bowls,
(6v1) Hoops,
(2) Timber,

---

4 Tackle for manoeuvring a lateen sail.

5 That is, the lumber to build a watermill or a windmill, as is clear in the Latin version in MS A_1: *De fusta unius molendini aure: V s.; de fusta unius molendini aque: X s.*, "For the wood of a windmill, 5s; for the wood of a water mill, 10s" (Baratier 386).

(3) Kegs,
(4) Struts,
(5) Spoons,
(6) pitchers,
(7) Two-handled jugs,
(8) Give, per hundred, four [pieces].
(9) ¶ Item, at Lubières they give, per hundred 2d
(10) or per bundle 0.5d
(11)
(12) A chest,
(13) A new box with feet,
(14) A vat,
(15) A cask,
(16) A new drain,
(17) A millstone,
(18) A barber's grindstone,
(19) A washbasin:
(20) For each one of these [things], it gives 4d
(21) Item, at Lubières, between the king and the lords, it gives 1d
(23)
(24) ¶ A bundle of pots,
(25) Jugs,
(26) Pitchers,
(27) Pans,
(28) Or any utensils of clay, gives, per bundle 4d

[Foods, etc.]

(7r1) ¶ A bundle of almonds in the shell,
(2) Walnuts,
(3) Hazelnuts, which contains eight heminas:
(4) the bundle gives 4.5d
(5) ¶ Item, at Lubières, between the king and the lords 0.5d
(7)
(8) ¶ A bundle of apples,
(9) Peaches,
(10) Sorb apples,
(11) Sour cherries,
(12) Fresh walnuts,
(13) Pears,

(14) Quinces,
(15) Medlars,
(16) Cherries,
(17) Chestnuts in the shell,
(18) Gives, per bundle 2d
(19) ¶ Item, at Lubières, between the king and the lords 0.5d
(20)
(21) ¶ A bundle of tanner's bark that contains nine heminas gives 1d
(23) At Lubières 0.5d
(24) ¶ A bundle of charcoal gives 1d
(25) Item, at Lubières, between the king and the lords [..........] 0.5d
(7v1) A bundle of rapes 0.5d
(2) It gives at Lubières 0.5d
(4) ¶ A bundle of large onions that contains two dozen, and [one of] small onions that contains three dozen;
(7)
(8) ¶ A bundle of garlic bulbs, which contains eight or ten dozen, gives in toll, per bundle .... 1 bunch
(12) ¶ Item, at Lubières, between the king and the lords 0.5d
(14)

[Materials: payment in kind or 18d]

(15) ¶ A sumpter's load of glass gives in toll, pieces 2
(17) And from the carrier, it gives 1 piece.
(18)
(19) ¶ A shipload of lime, gypsum, or rock, from twenty-five quarry stones up, pays at Lubières 18d
(22) Of which the king gets half,
(23) And the lords of the toll of Lubières, half.
(24–6)

[Exemptions]

(27) ¶ These things do not pay toll, that is:
(29) Soap,
(30) fish from the Rhône or a marsh,
(8r1) Cuttlefish,
(2) Liquorice,
(3) Galls,

(4) Verdigris,
(5) Haberdashery,
(6) furs,
(7) silver,
(8) Sulfur,
(9) Butter,
(10) Ochre,
(11) A funnel,
(12) Any product made of iron or copper or brass or tin,
(14) Gold,
(15) Coins,
(16) Except for the fair of Beaucaire in May, when furs, for the load of an animal, pay 6d
(19) And for [the load] of a man 3d
(20–1)

[Live cargo: horses, travellers, large animals]

(22) ¶ As for a horse bought or sold, wherever it is taken to sell, if it was worth £12 10s and up, and it crosses the Rhône, it pays 2s 6d
(8v1) ¶ Item, a Saracen or an ape pays 2s 6d
(2)
(3) All men riding, crossing the Rhône, except men of Tarascon and Beaucaire, and except nobles and their retinue,
(7) And except prelates – that is, from subdeacon up – if [the distance they travel] is less than eight leagues, pay 1.5d
(10) And if [the distance] is from eight leagues up, they pay 3.5d
(11)
(12) ¶ As for large animals coming from the regions of Provence, crossing the Rhône, if they are workhorses or mares or male mules or female mules, they pay as is said above.[6] And if they are oxen or asses, they pay 1d
(17) ¶ Item, ewes, goats, pigs, and their young: each animal pays 0.25d
(19–20)
(21) This is a fee for unloading cargo.
(22) As for animals coming from the regions beyond the Rhône, bought or sold or being taken to sell, if they are workmares or female mules, they pay 0.5d

---

6 Perhaps meaning that these large animals pay 1.5d if they come from within eight leagues and 3.5d if from farther away.

(26) ¶ Item, oxen, asses, ewes, goats, pigs pay 0.25d
(9r1) ¶ All Lombard pilgrims, men or women, going to visit Santiago [de Compostela], riding, give in toll 8d
(4) But if he or she is going elsewhere, he or she pays 3.5d
(5) And if he or she is walking or coming on the Rhône, he or she pays 1.5d
(6–7)
(8) ¶ Any Spaniard, Englishman, [or] German, and all pilgrims from Lyon and upstream going to visit Santiago or Saint-Gilles on horseback, pay 5d
(12)
(13) ¶ And if he is walking or coming on the Rhône, he pays 1d
(14)
(15) ¶ Any pilgrim from whatever region it may be, except Provençals: if he is walking, he gives 1d
(18)
(19) ¶ Coiners, as long as they work in a mint of the king our lord, or of the king of France, are exempt for their mounts.

[Rubric II]

[Tolls and *montazon* on salt]

(9v1) This is the toll on salt.
(2) One hogshead of salt going up the Rhône from Tarascon upstream, wherever it comes from, pays for the main tollhouse 20d
(6) Of which Johan Alba gets 1d
(7) And the king our lord 18d
(8) ¶ Item, it also gives for *montazon*, up to eight hogsheads .... 6d per hogshead,
(10) Of which the king our lord gets 3d
(11) And certain nobles of Tarascon [..] 4.5d
(12) From eight hogsheads up, it pays more as *montazon*, and it is divided in the same way.
(14) ¶ Item, it also gives for the toll of Lubières up to six hogsheads, 3d per hogshead. (16) And from six hogsheads up, for the whole boat, [........] 18d
(17) Of which the king our lord gets half,
(18) And half certain nobles of Tarascon.
(20) ¶ Item, it also gives at the rate of the toll of Lo Mujolans, which the king our lord bought: up to eight hogsheads, it gives per hogshead 1 .... 1.5d

(23) And from there up, for the whole boat 6d
(24)
(25) ¶ Total that a hogshead of salt pays for everything up to six hogsheads:
[....] 2s 5.75d

[Rubric III]

[Shares in the toll on salt]

[Table T1]

(10r1) These are the shares in the toll on salt.
(2–3)
(4) One hogshead of salt gives 2s 5.25d:
the king 22.75d, the knights 7d.

(6) Two hogsheads of salt give	4s 11.5d:	
the king 3s 9.5d,	the knights 14d.	
(9) ¶ Three hhd of salt give	7s 5.25d:	
the king 5s 8.25d,	the knights 1s 9d.	
(11) ¶ Four hhd of salt give	9s 11d:	
the king 7s 7d,	the knights 2s 4d.	
(13) ¶ Five hhd of salt give	12s 4.75d:	
the king 9s 5.75d,	the knights 2s 11d.	
(15) ¶ Six hhd of salt give	14s 10.5d:	
the king 11s 4.5d,	the knights 3s 6d.	
(17) ¶ Seven hhd of salt give	17s 1.25d:	
the king 13s 1.75d,	the knights 2s 11.5d.	
(19) ¶ Eight hhd of salt give	19s 4d:	
the king 14s 11d,	the knights 4s 5d.	
(21) ¶ Nine hhd of salt give	23s 8d:	
the king 17s 2d,	the knights 6s 6d.	
(23) ¶ Ten hhd of salt give	25s 10d:	
the king 18s 10.5d,	the knights 6s 11.5d.	
(25) ¶ Eleven hhd of salt give	28s 1d:	
the king £1 7d,	the knights 7s 5d.	
(27) ¶ Twelve hhd of salt give	30s 8d:	
the king £1 2s 5d,	the knights 8s 3d.	
(10v1) ¶ Thirteen hhd,	32s	10d:
the king	£1	4s 1.5d,
the knights	8s	8.5d.

(4) ¶ Fourteen hhd, 35s 1d:
the king £1. 5s 10d,
knights 9s 2d.

(7) ¶ Fifteen hhd, 37s 2d:
the king £1 7s 6.5d,
knights 9s 7.5d.

(10) ¶ Sixteen hhd, 39s 4d:
the king £1 9s 3d,
knights 10s 1d.

(13) ¶ Seventeen hhd, 41s 6d:
the king £1 10s 11d,
knights 10s 6.5d.

(16) ¶ Eighteen hhd, 44s 1d:
the king 12s 9.25d, £1,
knights 11s 3.75d.

(19) ¶ Nineteen hhd, 46s 3d:
the king £1 14s 5.75d,
knights 11s 9.25d.

(22) ¶ Twenty hhd, 48s 5d:
the king £1 16s 2.25d,
knights 12s 2.75d.

(25) ¶ Twenty-one hhd, 50s 7d:
the king £1 17s 10.75d, knights 12s 8.25d.

(11r1) ¶ Twenty-two hhd, 52s 9d: the king £1
19s 7.25d, knights 13s 1.75d.

(3) ¶ Twenty-three hhd, 54s 11d: the king £2
1s 3.75d, knights 13s 7.25d.

(5) ¶ Twenty-four hhd 57s 1d: the king £2
3s 0.25d, knights 14s 1.75d.

(7) ¶ Twenty-five hhd, 60s 3d: the king £2
4s 11.75d, knights 15s 3.25d.

(9) ¶ Twenty-six hhd, 62s 5d: the king £2
6s 7.25d, knights 16s 2.25d.

(11) ¶ Twenty-eight hhd, 66s 9d: the king £2
10s 1.25d, knights 16s 7.75d.

(13) ¶ Twenty-nine hhd, 68s 11d: the king £2
11s 9.75d, knights 17s 1.25d.

(15) ¶ Thirty hhd, 71s 1d: the king £2
13s 6.25d, knights 17s 6.25d.

(17) ¶ Thirty-one hhd, 73s 3d:	the king £2
15s 2.75d,	knights 18s 0.25d.
(19) ¶ Thirty-two hhd, 75s 5d:	the king £2
16s 11.25d,	knights 18s 5.75d.
(21) ¶ Thirty-three hhd, 77s 7d:	the king £2
18s 7.75d,	knights 18s 11.25d.
(11v2) ¶ Thirty-four hhd, 79s 9d:	the king £3
4.25d,	knights 19s. 4.75d.

(4) ¶ Thirty-five hhd,	£4	1s	11d:
the king	£3	2s	0.75d,
knights	19s	10d	0.25d.
(7) ¶ Thirty-six hhd,	£4	4s	1d:
the king	£3	3s	9.25d,
knights	20s	3d	0.75d.
(10) ¶ Thirty-seven hhd,	£4	7s	1d:
the king	£3	5s	8.25d,
knights	£1	1s	4.25d.
(13) ¶ Thirty-eight hhd,	£4	9s	3d:
the king	£3	7s	4.75d,
knights	£1	1s	10.75d.
(16) ¶ Thirty-nine hhd,	£4	11s	5d:
the king	£3	9s	1.25d,
knights	£1	2s	3.75d.
(19) ¶ Forty hhd,	£4	13s	10d:
the king	£3	10s	10d,
knights	£1	3s.	

(22)

(23) ¶ And if in the boat there were from forty hogsheads up, the forty hogsheads pay as is said above, and the excess gives, per hogshead, 22d only;

(12r 3) of which the king gets 19d;

(4) and Johan Alba, 1d;

(5) and the lords, 2d for the *montazon*.

(6)

(7) ¶ Any man who loads salt at Beaucaire pays 22d per hogshead, which are shared as [are] the 22d stated above.

(11) ¶ Item, it pays three *pogezas* [0.75d] per hogshead up to eight hogsheads for Los Mujolans, which now belong to the king our lord.

(14)

(15) ¶ And from eight hogsheads up, it gives, at the rate of the three *pogezas*, 6d for the whole boat and no more.
(18)
(19) ¶ Any man of Beaucaire or Tarascon who unloads salt at Beaucaire gives 4d per hogshead for *uzage*, of which the king our lord gets three halfpennies [1.5d] per hogshead, and the lords, 2.5d for the *montazon*.
(26) ¶ Item, at Lubières it gives 3d per hogshead up to six hogsheads, of which the king gets half.
(28) ¶ And the lords of Lubières, half. And from six hogsheads up, at Lubières it gives 18d for the whole boat, and 4d per hogshead in *usage*, however much there is.
(12v1) ¶ Item, any foreign man who loads salt in Tarascon pays in the same way.
(4)
(5) ¶ Any foreign man who unloads salt at Beaucaire pays 14.5d per hogshead, of which the king, all things considered, gets 9.5d; and the nobles 5d, of which Johan Alba gets 1d, and the lords of Lubières 1.5d, and the lords of the *montazon* 2.5d.
(11)
(12) ¶ And from six hogsheads up, it gives 11.5d per hogshead, and 18d for the whole boat for the toll of Lubières, of which the king gets 8d per hogshead and 9d for the whole boat. And the lords of the *montazon*, 2.5d per hogshead; and the lords of Lubières, 9d for the whole boat; and Johan Alba, 1d per hogshead.
(20)
(21) ¶ Item, all men who sell salt in the ports of Beaucaire or Tarascon pay as is said above about those who unload, local [men] or foreigners.
(25)
(26) ¶ A *caupol* laden with salt[7] that comes from the salt pans, if it is level, makes 8.5 hogsheads; and if it is heaping, it makes 12 hogsheads.

[Rubric IV]

[Tolls at Lubières]

(13r1) This is the toll of Lubières, of which the king our lord gets half, and certain nobles of Tarascon half.
(4–5)

---

7 Literally, a *caupolada* of salt. A *caupolada* is the load of a *caupol*, an oared barge.

[Goods, grain]

(6) On any load of goods from the Levant or elsewhere, going upstream or coming down, passing before Lubières, if there is toll, it gives [............] 2d
(10) Item, a bundle of any grain or any legumes or flour, of fifteen or sixteen setiers by the measure of Tarascon, pays [..] 2d
(13)
(14) ¶ However, if in one boat there were from twenty bundles upward, and it came from Avignon upstream, the shipload, however much there is in it, pays only 5s
(18)
(19) ¶ However, if in the boat there were grain belonging to two partners or more, and each one had twenty bundles or more in the hold, each one pays 5s
(24)

[Wood]

(25) ¶ A wooden log gives 2d
(26) ¶ However, if in the raft there were twenty logs, or from twenty up, it gives only 5s
(13v1) ¶ A ship's mast seven palms around and up pays .... 5[s]
(3)
(4) ¶ A yard of six and a half palms 5s
(5) Item, a tiller or round oak log 3s
(6) ¶ Item, a squared oak log or a pole less than six and a half palms [around] 2d
(8)

[Dye]

(9) ¶ Item, each hogshead of sumach, which contains three and a half *saqui-eras*, pays 7d
(11) ¶ However, if in the boat there were twenty *saquieras*, or from twenty up, it gives [only] 5s
(13)

[Materials]

(14) ¶ Item, a shipload of rock or lime or gypsum gives 18d.
(16)

[Food]

(17) ¶ Item, a bundle of apples, pears, or any other fruits, that pays toll 0.5d
(20)
(21) ¶ Item, a bundle of onions or garlic bulbs 0.5d
(22)
(23) ¶ Item, a bundle of tanner's bark or charcoal or rapes gives 0.5d
(25)
(26) ¶ Item, [likewise] a bundle of walnuts or almonds in the shell.
(28)

[Domestic objects]

(29) ¶ Item, a vat, cask, drain, new box or new chest, washbasin, millstone or [grindstone for] a smith or a barber 1d
(32)
(33) ¶ Item, hoops, struts, bowls,
(34) trenchers, small tubs, spoons,
(35) small bowls, wooden bowls, pitchers,
(36) two-handled jugs, kegs, roof tiles,
(37) timber, give, per bundle 0.5d

[Rubric V]

[Tolls at the Gates of Tarascon]

(14r1) This is the procedure of the toll at the Gates of Tarascon, which procedure Sir Pons del Prat, sometime tollkeeper, declared under oath.
(4–6)

[2s 2d (= 26d) per load]

(7) A load of cloths from France,
(8) cloths from Narbonne,
(9) cloths from Avignon, linen cloths,
(10) coarse muslin cloths, any other cloths;
(11) cordovan leather, indigo,
(12) pepper, ginger,
(13) clove, wax,
(14) silk, sendal,

(15) alum,	hides of lions or
(16)	camels or workmares
(17)	or the like;

(18) thread of inferior wool:
(19) of all these things abovesaid, a load is made of four quintals, and it pays, in *rials* 2s 2d
(22)

[19d]

(23) A load of oil, which contains eighteen canes;

(24) a load of hemp,	ropes,
(25) thread for ropes,	wool,
(26) lambswool,	sheepskins,
(27) lambskins,	kid[skins],
(28) cumin,	anise,
(29) peeled chestnuts,	shelled almonds,
(30) figs,	cheeses,
(31) rice, sugar,	powdered sugar,
(32) honey, tallow,	lard,
(33) iron, steel,	tin,
(34) Brazil wood,	fresh fish,
(35) salted [fish],	cotton,

(14v1) fustian, and the like: the load contains four quintals, which gives 19d

[Lead: 6d]

(3) ¶ A load of lead contains four quintals; it gives 6d

[Salt carried by animals: 2d]

(4) ¶ – of animals loaded with salt, gives 2d

[Food, domestic objects]

(5) ¶ – of animals loaded with fruits, gives 2d
(6) ¶ – of roof tiles, pitchers, goblets,
(7) ¶ – of hoops, gives, for a hundred, four [pieces].
(8) ¶ – of animals loaded with onions or garlic bulbs: they take one bunch.

(10) ¶ – of animals loaded with pitchers or two-handled jugs or kegs, gives 4d
(12) ¶ – of animals loaded with any grain, or any legumes, or flour: the bundle is made of eight setiers, and they give 4d
(15) ¶ – of animals loaded with bowls, trenchers, small tubs, large dishes, spoons, gives 4d
(18)
(19) ¶ – of a cask, vat, chest, new box, set of staves – that is, twenty-five staves with the wedges – gives 4d
(23) ¶ Item, – of a millstone or a washbasin, gives [........] 4d
(25) – of animals loaded with glass, gives pieces [........] 2
(27) ¶ Item, – of clay pots, gives, per hundred, [pieces] 4
(28) ¶ – of small animals, sold, gives, for four 1d
(30) ¶ – of large animals 0.5d
(31) ¶ A bundle of onions contains two dozen of the large ones or four dozen of the small ones.
(15r1) ¶ A bundle of garlic bulbs contains eight or ten dozen.

[Exemption]

(2) ¶ However, you must understand about all the things said above, [that] at the toll at the Gates there is an understanding if they have not paid at the tollhouse of Jarnègues; but if they had paid at Jarnègues, they would be exempt at the Gates.
(8)

[Rubric VI]

[Tolls at Saint-Gabriel]

(9) The proper and customary procedure of the toll of Saint-Gabriel, which is taken from the procedure of the toll of the Gate of Tarascon for the greater part of all the things written below.
(13)

[13d per load]

(14) A load of oil,	cumin,
(15) cinnamon,	honey,
(16) rice,	cheeses,
(17) almonds,	chestnuts,

(18) sugar,	ropes,
(19)	fustian,
(20) powdered sugar,	pitch,
(21) lard,	tin,
(22) tallow,	iron,
(23) hemp,	steel,
(24) tow,	tin,
(25) thread for ropes,	Brazil wood,
(26) cotton,	lambswool,
(27) sheepskins,	lambskins,

(28) kidskins, and similar things: the load is made of four quintals, on which half toll is taken at Tarascon, and they all give at Saint-Gabriel only 13d.

(15v1) ¶ As for all other things and other commodities, consider the proper and customary procedure of the toll of the Gate of Tarascon at this toll of Saint-Gabriel.

(6)

[Cloths, etc.: 2s 2d (= 26d)]

(7) ¶ A load of all kinds of cloths and linen cloths and coarse muslin cloths, cordovan leather, and other similar things gives 2s 2d. The load is made of four quintals.

(11)

[Rubric VII]

[The *Montazon* at Tarascon: first version]

[Table T2]

(12) This is the *montazon* of the knights of Tarascon, which they take from one hogshead of salt up to forty that does not remain in Tarascon or Beaucaire.

(16)

(17a) ¶ One	hhd	4.5d	(17b) Twenty-three	hhd	10s 11.25d
(18a) ¶ Two	hhd	9d.	(18b) Twenty-four	hhd	11s 3.75d
(19a) ¶ Three	hhd	13.5d	(19b) Twenty-five	hhd	12s 5.25d
(20a) ¶ Four	hhd	18d	(20b) Twenty-six	hhd	12s 9.75d
(21a) ¶ Five	hhd	22.5d	(21b) Twenty-seven	hhd	13s 3.25d
(22a) ¶ Six	hhd	2s 3d	(22b) Twenty-eight	hhd	13s 6.75d
(23a) ¶ Seven	hhd	2s 7.5d	(23b) Twenty-nine	hhd	13s 11.25d

(24a) ¶ Eight	hhd	3s	(24b) Thirty	hhd	14s 3.75d
(25a) ¶ Nine	hhd	5s	(25b) Thirty-one	hhd	14s 8.25d
(26a) ¶ Ten	hhd	5s 4.5d	(26b) Thirty-two	hhd	15s 1.75d
(27a) ¶ Eleven	hhd	5s 9d	(27b) Thirty-three	hhd	15s 5.25d
(28a) ¶ Twelve	hhd	6s 6d	(28b) Thirty-four	hhd	15s 9.75d
(16r1a) ¶ Thirteen	hhd	6s 10.5d	(1b) Thirty-five	hhd	16s 2.75d
(2a) ¶ Fourteen	hhd	7s 3d	(2b) Thirty-six	hhd	16s 6.75d
(3a) ¶ Fifteen	hhd	7s 7.5d	(3b) Thirty-seven	hhd	17s 6.75d
(4a) ¶ Sixteen	hhd	8s	(4b) Thirty-eight	hhd	17s 11.25d
(5a) ¶ Seventeen	hhd	8s 4.5d	(5b) Thirty-nine	hhd	18s 3.75d
(6a) ¶ Eighteen	hhd	9s 0.75d	(6b) Forty	hhd	18s 11d
(7) ¶ Nineteen	hhd	9s 5.25d			
(8) ¶ Twenty	hhd	8s 10.75d			
(9) ¶ Twenty-one	hhd	10s 2.25d			
(10) ¶ Twenty-two	hhd	10s 6.75d			

[Rubric VIII]

[The *Montazon* at Tarascon: second version]

[Table T3]

(16r11) This is the *montazon* of the knights of Tarascon, which they take for one hogshead up to forty that does not remain in Tarascon or Beaucaire.
(15–18)

(19) ¶ One	hhd	4.5d	
(20) ¶ Two	hhd	9d	
(21) ¶ Three	hhd	13.5d	
(22) ¶ Four	hhd	18d	
(23) ¶ Five	hhd	22.5d	
(24) ¶ Six	hhd	2s 3d	
(25) ¶ Seven	hhd	2s 7.5d	
(26) ¶ Eight	hhd	3s	
(16v1) ¶ Nine	hhd	5s	
(2) ¶ Ten	hhd	5s	4.5d
(3) ¶ Eleven	hhd	5s	9d
(4) ¶ Twelve	hhd	6s	8d
(5) ¶ Thirteen	hhd	6s	10.5d
(6) ¶ Fourteen	hhd	7s	3d
(7) ¶ Fifteen	hhd	7s	7.5d

(8) ¶ Sixteen	hhd	8s	
(9) ¶ Seventeen	hhd	8s	4.5d
(10) ¶ Eighteen	hhd	9s	
(11) ¶ Nineteen	hhd	9s	5.25d
(12) ¶ Twenty	hhd	9s	9.75d
(13) ¶ Twenty-one	hhd	10s	2.25d
(14) ¶ Twenty-two	hhd	10s	6.75d
(15) ¶ Twenty-three	hhd	10s	11.25d
(16) ¶ Twenty-four	hhd	11s	3.75d
(17) ¶ Twenty-five	hhd	12s	5.25d
(18) ¶ Twenty-six	hhd	12s	9.75d
(19) ¶ Twenty-seven	hhd	13s	2.25d
(20) ¶ Twenty-eight	hhd	13s	6.75d
(21) ¶ Twenty-nine	hhd	13s	11.25d
(22) ¶ Thirty	hhd	14s	3.75d
(23) ¶ Thirty-one	hhd	14s	8.25d
(24) ¶ Thirty-two	hhd	15s	0.75d
(25) ¶ Thirty-three	hhd	15s	5.25d
(26) ¶ Thirty-four	hhd	[15]s	9.75d
(17r1) ¶ Thirty-five	hhd	16s	2.75d
(2) ¶ Thirty-six	hhd	16s	6.75d
(3) ¶ Thirty-seven	hhd	17s	6.75d
(4) ¶ Thirty-eight	hhd	17s	11.25d
(5) ¶ Thirty-nine	hhd	18s	3.75d
(6) ¶ Forty	hhd	18s	11d

Text of MS N: Newberry Library (Chicago) / Northwestern University (Evanston) MS 1; Newberry Library, Vault Case MS 220

(Front cover)

Pancarte

(1r1–14 blank)

[Rubric I]

[John 1–14]

(1r15) Inicium sancti evangelii secundum Johannem.

(17) In principio erat verbum, et ver-(18)bum erat apud deum, et deus erat (19) verbum. Hoc erat in principio apud deum. (20) Omnia per ipsum facta sunt, et sine ipso (21) factum est nichil quod factum est. In ipso (22) vita erat, et vita erat lux hominum. Et lux (23) in tenebris lucet, et tenebre eam non compre-(24)henderunt. Fuit homo missus a deo, cui no-(25)men erat Johannes. Hic venit in testimonium, (1v1) ut testimonium perhiberet de lumine, ut omnes (2) crederent per illum. Non erat ille lux, sed (3) ut testimonium perhiberet de lumine. Erat (4) lux vera que illuminat omnem hominem (5) venientem in hunc mundum. In mundo erat, (6) et mundus per ipsum factus est, et mundus (7) eum non cognovit. In propria venit, et sui eum (8) non receperunt. Quocquod autem receperunt (9) eum, dedit eis potestatem filios dei fieri, his (10) qui credunt in nomine eius. Qui non ex san-(11)guinibus, neque ex voluntate carnis, neque ex (12) voluntate viri, sed ex deo nati sunt. Et verbum (13) caro factum est, et habitabit in nobis, et vi-(14)dimus gloriam eius, gloriam quasi unigeniti (15) a patre, plenum gracie et veritatis.

[Rubric II]

[Register of the tollhouse at Tarascon:

Tolls on salt and shares in the toll]

(17) Sec si lo registre del peage de Tarascon. Et pre-(18)mierament se tracta de la sal, lo peage et la di-(19)visio d'aquel entre lo rey et los gentils homens.

(21) Lo muey petit de la mesura de (22) Tharascon, montant de qualque (23) luoc que vengua d'aval en montant (24) amont, pagua .ij. s/ v. d' e iij. pogesas, de (25) que en ven al rey .xxii d'., e a ma dama Elis (2r1) .i. d'. E dels vi. d'., d'aquel lo quart es del rey, (2) e la resta dels gentils homens; e iij. pogesas (3) del peage dels Violans, lo qual es aras del (4) rey; .iij. d'aquelos son de Lobieras, dont la (5) mitat es del rey.

(6) Soma, la part del rey per muy .xxij. (7) d'. et iij. pogesas, et la part dels gen-(8) tils homens .vj. d'., et la part de ma dama Elis (9) .i. d'. Et de vj. muy en sus non pagua a Lobieras (10) si non xviij. d'. tot lo navey. Et las .iij. pogesas (11) del peage dels Violans pagua entro a viij. muy.

(12) Aysi apres si tracta del peage de la sal et de (13) la division d'aquel entre lo rey et los gentils (14) homens montant de .i. muy petit entro .xl. (15) muy petit.

(16) La part de ma dama Elis es .i. d' per cascun (17) muy petit.

[Table N1]

[Tolls on Salt in Small Hogsheads]

(18) Lo muy petit de la mesura de Tharascon (19) pagua .ij. s/ v. d'. iij. pogesas, de que (20) en ven al rey .xxij. d'. iij. pogesas, et a tos los (21) gentils homens .vij. d'.

(22) [II][8] Muy pagan .iiij. s/ .xi d' et mi[a]gla de que en (23) ven al rey iij. s/ .ix. d'. et miagla, et als gentils (24) homens .xiiij. d'.

(25) [III] Muy pagan .viij. s/ .v. d'. e .i. pogesa: al rey (2v1) .v. s/ .viii. d'. e pogesa, als gentils homens .xxj. d.

(2) [IV] Muy pagan .ix. s/ .xj. d'.: al rey .vij. s/ .vij d'., (3) als gentils homes .ij. s/ .iiij. d'.

8 The number of hogsheads at the beginning of each entry in Tables N1 and N2 was omitted by scribal error. See discussion in §4.4.4.

(4) [V] Muy .xij. s/ .iiij. d'.iii. pogesas: al rey .ix. s/ (5) .v. d' .iij. pogesas, als gentils homens .ij. s/ .xij. d'.

(6) [VI] Muy, xiijj. s/ .x. d'. e miagla: [...], als gentils ho-(7)mens s/ .iiij. d'. vj.

(8) [VII] Muy, .xvij. s/ .i. d'. i. pogesa: al rey .xiij. s/ .i. d'. (9) .iij. pogesas, als gentils homes .iij. s/ .xj. d. et (10) miagla.

(11) [VIII] Muy, .xix. s/ .iiij. d'.: al rey .xiiij. s/ .xj. d'., als gen-(12)tils homes .iiij. s/ .v. d'.

(13) [IX] Muy, .xxiij. s/ .viij. d'.: al rey .xvij. s/ .ij. d'., als (14) gentils homes .vj. s/. .vj. d'.

(15) [X] Muy, .xxv. s/ .x. d'.: al rey xviij. s/ .x. d'. et i. (16) miagla, [...].

(17) [XI] Muy, .xxviij. s/ .x. d'.: al rey .xx. s/ .vij., als (18) gentils homes .vij. s/ .v. d'.

(19) [XII] Muy, .xxx. s/ .viij. d'.: al rey .xxij. s/ .v. d'., als (20) gentils homes .viij. s/ .iij. d'.

(21) [XIII] Muy, .xxxij. s/ .x. d'.: al rey .xxiiij. s/ .i. d'. et mi-(22)agla, [...].

(23) [XIV] Muy, .xxxv. s/.: al rey .xxv. s' .x. d'., als gentils (24) homes .ix. s/ .ij. d'.

(25) [XV] Muy, .xxxvij. s' .ij. d'.: al rey .xxvij. s/ .vj. d'. (3r1) et miagla, als gentils homes .viij. s/ .vij. d'. et (2) miagla.

(3) [XVI] Muy, .xxxix. s/ .iiij. d'.: al rey .xxix. s/ .iij. d'., als (4) gentils homes .x. s/ .i. d'.

(5) [XVII] Muy, .xlj. s/ .vj. d'.: al rey .xxx. s/ .xj. d'. e mia-(6)gla, als gentils homes .x. s/ .vj. d'. et miagla.

(7) [XVIII] Muy, .xliiij. s/ .i. d'.: al rey .xxxij. s/ .ix. d' .i. po-(8)gesa, als gentils homes .xj. s/ .iij. d' .i. pogesa.

(9) [XIX] Muy, .xlvj. s/ .iiij. d'.: al rey xxxiiij. s/ .v. d' .iij. (10) pogesas, als gentils homes .xj. s/ .ix. d'. i. pogesa.

(11) [XX] Muy, .xlviij. s/ .v. d'.: al rey xxxvj. s/ .ij. d'. (12) .j. pogesa, als gentils homes .xij. s/ .ij. d' .iij. po-(13)gesas.

(14) [XXI] Muy, .l. s/ .vij. d'.: al rey .xxxvij. s/ .x. d' .iij. po-(15)gesas, als gentils homes .xij. s/ .viij. d' .i. po-(16)gesa.

(17) [XXII] Muy, .lij. s/ .ix. d'.: al rey .xxxix. s/ .viij. d' .i. (18) pogesa, als gentils homes .xiij. s/ .i. d' .iij. pogesas.

(19) [XXIII] Muy, .liiij. s/ .xj. d'.: al rey .xlj. s/ .iij. d' et .iij. po-(20)gesas, als gentils homes .xiij. s/ .vij. d' .i. pogesa.

(21) [XXIV] Muy, .lvij. s/ .i. d'.: al rey .xliij. s/ .i. pogesa, als (22) gentils homes .xiiij. s/ .iij. d'.

(23) [XXV] Muy, lx. s/ .iij. d'.: al rey xliij. s/ .xj. d' .iij. poge-(24)sas, als gentils homes .xv. s/ .iij. d' .i. pogesa.

(25) [XXVI] Muy, .lxij. s/ .v. d'.: al rey .xlvj. s/ .viij. d' .i. po-(3v1)gesa, als gentils homes .xv. s/ .viij. d' .iij. poge-(2)sas.

(3) [XXVII] Muy, lxiiij. s/ .vij. d'.: al rey .xlviij. s/ .iiij. d'. (4) .iij. pogesas, als gentils homes .xvj. s/ .ij. d'. (5) e .i. pogesa.

(6) [XXVIII] Muy, .lxvj. s/ .ix. d'.: al rey .l. s/ .i. d' .i. pogesa, (7) als gentils homes .xvj. s/ .vij. d' .iij. pogesas.

(8) [XXIX] Muy, .lxviij. s/ .xj. d'.: al rey .lj. s/ .ix. d' .iij. (9) pogesas, als gentils homes .xvij. s/ .i. d' .i. pogesa.

(10) [XXX] Muy, .lxxj. s/ .i. d'.: al rey .liij. s/ .vj. d' .i. pogesa, (11) als gentils homes .xvij. s/ .vj. d' .iij. pogesas.

(12) [XXXI] Muy, .lxxiij. s/ .iij. d'.: al rey .lv. s/ .ij. d' .iij. po-(13)gesas, als gentils homes .xviij. s/ .i. pogesa.

(14) [XXXII] Muy, .lxxv. s/ .v. d'.: al rey .lvj. s/ .xj. d' .i. pogesa, (15) als gentils homes .xviij. s/ .v. d' .iij. pogesas.

(16) [XXXIII] Muy, .lxxvij. s/ .vij. d'.: al rey .lviij. s/ .vij. d'. (17) .i. pogesa, als gentils homes .xviij. s/ .xj. d' .i. (18) pogesa.

(19) [XXXIV] Muy, .lxxix. s/ .xj. d'.: al rey .lx. s/ .iiij. d'., als (20) gentils homes .xix. s/ .iiij. d'. una pogesa.

(21) [XXXV] Muy, .iiij. lib/ .xxxiij. d'.: al rey .lxij. s/ .iij. po-(22)gesas, als gentils homes .xix. s/ .x. d'. una (23) pogesa.

(24) [XXXVI] Muy, [.iiij.] lib/ .iiij. s/ .i. d'.: al rey .lxiij. s/ .ix. d' .i. (25) pogesa, als gentils homes .xxj. s/ .iij. d' .iij. poge-(26)sas.

(4r1) [XXXVII] Muy, .iiij. lib/ .vij. s/ .i. d'.: al rey .lxv. s/ .viij. d'. (2) .i. pogesa, als gentils homes .xxj. s/ .iij. d' .iij. (3) pogesas.

(4) [XXXVIII] Muy, .iiij. lib/ .ix. s/ .iij. d'.: al rey .lvij. s/ .iiij. (5) d' .iij. pogesas, als gentils homes .xxj. s/ .x. d'. (6) et una pogesa.

(7) [XXXIX] Muy, .iiij. lib/ .xj. s/ .v. d'.: al rey .lxix. s/ .i. d'. (8) .i. pogesa, als gentils homes .xxij. s/ .iij. d'. (9) .iij. pogesas.

(10) [XL] Muy, .iiij. lib/ .xiij. s/ .x. d'.: al rey .lxx. s/ .x. (11) d'., als gentils homes .xxiij. s/.

(12) De .xl. muy petis en sus, si monton (13) en un navey pagua coma desus es (14) dit, e so que y aura mais de xl. muy si part (15) tot l'argent que sera desus las .iiij. lib/ .xiij. s/ (16) .x. d'. a rason de xxij. d'. lo muy: la part del (17) rey, .xix. d'. per cascun muy, e la part dels gen-(18)tils homes, .iij. d'., so es assaber .ij. d'. als gen-(19)tils homes de la montason et .i. d'. a ma da-(20)ma Elis.

(21) La sal que se carga a Belcayre per mon-(22)tar amont per aygua pagua lo muy (23) petit de la mesura de Tharascon .xxij. d'., e se (24) part en la forma sobredita de xl. muy en sus, (25) so es assaber .xix. d'. al rey et .ij. d'. als gentils (4v1) homes de la montason, e .i. d'. a ma dama Elis.

(2) Item plus paga lo muy .iij. pogesas (3) jusques a viij. muy, et de viij. muy en (4) sus paga lo navey al rey .vj. d'.

(5) La sal que si descargua a Belcayre, si es (6) de home de Belcayre o de Tharascon, paga (7) per muy petit, mesura de Tharascon, per l'u-(8)sage .iiij. d'. per muy petit, en que a lo rey .iij. (9) mieaglas, et los gentils homes .ij. d'. e miagla.

(10) Item plus pagua .iij. d'. del peage de Lobie-(11)ras entro a vj. muy, e si parten per aiguals (12) pars lo rey e aquelos de Lobieras. E de vj. a (13) en sus pagua xviij. d'. tot lo navey per lo (14) peage de Lobieras, en que lo re a la mitat. (15) Et ma dama Elis non pren ren en l'usage.

(16) Item la sal que si descargua a Belcayre de (17) home estrany pagua, lo muy de la mesura (18) de Tarascon, .xj. d'. e miagla; pagua al rey .viij. (19) d'., .ij. d'. e miagla senhors de la montaison, et (20) .j. d'. a ma dama Elis.

(21) Item pagua plus lo muy .iij. d'. a Lobie-(22)ras entro a vj. muy, et de vj. muy en sus (23) xviii. d'. tot lo navey, la mitat al rey e l'altra (24) mitat als gentils homes de Lobieras.

(25) Tot home que met sal a Tarascon, si non (5r1) es de Tarascon, pagua per muy de la mesura (2) de Tarascon .iiij. d'. de usage, et xviij. d'. al peage (3) de Lobieras, per la forma que pagua la sal que (4) si descargua a Belcayre per man de home de (5) Tharascon o de Belcayre, et aisins si part l'ar-(6) gent entre lo rey et los gentils homes de la (7) montaison et de Lobieras.

(8) Tout home de Tarascon que met sal a Ta-(9)rascon non pagua peage de Tarascon si (10) non lo peage de Lobieras, so es a saber .iiij. d'. (11) per muy entro a vj. muy, et de vj. muy en (12) sus pagua xviij. d'. tot lo navey, la mitat (13) al rey et l'altra mitat a Lobieras. Et si la dita (14) sal si tira fora de la vila de Tarascon per aygua, (15) pagua aisins coma la sal que si carga a Belcaire; (16) et aisins tot home que carga sal a Tarascon (17) paga en la maniera que paga la sal que si carga (18) a Belcaire.

(19) Aysi si sec la maniera de levar lo peage (20) de la sal que monta contramont lo Rose (21) a muey gros, et aquo que si paga tant al rey (22) quant als gentils homes.

(23) Et es a saber que lo muy gros es de .xl. (24) sestiers comols de la mesura de Pecays, (25) o de xlij. sestiers de la mesura de la mar, que (5v1) pesa environ .lxxv. quintals.

[Table N2]

[Tolls on salt in large hogsheads]

(2) Lo muy gros montant amont, lo qual (3) es .iij. muy petis meyns la xxj^{e}. part, (4) pagua .v. tornes d'argent. Et cascun d'aquelos (5) torneses val .xvj.

d'. et monton los dits .v. (6) torneses .vj. s/ .viij., que es mieç florin de Flor-(7)rensa, car los .x. torneses valen .j. florin de (8) Florensa. Et paga al rey .v. s/ .i. d'. ij. pogesas, (9) et als gentils homes .xviij. d'. ij. pogesas.

(10) [II] Muy gros son .v. petis et calque causa (11) mais, et paga xiij. s/ .iiij. d'.: al rey .x. s/ .ij. d'. (12) .j. pogesa, als gentils homes .iij. s/ .i. d'. .iij. po-(13)gesas.

(14) [III] Muy gros son viij. petis; pagan .xx. s/, dont (15) ne ven al rey .xv. s/ .v. d'., et als gentils homes (16) .iiij. s/ vj. d.

(17) [IV] Muy [gros], .x. petis, .xxvj. s/ .viij. d'.: al rey .xix. s/ .vj. (18) d'., als gentils homes .vij. s/ .ij. d'.

(19) [V] Muy gros, xiij. petis, xxxiij. s/ .iiij. d'.: al rey (20) xxiiij. s/ .vj. d'., als gentils homes .viij. s/ .x. d'.

(21) [VI] Muy gros, .xvj. petis, xl. s/: al rey xxix. s/, als (22) gentils homes .x. s/ .iij. d'.

(23) [VII] Muy gros, .xix. petis, .xlvj. s/ .viij. d'.: al rey .xxxiij. (24) s/ .ix. d'. et .i. miagla, als gentils homes .xj. s/ (25) .x. d'. et una miagla.

(6r1) [VIII] Muy gros, xxij. petis, .liij. s/ .iiij. d'.: al rey .xl. s/ (2) et una miagla, als gentils homes .xiij. s/ .iij. d'. (3) et una miagla.

(4) [IX] Muy gros, xxv. petis, .lx. s/: al rey .xliiij. s/ .ix. d'. (5) una miagla, als gentils homes .xv. s/ .ij. d'. i. mi-(6)agla.

(7) [X] Muy g[r]os, .xxv. petis, .lx. s/: al rey .xliiij. s/ .ix. d'. (8) et una miagla, als gentils homes .xvj. s/ .vij. d'. (9) doas pogesas.

(10) [XI] Muy gros, .xxxj. petit, pagua .lxiij. s/ .iiij. [d'.]: al rey (11) .lv. s/ .iij. d' .i. miagla, als gentils homes .xviij. s/ (12) una miagla.

(13) [XII] Muy gros, xxxiiij. petis, .iiij. lib/: al rey .lxv. s/ (14) iiij. d' .i. miagla, als gentils homes .xix. s/ (15) .v. d'. una miagla.

(16) [XIII] Muy gros, .xxxvij. petis, .iiij. lib/ .vj. s/ .viij. d'.: (17) al rey .lxv. s/ .iiij. d'. .i. miagla, als gentils ho-(18)mes .xxj. s/ .iiij. d'. una miagla.

(19) [XIV] Muy gros, .xl. petis, pagan .iiij. lib/ .xiij. s/ .iiij. d'.: (20) al rey .lxx. s/ .iiij. d'., als gentils homes .xxiij. s/.

(21) De xiiij. muy en sus si metan en un (22) navey; tot l'argent des xiiij. muy si part (23) entre lo rey et los gentils homes coma es (24) diç, e lo sobreplus de xiiij. muy gros pagan (25) ausi ben per cascun gros muy .vj. s/ .viij. d'., (6v1) et si part lo dit argent a xxij. d'., dont lo rey (2) pren .xix. d'. et los gentils homes .iij. d'., so es (3) a saber .ij. d'. als gentils homes de la montaison (4) et .i. d'. a Johan Alba.

(5) La sal que si descarga a Belcayre, sia de ho-(6)me de Belcayre o de Tharascon, paga per muy (7) gros .viij. d'.: al rey iij. d'., als gentils homes (8) .v. deniers.

(9) Item paga plus a Adaul .v. d'. et pogesa, si (10) lo nocier non es de Belcayre.

(11) La sal que si descarga a Belcayre que es (12) de home estrani et non de Belcayre ny de (13) Tharascon paga per muy gros .iij. s/. iiij. d'., (14) lo qual s'apella mieç peage: del rey .ij. s/ .iiij. d'., (15) gentils homes .j. s/.

(16) Item plus paga al peage de Lobieras per (17) lo navec .xviij. d'., dont la mitat es del rey (18) et l'autra dels ditz de Lobieras. Item plus Adaul (19) .v. s/ una pogesa.

(20) La sal que si descarga a Tharascon d'ome (21) estrange que non sia de Tharascon paga (22) lo muy gros en la forma que paga la sal que (23) si descarga a Belcayre de home de Belcayre ho (24) de Tharascon: paga en la maniera que dit est (25) dessus.

(7r1) Si home de Tharascon met sal en Tharas-(2)con, non pagua si non xviij. d'. al peage (3) de Lobieras; totas vegadas si la tira fora de Ta-(4)rascon, paga coma home estrangier, coma (5) escriç es en lo peage de la sal que si carga a Belcay-(6)re; et si l'aporta a Belcayre, paga per la maniera (7) coma la sal que si descarga a Belcayre.

(8) La sal que si carga a Tharascon o a Belcayre, (9) ho per home estrangier ho per home de vila, (10) et monta contramont lo Rose, paga per muy (11) gros .v. s/ .iiij. d'., dont ven al rey .iiij. s/. vij. d'. (12) una pogesa .ij. grans, et als gentils homes (13) .viij. d' .i. miagla .iij. grans. Et non paga ren (14) a Lobieras ny a Adaul, per so que non passe per lur (15) termine.

[Rubric III]

[Tolls on commodities at Tarascon and Lubières]

(16) Sec si lo peage de las mercandisas.

[2s 6.5d (= 30.5d) per load]

(17) Carga de draps d'Avingno, la qual es de (18) nou draps la carga; et carga de draps (19) de França de xij. draps, et de draps de Nar-(20)bona de xxiiij. pessas, d'estamenha de xxiiij. (21) pessas, de bruns de .iiij. draps. De cuers de (22) buou, de camel, [hole in MS] de chival, et de lur semblant, (23) adobas o non adobas, es la carga de xx. quers. (24) Carga de cordovan la qual es de .iiij. quintals (25) ho de xij. dogenas; de telas, de indi, de siera, (7v1) de sendal, de pluma, de gingibre, de alum de (2) pluma, de alum de roca, de alum d'Alaf, de (3) alum de cico tonip, de fil, de pelliceria, ne de (4) girofle, de pebre, de safran, de coton no[u], de seda, (5) de pels de conils, et lurs senblans. De las cau-(6)sas sobredichas, la carga de iiij. quintals, et (7)

paga .ij. s/ .vj. d'. e miagla, dont enpren lo rey (8) .ij. s/. iij. d'. e miagla, Johan Alba .i. d'., et Lobieras (9) .i. denier.

[19d per load]

(10) Carga de lana, de lin, de bresil, de blan-(11)quet, de peyson de mar fresc ho salat, (12) de castangnias peladas, d'amella[s] pessadas, de (13) figas secas, d'agibes, de comin, de sucre, de (14) polvera de sucre, de stopas, de fil de cordas, (15) et de cordas de cassia fistula, d'acier, de mel, (16) de datils, de ris, de canela, de canebe, de mos-(17)tarda, de coure, de coton, de pega, de fustani, de (18) torras, de graissa de porc, de sieu, d'estanh, de (19) roge, de carn salada, de ferre, de fromages, (20) d'oli lo qual es de xvj. o de xvij. canes la car-(21)ga, de pels de mouton, d'anhel, de pels de ca-(22)bris, et de lur semblant, [hole in MS] si fa la carga de (23) iiij. quintals, et paga la carga .xix. d'., dont (24) pren Johan Alba .i. d'. Item plus al peage de (25) Lobieras .ij. d'., dont lo rey n'a .i. d'.

[Cloth and leather: from 2d to 0.5d]

(8r1) Una dogena de pels de mouton e lur semblant (2) pagua .iij. miaglas.

(3) Item una dogena de cordovan paga .ij. d'. (4) [U]n cuer de buou o de chival o de camel, o (5) lur senblant, pagua .j. d'. e miagla.

(6) Un cuer d'ors paga .j. d'. [U]na cota paga (7) .j. miala. [U]na pessa d'estamenha paga .i. mi-(8)agla. [U]na corda de tela, .j. miagla. [U]na fais-(9)sa, .j. miagla.

[Woad: 14d per load]

(10) Carga de caida de .iiij. quintals paga .xiiij. d'., (11) dont pren Johan Alba .j. d'. Item plus paga (12) al peage de Lobieras .ij. d'., dont lo rey a la (13) mitat.

[9d per load]

(14) Carga de graissa, d'alum de Boulcan, aludas (15) de que si fan los pargamins, et lur senblant, (16) la carga de .iiij. quintals paga .ix. d'., dont Jo-(17)han Alba pren .j. d'.

(18) Item plus per lo peage de Lobieras .ij. d'., dont (19) lo rey a la mitat.

(20) Teules paga lo millier .ix. d'., dont a Johan (21) Alba .j. d'.

(22) Carga de cordas viellas paga .ix. d'., dont (23) Johan Alba a .j. d'. Item mais al peage de (24) Lobieras .ij. d'., dont lo rey a la mitat.

[Grain, vegetables: 9.5d per load]

(25) Carga de syvada, ordi, segla, faves, seses, (8v1) et tota maniera de blas et de liolmes: es la car-(2)ga o la somada de xv. o de xvj. sestiers a la (3) mesura de Tarascon, et paga .ix. d'. e miagla (4) per saumada, dont en ven a Johan Alba .j. d'.

(5) Item plus paga a Lobieras .ij. d'., dont (6) la mitat es del rey, fin a xxx. saumadas. (7) Et de xxx. saumadas en sus, non paga al pe-(8)age de Lobieras tot lo navec si non .v. s/, (9) dont la mitat es del rey.

[Lead, alum, wine: 6d per load or butt]

(10) Carga de plomb de iiij. quintals paga (11) vj. d'., de que pren Johan Alba .j. miagla.

(12) Item paga a Lobieras .ij. d'., dont lo rey n'a (13) la mitat.

(14) D'alum que ven per Rose, venga d'amont (15) o d'aval, cascuna bota, sia grossa o petita, pa-(16)ga .vj. d'.

[Wine: payment in kind plus 6d per butt]

(17) Item paga d'una bota mieç barral de vin, (18) et doas botas un barral de vin. Et de .iij. bo-(19)tas en sus, paga tot lo navec una saumada (20) de vin.

(21) Item mais paga de cascuna bota .vj. d'., (22) et si lo vin ven en barrals, paga lo muy (23) de la mesura de Tarascon en la maniera co-(24)ma si venia en botas. Et si home de Taras-(25)con fa compania anbe home estrange, et que (9r1) lo vin sia ensenble ho en divisament, paga (2) conplidament coma home estrange. Totas (3) vegadas si lo vin es en botas saupudas, l'es-(4) trange es tengut de pagar lo peage tant (5) solament.

[Dye: 6s 5d (= 77d) per hogshead]

(6) Lo muy del ros son de lxxij. quintals, que (7) son tres sequieras e miega; paga .vj. s/ .v. (8) d'., dont ven a Johan Alba de .i. d'. de cascun (9) muy. Et de .xx. sequieras en sus, paga .v. s/ a (10) Lobieras tot lo navey, dont la mitat es del rey.

[Materials: 18d]

(11) Lo navec cargat de peyras, de xxv. pey-(12)ras en sus, paga xviij. d'. tot lo navey (13) per lo peage de Lobieras tant solament, dont (14) lo rey a la mitat.

(15) Lo navec cargat de caus o de gip paga (16) xviij. d'. tot lo navec a Lobieras, dont la (17) mitat es del rey.

[Live cargo: horses, travellers, large or small animals: tolls vary]

(18) Un chival, que sie vendut o que si me-(19)ne per vendre, si passa lo Rose et val .xij. (20) lib/ e .x. s/ en sus, paga .ij. s/ .vj. d'. Et si val (21) meins paga .iiij. d'. tant solament.

(22) Et aussi un sarrazin, esclau o esclava, (23) o mastina, paga cascun .ij. s/ .vj. d'.

(24) Bestia grossa que ven de Provensa, co-(25)ma buou, ase, mul, et lur semblant, et passa (9v1) Rose, paga cascuna pessa .i. d'.

(2) Bestias menudas coma moutons, porcs, (3) cabras, bocs, et lurs senblans, cascun paga (4) una pogesa.

(5) Bestias grossas que si compran a Belcayre (6) et venon aissi de home estrange, ainsi co-(7)ma chival, mul, paga .j. d'.

(8) Buous et ases pagan una miagla.

(9) Bestias menudas coma moutons, porcs, (10) cabras, et lur senblant, paga .j. pogesa.

(11) Tot cavalcador que non sia de Tharas-(12)con ho de Belcayre, passant lo Rose, si (13) es de luoc pres d'aisi denfra .xx. legas, pa-(14)ga .vij. d'. et miagla; et si el es de .viij. legas (15) en [ba]s, paga .iij. d'. et miagla.

(16) Et quant lo pont d'entre Belcayre et (17) Tharascon era entier, pagavan los pro-(18)cans .ij. d'., et los luehn .iiij. d'. et los pea-(19)giers devian lo pont .j. miagla.

(20) Tot capelan, clerc, que non sie privile-(21)giat, que sia subdiaque, paga coma (22) los autres cavalcadors. Totas vegades, si (23) el es diaque ho de deiaque en sus, ho chiva-(24)lier ho filz de chivalier, ho que sia de na-(25) tura de chivalier, et aquels que van amb els (10r1) a lur despens et a lur vestir, son francs del (2) peage.

(3) Maistres de moneda que se apelan mone-(4)diers, et tos hobrans de moneda au (5) tems que fan moneda, tant per lo rey de Si-(6)cilia coma per lo rey de França: elos et lurs (7) chivals son francs. Et quant elos non obran (8) de moneda, pagan coma los autres cavalca-(9)dors, coma dit es davant.

(10) Tot romiou ho romia que sia defora pais (11) de Provença paga .j. d'. Et si el es de Pro-(12)vença, non paga ren.

(13) Tot romieu que ven de Lion en sus, caval-(14)cant a Sant Jaume ho a Sant Gile, paga .v. d'. (15) Et si va a pe, non paga sinon .j. d'.

(16) Tot Lombart ho Lombarda romiou, caval-(17)cant a Sant Jaume, paga .viij. d'. Et si va au-(18)tra part, paga .iiij. d. Et si va a pe ho per ay-(19)gua, paga .iij. miaglas.

(20) Tot Espanhol, Angles, ho Alaman, cavalcant, (21) paga .v. d'. Et a pe, paga .j. d'.

(22) Et es de costuma d'estre franc tot romio (23) ho romieua cavalcant, passant Rose, ve-(24)nent a Sancta Martha tos los tres jors pre-(25)miers de Sancta Martha.

[Wood and wood products: tolls vary]

(10v1) Tout arbre redon si deu mesurar al ters so-(2)tterran de la rais.

(3) Arbre de nau que aga .vij. palms en sus (4) de redon paga lxx. s/, de que en ven a Johan (5) Alba .ij. s/.

(6) Item paga a Lobieras .v. s/, dont la mitat (7) es del rey.

(8) Entena que age .vj. palms et mieç de re-(9)don paga .xxx. s/, de que en ven a Johan Alba .ij. s/ .vj. d'.

(10) Item plus paga a Lobieras .v. s/, de que la (11) mitat es del rey.

(12) Entena de .vj. palms paga .xx. s/, de que (13) pren Johan Alba .viij. d'. Item plus a Lobi-(14)eras .ij. d'., de que la mitat es del rey.

(15) Entena de .v. palms et mieç paga .xv. s/, en que (16) pren Johan Alba .v. d'. Item plus paga a Lo-(17)bieras .ij. d'., de que la mitat es del rey.

(18) Entena de .v. palms .x. s/, dont ven a Johan (19) Alba .iij. d'. Item plus a Lobieras .ij. d'., et la (20) mitat al rey.

(21) Entena de .iiij. palms e mieç paga .v. s/. (22) Et de iiij. palms, .iiij. s/. Et de .iiij. palms en (23) bas, segons l'avis del peagier. Et en tot pren (24) Johan Alba .j. d'. Et Lobieras .ij. d'., de que lo rey (15) a la mitat.

(11r1) Timon de nau et roure redon paga .xv. (2) s/, don ven a Johan Alba per .v. travadas (3) .v. d'. Item paga a Lobieras .iij. s/, la mitat al rey.

(4) Roure cayrat paga .v. s/, don ven a Johan (5) Alba per .iij. travadas .iij. d'. Item plus a Lobie-(6)ras .ij. d'., la mitat al rey.

(7) Una travada de fusta paga .i. s/ et miagla, (8) don ven a Johan Alba .j. d'.

(9) Item plus paga per lo peage dels Violans (10) .iij. pogesas entro a .viij. travadas, et de .viij. (11) travadas en sus paga tot lo radel per lo pea-(12)ge dels Violans .v. d'., lo qual es del rey.

(13) Item plus paga la travada a Lobieras .ij. d'. (14) entro a .xx. travadas, et de .xx. travadas en (15) sus paga a Lobieras .v. s/ tot lo radel et non (16) plus, et a Johan Alba per cascuna travada.

(17) Un carrat de sasel ho melle es travada. .Xij. (18) bigas redonas primas es una travada.

(19) Doze jainas coladieras fan una travada.

(20) Quatre ho .vj. jainas bastardas fan una (21) travada.

(22) De .ij. cairas redons es una travada.

(23) De .iiij. cairas que tiran un parelh de buous (24) es travada.

(25) De .xx. taulas de sapin es travada.

(11v1) De .x. taulas de roure es una travada, ho de (2) .iiij. si son grandes.

(3) De .vj. taulas de noguier es travada.

(4) De orsas ho corbas de barca, de viij. ho de (5) .ix. es travada.

(6) Molin d'aygua paga .x. s/.

(7) Molin d'aura paga .v. s/.

(8) Barca, .v. s/.

(9) Nau.

(10) Navec conprat ho vendut ho que si me-(11)ne per vendre, de cascun fill paga .ij. d'. (12) Del sol del navec et de .ij. peyrons si fa lo fil. (13) Item paga una rema ho son pres, al plaser (14) del peagier. Et aysin paga peage de Lobieras (15) .ij. d'. de cascun fil et una rema, et la mitat (16) es del rey.

[Domestic objects, foods: payment in kind plus various tolls]

(17) Lausas, escudellas, talhadors, culhiers, (18) grasals, brocs, cornudas, sistras, pany-(19)eras, seucles redons, et totas aysinas de fus-(20)ta: de c[ent], .iiij. Et de la saumada paga a Lobieras (21) miagla, la mitat al rey. Et ausi de ramas: de (22) sent iiij°., et [miagla] a Lobieras, la mitat al rey.

(23) Sarrias que son fachas de vergans paga (24) per pessa .i. d'.

(25) Banastons, tot lo navec paga .j. banaston. (12r1) Totas vegadas sarrias de gioncs, cabasses ne (2) cordas de gonc, non paga ren.

(3) Saumadas d'ollas, et tota aysina de terra, pa-(4)ga .iiij. d'. Totas vegadas aisinas de terra que (5) si fan a Tarascon, et tot obrage de terra, paga (6) de cent .iiij., ho lo pres de las .iiij.°

(7) Saumada de amellas an lo croveilh, noses, (8) avelanes, et lur senblant, que es la saumada (9) de .viij. sestiers mesura de Tarascon, paga (10) .iiij. d'. et .j. miagla, et a Lobieras .j. miagla, (11) et la mitat al rey.

(12) Una saumada de castanhas an la pelanha, (13) pomas, peras, codons, persegues, sorbas, a-(14)griotas, seriesas, citrons, limons, ponsiris, rosas (15) frescas, et tota fruta fresca salvat figuas menu-(16)das, granas et cormas: paga la somada .ij. d'. (17) Et a Lobieras miagla, la mitat al rey.

(18) Saumada de rabas et de carbon, de ruscla, (19) de nerta, de lentiscle, paga .j. d'. Et a Lobieras (20) miagla, la mitat al rey.

(21) Cayssa nova, escrins, armaris, et lur sen-(22)blant, tinas, tots vayssels, dogan no[u], (23) molas de molin, mola de barbier, porcs salas: (24) cascun d'aquellos paga .iiij. d'. Item a Lobieras (25) .j. d'., la mitat al rey.

(12v1) Cebas: la saumada de .iij. dogenas de petitas. (2) La saumada dels aills es de .viij. ho de .x. dogenas; (3) paga la saumada .j. rest, et .j. miagla a Lobieras, (4) la mitat al rey.

(5) La copiera de las aisinas del veire paga .ij. (6) pessas, et lo colher paga una pessa.

[Rubric IV]

[Exempt items]

Segon si (7) las causas que son francas et non pagan point (8) de peage.

(9) L'aur et l'argent monedat, verdet, (10) mersaria, galas, regalicia, sabon, glassa, (11) peysson de Rose ho de palum fresc, sipias, sol-(12)pre, burre, arsiqua, obrage faç de ferre ho (13) de coure ho de loton ho d'estanh, raubas fa-(14)chas que se apelan plagarias–totas vegadas (15) a la fiera de Belcayre, que es de may, pagan (16) de raubas fachas del fais d'un home .iij. d'., (17) et d'una bestia .vj. d'. Et ausi es frauc, gron, (18) ful, fauda, libres, cabasses, papier, sarrias (19) de gonc, et cordes de jonc, et seu.

(20) Totas mercadarias que non sian en lo (21) capitol de las causas francas pagaran lo (22) peage en la forma de las mercadarias que (23) son plus pres de lur pres.

(24) Nota que l'an mil ccc. xxv. et lo ix. jour (25) del mes d'octubre, passet par dessus lo Rose (13r1) un navech cargat de sendres, et li fon deman-(2)dat lo peage; lo qual respondet que non devie ren (3) per so car non era trobat al registre que degessa. (4) Et en aquel temps nostre senhor lo rey era aisi, (5) et la question venc davant el. Et fon cove-(6)gut que, vesent que las cendres non [son] pont (7) ambe las autras causas francas, que deguessan (8) pagar segons la mercadaria que fora plus pro-(9)pia et plus senblant a las cendres, et que (10) pagessa coma caus ho gip.

[Rubric V]

[Currencies]

Segon si la de-(11)claracion de las monedas.

(12) Totas las monedas que si levan als (13) peages sobredits, sia al peage de l'aygua (14) et del Portal de Tarascon, de Sant Gabriel, de (15) Lobieras, es a moneda de tornes d'argent (16) fin, que sa liga es xj. d'. et miagla, et son (17) pres iij. d'. et miagla. Et cascun tornes val (18) xvj. d'., et los x. tornes valon j. florin de (19) Florensa de bon aur et de xxiiij. cayras, et (20) pesa iij. d'. Et los tornes contant a xij. fl. (21) viij. d'. val .xv. d'. et v. grans. Et lo blanc que (22) que s[a] ligua es .x. d'. et v. grans et ters, (23) et son pes .ij. d'. et ij. grans, dont val lo (24) blanc .vij. d' .iij. pogesas et j. quart de po-(25) gesa. Et lo patac val .iij. miaglas et quart (26) de pogesa.

(13v1) En la partison del peage de la sal entre (2) lo rey et los gentils homes, si conta lo (3) florin de Florença desus dit a xiij. s/ iiij d'., (4) et a quel conte val lo tornes .xvj. d'. Et a-(5)donc si conta lo blanc .viij. d' .viij. grans, (6) et lo patac del dit blanc val .v. patacs (7) d'aquels de .iij. miaglas et iiij.° grans. Et (8) per so per egalar los coronas a la moneda (9) dels tornes que foren fach davant los coro-(10)nas, fon mes l'argent que si levava a (11) [x]ij. s/ .viij d'. lo florin de Florensa, et lo (12) blanc a .viij. d'., et los .xix. blancs valon (13) lo florin de Florensa desus ditz. Totas ve-(14)gadas los peagiers ordeneron que lo peage (15) de la sal si levessa a xiij. s/ .iiij. d'., los quals (16) son .x. tornes, et lo peage de las mercada-(17)rias a xii. s/ viij. d'., dels quals .xix. blancs (18) valon lo florin desus dit, contant lo blanc (19) a .viij. deniers.

(20) Item lo muy gros de la sal que monta (21) amont per Rose paga .v. tornes d'argent (22) que valon miech florin de Florensa, lo (23) qual val .vj. s/ viij. d'. a rason de .xvj. d'. los (24) tornes.

[Rubric VI]

[Tolls at the Gate of Tarascon]

La forma et la maniera del peage (25) del Portal de Tarascon.

[2s 2.5d (= 26.5d) per load]

(14r1) Carga de draps de França, de Narbona, (2) d'estamenha, de tela et de tos autres (3) draps; de cordoan, d'indi, de pebre, de siera, (4) de seda, de sendat, d'alum, de gingibre, (5) de girofles et de tota maniera d'espiceria; (6) d'ensens, de mastec, de citoal; de pena vay-(7)ra, de pelisaria, de pel de buou, de camel, (8) de chival; de fil de Colonha, de vels et de lin (9) et de lur semblant: de las causas sobredi-(10)chas es facha la carga de .iiij. quintals. (11) Paga .ij. s/ ij. d'. et miagla. Item mais a (12) Johan Alba .j. d'.

[18d]

(13) Carga de lana, de bresill, de peyson (14) de mar salat ho non salat, de casta-(15)nhas peladas, d'amellas pessadas, de comin, (16) de sucre et de pols de sucre, de cassia fistula, (17) d'acier, de datils, de mostarda, de eruga, de (18) figas sequas, de agibes, d'estopa, de mel, (19) de ris, de canebe, de coure, d'anis, de fill (20) de corda, de carda, de pega, de coton, de fus-(21) tani, de boras, de sayn, de seu, d'estanh, de (22) roga, de ferre, de loton, de oli, de fromage, (23) de pels de mouton, d'estam filat, de grana (24) de caules, et de tota maniera de granas (25) et de lur senblant: es facha la carga de (14v1) .iiij. quintals, et paga .xviij. d'. Item a Johan (2) Alba .j. d'.

[8d]

(3) Carga de gresa, d'alum de Bolcam, d'aludas (4) que on fa pargamins et lur senblant: es (5) facha la carga de .iiij. quintals. Paga .viij. (6) d'. Item a Johan Alba .j. d'.
(7) Sarcia vielha: paga la carga de iiij. quintals (8) viij. d'. Item a Johan Alba .j. d'.
(9) Teules: paga lo millier .viij. d'., et a Johan (10) Alba .j. d'.

[Grains: 4d]

(11) Saumada de tot blat, farina, milh, et de (12) tot liomes: es la saumada de viij. sestiers de (13) la mesura de Tarascon. Paga .iiij. d'.

[Lead: 6d]

(14) Carga de ploms paga .vj. d'.

[Salt carried by animals: 2d]

(15) De bestia cargada de sal: paga .ij. d'.

[Food, domestic objects]

(16) Fruchas coma es pera, poma, castanhas (17) an la scorsa, codons, pesseges, agriota, seriesas, (18) citrons, noses frescas, et tota maniera de fru-(19)cha salvat figas frescas: la somada .ij. d'.
(20) Saumada d'amellas an lo crovelh, noses, (21) et avelana[s] et lur senblant, paga .iiij. d'.
(22) Saumada de rabas et de ruscla, lentilhas, (23) riorta, carbon, paga .j. d'.
(24) Saumada de seba et d'alhs paga .j. rest.
(25) De bestia cargada de brocs, de barrals, et (15r1) de tota aisina de fusta, paga .iiij. d'.
(2) Vaysel, bota, tina de xxv. dogas, caissa, escrin, (3) mola de molin, mola de barbier, de bacon: paga cascun .iiij. d'.
(5) Saumada de veire et tota aisina de veire (6) paga .ij. pessas, et colier .j. pessa.
(7) Saumada d'ollas et tota aisina de terra paga (8) de cent .iiij.
(9) De bestia grossa, paga cascuna .j. miagla.
(10) De bestia menuda, paga de .iiij. i. d'.

[Exemptions]

(11) Totas fes si las causas davan dichas a-(12)guesson pagat al peage de Gernega, non pa-(13)gan ren al Portal.
(14) Totas las causas que son francas a Lau-(15)biera son francas al Portal.
(16) Totas las mercadarias las quals si ven-(17)don a Tarascon ho en son terratori, salvat (18) la sal, son francas del peage de Tarascon mas (19) que resten en Tarascon. Totas fes apres que (20) aguessan vendudas las dichas mercadari-(21)as a Tarascon et pueis la traguessan de Taras-(22)con, so es a saber home estrange que non (23) sie de Tarascon ny de Belcaire, pagaria lo pe-(24)age ho per aiga ho per terra que la porta-(25)son.
(15v1) Totas las causas venent per aigua de (2) montada ou de deisenduda et se des-(3)carga a Belcaire de home estrangier per por-(4)tar per terra en qualque part que sia al re-(5)alme paga al peage del rey et de Lobieras (6) tot entierament. Et ausi parelhament totas (7) las causas que si cargan a Belcaire per portar (8) per la ribiera, montant ho dese[n]dent, deu lo (9) peage conplidament.

[Rubric VII]

[Tolls at Saint-Gabriel]

Lo peage de sant (10) Gabriel, dont la gent d'Arle et de Tarascon son francs.

[13d]

(11) Carga d'oli, de canebe, d'anhinas, de pel (12) de cabrit, de pel de mouton, de conilh, de (13) castanha pelada, de ferre, d'estanh, de figas (14) secas, d'agibes; de peisson de mar salat ho non; (15) de coton, de fustani, de bresilh, et lur senblant: (16) es la carga de .iiij. quintals. Paga .xiij. d'.

[2s 2d (= 26d)]

(17) Carga de draps d'Avihon de .ix. draps, (18) de draps de Fransa de .xij. draps, de draps (19) de Narbona de xxiiij. draps, d'estamenhas, (20) de bruns, de pel de buou ho de camel ho de (21) chival, de cordovan, d'alum de roqua, de tela, (22) de pels de conilz, de fil, de vars, de tota pena (23) vana, de veuls, de ciera, d'indi, de pelliceria, (24) de pebre, de gingibre, de girofle, de cendat, (25) de citoal, d'alun de pluma, de roqua, d'Alap, d'a-(16r1) lum de sitrum: totas las causas sobredichas (2) et lur senblant paga de .iiij. quintals .ij. s/. ij. d.

(3) Et totas las autras causas menudieras (4) que non son escrichas aisi: regarda la (5) forma et la maniera del peage del Portal de (6) Tarascon, et segons aquella forma leva lo pea-(7)ge de sant Gabriel.

[Exemptions]

(8) Totas las causas que son franquas al (9) peage del Portal de Tarascon son francas (10) al peage de sant Gabriel, exceptat gens de (11) Belcaire que non son pont francs jamais al (12) peage de sant Gabriel.

[Currencies]

(13) Totas las monedas que se levon als peages (14) mantegus, tant al peage de l'aigua coma (15) al peage del Portal de Tarascon et sant Gabriel, (16) si leva a moneda de tornesos d'argent fin, que (17) sa ligua es xj. d' et miagla, que los .x. tornes va-(18)len .j. florin de Florença d'aur de xxiiij. cayras, (19) et son pes es de .iiij. d'. Et lo tornes val xv. d. (20) et v. grans de la moneda nomada au dit pe-(21)age. Et per aisins lo florin de Florença val de (22) la dicha moneda .xij. s/. viij. d':–/-/-

Translation of MS N

(Front cover)

Schedule of Tolls

(1r1–14 blank)

[Rubric I]

[John 1–14]

(1r15) The beginning of the holy gospel according to John.
(17) In the beginning was the word, and the word was with God, and the word was God. This was in the beginning with God. All things were made by him, and without him was made nothing that was made. In him was life, and the life was the light of men. And the light shines in darkness, and the darkness did not comprehend it. There was a man sent from God, whose name was John. This man came for a witness, to give testimony of the light, that all men might believe through him. He was not the light, but was to give testimony of the light. That was the true light, which enlightens every man that comes into this world. He was in the world, and the world was made by him, and the world knew him not. He came unto his own, and his own received him not. But as many as received him, he gave them power to be made the sons of God, to them that believe in his name. Who are born, not of blood, nor of the will of the flesh, nor of the will of man, but of God. And the word was made flesh, and will dwell among us – and we saw his glory, the glory as it were of the only begotten of the father – full of grace and truth.

[Rubric II]

[Register of the tollhouse at Tarascon:

Tolls on salt and shares in the toll]

(1v17) Here follows the register of the tollhouse at Tarascon. And first is dealt with salt, the toll and the division of that between the king and the nobles.

(21) The small hogshead by the measure of Tarascon, coming from whatever place it may come from downstream as it comes upstream, pays 2s 5.75d [29.75d], of which 22d comes to the king, and to Madame Elis 1d. And as for the 6d [that remain, not counting the 0.75d], one-fourth of that is the king's. And the rest [is] the nobles'; and [so are] three *pogezas* [0.75d] from the Fiddlers' Toll, which is now the king's; three of those [deniers] are from Lubières, of which half is the king's.[9]

(2r6) In total, the king's share per hogshead: 22.75d, and the nobles' share: 6d, and Madame Elis's share: 1d. And from six hogsheads up, [salt] pays only 18d at Lubières for the whole boat. And it pays the 0.75d of the Fiddlers' Toll up to eight hogsheads.

(12) Hereafter are set forth the toll on salt and the division of that between the king and the nobles, going up from one small hogshead to forty small hogsheads.

(16) The share of Madame Elis is 1d for each small hogshead.

[Table N1]

[Tolls on salt in small hogsheads]

(18) The small hogshead by the measure of Tarascon pays 2s 5.75d, of which 22.75d comes to the king, and to all the nobles 7d.[10]

(22) [Two] hogsheads pay 4s 11.5d, of which 3s 9.5d comes to the king, and to the nobles 14d.

(25) [Three] hogsheads pay 8s 5.25d: to the king 5s 8.25d, to the nobles 21d.

---

9 Toll of 29.75d – 22d to king – 1d to Madame Elis leaves 6.75d to be shared, or 6d not counting the *pogezas* (0.75d). One fourth of 6d = 1.5d for the king, but only half of this amount (because the king owns half of the tolls from Lubières), so 0.75d, which makes a total of 22.75d for the king, as below. This leaves 5.25d for the nobles, plus 0.75d (the three *pogezas*), which makes a total of 6d for the nobles, as below. Of the 5.25d for the nobles, 3d come from Lubières.

10 All the nobles: that is, including Madame Elis, as is explained at N2r7–9.

(2v2) [Four] hogsheads pay 9s 11d: to the king 7s 7d, to the nobles 2s 4d.
(4) [Five] hogsheads, 12s 4.75d: to the king 9s 5.75d, to the nobles 2s 12d.
(6) [Six] hogsheads, 14s 10.5d: [...], to the nobles 4s 6d.
(8) [Seven] hogsheads, 17s 1.25d: to the king 13s 1.75d, to the nobles 3s 11.5d.
(11) [Eight] hogsheads, 19s 4d: to the king 14s 11d, to the nobles 4s 5d.
(13) [Nine] hogsheads, 23s 8d: to the king 17s 2d, to the nobles 6s 6d.
(15) [Ten] hogsheads, 25s 10d: to the king 18s 10.5d, [...].
(17) [Eleven] hogsheads, 28s 10d: to the king 20s 7[d], to the nobles 7s 5d.
(19) [Twelve] hogsheads, 30s 8d: to the king 22s 5d, to the nobles 8s 3d.
(21) [Thirteen] hogsheads, 32s 10d: to the king 24s 1.5d, [...].
(23) [Fourteen] hogsheads, 35s: to the king 25s 10d, to the nobles 9s 2d.
(25) [Fifteen] hogsheads, 37s 2d: to the king 27s 6.5d, to the nobles 8s 7.5d.
(3r3) [Sixteen] hogsheads, 39s 4d: to the king 29s 3d, to the nobles 10s 1d.
(5) [Seventeen] hogsheads, 41s 6d: to the king 30s 11.5d, to the nobles 10s 6.5d.
(7) [Eighteen] hogsheads, 44s 1d: to the king 32s 9.25d, to the nobles 11s 3.25d.
(9) [Nineteen] hogsheads, 46s 4d: to the king 34s 5.75d, to the nobles 11s 9.25d.
(11) [Twenty] hogsheads, 48s 5d: to the king 36s 2.25d, to the nobles 12s 2.75d.
(14) [Twenty-one] hogsheads, 50s 7d: to the king 37s 10.75d, to the nobles 12s 8.25d.
(17) [Twenty-two] hogsheads, 52s 9d: to the king 39s 8.25d, to the nobles 13s 1.75d.
(19) [Twenty-three] hogsheads, 54s 11d: to the king 41s 3.75d, to the nobles 13s 7.25d.
(21) [Twenty-four] hogsheads, 57s 1d: to the king 43s 0.25d, to the nobles 14s 3d.
(23) [Twenty-five] hogsheads, 60s 3d: to the king 43s 11.75d, to the nobles 15s 3.25d.
(25) [Twenty-six] hogsheads, 62s 5d: to the king 46s 8.25d, to the nobles 15s 8.75d.
(3v3) [Twenty-seven] hogsheads, 64s 7d: to the king 48s 4.75d, to the nobles 16s 2.25d.
(6) [Twenty-eight] hogsheads, 66s 9d: to the king 50s 1.25d, to the nobles 16s 7.75d.
(8) [Twenty-nine] hogsheads, 68s 11d: to the king 51s 9.75d, to the nobles 17s 1.25d.
(10) [Thirty] hogsheads, 71s 1d: to the king 53s 6.25d, to the nobles 17s 6.75d.

(12) [Thirty-one] hogsheads, 73s 3d: to the king 55s 2.75d, to the nobles 18s 0.25s.
(14) [Thirty-two] hogsheads, 75s 5d: to the king 56s 11.25d, to the nobles 18s 5.75d.
(16) [Thirty-three] hogsheads, 77s 7d: to the king 58s 7.25d, to the nobles 18s 11.25d.
(19) [Thirty-four] hogsheads, 79s 11d: to the king 60s 4d, to the nobles 19s 4.25d.
(21) [Thirty-five] hogsheads, £4 33d: to the king 62s 0.75d, to the nobles 19s 10.25d.
(24) [Thirty-six] hogsheads, £[4] 4s 1d: to the king 63s 9.25d, to the nobles 21s 3.75d.
(4r1) [Thirty-seven] hogsheads, £4 7s 1d: to the king 65s 8.25d, to the nobles 21s 3.75d.
(4) [Thirty-eight] hogsheads, £4 9s 3d: to the king 57s 4.75d, to the nobles 21s 10.25d.
(7) [Thirty-nine] hogsheads, £4 11s 5d: to the king 69s 1.25d, to the nobles 22s 3.75d.
(10) [Forty] hogsheads, £4 13s 10d: to the king 70s 10d, to the nobles 23s.
(12) From forty small hogsheads up, if they go upstream in a boat, it pays as is said above; and [as for] what there is over forty hogsheads, all the money there is over the £4 13s 10d is divided at the rate of 22d per hogshead: the king's share, 19d for each hogshead; and the nobles' share, 3d, that is, 2d to the nobles of the *montazon* and 1d to Madame Elis.
(21) Salt that is loaded at Beaucaire to go upstream by water pays 22d per small hogshead by the measure of Tarascon, and it is shared on the model abovesaid from forty hogsheads up, that is, 19d to the king and 2d to the nobles of the *montason* and 1d to Madame Elis.
(4v2) Item, it also pays 0.75d per hogshead up to eight hogsheads, and from eight hogsheads up the boat pays the king 6d.
(5) Salt that is unloaded at Beaucaire, if it belongs to a man of Beaucaire or Tarascon, pays per small hogshead, measure of Tarascon, 4d per small hogshead for *uzage*, in which the king has 1.5d and the nobles 2.5d.
(10) Item, it also pays 3d at the toll of Lubières up to six hogsheads, and they are shared equally [between] the king and those of Lubières. And from six [hogsheads] up, it pays 18d for the whole boat at the toll of Lubières, in which the king has half. And Madame Elis takes nothing in the *uzage*.
(16) Item, salt that is unloaded at Beaucaire belonging to a foreigner pays, per hogshead by the measure of Tarascon, 11.5d: it pays 8d to the king, 2.5d [to] the lords of the *montaizon*, and 1d to Madame Elis.

(21) Item, the hogshead also pays 3d at Lubières up to six hogsheads, and from six hogsheads up 18d for the whole boat, half to the king and the other half to the nobles of Lubières.

(25) Any man who loads salt at Tarascon, if he is not from Tarascon, pays, per hogshead by the measure of Tarascon, 4d of *uzage,* and 18d at the tollhouse of Lubières on the model that salt pays that is unloaded at Beaucaire by order of a man of Tarascon or Beaucaire, and the money is shared in the same way between the king and the nobles of the *montaizon* and [those] of Lubières.

(5r8) Any man of Tarascon who loads salt at Tarascon does not pay the toll of Tarascon but the toll of Lubières, that is, 4d per hogshead up to six hogsheads, and from six hogsheads up he pays 18d for the whole boat, half to the king and the other half to Lubières. And if the said salt is taken out of the town of Tarascon by water, it pays in the same way as does the salt that is loaded at Beaucaire; and in the same way, any man who loads salt at Tarascon pays in the manner that salt pays that is loaded at Beaucaire.

(19) Here follows the manner of levying the toll on salt that comes up the Rhône against the current by the large hogshead, and what is paid to both the king and the nobles.

(23) And one must know that the large hogshead contains forty heaping setiers by the measure of Peccais, or forty-two setiers by the measure of the sea, [and] that it weighs about seventy-five quintals.

[Table N2]

[Tolls on salt in large hogsheads]

(5v2) The large hogshead going upstream, which is three small hogsheads minus 1/21, pays 5 silver tournois.[11] And each one of those tournois is worth 16d, and the said five tournois come to 6s 8[d], which is half a florin of Florence, because every ten tournois are worth one florin of Florence.[12] And it pays the king 5s 1.5d, and the nobles 18.5d.

(10) [Two] large hogsheads are five small ones and something more, and pay 13s 4d: to the king 10s 2.25d, to the nobles 3s 1.75d.

(14) [Three] large hogsheads are eight small ones; they pay 20s, of which 15s 5d come to the king, and 4s 6d to the nobles.

11 One large hogshead = 2.95 small hogsheads.

12 If one tournois = 16d, then five tournois = 80d, i.e. 6s 8d. Ten tournois = 160d, i.e. 13s 4d = one florin of Florence.

(17) [Four] [large] hogsheads, ten small, 26s 8d: to the king 19s 6d, to the nobles 7s 2d.
(19) [Five] large hogsheads, thirteen small, 33s 4d: to the king 24s 6d, to the nobles 8s 10d.
(21) [Six] large hogsheads, sixteen small, 40s: to the king 29s, to the nobles 10s 3d.
(23) [Seven] large hogsheads, nineteen small, 46s 8d: to the king 33s 9.5d, to the nobles 11s 10.5d.
(6r1) [Eight] large hogsheads, twenty-two small, 53s 4d: to the king 40s 0.5d, to the nobles 13s 3.5d.
(4) [Nine] large hogsheads, twenty-five small, 60s: to the king 44s 9.5d, to the nobles 15s 2.5d.
(7) [Ten] large hogsheads, twenty-five small, 60s: to the king 44s 9.5d, to the nobles 16s 7.5d.
(10) [Eleven] large hogsheads, thirty-one small, pay 63s 4[d]: to the king 55s 3.5d, to the nobles 18s 0.5d.
(13) [Twelve] large hogsheads, thirty-four small, £4: to the king 65s 4.5d, to the nobles 19s 5.5d.
(16) [Thirteen] large hogsheads, thirty-seven small, £4 6s 8d: to the king 65s 4.5d, to the nobles 21s 4.5d.
(19) [Fourteen] large hogsheads, forty small, pay £4 13s 4d: to the king 70s 4d, to the nobles 23s.
(21) From fourteen hogsheads up, let them be loaded in one boat; all the money of the fourteen hogsheads is shared between the king and the nobles as has been said, and what is more than fourteen large hogsheads pays also for each large hogshead 6s 8d, and the said money is shared [in increments of] 22d, of which the king takes 19d and the nobles 3d, that is, 2d for the nobles of the *montaison* and 1d for Johan Alba.
(6v5) Salt that is unloaded at Beaucaire, whether it belongs to a man of Beaucaire or Tarascon, pays 8d per large hogshead: to the king 3d, to the nobles 5d.
(9) Item, it also pays at Adaul 5.25d, if the skipper is not from Beaucaire.
(11) Salt that is unloaded at Beaucaire that belongs to a foreigner, and not [a man] from Beaucaire or Tarascon, pays 3s 4d per large hogshead, which is called half toll: the king's 2s 4d, the nobles' 1s.
(16) Item, at the toll of Lubières it also pays 18d for the boat, of which half belongs to the king and the other to the said men of Lubières. Item, also at Adaul, 5s 0.25d.
(20) Salt that is unloaded at Tarascon belonging to a foreign man, who is not from Tarascon, pays for the large hogshead on the model that salt pays that

is unloaded at Beaucaire, belonging to a man from Beaucaire or from Tarascon: it pays in the manner that is said above.

(7r1) If a man from Tarascon loads salt at Tarascon, he pays only 18d at the toll of Lubières; however, if he takes it out of Tarascon he pays like a foreigner, as is written in the toll for salt that is loaded at Beaucaire; and if he takes it to Beaucaire, he pays in the manner of salt that is unloaded at Beaucaire.

(8) Salt that is loaded in Tarascon or Beaucaire, either by a foreigner or by a man from the town, and goes upstream on the Rhône, pays 5s 4d per large hogshead, of which 4s 7.25d and 2 grains comes to the king, and 8.5d 3 grains to the nobles. And it pays nothing at Lubières or Adaul because it does not pass their border.

[Rubric III]

[Tolls on commodities at Tarascon and Lubières]

(16) Here follows the toll on commodities.

[2s 6.5d (= 30.5d) per load]

(17) A load of cloths from Avignon, which contains nine bolts the load; a load of cloths from France, twelve bolts; cloths from Narbonne, twenty-four pieces; coarse muslin, twenty-four pieces; brown cloth, four bolts. The load of hides of ox, camel, [hole in MS] horse, and the like, tanned or not tanned, contains twenty hides. A load of cordovan leather, which contains four quintals or twelve dozen [pieces]; of linen cloths, indigo, wax, sendal, feathers, ginger, plume alum, rock alum, alum from Aleppo, sugar alum, thread, fur skins, or cloves, pepper, saffron, new cotton, silk, rabbit furs, and the like. Of the abovesaid things, the load [contains] four quintals and pays 2s 6.5d, of which the king takes 2s 3.5d, Johan Alba 1d, and Lubières 1d.

[19d per load]

(7v10) A load of wool, tow, Brazil wood, white cloth, fish from the sea, fresh or salted; peeled chestnuts, almonds in pieces, dry figs, raisins, cumin, sugar, powdered sugar, tow, thread for ropes, ropes made from pudding pipe tree, steel, honey, dates, rice, cinnamon, hemp, mustard, copper, cotton, pitch, fustian, pots, hog fat, tallow, tin, madder dye, salted meat, iron, cheeses, oil – which contains sixteen or seventeen canes per load –, sheepskins, lamb[skins], kidskins, and the like: [hole in MS] the load is made of four quintals, and the load pays 19d, of which Johan Alba takes 1d. Item, also at the toll of Lubières, 2d, of which the king gets 1d.

[Cloth and leather: from 2d to 0.5d]

(8r1) A dozen sheepskins, and the like, pay 1.5d.
(3) Item, a dozen cordovan hides pay 2d. A hide of an ox, a horse, or a camel, or the like, pays 1.5d.
(6) A bearhide pays 1d. A tunic pays 0.5d. A piece of coarse muslin cloth pays 0.5d. A cord of linen, 0.5d. A strap, 0.5d.

[Woad: 14d per load]

(10) A load of woad containing four quintals pays 14d, of which Johan Alba takes 1d. Item, it also pays 2d at the toll of Lubières, of which the king gets half.

[9d per load]

(14) A load of grease, alum from Vulcano, sheepskins for making parchments, and the like: the load of four quintals pays 9d, of which Johan Alba takes 1d.
(18) Item, also 2d for the toll of Lubières, of which the king gets half.
(20) [A load of] tiles pays 9d per thousand, of which Johan Alba gets 1d.
(22) A load of old ropes pays 9d, of which Johan Alba gets 1d. Item, also 2d at the toll of Lubières, of which the king gets half.

[Grain, vegetables: 9.5d per load]

(25) A load of oats, barley, rye, beans, chickpeas, and all manner of grains and legumes: the load or bundle contains fifteen or sixteen setiers by the measure of Tarascon, and pays 9.5d per bundle, of which 1d comes to Johan Alba.
(8v5) Item, it also pays 2d at Lubières, half of which belongs to the king, up to thirty bundles. And from thirty bundles upwards, at the toll of Lubières the whole boat pays only 5s, half of which belongs to the king.

[Lead, alum, wine: 6d per load or butt]

(10) A load of lead of four quintals pays 6d, of which Johan Alba takes 0.5d.
(12) Item, it pays 2d at Lubières, of which the king gets half.
(14) Of alum that comes by the Rhône, whether it comes from upstream or downstream, each butt, either large or small, pays 6d.

[Wine: payment in kind plus 6d per butt]

(17) Item, for one butt it pays half a keg of wine, and for two butts one keg of wine. And from three butts up the whole boat pays a bundle of wine.

(21) Item, it also pays 6d for each butt, and if the wine comes in kegs, the hogshead, by the measure of Tarascon, pays in the manner as if it came in butts. And if a man of Tarascon makes a partnership with a foreigner, whether [their] wine is mixed together or separate, it pays in full as of a foreigner. However, if it is common knowledge that the wine is in butts [belonging to either the Tarascon man or the foreigner], only the foreigner is obliged to pay the toll.[13]

[Dye: 6s 5d (= 77d) per hogshead]

(9r6) A hogshead of sumach contains seventy-two quintals, which are three *saquieras* and a half; it pays 6s 5d, of which 1d comes to Johan Alba for each hogshead. And from twenty *saquieras* up, it pays 5s at Lubières for the whole boat, half of which belongs to the king.

[Materials: 18d]

(11) A boat loaded with rocks, from twenty-five rocks up, pays only 18d for the whole boat at the toll of Lubières, of which the king gets half.

(15) A boat loaded with lime or gypsum pays 18d for the whole boat at Lubières, half of which belongs to the king.

[Live cargo: horses, travellers, large or small animals: tolls vary]

(18) A horse, whether it has been sold or is being taken to be sold, if it crosses the Rhône and is worth £12 10s and up, pays 2s 6d. And if it is worth less, it pays only 4d.[14]

---

13 Compare T5r8–12; MS N makes the distinction subtler, possibly out of confusion, by adding *ho en divisament*, "or separate." The distinction as made seems to depend on common knowledge versus its implicit opposite, mere assertion. If the men in a partnership pool their holding or merely assert that they have divided their wine by owner, they must pay toll on all of it; but if such a division is confirmed by common knowledge, they pay toll only on the wine belonging to the foreigner. The partnership (*compania*) may be treated as a transparent fiction for the purpose of reducing the toll.

14 The large difference between the two tolls (30d versus 4d) implies a large difference between two types of horse, presumably a noble steed versus a workhorse.

(22) And also a Saracen slave, man or woman, or a female mastiff: each one pays 2s 6d.

(24) A large animal that comes from Provence such as an ox, ass, mule, or the like, and crosses the Rhône, pays 1d for each piece.

(9v2) Small animals such as sheep, pigs, female goats, male goats, and the like pay 0.25d apiece.

(5) Large animals such as a horse or a mule that are bought at Beaucaire and come here [brought] by a foreigner pay 1d.

(8) Oxen and asses pay 0.5d.

(9) Small animals like sheep, pigs, goats, and the like pay 0.25d.

(11) Any rider who is not from Tarascon or Beaucaire, crossing the Rhône, if he is from a place near here, within twenty leagues, pays 7.5d; but if he is from eight leagues down, he pays 3.5d.

(16) And when the bridge beteween Beaucaire and Tarascon was whole, those from nearby paid 2d, and those from far away 4d, and the tollkeepers owed the bridge 0.5d.[15]

(20) Any chaplain [or] clerk who has no privilege, be he [as high as a] sub-deacon, pays like other riders. However, if he is a deacon or from a deacon up, or a knight or a son of a knight, or if he is of the family of a knight, and those who go with them at their expense and in their clothes, they are exempt from toll.

(10r3) Masters of a mint, who are called coiners, and all workers in a mint in the season when they are making coins, either for the king of Sicily or for the king of France: they and their horses are exempt. But when they are not working in a mint, they pay like the other riders, as was said before.

(10) Any pilgrim, man or woman, who is from outside the region of Provence pays 1d. But if he is from Provence, he pays nothing.

(13) Any pilgrim who comes from above Lyon, riding to Santiago [de Compostela] or Saint-Gilles, pays 5d. But if he is walking, he pays only 1d.

(16) Any Lombard pilgrim, man or woman, riding to Santiago, pays 8d. But if he is going elsewhere, he pays 4d. And if he is walking or going by river, he pays 1.5d.

(20) Any Spaniard, Englishman, or German who is riding pays 5d. But by foot, he pays 1d.

(22) And it is customary that any pilgrim is exempt, man or woman, riding, crossing the Rhône, coming to [the church of] Sainte Marthe [in Tarascon] on the first three days of [the festival of] Saint Martha.

---

15 The corporation of the toll retained the larger portion of a toll for crossing the bridge, but remitted 0.5d to the corporation of the bridge.

[Wood and wood products: tolls vary]

(10v1) Any round tree must be measured one-third up from the root.
(3) A ship's mast that is seven palms or more around pays 70s, of which 2s comes to Johan Alba.
(6) Item, at Lubières it pays 5s, half of which is the king's.
(8) A yard that is six palms and a half around pays 30s, of which 2s 6d comes to Johan Alba.
(10) Item, at Lubières it also pays 5s, half of which is the king's.
(12) A yard of six palms pays 20s, of which Johan Alba takes 8d. Item, also at Lubières 2d, half of which is the king's.
(15) A yard of five and a half palms pays 15s, of which Johan Alba takes 5d. Item, at Lubières it also pays 2d, half of which is the king's.
(18) A yard of five palms, 10s, of which 3d comes to Johan Alba. Item, also at Lubières 2d, and half to the king.
(21) A yard of four and a half palms pays 5s. And of four palms, 4s. And from four palms down, according to the judgment of the tollkeeper. And in everything Johan Alba takes 1d. And Lubières 2d, of which the king gets half.
(11r1) A ship's tiller or a round oak log pays 15s, of which, for five logs, 5d comes to Johan Alba. Item, at Lubières it pays 3s, half to the king.
(4) A squared oak log pays 5s, of which, for three logs, 3d comes to Johan Alba. Item, at Lubières also 2d, half to the king.
(7) A stack of timber pays 1s 0.5d, of which 1d comes to Johan Alba.
(9) Item, at the Fiddler's Toll it also pays 0.75d up to eight logs, and from eight logs up it pays 5d for the whole raft at the Fiddler's Toll, which is the king's.
(13) Item, at Lubières it also pays 2d per log up to twenty logs, and from twenty logs up it pays 5s at Lubières for the whole raft and no more, and to Johan Alba [1d][16] for each log.
(17) A squared log of timber from Seyssel or one of larch wood is a stack. Twelve thin, round poles is one stack.
(19) Twelve portable logs make one stack.
(20) Four or six small, irregular logs make one stack.
(22) Two round, squared timbers is one stack.
(23) Four squared timbers that a pair of oxen [can] pull is one stack.
(25) Twenty boards of fir is a stack.
(11v1) Ten boards of oak is a stack, or four if they are large.

16 As in N11r8, T5v19.

(3) Six boards of walnut is a stack.
(4) Eight or nine mizzen yards or curved planks for a bark is a stack.
(6) A watermill pays 10s.
(7) A windmill pays 5s.
(8) A bark, 5s.
(9) A ship.
(10) A boat [recently] bought or sold, or that is being taken to sell, pays 2d for each strake. The strake is counted from the tier [of goods in the hold] of the boat, plus two sheer-rails. Item, it pays one oar or its price, at the discretion of the tollkeeper. And thus it pays, [at the] toll of Lubières, 2d for each strake and one oar, and half is the king's.

[Domestic objects, foods: payment in kind plus various tolls]

(17) Roof tiles, bowls, trenchers, spoons, bowls, pitchers, two-handled jugs, baskets, breadbaskets, round hoops, and all utensils of wood: 4 [pieces] per hundred. And at Lubières it pays 0.5d the bundle, half to the king. And also for oars: 4 [pieces] per hundred, and [0.5d] at Lubières, half to the king.
(23) Baskets that are made of twigs pay 1d per piece.
(25) Hampers: the whole boat pays one hamper. However, baskets made of rushes, plaited shopping baskets, and ropes made of rush pay nothing.
(12r3) Bundles of clay pots, and all utensils of clay, pay 4d. However, utensils of clay that are made in Tarascon, and all products of clay, pay 4 [pieces] per hundred, or the price of the four.
(7) A bundle of almonds in the shell, walnuts, hazelnuts, and the like, the load of which contains eight setiers, measure of Tarascon, pays 4.5d, and at Lubières 0.5d, and half to the king.
(12) A bundle of chestnuts in the shell, apples, pears, quinces, peaches, sorb apples, sour cherries, cherries, lemons, limes, large lemons, fresh roses,[17] and all fresh fruit except small figs, seeds and cornel berries: the bundle pays 2d. And at Lubières 0.5d, half to the king.
(18) A bundle of rapes or charcoal, tanner's bark, myrtle, [or] mastic, pays 1d. And at Lubières 0.5d, half to the king.
(21) A new chest, boxes, armoires and the like, vats, all receptacles, a [new] set of staves, millstones, a barber's grindstone, salt pork: each of these pays 4d. Item, at Lubières 1d, half to the king.

---

17 *Rosas frescas*, N12r14, may be an error for *noses frescas*, fresh walnuts (see Glossary).

(12v1) Onions: the bundle [contains] three dozen small ones. The bundle of garlic bulbs contains eight or ten dozen; the bundle pays one bunch, and at Lubières 0.5d, half to the king.

(5) The sumpter's load of utensils of glass pays two pieces, and the carrier pays one piece.

[Rubric IV]

[Exempt items]

(6) Here follow the things that are exempt and pay no toll at all.

(9) Coined gold and silver, verdigris, haberdashery, gallnuts, liquorice, soap, gum arabic, fish from the Rhône or a freshwater marsh, cuttlefish, sulphur, butter, sheepsbelly, products made of iron or copper or brass or tin, ready-made dresses that are called *plagarias*; however, at the fair of Beaucaire, which is in May, they pay 3d for a man's load of ready-made dresses, or 6d for an animal's. And it is the same for a frock, garment, purse, skirt, books, plaited shopping baskets, paper, baskets made of rushes, and ropes made of rushes, and tallow.

(20) All commodities that are not in the chapter of exempt things will pay the toll on the model of the commodities that are nearest their price.

(24) Note that in the year 1325 and the ninth day of the month of October, a boat loaded with ashes passed over the Rhône, and the toll was asked of it; which [the ship, viz. the ship's captain] answered that it owed nothing, because it was not found in the register that it owed [anything]. And at that time our lord the king[18] was here, and the question came before him. And it was agreed, seeing that ashes are not at all with the other exempt things, that it must pay according to the commodity that was closest and most like ashes, and that it would pay like lime or gypsum.

[Rubric V]

[Currencies]

(13r10) Here follows the explanation of currencies.

(12) All the coins that are levied at the abovesaid tolls, either the tollhouse by the river or the ones at the Gate of Tarascon, Saint-Gabriel, or Lubières, are

18 The king in 1325 was Robert of Anjou, king of Naples, count of Provence and Forcalquier, who ruled 1309–43.

in currency of tournois of pure silver; its fineness is 11.5d,[19] and its silver [weighs] 3.5d.[20] And each [large] tournois is worth 16d, and ten tournois are worth one florin of Florence of good gold and twenty-four carats, and it weighs 3d.[21] And the [small] tournois, counting as twelve per florin [plus] 8d, are worth 15d and 5 grains.[22] And [as for] the *blanc*, if its fineness is 10d and 5 grains and a third,[23] and its weight 2d and 2 grains,[24] then the *blanc* is worth 7.75d and one-fourth of a *pogeza*.[25] And the *patac* is worth 1.5d and one-fourth of a *pogeza*.[26]

(13v1) In dividing the toll on salt between the king and the nobles, the said florin of Florence counts as 13s 4d,[27] and by that count the tournois is worth 16d. And then the *blanc* is counted as 8d and 8 grains;[28] and [as for] the *patac* of the said *blanc*, it [the *blanc*] is worth five *patacs* of those of 1.5d and 4 grains.[29] And so, to compare *coronats* to currency in the tournois that were made before the *coronats*,[30] the money that was levied was put at [1]2s 8d per florin of Florence,[31] and the *blanc* at 8d, and nineteen *blancs* are worth the said florin of Florence. However, the tollkeepers ordered that the toll on salt be levied at 13s 4d,[32] which are ten tournois,[33] and the tolls on commodities at 12s 8d,[34] of which nineteen *blancs* are worth the abovesaid florin, counting the *blanc* at 8d.[35]

---

19 Silver of 11.5d fineness was defined conventionally as pure; that is, its fineness was considered as 1000/1000 in terms of *argent le roi*.

20 3.5 x 1.27 grams = 4.45 grams.

21 3 x 1.27 grams = 3.81 grams.

22 15d + 5/24d = 15.21d.

23 10d + 5.3/24d = 10.22d. 10.22/11.5 *argent le roi* = fineness 889/1000.

24 (2 x 1.27 grams) + (2 x 0.053 grams) = 2.65 grams.

25 One-fourth of a *pogeza* is 0.06d. Total value of the *blanc*: 7.81d.

26 Value of the *patac*: 1.56d.

27 13s 4d = (13 x 12d) + 4d = 160d.

28 8.33d.

29 One *patac* = 1.67d. Five *patacs* = 5 x 1.67d = 8.33d = one *blanc*.

30 The *coronat* appeared in 1330 (see Glossary).

31 12s 8d = (12 x 12d) + 8d = 152d. MS N13v11 reads .xxij., an error for .xij. The correct reading is assured by what follows in N13v12–13: "The money that was levied was put at 12s 8d [152d] per florin of Florence and ... the *blanc* at 8d, and nineteen *blancs* are worth the said florin of Florence" (19 x 8d = 152d).

32 13s 4d = (13 x 12d) + 4d = 160d, the new rate for the florin of Florence as of 1330.

33 At 16d per tournois, as above.

34 12s 8d = (12 x 12d) + 8d = 152d, the old rate.

35 19 x 8d = 152d, the old rate. In 1330, with the introduction of the *coronat* and a new rate of exchange for deniers to florins of Florence, the tollkeepers ordered that the toll on salt be calculated in terms of the new rate and the tolls on commodities in terms of the old rate.

(20) Item, the large hogshead of salt that goes upstream on the Rhône pays 5 silver tournois,[36] which are worth half a florin of Florence, [and half a florin] is worth 6s 8d at the rate of 16d per tournois.[37]

[Rubric VI]

[Tolls at the Gate of Tarascon]

(24) The proper and customary procedure of the toll at the Gate of Tarascon.

[2s 2.5d (= 26.5d) per load]

(14r1) A load of cloths from France [or] Narbonne, coarse muslin, linen cloth, and all other cloths; cordovan leather, indigo, pepper, wax, silk, sendal, alum, ginger, cloves, and any kind of spice; incense, mastic, zedoary; varicoloured fur lining, fur skins, oxhide, camel[hide], horse[hide]; thread from Cologne, fleece, and flax, and the like: a load of the abovesaid things is made of four quintals. It pays 2s 2.5d. Item, also to Johan Alba, 1d.

[18d]

(13) A load of wool, Brazil wood, fish from the sea (salted or not salted), peeled chestnuts, almonds in pieces, cumin, sugar, powdered sugar, pudding pipe tree, steel, dates, mustard, roquette, dry figs, raisins, tow, honey, rice, hemp, copper, anise, thread for ropes, fine flannel, pitch, cotton, fustian, borax, lard, tallow, tin, madder dye, iron, brass, oil, cheese, sheepskins, fine-spun wool, cabbage seed, and all kinds of seeds and the like: a load is made of four quintals and pays 18d. Item, to Johan Alba, 1d.

---

36 Cf. Table N2, Tolls on Salt in Large Hogsheads: "The large hogshead going upstream, which is three small hogsheads minus 1/21, pays 5 silver tournois. And each one of those tournois is worth 16d, and the said five tournois come to 6s 8d, which is half a florin of Florence, because every ten tournois are worth one florin of Florence. And it pays the king 5s 1.5d and the nobles 18.5d" (N5v2–9).

37 If one tournois = 16d, then five tournois = 80d, which is 6s 8d. Ten tournois = one florin, as stated above.

[8d]

(14v3) A load of tartar, alum from Vulcano, sheepskins that are made into parchments, and the like: the load is made of four quintals. It pays 8d. Item, to Johan Alba, 1d.
(7) Old ropes: the load of four quintals pays 8d. Item, to Johan Alba, 1d.
(9) Tiles: [a load] pays, per thousand, 8d. And to Johan Alba, 1d.

[Grains: 4d]

(11) A bundle of any grain, flour, millet, and any legume: the bundle contains eight setiers by the measure of Tarascon. It pays 4d.

[Lead: 6d]

(14) A load of lead weights pays 6d.

[Salt carried by animals: 2d]

(15) [A load] of an animal loaded with salt pays 2d.

[Food, domestic objects]

(16) Fruits such as pears, apples, chestnuts with the shell, quinces, peaches, sour cherries, cherries, lemons, fresh walnuts, and every kind of fruit except fresh figs: the bundle, 2d.
(20) A bundle of almonds with the shell, walnuts, hazelnuts, and the like, pays 4d.
(22) A bundle of rape or tanner's bark, lentils, withes, [or] charcoal, pays 1d.
(24) A bundle of onions or garlics pays one bunch.
(25) [A bundle] of an animal loaded with pitchers, kegs, and all utensils of wood, pays 4d.
(15r2) A cask, butt, vat of twenty-five staves, chest, box, millstone for a mill, barber's grindstone, washbasin: each one pays 4d.
(5) A bundle of glass and any utensil of glass pays two pieces; and a carrier, one piece.
(7) A bundle of clay pots and any utensil of clay pays 4 [pieces] per hundred.
(9) Each large animal pays 0.5d.
(10) A small animal pays 1d for four.

[Exemptions]

(11) However, if the aforesaid things have paid at the tollhouse of Jarnègues, they pay nothing at the Gate.
(14) All the things that are exempt at Lubières are exempt at the Gate.
(16) All the commodities that are sold in Tarascon or its territory, except salt, are exempt from the toll at Tarascon, provided that they remain in Tarascon. However, after they have sold the said commodities in Tarascon and then taken them out of Tarascon – that is, a foreigner who is not from Tarascon or Beaucaire – he would pay the toll, whether they carried it by water or by land.
(15v1) All the things coming by water, going upstream or downstream, and that are unloaded at Beaucaire by a foreigner to be carried by land in any direction in the kingdom,[38] pays in full at the king's toll and at Lubières. And likewise, all things that are loaded at Beaucaire to be carried on the bank, upstream or downstream, owe the toll in full.

[Rubric VII]

[Tolls at Saint-Gabriel]

(15v9) The toll of Saint-Gabriel, from which the people of Arles and Tarascon are exempt.

[13d]

(11) A cargo of oil, hemp, lambskins, kidskins, sheepskins, rabbit [skins], peeled chestnuts, iron, tin, dry figs, raisins; fish from the sea, salted or not; cotton, fustian, Brazilwood, and the like: the load contains four quintals. It pays 13d.

[2s 2d (= 26d)]

(17) A load of cloths from Avignon of nine bolts, cloths from France of twelve bolts, cloths from Narbonne of twenty-four bolts, coarse muslins, brown cloth, hide of ox or camel or horse, cordovan leather, rock alum, linen cloth,

38 *Al realme*: in the kingdom. That is, starboard, on the right bank (Languedoc); opposed to the *empire*, port, the left bank (Provence).

rabbit skins, thread, squirrel furs, any irregular fur lining, calves, wax, indigo, fur skins, pepper, ginger, cloves, sendal, zedoary, feather alum, rock alum, alum from Aleppo, sugar alum: all the things abovesaid and their like pay 2s 2d for four quintals.

(16r3) And [as for] all the other small things that are not written here, look at the proper and customary procedure of the toll at the Gate of Tarascon, and levy the toll at Saint-Gabriel according to that procedure.

[Exemptions]

(8) All the things that are exempt at the toll of the Gate of Tarascon are exempt at the toll of Saint-Gabriel, except people from Beaucaire, who are never ever exempt at the toll of Saint-Gabriel.

[Currencies]

(13) All the coins that are levied at the tolls mentioned, both the tollhouse by the river and the tollhouse of the Gate of Tarascon and [the one at] Saint-Gabriel, are levied in currency of pure silver tournois; its fineness is 11.5d, ten tournois are worth one florin of Florence in twenty-four carat gold, and its weight is 4d. And the tournois is worth 15d and 5 grains of the coin named at the said toll. And thus the florin of Florence is worth, in the said currency, 12s 8d.[39]—

39 If one tournois is worth 15d plus 5 grains (15d + 5/24d = 15.208d), then ten tournois are worth 152.08d, which is one florin. The florin of 152.08d/12 = 12.67s = 12s 8d.

Marginalia

MS T

- *T13r, left margin*: blat. *Occitan. "Grain." Refers to T13r10:* blat.
- *T15r, left margin, in decorative sworls ascending from the capital* C *of* Cargua, *T15r14: a face.*
- *T15r, left margin, in decorative sworls descending from the capital* C *of* Cargua, *T15r14: a bird.*

MS N

- *N1v, lower left margin*: Cj [= Ci] appres / est designee / la portion du / Roy sur le / peage & la / portion des gentilshomes. *French hand 2 (loose). "Hereafter is designated the share of the king in the toll and the share of the noblemen." Refers to N1v18:* Se tracta de la sal, lo peage et la divisio d'aquel entre lo rey et los gentils homes.
- *N4v, left margin*: nota. *Latin hand 1 (thin line). "Take note." Refers to N4v7–8:* Per lu / sage.
- *N5v, upper left margin:* ¶ Lestimasion / de largent / pour le peage / du sel. *French hand 3 (framed within horizontal line above and decorative tail of the* l *in* sel*). "The determination of the money for the toll on salt." Refers to N5v19:* Aysi si sec la maniera de levar lo peage de la sal.
- *N6v, left margin:* nota. *Latin hand 1 (thin line). "Take note." Refers to N6v11:* La sal que si descarga a Belcayre.
- *N7r, left margin:* sel. *French hand 4. "Salt." Refers to N7r8:* La sal.
- *N8r, lower right margin:* bled. *French hand 5 (thick line). "Grain." Refers to N8v1 overleaf:* blas.

- *N8r, lower right margin (continues the word* bled *from preceding note):* z et liormes. *Occitan hand 1 (thin line). "(Grain)s and legumes." Refers to N8v1 overleaf:* et de liolmes.
- *N8v, left margin:* Alun. *French hand 6. "Alum." Refers to N8v14:* D'Alum.
- *N9r, left margin:* Nota. *Latin hand 2. "Take note." Refers to N9r18:* Un chival que sie vendut.
- *N9r, right margin:* Sarrasin / esclau. *Occitan hand 2 (pencil). "Saracen slave." Refers to* N9r22: Sarrazin esclau.
- *N9v, left margin:* no[ta]. *Latin hand 3. "Take note." Refers to N9v16:* Et quant lo pont dentre ...
- *N11v, left margin:* 4 pour cent. *French hand 7 (court hand). "Four per cent." Refers to N11v21:* de c'. iiij.
- *N12r, upper left margin:* miellas. *Occitan hand 3. "Almonds." Refers to N12r7:* amellas. *Compare* melas *T4r4.*
- *N12v, left margin:* no[ta]. *Latin hand 3. "Take note." Refers to N12v15:* a la fiera de Belcayre.
- *N14v, left margin:* bestia ga[r]gada / de sal. *Occitan hand 4. "An animal loaded with salt." Refers to N14v15:* De bestia cargada de sal.
- *N15r, left margin:* c 4. *French hand 7 (court). "Four per cent." Refers to N15r8:* de cent .iiij.
- *N15r, left margin:* notat. *Latin hand 4. "He (she, it) takes note." Refers to N15r12:* Totas fes si las causas davan dichas aguesson pagat al peage de Gernega ...
- *N15r, left margin:* no[ta]. *Latin hand 3. "Take note." Refers to N15r18:* Totas las mercadarias ... son francas del peage de Tarascon.
- *N15v, upper left margin:* no[ta]. *Latin hand 3. "Take note." Refers to N15v1:* Totas las causas venent per aigua ...
- *N16r, top margin, above the word* sitrum: *a question mark. Cf. Textual Note, N15v25–16r1.*
- *N16r, left margin:* no[ta]. *Latin hand 3. "Take note." Refers to N16r8:* Totas las causas que son franquas ...
- *N16r, left margin:* Nota. *Latin hand 2. "Take note." Refers to N16r10:* al peage de sant Gabriel.
- *N16r, left margin:* benque [?]. *French hand 4 (?). Reading and meaning uncertain. See Glossary s.v.* be(nque) [?].
- *N16r, left margin:* Monede. *Italian (?) hand 1. "Currencies." Refers to N16r13:* monedas.
- *N16v, bottom, upside down*: Memoyre de descendre [?] le livre pour m'aider au St-Esperit. "Memo to take down the book to help me at Saint-Esprit." *May refer to Pont-Saint-Esprit, the town upstream from Tarascon.*

Textual Notes

MS T

- T3r1–3: *in red.*
- T3r1 form[a]: form *T, Bondurand*; *cf.* forma *passim.*
- T3r2 pesage: pesage *T, in red with a brown speck below the* s *that may indicate expunctuation. The forms* pesage, pezage, *and* peage *all occur elsewhere in T.*
- T3r26 sendat: sondat *Bondurand.*
- T3r29 indi: judi *Bondurand.*
- T3v7 o.: ob. *Bondurand passim.*
- T3v27–30: *A triangular piece of parchment has been torn out, and what remains shows a tear. These deteriorations do not influence the text on T3r, but on T3v they delete the words in brackets;* de pegua *T3v29 is legible through a white substance, perhaps a glue.*
- T3v28 seu: fen *Bondurand.*
- T3v33 aninas: auvias *Bondurand.*
- T4r12 piatta *T*, piacta *Bondurand. The digraph* -tt- *recurs in* mattafellon T4r13 (mactafellon *Bondurand*), botta T4v32 (botta *Bondurand*).
- T4r13 mattafellon *T*, mactafellon *Bondurand.*
- T4r15 argento: argent *Bondurand.* vivo: vivono *Bondurand. MS T reads* argento vivovo, *a dittography of the last syllable. Bondurand reads* argent vivono,*"vif-argent, mercure" (140n5). Thomas notes, "argent vivono: lire* viu o no, *vif ou non" (1891, 420), which is unacceptable because quicksilver pays a toll of 21d (T4r15) while silver is toll free (T8r7, N12v9).*
- T4r16: *Contrasting, blacker ink and thinner line; a second hand, or a different pen and ink.*
- T4v2 sarsia vielha: sarsiamelha *Bondurand.*
- T4v7 senors: senhors *Bondurand.*

- T4v12 Carga: Cargua *Bondurand.* et tota: e tota *Bondurand.*
- T5r4 ven: venj *T, corrected to* ven.
- T5r5 m[ie]g: mueg *T, emended by Bondurand in a note, although he prints* mueg *in the text: "Il faut lire* mieg *et sous-entendre barral. Le sens est: si le vin vient en barraux, il paiera un demi-barral par tonneau, comme il est dit plus haut" (142n1). Disputed by Thomas: "Art. 80,* mueg *veut dire* muid *et non* demi" *(1891, 420).*
- T5r20 navei: nave i *Bondurand, cf.* navei *passim.*
- T5r30 Lubieras: *Marks in the left margin at T5r31 (*b+*) and T5r37 (*a b a*) indicate that T5r37 should precede T5r32. Moving these lines creates a progression downward from seven hands to six, five and a half, and so on, which must have been intended. Accordingly T5r37–42 have been moved and renumbered as T5r[32–7], and lines T5r32–6 as T5r[38–42].*
- T5r[32] Albre: Aalbre *T*, a[l]bre *Bondurand.*
- T5r[36] lo senhors: lo[s] senhors *Bondurand.*
- T5v17. The words *a Lubieras* seem to have been inserted erroneously; in their absence, the passage would have referred implicitly to Tarascon instead. The passage on wood lists the toll for a *timon de nau* or *roure rodon*, first at Tarascon (implicitly) (T5v12), then at Lubières (T5v14). Next it gives the toll for a *travada* of timber erroneously for Lubières (T5v17), then correctly at Los Mujolans (T5v20) and Lubières (T5v27). If we understand the toll of 12.5d (T5v18) as applying to Tarascon rather than Lubières, it matches the corresponding tolls for all ten wood products in MS A_1 (Baratier 386b, lines 11–24), eight in MS P (Guérard 1:lxxxii, lines 15–25; two are omitted), two in MS A_2 (Martin-Portier 2:42), and eight in MS N (N11r17–11v4; two others are omitted).
- T5v34 faita: facta *Bondurand.*
- T5v35 roans: roaus *Bondurand.*
- T5v36 facha: facta *Bondurand.*
- T6r2 vi: V *Bondurand.*
- T6r26 talhador[s]: talhador *T.*
- T6v1 selcles: selclees *Bondurand.*
- T6v3: *Blacker ink, thinner line; a second hand or a different pen.*
- T6v21 lo senhors: los senhors *Bondurand.*
- T7r5 lo: los *Bondurand.*
- T7r16: *Blacker ink, thinner line; a second hand or a different pen.*
- T7v1 rabas: rabas dona a lubieras o. *T, with* dona a lubieras *expunctuated in brown and lined out in red.*
- T8r9 buire: coure *Bondurand.*
- T8r10 arzita: zozita *Bondurand.*
- T8r22 vendre: per vendre vendere *T, with* vendre *lined out.*

- T8v5 eisseptat: eisseptat prelatz so es *T, with* prelatz so es *expunctuated in brown ink and lined out in red.*
- T8v10: *Blacker ink, thinner line; a second hand or a different pen.*
- T8v21: *in red.*
- T9r11: pagua de, *with* de *lined out in black.*
- T9r21 cavalcaduras: cavalcadas *T,* cadas *expunctuated; corrected to* cavalcaduras.
- T9r22: cadas *T, expunctuated in brown.*
- T9v1: *in red.*
- T10r1: *in red.*
- T10r6 sal dona: *transposed to the beginning of T10r7.*
- T10v17 libr. i: *scribal correction, out of normal order (£ s d).*
- T11v16 [X]XXIX: XXIX *T.*
- T11v24 dis: dis dis *T.*
- T11v24 lo: la *Bondurand.*
- T12r27 lu: lo *Bondurand.*
- T12r28 lo: lo[s] *Bondurand.*
- T12r30 iiii: III *Bondurand.*
- T12v8 de.: de[n.] *Bondurand.*
- T12v19 d.: s d. *T, with the* s *crossed out in red.*
- T12v27 fau: faù *Bondurand.*
- T12v28 fau: faù *Bondurand.*
- T13r1–3: *in red.*
- T13r2 nostre: noste nostre *T, with* noste *expunctuated.*
- T13r10 e de tot: e de tot lo *T, with* lo *lined out in black.*
- T13r20 avia: avia blat (21) de .ij. paries o de plus a cascun (22) avia *T. Dittography, as Bondurand saw (p. 154n4).*
- T13v1 nau: naù *Bondurand.*
- T13v2 [s/] .v.: .v. *T,* V l. (?) *B. The toll of 5s recurs in MSS* A_2 *(*arbore navium, *Martin-Portier 2:48) and N (*arbre de nau, *N10v6), both for Lubières.*
- T13v6 e: et *Bondurand.*
- T13v12 tant [solament]: tant *T*, tant [solamens] *Bondurand.*
- T13v17 saumada: saumadas *T, with* -s *crossed out.*
- T13v18 pezag: pez pezag *T, with the first* pez *lined out.*
- T13v30 nou: noù *Bondurand.* mol[a]: molo *T.*
- T13v31 o de fabre: o de fabre o de fabre *T.*
- T14r1–3*: in red.*
- T14r11 indi: Jndi *T*, judi *Bondurand.*
- T14r32 seu: sèu *Bondurand.*
- T14v7 [d.]: *om. T*, [d.]? *Bondurand.*
- T14v19 escrin/h nou: escrin hnoù *Bondurand. Cf.* escrinh nou *T6v13, T13v29.*

- T14v21 an: en *Bondurand.*
- T14v27 [d.]: *om. T*, [d.](?) *Bondurand.*
- T14v28 menuda[s]: menuda *T*, menuda[s] *Bondurand.*
- T15r2 deves: devès *Bondurand.*
- T15r9–12: *in red.*
- T15r22 seu: sèu *Bondurand.*
- T15r26 anhnis: anhis *Bondurand.*
- T15r29 facha: fachas *T*, facha(s) *Bondurand.*
- T15r30 thar& *T*, Tharascon *Bondurand.*
- T15v–16r: *Table T2 is presented in two columns.*
- T15v1 tota[s]: tota *T, Bondurand.*
- T15v12–15: *in red.*
- T15v26a iiii: ix iiii *T, with* ix *crossed out (scribal correction).*
- T16r3a: *Table T2 skips* XVI mo.
- T16r10–13: *in red.*
- T16r10 cavalhers: cavalliers *Bondurand.*
- T16r22 xiiij: ixiiij *T.*
- T16r23 v[j]: v *T.*
- T16v26 [xv]: *om. T.*
- T17r6. *The rest of T17r and all of T17v are blank. Folio T18r begins in red:* Transactio inhita inter nobiles et burgenses consilii Tharasconis super multis causis, "An agreement undertaken among the nobles and the townspeople of the council of Tarascon on many subjects."

MS N

- *The inside front cover contains the mirror image of the verso of a removed pastedown. The text extends over 23 lines. Despite considerable damage, it can be read well enough to determine that the first 22 lines reproduce John 1–14, the same passage that occurs on N1r15-v15 (facing), followed at line 23, perhaps, by* I n d js [...] gracias, *that is* In nomine domini Jesu gratias *(Col. 3:17). The hand is a* cursiva formata, *perhaps slightly earlier than the hand of MS N itself or of the same date (Paul Saenger, e-mail to the author, 15 August 2014). The inside back cover shows no text.*
- N1v13 habitabit: habitavit *Vulgate.*
- N1v25 .xxii d'.: .xixii° d'. *N. The number in N is nonsense; the correct reading* (.xxii.) *is assured by what follows in N2r6–9.*
- N2r22-N4r10. *The number of small hogsheads for each entry in Table N1 from two to forty is omitted.*
- N3v24 [.iiij.]: *om. N.*

- N4v12 [entre]: *om. N.*
- N4v19 [als]: *om. N.*
- N5v2-N6r19. *The number of large hogsheads for each entry in Table N2 from one to fourteen is omitted.*
- N5v17 Muy [gros]: Muy *N.*
- N6r7 g[r]os: gos *N.*
- N6v15 [dels]: *om. N.*
- N7v4 no[u]: nõ *N* (= non).
- N7v6 [es]: *om. N.*
- N7v12 amella[s]: amella *N.*
- N8r4 [Un]: n *N.*
- N8r6 [U]na: na *N.*
- N8r7 [U]na: na *N.*
- N8r8 [U]na: na *N.*
- N8r9 [U]na: na *N.*
- N9v15 en [ba]s: en sus *N. MS N makes no sense: a rider from within 20 leagues pays 7.5d, while one from more than 8 leagues pays 3.5d. The meaning must be that one from within 8 leagues pays the lower rate.*
- N11v22 [miagla]: viij. d'. *N. The emendation, based on the initial minims in* viij *and* miagla, *makes sense of this passage in its own terms* (de c[ent] .iiij. ... et ... a Lobieras miagla ... et ansi ... de sent iiijo. et [miagla] a Lobieras, *N11v20–2), and restores partial coherence with MS T* (de c[ent], iiij ... a Lubieras, lo c[ent], d' .ij., o la saumada o', *T6v8–10).*
- N12r22 dogan no[u], molas: *N reads* "dogan. non molas" *under Rubric III, Tolls on Commodities at Tarascon and Lubières; cf.* dogas, caissa, escrin, mola de molin, mola de barbier, *N15r2–3, under Rubric VI, Tolls at the Gate of Tarascon;* dogat nou, mola de molin, *T6v16–17, under Rubric I, Tolls on Commodities at Tarascon and Lubières.*
- N12v18 sarrias *N, with the* i *inserted above the line.*
- N13r6 non [son] pont: non pont *N; cf.* non son pont *N16r11. Eye-skip from the* -on *of* non *to that of* son.
- N13r22 s[a] ligua: si ligua *N. Cf.* sa ligua, *N16r17.*
- N13v11 [x]ij. s/: xxij. s/ *N. The correct reading is assured by what follows in N13v12–13: "the money that was levied was put at 12s 8d [152d] per florin of Florence and ... the* blanc *at 8d, and nineteen* blancs *are worth the said florin of Florence" [19 x 8d = 152d].*
- N14r8 fil de Colonha: *cf.* fil de cohanha, T14r18. *Scribal error in N (?); compare Glossary.*
- N14v21 avelana *N.*
- N15v8 dese[n]dent: deseident *N.*

- N15v25–16r1 a / lum de sitrum. *At first glance the phrase looks like* alum de sititim, *which is meaningless; hence the question mark over* sititim / sitrum. *However, one should read not* siti- *but* sitr-, *with the horizontal tick of the* r *displaced, leaving the minim to look like an* i. *The tick is similarly displaced, though not so far, in* traguessan *N15r21 and* estranger *N15v3; the sequence* tri *does not occur elsewhere in MS N. The tick caps the first minim of the* u *in* -um *(not* -tim*). Compare* alum sicrum, *T3v3. In T, the letters* t *and* c *sometimes appear to be identical; in N they do not.*
- N16r22. *The rest of N16r and all of N16v are blank.*

Glossary

The glossary is selective. Each entry gives forms encountered in MSS T and N with folio and line numbers, English meanings with explanations of less familiar terms, and references to Occitan dictionaries. Many entries also provide selected equivalent terms from the Latin registers (MSS A_1PA_2), which may or may not be etyma of the Occitan form. Headwords are provided for nouns in the singular, adjectives in the masculine singular, and verbs in the infinitive, when such forms are lacking in the registers; such headwords are followed by a colon. Occitan words are italicized; translations into French or German are put in quotation marks. In determining the meaning of words, recourse has been made sparingly to context as the registers often provide lists of dissimilar objects that happen to pay the same toll (see Introduction, §4.2).

An asterisk (*) marks a word, a form, or a meaning that was not recognized in *LR, SW,* or *PD*. (Proper nouns, not included in these works, are not so marked.) See *adobar, agibe, arsiqua, arzica, avis, bon, boras, buguet, cairat* (3), *carda, caule, citron, clovel, colier* (2), *corba, dela, denier* (2, 3, 4), *descendre, divisament, dos* (2), *drap* (2), *eiseptat, espiceria, estanh, fil* (2), *fresc, ful, gaida, gran* (2), *grazali(n), grazulo(n), gron, gros* (3), *leon, liga, liome, lu, mattafellon, mais, mastina, metre* (2), *moneda* (3, 4), *montar, naviada, obol, octubre, paniera, peiron, pelanha, pezage* (2, 3), *plagaria, plus, pol, rama, rason, roans, sarcia, sauput, sauputament, seton, sistra, sol* (1), *tornes, torra, tot, travada* (2), *uleta, vestir.* In Latin words, the asterisk marks forms not listed by Du Cange or Niermeyer.

The alphabetical order includes index entries for Animals (1), products of; Animals (2), types of; Building materials; Cities and regions; Cloth, materials; Clothing, garments; Coins, money, currency; Dyes; Fees; Foods; Furniture, utensils, containers, tools; Measures; Metals, minerals, chemicals; Passengers; Payment in kind; Plants and plant products; Ships (1), parts of; Ships (2), types of; Spices and medicines; Tollhouses; Tollkeeper; Wood and wood products.

abre, see *arbre*

acier, N7v15, N14r17; *assier*, T14r33, T15r23. Steel (*LR* 2:20, *DAO* 166, *DAOS* 76). Med. Lat. *aciarium, acer-* (Niermeyer); abl. *ascerio* (Baratier 385).

Adaul, N6v9, N6v18, N7r14. Saint-Andiol (canton Orgon, arrondissement Arles, Bouches-du-Rhône), site of a tollhouse, *pedagium* (Pécout 285, s.v. Sanctus Andeolus). Orgon and Saint-Andiol were situated in the *viguerie* of Tarascon (Hébert 1979, 81; Pécout 2010, fig. 29). Lat. *Andeolus, Antiolus*; *forma et modus pedagii de Orgono et Sancti Antiol* (Baratier 393, Guérard 1:lxxxix).

adobar, past part., masc. pl. (*cuors*) *adobatz o non adobatz* T3r17, (*cuers*) *adobas o non adobas* N7r23. To prepare (*PD* 7, Pansier 3:5); *to tan, "to convert (skin or hide) into leather by steeping in an infusion of an astringent bark, as that of the oak" (*OED*). *Adobatz o non adobatz*, T3r17; *adobas o non adobas,* N7r23. Tanned or not tanned (raw). "Le cuir tanné (*adobat*)" (Bourilly 1928, 80). Lat. *aptare*, to prepare, past part. *aptatus*; abl. pl. masc. *coriis abtamptis ... coriis non abtatis* (Baratier 385), *coriis abtamptis ... non aptatis* (Guérard 1:lxxxiii).

adonc, N13v4. Then (*PD* 7).

***agibe**: pl. *agibes* N7v13, N14r18, N15v14. A type of raisin (dried grape). *Agibis*, "variété de raisins secs" (Pansier 3:6; Stempel 1996, 4:302); "variété de raisin blanc ... que l'on fait sécher" (Mistral 1:47). *Agibit*, "raisin sec" (Alibert 83); "fruit séché sur l'arbre, très-mur; on le dit particulièrement d'une espèce de raisin à gros grains" (Honnorat 1:50–1). *FEW* 19:201b. It. *zibibbo* (Pegolotti 1936, 434).

agriota, N14v17; pl. *agriotas*, T7r11, N12r13. Sour cherry. "Griotte, cerise aigre" (*PD* 11). Lat. *aigriota* (= Occ.); abl. pl. *aigriotis* (Baratier 387).

aigua, T6r12, N15v1, N16r14; *aiga*, N15r24; *aygua*, N4r22, N5r14, N10r18, N11v6, N13r13. Water. *Aiga* (*PD* 12). *Peage de l'–*, N13r13, N16r14. Tollhouse by the river. *Per –*, N10r18. By river.

aigual: fem. pl. *aiguals*, N4v11. *Egal, ai-*, (*PD* 134). *Per aiguals*, equally.

aills, see *alh*

aisi (1), N13r4. Here (*PD* 13).

aisi (2), *aisins*, see *ausi*

aizina: *aisina*, N12r3, N15r1, N15r5, N15r7; pl. *aizinas*, T6v28; *aisinas*, N11v19, N12r4, N12v5; *aysinas*, N11v19, N12r3. Utensil (*PD* 13, Alibert 88). – *de fusta*, N11v19, N15r1. Utensil of wood. – *de terra*, T6v28,

N12r3, N12r4, N15r7. Utensil of clay, earthenware. – *de veire*, N12v5, N15r5. Utensil of glass.

Alaman, T9r8, N10r20. German. Lat. *Alamandus* (Baratier 387).

Alap, T3v2, N15v25; *Alaf*, N7v2. Aleppo (Arabic *Halab*), city in Syria. See *alum d'Alap*

albire, T5v5. Judgment (*PD* 15). *A l'albire del peagier*, in the judgment of the tollkeeper; "à l'appréciation du péager" (Bondurand 143n3). Lat. *ad arbitrium pedejarii* (Baratier 387). Cf. *plaser*

albre, see *arbre*

alh: pl. *alhs*, T7v8, T13v21, T14v8, T15r1, N14v24; *aills*, N12v2. Garlic bulb (*PD* 16, *DAO* 425, *DAOS* 354). Lat. *alium*; abl. pl. *alleis*, "aulx" (Baratier 388).

aluda: pl. *aludas*, T4v4, N8r14, N14v3. Sheepskin (*PD* 17), of quality suitable for making parchment. "Peaux dont on fait le parchemin" (Bondurand 141n2). Lat. *aluta*; abl. pl. *aludis*, influenced by Occ. (Baratier 386).

alum, T3v2, T3v3, T4v3, T14r15, N7v1, N7v2, N7v3, N8r14, N8v14, N14r4, N14v3, N15v21, N15v25; *alun*, N15v25. Alum (*PD* 17, *DAO* 158, *DAOS* 65), "an astringent mineral salt, typically occurring as colourless or whitish crystals, that is used as a mordant for dyeing, in tanning, for sizing paper and fireproofing materials, in water purification, and in medicine (esp. as a styptic)" (*OED*). Lat. *alumen,* Med. Lat. **alupnum*; abl. *alupno* (Baratier 386); abl. *alump*, *alup*, influenced by Occ. (see following entries).

alum d'Alap, T3v2, N15v25; *alum d'Alaf*, N7v2 (*DAO* 158, *DAOS* 66). Alum from Aleppo. Exported from that city but not produced there; it "came perhaps from Edessa or from even farther afield. Aleppo alum is probably identical with Roche alum" (Singer 1948, 88; see also *alum de roca*). Aleppo alum is now used in deodorant spray. Lat. abl. *alupno ... de Alamp* (Baratier 386, Guérard 1:lxxxiv); *alup de Alamp* (Baratier 396, 399, Guérard 1:xcv), *alup de Alomp* (Guérard 1:xci).

alum de cico tonip, N7v3. A form of alum; probably *alum sicrum* (which see) in MS T, sugar alum. Or *cico* might be a corruption of *chisico*, "Cyzican alum ... from an island in the Sea of Marmora [in Turkey, between the Black Sea and the Aegean], presumably the peninsula of Cyzicus, now Kapu Dagh" (Pegolotti 1936, 411, s.v. Cassico).

alum de pluma, T3v3, N7v1; *alun de pluma*, N15v25 (*DAO* 158, *DAOS* 65). Feather alum or halotrichite, "a mineral consisting of a hydrated sulphate of iron and aluminium, occurring in yellowish-white, fibrous masses" (*OED*). Lat. abl. *alupno de pluma* (Baratier 386, Guérard 1:lxxxiv), *alump de pluma* (Guérard 1:xcv), *alup de pluma* (Baratier 396, 399, Guérard 1:xci. It. *allume di piuma*, "plume alum, the finest kind of alum" (Edler 27).

alum de roca, N7v2; *de roqua*, N15v21, N15v25 (*DAO* 158, *DAOS* 65). Rock alum, "crystalline alum of high purity, *esp.* that prepared from Italian alunite" (*OED*).

alum de Volcan, T4v3; – *de Bolcam*, N14v3, – *de Boulcan*, N8r14 (*DAO* 158, *DAOS* 66). Alum from Vulcano, an island north of Sicily (Singer 1948, 58); used today in deodorant. Lat. *alup de Bolca, Bolcan, Bolcano, Balcano* (Baratier 386, 393, Guérard 1:lxxvi, lxxviii, lxxix, lxxx, xci, xcvi).

alum sicrum, T3v3 (*DAO* 158); *alum de sitrum*, N15v25 (see Textual Note). Sugar alum. In view of Lat. abl. *alupno ... de sucrino* (Baratier 386, Guérard 1:lxxxiv), Thomas (1891, 420) suggested "alun *zuccharino*, comme disent les Italiens, c'est-à-dire en forme de pain de sucre," in the form of a sugarloaf, "a moulded conical mass of hard refined sugar (now rarely made)" (*OED*). Cf. Occ. *sicrepan*, "sucre en pain" (Pansier 3:156); *alum securum* (*DAO* 159, *DAOS* 66); It. *allume zuccherino*, "Sugar Alum ... this material is said to have been manufactured by heating alum with rose-water and white of egg" (Pegolotti 1936, 412). Levy accepted Thomas's suggestion (*SW* 1:53).

amella: pl. *amellas*, T7r1, T13v26, T14r29, T15r17, N12r7, N14r15, N14v20; *amella[s]*, N7v12. Almond. *Amela* (*PD* 18, *DAO* 307, *DAOS* 206). Lat. *amygdala*; nom. pl. *amigdale* (Baratier 387), abl. pl. *amigdalis* (385). See also *mela*

amon, T9r9; *amont*, N1v24, N4r22, N13v21, etc.; *en amont*, T11v24, T12r15. Upstream (*PD* 19). Lat. *superius* (Baratier 386, Guérard 1:lxxxiv).

Angles, see *Engles*

anhel, N7v21; pl. *anhels*, T15r27; *anels*, T14r27. Lamb (*PD* 21). Lat. *agnus*; gen. pl. *agnorum* (Baratier 388).

anhina (1): pl. *aninas*, T3v33. *Lamb. *Pels d'aninas*, T3v33 (paid 21d at Tarascon), is equivalent in meaning to *pels d'anhel*, N7v21 (paid 19d at Tarascon: the change in rate is standard), which implies that *anhina* here is synonymous with *anhel*, lamb. Cf. *pel anina*, "peau d'agneau" (*DAO* 547, *DAOS* 471).

anhina (2): pl. *anhinas*, N15v11. Lambskin. "Peau d'agneau" (PD 22, *DAO* 547, *DAOS* 471). *Carga ... d'anhinas*, N15v11. Load of lambskins. Lat.

agninus, of a lamb; abl. pl. masc. *agninis* (Baratier 385, Guérard 1:lxxxiii), *anginis* (Baratier 388, Guérard 1:lxxvi, lxxxi, lxxxvi, lxxxvii, xci).

Not *auvias,* "comme *ouviho*, brebis" (Bondurand 139n8). Meyer (1891, 482) suggested *anujas*, Mod. Occ. *anouge*, "agneau de l'année," i.e., *anotge*, "agneau de l'année" (*PD* 22), yearling lamb, the biblical *agnum anniculum.*

anhis, T14r26; *anhnis*, T15r26. Lambswool (*PD* 22).

Animals (1), products of: see *aluda, anhis, anina, carn, cera, cohanha, cordovan, cuer, lana, moutonina, pel, pelharia, pelisaria, pergamin, vair (1), vel*

Animals (2), types of: *anhel, aze, bestia, boc, buou, cabra, cabret, cabrit, camel, caval, cavalcadura, conil, egua, feda, isime, leon, mastina, mouton, mul, mula, ors, porc, rossa, rossin, veul*

aninas, see *anhina*

anis, T3v18, N14r19; *anise*, T14r28. Anise (*LR* 2:89, *DAO* 438, *DAOS* 373).

ansi, see *ausi*

antenna, T5r[38], T5r[42], T13v4; *entena*, N10v8, N10v12, N10v15, N10v18, N10v21. Yard supporting a lateen sail, which is "a triangular sail suspended by a long yard at an angle of about 45 degrees to the mast" (*OED*). "By the thirteenth century, the yards of large sailing ships could weigh up to 6.5 metric tonnes. To manage such yards and the huge sails hung from them, some over 800 square metres in area, required many men and complex block and tackle systems" (Pryor 1994, 71); for such tackle, see *orsa*. Fr. *antenne* (*PD* 22, Jal 145). It. *antenna* (Reale Accademia d'Italia 1937, 35). Lat. *antena* (Baratier 386).

antic, T14r3. Former, sometime (*PD* 22). Lat. *antiquus* (Baratier 388).

apelar: pres. 3rd pers. sg. *apella*, N6v14; pl. *apelan*, N10r3, N12v14. To call (*PD* 23).

aportar: pres. 3rd pers. sg. *aporta*, N7r6. To take (*PD* 25).

aquel (1), N1v19, N2r1, N2r13, N13v4; pl. *aquels*, N9v25, N13v7; *aquelos*, N2r4, N4v12; *aquellos*, N12r24. Demonstrative pronoun. That, that one ("ce," *PD* 26).

aquel (2), N13r4; pl. *aquelos*, N5v4; fem. *aquella*, N16r6. Demonstrative adj. That (*PD* 26). See also *elos*

aquest, T15v4. Demonstrative adj. This (*PD* 26).

aqui, T5v5; *aquei,* T9v23. There (*PD* 26). Lat. *ibi* (Baratier 381). *D'aqui en avalle*, T5v5. From there (that amount) down. *D'aquei ensus*, T9v23. From there (that amount) up.

aras, T12r12, N2r3. Now. *Ar, ara, -as* (PD 26). Lat. *modo* (Baratier 381).

arbre, N10v1, N10v3; *abre*, T5r[33]; *albre*, T5r[32], T13v1. Tree (*DAO* 203, *DAOS* 100). – *de nau*, T13v1, N10v3. Mast (*PD* 26), serving to support either sails or the hawser by which the ship was towed upstream (Rossiaud 2002, 2:20). Lat. *arbor*; abl. *albore*, influenced by Occ. (Baratier 386).

arca, T6v12, T13v30, T14v19. Chest (*PD* 27). Lat. *archa* (Baratier 388).

argent (1), T8r7, N5v4, N12v9, N13r15, N13v21, N16r16. Silver (*LR* 2:119, *DAO* 162, *DAOS* 70). – *fin*, N16r16. Pure silver. *Tornes d'–*, N5v4, N13r15, N13v21, N16r16. Silver tournois (coins).

argent (2), N4r15, N5r5, N6r22, N6v1, N13v10. Money (*LR* 2:119). Lat. *argentum* (Baratier 386).

argento vivo (It.), T4r15. Quicksilver (on the form, see Textual Notes). It. *argento vivo* (Battaglia 1:645; Pegolotti 1936, 413), in contrast with Occ. *argen viu* (*LR* 119, *DAO* 165, *DAOS* 75). Lat. *argentum vivum*; gen. *argenti vivi* (Baratier 396, Guérard 1:xcii, xciv), abl. *argento vivo* (Baratier 396, Guérard 1:xci). Lat. blended with Occ.: acc. *argent vivum,* abl. *argent vivo* (Baratier 385).

Arle, N15v10. Arles (Bouches-du-Rhône).

armari: pl. *armaris*, N12r21. Armoire. Fr. "armoire" (*PD* 28). "Grand meuble, ordinairement plus haut que large, garni de tablettes et fermé par une ou plusieurs portes, destiné à renfermer les objets de ménage, le linge, les vêtements" (*TLFi*).

arribage, T8v21. Fee for unloading cargo. *Aribatge*, "droit d'arrivage" (*PD* 28); Fr. *arrivage*, "droit pour abord et débarquement des marchandises, droit d'aborder dans un port" (*TLFi*). The following two entries concern animals brought to Tarascon and unloaded there, in contrast to preceding entries on animals being shipped past the town.

Not "arrivage, Lieu où l'on arrive, où l'on aborde. Point de transbordement, port" (Rossiaud 2002, 2:28).

***arsiqua**, N12v12. Sheepsbelly (?): "Sheeps Belly, or Intrels [entrails], the puddings called strings, or Rope," citation dated 1688 (*OED* s.v. sheep, *n.*). *Archican*, "nom qu'on donne aux boyaux du mouton et du boeuf, particulièrement à la panse" (Honnorat 1:137; Mistral 1:124; *FEW* 22/2:142b). Context suggests that this *arsiqua* is either edible entrails, like butter (*burre*, the preceding item), or mineral ochre (see *arzica*), like iron (*obrage faç de ferre*, the following one).

***arzica**, T8r10. Ochre, "any of various natural earthy materials or clays which are rich in iron oxides and vary in colour from light yellow to deep orange-red or brown; a pigment made from such a material" (*OED*). Med. Lat. *archica* (Du Cange 1:363), *arzisca* (Guérard 1:lxxxxix); "terre jaune, sorte d'ocre" (Baratier 399n1). This meaning is confirmed by Lat. *excepta archica et sulfure* (Baratier 400, Guérard 1:xcvii); but Baratier (400n1) suspects an error for *argent*. Italian *arzicco* or *arzica*, "a yellow pigment ... either yellow lake from weld, or a yellow earth yielding ochreous pigment, most likely the first" (Pegolotti 1936, 413). Bondurand reads *zozita* (149n4), corrected to *arzica* by Pansier (5:161). See also *arsiqua*

ase, *ases*, see *aze*

assaber, T7v28, T8v7, T14v20, N4r18, N4r25. Abbreviated form of *so es assaber*, that is to say (*SW* 7:402): *so es a saber*, N5r10, N5r23, N6v3, N15r22. Lat. *scilicet* (Baratier 386, 388, Guérard 1:lxxxvii), *sciendum* (Guérard 1:lxxxvi).

assier, see *acier*

aur, T8r14, N12v9, N13r19, N16r18. Gold (*PD* 33, *DAO* 161, *DAOS* 69). – *de xxiiii cayras*, N16r18. Twenty-four carat gold. Lat. *aurum* (Baratier 386).

aura, T6r13, N11v7. Wind (*PD* 33). Lat. *aura*; gen. *aure* (Baratier 386).

ausi, N11v21, N12v17, N15v6; *aussi*, N9r22; *aissi*, T98v15, T11v24, T12v23; *aysin*, N11v14; *aisins*, N5r5, N5r15, N5r16, N16r21. MS N blends the cognates of Fr. *ainsi*, thus, and *aussi*, also:

(1) In a like manner, in the same way, so, thus: *aysin*, N11v14; *aisins*, N5r5, N5r16; *ansi*, N12v17.

(2) As, as much as: *aissi quant*, T98v15, T11v24, T12v23. Just as: *aissi quant*, T12r9.

(3) Also: *aisins*, N16r21; *ausi*, N15v6, N11v21; *aussi*, N9r22; *per aisins*, N16r21.

PD does not recognize the forms in *au-* or the meaning "also": *aisi, aisins, ansins*, "ainsi" (*PD* 13). Cf. *ensins*, "ainsi" (Pansier 3:71); *aussi*, "aussi, pareillement" (Honnorat 1:189, Mistral 1:184).

aval, N1v23, N8v15; *avalle* (It. form), T5v5. Down. *aval*, "en bas" (*PD* 35). *d'aval*, N1v23, N8v15. From downstream. *En avalle*, T5v5. Down, downward (below a girth of four palms, speaking of a yard). Cf. archaic It. *avale*, now (Battaglia 1:864). Lat. *inferius* (Baratier 386, Guérard 1:lxxxiv).

avelana: pl. *avellanas*, T7r3; *avelana[s]*, N14v21; *avelanes*, N12r8. Hazelnut (*PD* 36, *DAO* 301, *DAOS* 198). Lat. *abellana, avel-*; nom. pl. *avellane* (Baratier 387).

aver, n.m., T13r6. Goods (*PD* 36).

Avinhon, T13r15, T14r9, T4v17; *Avignon*, T4v25; *Avigno*, T3r7; *Avihon*, N15v17; *Avingno*, N7r17. Avignon (Vaucluse).

avis, N10v23. *Judgment. "Croyance, semblant" (*LR* 5:536); "avis, opinion" (Pansier 3:18). For "judgement" in Fr. but not Occ., *FEW* 14:535a.

aygua, see *aigua*

aysina, see *aizina*

aze: *ase*, N9r25; pl. *ases*, N9v8; *azes*, T8v16, T8v26. Ass (*PD* 37, *DAOS* 558). Lat. *asinus* (Baratier 387, 388).

bacon, T6v19, T13v30, T14v23, N15r3. Washbasin (?). "Bac, auge," vat, trough (*PD* 38); Ger. "Trog, Mulde," trough, basin (*SW* 1:118). "Vanne de moulin," sluice gate of a mill (Bondurand 146n13). Med. Lat. *baco* (Niermeyer); abl. *bacono* (Baratier 388, Guérard 1:xcvii), *baccone* (Guérard 1:xcviii), *baccono* (xcix), pl. *baconis* (xcii). "En général bacco veut dire lard, mais ici il s'agit probablement du bas latin: *baccinus*, en provençal *bacho* ou *bacholo*: dans le sens de cuvier à lessive, bassin, auge" (Baratier 388n3).

banaston, N11v25; pl. *banastons*, N11v25. Hamper. "Mannequin, panier en forme de hotte" (*PD* 40).

baral, see *barral*

barbier, T6v18, T13v31, N12r23, N15r3. Barber (*PD* 41), surgeon (Fourquin and Rigaud 1994, 41).

barca, N11v4, N11v8; *barcha*, T6r15. Bark, small ship; also applied to any sailing vessel. "Barque" (*PD* 41). For Baratier and Reynaud (1951, 743–4), the *barque* was the smallest and most numerous type of ship, for example the *caupol* (see *caupolada*). "Un peu tout ce qui flotte; au moins dans la langue commune qui applique barque aux plus gros navires de commerce" (Rossiaud 2002, 2:37; cf. Fourquin and Rigaud 1994, 41). Lat. *barca* (Baratier 386).

barral, N8v17, N8v18; *baral*, T4v33, T5r1; pl. *barrals*, T13v36, N8v22, N14v25; *barals*, T5r4, T6v3, T14v11. Keg. "Baril" (*PD* 42), a liquid measure that varied by town from 40 to 50 litres (Rossiaud 2002, 2:212). Used to contain wine, passim; empty keg, T6v3, T13v36, T14v11, N14v25. The larger recipient was the *bota*, butt (which see). Med. Lat. *barrale*, *barralus* (Du Cange 1:588), *barral* (Niermeyer); acc. *barral* (= Occ.) (*barral de vino, medium barral)* (Baratier 386); abl. *barralo* (386); abl. pl. *barrals* (= Occ.) (388).

bas, N10v23; *[ba]s*, N9v15 (see Textual Notes). *En bas*, down.

bastart: fem. pl. *bastardas*, T6r2, N11r20. Irregular. "Bâtard; faux, irrégulier; d'une largeur moyenne" (*PD* 43). Med. Lat. *bastardus* (Niermeyer); abl. pl. *bastardis*, "grosses" (Baratier 386).

Belcaire, T8v4, N5r15, etc.; *Belcayre*, T8r16, N4r21, etc.; *Bellcayre*, T12r20; *Belcare*, T16r13; *Belcari*, T15v15. Beaucaire (Gard). Med. Lat. *Belliquadrum, Bellicadrum*; abl. *Bellicadro* (Baratier 386).

be(nque) [?], N16r margin. Currency exchange (?). If the MS reads *benque* (and not *beugus, bengns, beague*, and so on, other possible readings that I cannot interpret), perhaps this word is a form, which I find attested nowhere else, of Fr. *banque*, bank. Occ. *banca*, "banc, siège" (*PD* 40), had the sense "comptoir" (Pansier 3:20, Mistral 1:218), "trafic d'argent" (Honorat 1:223). This meaning would refer to the adjacent text, N16r13: *Totas las monedas que se levon als peages ...* OFr. *banque* (Godefroy 8:286); Cat. *banca*, pl. *banques* (Faraudo); It. *banco*, "the stall or shop of a money-changer or banker, a bank" (Edler 40). It. *banco, banca* has variants with stressed *e* (*benc*, etc.), cited by Pfister 1979, Germanismi I.3.398, I.3.433.

On meaning, cf. English *bank*, from French *banque*, which is from Italian *banca*: "The original meaning 'shelf, bench' ... was extended in Italian to that of 'tradesman's stall, counter, money-changer's table ... whence 'money-shop, bank,' a use of the word which passed, with the trade of banking, from Italy into other countries ... –The table or counter of a money-changer or dealer in money.... –The shop, office, or place of business of a money-dealer" (*OED*).

bestia, T8r18, T8v18, etc., N12v7; pl. *bestias*, T8v22, etc. Animal (*PD* 46, *DAO* 542, *DAOS* 490). – *grossa*, N9r24, N15r9; *bestias grossas*, T8v12, T14v30, N9v5. Large animal. – *menuda*, T14v28, N15r10; *bestias menudas*, T14v28, N9v2, N9v9. Small animal. Lat. *bestia*, which could mean "horse": *bestie brave, antequam equitetur*, "unbroken animals, before they are ridden" (Baratier 388, Guérard 1:lxxxvii).

bestia cargada, T14v15, N14v15, N14v25; *bestia carguada*, T14v4, etc. Loaded animal. Toll may be calculated per animal, loaded (*bestia cargada, lo fais de una bestia*) with merchandise (salt, fruit, vegetables, domestic objects, grain, furs), or per animal for sale or recently sold (horse, slave, mastiff, ox, ass, mule). The *bestia cargada* and the *saumada* are both applied to measure grains, fruit, vegetables, and domestic objects, but only the *bestia cargada* to salt, which is more often measured in hogsheads (*mog*). See also *carga, saumada*

biga: pl. *bigas*, N11r18. Long, thin pole. "Les bigues sont sans aucun doute les *grandes pertegues rondes* des tarifs de Beaucaire et Tarascon (ADV [Archives départementales Vaucluse] 1 J 163) ... Poteaux très longs et minces (et non poutres comme l'écrivent Jal et Pansier), les bigues sont employées dans la construction des engins et des échafaudages; certaines doivent servir d'antennes" (Rossiaud 2002, 2:57). "Forte pièce de bois de sapin dont on se sert seule ou ajustée avec une autre pour soulever de gros fardeaux, à l'aide de palans attachés au sommet de ladite pièce" (Jal 291 s.v. "bigue").

Not a small beam, "petite poutre longue et grèle, poutrelle" (*PD* 47).

blanc, N13r21, N13r24, N13v5, N13v6, N13v12, N13v18; pl. *blancs*, N13v12, N13v17. Blank, "a small French coin, originally of silver, but afterwards of copper" (*OED*). *Blanc* (*PD* 47; Pansier 3:24; Rolland 1956, 84). Counted as 8d 8 grains (8.33d), N13v5; equal to five *patacs*, N13v6; counted as 8d before 1330, N13v12; nineteen *blancs* at 8d made a florin of Florence at 152d, N13v17–19.

blanquet, N7v10. White woollen cloth. "Drap blanc" (*PD* 47). "Drap de laine blanc" (Enlart 1902-16, 3:541).

blat, T4v12, T4v17, T4v23, etc.; N14v11; pl. *blas*, N8v1. Grain (*PD* 48, *DAO* 368, *DAOS* 273). Med. Lat. *bladum* (Niermeyer); gen. *bladi* (Baratier 385), abl. *blado* (Baratier 388).

bled (Fr.), N8r margin. Grain. The spelling *bled* survived into the eighteenth century (*TLFi* s.v. *blé*).

boc: pl. *bocs*, N9v3. Male goat (*PD* 48).

bon, N13r19. Good. *bon aur*, N13r19. Good (*not debased) gold.

***boras**, N14r21. Borax (*DAO* 160, *DAOS* 68), "a native salt; the acid borate of sodium" (*OED*). *Boràs* (Alibert 169), *boraytz* (*FEW* 19:32b).

borrassa: pl. *borrassas*, T4r3. Coarse woollen cloth (*PD* 51). Med. Lat. *borrachia* (Du Cange 1:709); abl. pl. *borrassis* (Baratier 385), *borrasciis* (Guérard 1:xcii).

bota, T4v33, T5r5, N8v15, N15r2; *botta*, T4v32, etc.; pl. *botas*, T5r1, T5r2, N8v18, N9r3, etc. Butt, cask. "Tonneau, baril" (*PD* 52). Used to contain wine, passim; alum, N8v15. Empty butt, N15r2. – *grossa o petita*, N8v15.

Butt, large or small. At Lyon the *bota* of wine held 465 litres, but in other towns of the Midi it varied from 4 to 17 *barrals* (which see), or kegs (Rossiaud 2002, 2:212). "450 litres environ" (Baratier and Reynaud 1951, 904). "À Lisle [L'Isle-sur-la-Sorgue, Vaucluse (?)] en 1394 la *bota* de vin contenait 4 salmées ou 800 litres" (Pansier 5:164). "Tonneau ...; unité de volume équivalent à ca. 9,5 qtx soit ca. 0,36 m3" (Fourquin and Rigaud 1994, 58).

botta, see *bota*

Boulcan, see *Volcan*

bresilh, T14r34, N15v15; *brezilh*, T15r25; *brecilh*, T3v30; *bresil*, N7v10; *bresill*, N14r13. Brazil wood (*PD* 54, *DAO* 463, *DAOS* 400), "the hard brownish-red wood of an East Indian tree ... from which dyers obtain a red colour. After the discovery of the New World, the name was extended and gradually transferred to the similar wood of a South American species (*C. echinata*), which has given its name to the land of Brazil" (*OED*). Med. Lat. *brasile, bresile* (Niermeyer); abl. *bresil* (= Occ.) (Baratier 388).

broc: pl. *brocs*, T6v6, T13v35, T14v10, N11v18, N14v25. Pitcher (*PD* 55). Med. Lat. *brochus* (Niermeyer); gen. pl. *brocorum* (Delebecque 3:54; *brecorum* Martin-Portier 2:46), abl. pl. *brocquis* (Baratier 377), *brocs* (= Occ.) (Baratier 388).

brocat: pl. *brocatz*, T6v25. Jug. "Espèce de grande cruche" (*PD* 55). "Vases à robinet," pots with a spigot (Bondurand 146n16).

brun: pl. *bruns*, T3r13, N7r21, N15v20. Brown woollen cloth. "Drap brun" (*PD* 55). "Brun, drap de laine" (Enlart 1902-16, 3:545). "Autre drap grossier de couleur brune, comme la *bure* ou le *cadis*" (Bourilly 1928, 43n16).

buguet (?): pl. **buetz*, T14v21. Perhaps a wedge used in assembling staves into a barrel, or to prevent a barrel from rolling. *Buguet*, "petit bois" (*LR* 2:240). *Buget, buyet*, "mur de refend, cloison [Eng. partition]; variété de cairon ["pierre molle qui sert à bâtir, et que l'on peut acheter toute taillée en petits cubes" (Littré)]; blochet [Eng. "block, stop block"] ou coyer ["morceau de bois qui porte sur la partie inférieure des chevrons et sur la saillie de l'entablement, pour former l'avance de l'égout d'un toit" (Littré)]" (Pansier 3:30). *De dogan (so es assaber de xxv dogas an los buetz)*, T14v21, a set of staves (that is, twenty-five staves with the wedges). Med. Lat. *buga*, "minutum lignum. Gall. buchette" (Du Cange 1:770), stick, bit of dry wood; abl. pl. *bugis* in *de donga sciliget de xxv dogilis cum bugis* (Guérard 1:lxxxvi); *donga, scilicet de XXV dogis cum bugis*, "douve de tonneau avec du bois neuf" (Baratier 388). Cf. *unum cadum* *de salmata cum uno buey,* "un tonneau d'une salmée avec son support" (Pansier 5:165, s.v. *buei*); *buey*, "partie en fer d'un grand coffre" (*FEW* 22/2:106a).

Building materials: *cairon, lausa, mola, peira, teule, veire*. See also Wood and wood products.

buire, T8r9; *burre*, N12v12. Butter (*PD* 56, Alibert 185). Lat. *buturum.*

buou, T4r32, N7r22, N8r4, N9r25, N14r7, N15v20; pl. *buous*, T6r5, T8v26, N9v8, N11r23; *buos*, T8v16. Ox (*DAOS* 494). *Bou* (*PD* 52). *Cuer de –*, N8r4; *pel de –*, N14r7, N15v20. Oxhide. Lat *bos*; abl. *bove* (Baratier 377).

burre, see *buire*

c., c', see *cent*

cabas: pl. *cabasses*, N12r1, N12v18. Plaited shopping basket (*PD* 57).

cabra: pl. *cabras*, T8v17, T8v26, N9v3, N9v10. Goat (*PD* 58). N9v3. Female goat, in contrast to *boc*.

cabret, T3v32. Kid, young goat (*PD* 58). *Pels de cabret*, T3v32 (paying 21d at Tarascon), is equivalent in meaning to *pels de cabris*, N7v21 (paying 19d at Tarascon; the change in rate is standard). Lat. *haedus*, *edus*; gen. pl. *edorum* (Baratier 385, 388).

cabrit, N15v12; pl. *cabritz*, T14r27, T15r28; *cabris*, N7v21. Kid, young goat (*PD* 58). *Pels de –*, N7v21, N15v12. Kidskin. See also *cabret.*

çafarame (It.; mod. It. zafferano), T3r28. Saffron. This spelling recurs in an early fifteenth-century Italian cookbook, among other forms that include *çaffarana, çaffarano, saffarame* (Boström [1985], A 2:3, p. 5, and glossary, p. 120), and, without the cedilla, in Malacarne 2000, 296. *Çafarame* at T3r28, taxed at 29.5d for one *carga* (four quintals), is synonymous with *safran* at N7v4, taxed at 30.50d for one *carga*. The increase from 29.5d in MS T to 30.5d in MS N is standard at Tarascon. See also *safran*

Read as *tafarame* by Bondurand and glossed as "taffetas," with the comment "de *tafatanus*" (p. 138n5). "La forme *tafarame* est bien extraordinaire, s'il s'agit réellement de taffetas, comme le pense l'éditeur" (Thomas 1891, 420).

caida, see *gaida*

cairas, see *cairat* (2) and (3)

cairat (1), adj.: *quairat*, T5v15, T13v6; *cayrat*, N11r4. Squared.

cairat (2), n.: *quairat*, T5v33; *carrat*, N11r17; pl. *quairatz*, T5v35, T6r5; *cairas,* N11r22, N11r23, stressed *cairás*, the late form of the past participle plural, assured by masculine *cairás redons*, N11r22. Large squared timber (*PD* 58; Rossiaud 2002, 2:285). "Planche" (Fourquin and Rigaud 1994, 79). *Cairas redons*, N11r22. Round squared timbers, perhaps timber suitable for squaring, but not yet squared (?); or *cairat* here may mean "la plus grosse pièce de l'antenne, celle qui, liée à la penne, se rapproche du pont (et de la proue) du navire par son extrémitée inférieure" (Rossiaud 2002, 2:78–9, s.v. *carra, cayrat*). *Quairatz de roans*, T5v35. Squared logs of timber from Le Royans. *Quairat de saisel*, T5v33. Squared log of timber from Le Seyssel. Lat. *quadratus*; abl. *cadrato* (Martin-Portier 2:48); *cairato*, pl. *cairatis*, influenced by Occ. (Baratier 386).

cairat (3): n., pl. *cayras* (stressed *cayrás*), N13r19, N16r18. *Carat, the measure of fineness in gold. *Xxiiii cayras*, N13r19, N16r18. Twenty-four carat (gold). "L'or parfaitement pur serait à 24 carats" (Honnorat 1:414, s.v. *carat*).

cairon: pl. *cairons*, T7v20. Quarry stone (*PD* 59).

caissa, N15r2; *cayssa*, N12r21. Chest. *Caisa* (*PD* 59).

camel, N7r22, N8r4, N14r7, N15v20; pl. *camels*, T14r16. Camel (*PD* 61). *Pel ... de –*, N14r7, N15v20. Camelhide. Lat. *camelus*; gen. pl. *camelorum* (*coriis camelorum,* Guérard 1:xci).

cana: pl. *cannas*, T4r11, T14r23; *canes*, N7v20. Cane, a liquid measure used for oil, etc. (*PD* 62). Equal to 9.019 litres at Tarascon in 1841 (Zupko 1978, 35). Mod. Occ. *cano*, "mesure de capacité usitée pour l'huile, valant un dékalitre, plus ou moins selon le pays" (Mistral 1:447). Med. Lat. *canna* (Niermeyer), a measure of honey and oil; *canna melis et olei* (Baratier 390, Guérard 1:lxxxviii). *Cana* also referred to a measure of length; see *corda* (2).

canape, T3v13, T14r24; *canabe*, T15r23; *canebe*, N7v16, N14r19, N15v11. Hemp. *Cambe* (*PD* 61), *canebe* (*DAO* 452, *DAOS* 391). Lat. *cannabis*; gen. *canapis* (Martiñ-Portier 247), abl. *cannebe* (Baratier 385, 388), *canebe* (Guérard 1:lxxxvii).

canebe, see *canape*

canela, T15r15, N7v16; *canella*, T3v19. Cinnamon (*PD* 62). Med. Lat. *cannella* (Niermeyer); abl. *cannella* (Baratier 385, 388), *cannello* (Baratier 388); synonymous with *cinnamomum*, gen. *cinamomi* (Martin-Portier 2:41).

canes, see *cana*

capelan, N9v20. Chaplain (*PD* 65).

capitol, N12v21. Chapter (*PD* 65).

carbon, T7r24, T13v23, N12r18, N14v23. Charcoal (*PD* 67). Lat. *carbo*, Med. Lat. **carbonum* (Martin-Portier 2:45); gen. *carboni* (Guérard 1:lxxxvi), abl. *carbono* (Baratier 387, 388).

carda, N14r20. *Molleton, swanskin, "a fine thick kind of flannel" (*OED*). "Carde" (Pansier 3:36). "Carde (*carda*), sorte de molleton" (Enlart 1902-16, 3:547). "Molleton" seems rather more likely in context than "card, carding-comb," Fr. "peigne de cardeur" (*PD* 67), "an implement for raising a nap on cloth, consisting of teasel-heads set in a frame" (*OED*).

carga (1), T3v2, N7r17, etc.; *cargua* T3r7, etc. Load, cargo. "Charge" (*PD* 68). It is often uncertain whether a given usage refers simply to a load (1) or to the conventional measure (2). "Charge, fardeau, faix, ce que porte ou peut porter un homme ou un animal ... aussi une mesure de convention" (Honnorat 1:419).

carga (2), T4v12, T14v1, N8v1; *cargua*, T14r20, T14v3, T15r29. A conventional measure used as the basis for calculating tolls; defined for each commodity, most often as four quintals (about 180 kilograms), or as a certain number of *cannas* of oil, *sestiers* of grain, *costas* (bars) of iron, *saumadas* of grain (T4v17, N8v2), or pieces of other commodities (bolts of cloth, hides, objects of glass). *Carga*, "charge: unité de poids de 4 quintaux" (Rossiaud 2002, 2:77). "Entre deux et quatre quintaux" (Baratier and Reynaud 1951, 902). See also *bestia cargada, saumada*

cargar: pres. 3rd pers. sg. *carga*, N4r21, etc.; *cargua*, T12r7; pl. *cargan*, N15v7; past part., masc., *cargat*, N9r11, etc.; *carguat*, T4v17, T4v25; fem., *cargada*, N14v15, etc.; *carguada*, T14v4, etc.; *ga[r]gada*, N14v margin (the initial *ga-* by assimilation; cf. *disgargatus*, Guérard 1:lxxxvii). To load (*PD* 68). See also *bestia cargada*

carn, N7v19. Meat (*PD* 68). – *salada*, N7v19. Salt meat.

carrat, see *quairat*

cassia fistula (Lat.), N7v15, N14r16. *Cassia fistula*, "the pods of the pudding-pipe tree, the pulp of which forms purgative cassia ..., a product of India and Egypt" (Pegolotti 1936, 415–6). *Cassia fistola* (Occ.) in the *Elucidari de las proprietatz*, trans. Fr. *casse fistole* (*LR* 2:352). *Cordas de –*, N7v15. Rope made of pulp from the pudding pipe tree.

castanha, N15v13; pl. *castanhas*, T4r5, T7r17, T14r29, T15r17, N12r12, N14r14, N14v16; *castangnias*, N7v12. Chestnut (*PD* 71, *DAO* 303, *DAOS* 202). – *am escorsa*, T7r17; – *an la scorsa*, N14v16; – *an la pelanha*,

N12r12. Chestnut in the shell. – *pelada*, T4r5, T14r29, N7v12, N14r14, N15v13. Peeled chestnut. "Châtaignes sèches (l'opération du blanchissage les prive de leur peau)" (Bondurand 139n13). Lat. *castanea*; nom. pl. *castage cum scorcha* (Baratier 387), abl. pl. *castagis pelatis* (385).

caulet: pl. *caules* (stressed *caulés*), N14r24. Cabbage. *Grana de caules*, N14r24. Cabbage seed. *Caulet*, "chou, petit chou" (*PD* 72, *DAO* 411, *DAOS* 338); *cau, caul, caulet*, "chou" (Pansier 3:38).

caupolada, T12v26. Cargo of a *caupol*, a small, short boat (*PD* 72); "allège, petit navire à fond plat ... naviguant sur la côte et dans les étangs" (Fourquin and Rigaud 1994, 95). Baratier and Reynaud (1951, 743) describe a *caupol* as a flat-bottomed barge with one mast and four to fourteen oars. A *caupolada* of salt measured 8.5 hogsheads by even measure or 12 by heaped measure, T12v26–8 (Bondurand 153n6). Med. Lat. *caupolata* (Jal 440–1).

caus, T7v19, T13v14, N9r15, N13r10. Lime (*PD* 72), "the alkaline earth which is the chief constituent of mortar" (*OED*).

caval, T8r22, T9r10. Horse (*PD* 72, *DAOS* 517). *Ad* –, T9r10. On horseback. Lat. *equus*; abl. *equo* (Baratier 377, 386). *Caval* in MS T, *chival* in MS N (which see).

cavalcador, N9v11; pl. *cavalcadors*, N9v22, N10r8. Rider (*PD* 73). *Cavalcador*, N9v11, is equivalent in meaning to *homs cavalcans*, T8v10 (both pay 3.5d at Tarascon). Lat. *eques* (Guérard 1:lxxxv).

cavalcadura: pl. *cavalcaduras*, T9r21. Mount (*PD* 73).

cavalcan, *cavalcant*, see *cavalcar*

cavalcar: pres. part. *cavalcant*, T9r2, N10r13, N10r16, N10r20, N10r23; masc. pl. *cavalcans*, T8v3. To ride (*PD* 73). Lat. *equitare*; pres. part. *equitans* (Baratier 389, Guérard 1:lxxxv).

cavalier: pl. *cavaliers*, T10r5, etc.; *cavalliers*, T10r7, T15v12; *cavalhers*, T16r11. Knight (*PD* 73). Lat. *miles* (Baratier 385); gen. pl. *militum* (387, Guérard 1:lxxxiv). Lat. *nobilis*; gen. pl. *nobilium* (Baratier 387, Guérard 1:lxxxv). See also *chevalier*

cayras, see *cairat* (3)

cayrat, see *cairat* (1)

cayssa, see *caissa*

cebas, see *seba*

cendat, see *sendat*

cendre: pl. *cendres*, N13r6, N13r9; *sendres*, N13r1. Ash (*PD* 75).

cent, N12r6, N15r8; *c[ent]*, T6v8, T6v9, T14v7, N11v20; *sent*, N11v22; *c[ent]*º (It. *cento*), T5r27, T14v27. Hundred. *Cen* (*PD* 74). *De* –, passim; *lo* –, T6v9; *en* –, T5r27. Per hundred. Lat. *de cento*; *de C* (Baratier 387).

cento (It.), see *cent*

cera, T3r21; *sera*, T14r13; *ciera*, N15v23; *siera*, N7r25, N14r3. Wax (*PD* 75). Lat. *cera*; abl. *cera* (Guérard 1:lxxxi, lxxxvi), *sera* (Guérard 1:lxxxiii, Martin-Portier 2:40), *ceira* (Baratier 377, 385, 388); *ceira* shows influence from northwestern It. dialects of Piedmont and Liguria (Maiden and Parry 1997, 239, 248).

cercle: pl. *cercles*, T14v7; *selcles*, T6v1, T13v33; *seucles*, N11v19. Hoop. *Celcle* (*PD* 74, *SW* 1:240, Pansier 3:39); *cercle (LR* 2:381). Lat. *circulus*; abl. pl. *circulis* (Baratier 387), *circlis* (Baratier 388), *cilclis* (Guérard 1:lxxxvi); *cercles* (Baratier 377), *sercles* (= Occ.) (Guérard 1:lxxxi).

che (It.), T12v5. That. Spelled *que* elsewhere in MSS TN.

Chemicals, see Metals

chival, N7r22, N8r4, N9r18, N9v7, N14r8, N15v21; pl. *chivals*, N10r7. Horse (*PD* 72, *DAOS* 517). *Pel ... de* –, N14r8, N15v21. Horsehide. Lat. *equus*; abl. *equo* (Baratier 386). Cf. *chivalier* in MS N, but also *cavalcador* in MS N; *caval* in MS T; *cavalcar* in both MSS. Occ. *chival* is probably a loan from Francoprovençal *chival*, not from Old French *cheval, chival*, according to Ronjat (1930–41, 1:57–8, §31), who points out that *chivau* occurs in Guilhem IX and *chival* in the *Chanson de la croisade albigeoise* and several fifteenth-century sources. For Pasero, *chivau* in Guilhem IX (beside *caval*) is a Poitevinism (1973, 97, note to poem 4, line 5). *FEW* (2:12) gives the etymon as "fr. *cheval* (oder frpr. *chival*?)."

chivalier, N9v23, N9v24, N9v25. Knight (*PD* 73). *Filz de* –, N9v24. Son of a knight. See also *cavalier*

ci-appres (Fr.), N1v margin. Hereafter, in following text (*TLFi*, Littré).

cico tonip, see *alum de cico tonip*

ciera, see *cera*

citeal, T3r27; *citoal*, N14r6, N15v25. Zedoary, "an aromatic tuberous root ... of the East Indies and neighbouring countries ... having properties resembling those of ginger" (*OED*), also called setwall. *Citoal* (*PD* 77, *DAO* 538, *DAOS* 462). It. *zettoara* (Pegolotti 1936, 434). Med. Lat. *zedoarium*, from Arabic *zedwar* (*OED*); abl. *sitoal* (= Occ.) (Baratier 325).

Cities and regions: see *Adaul, Alap, Arle, Avinhon, Belcaire, Colonha, Florensa, Fransa, Gernegua, Levant, Lion, Lubieras, Narbona, non-Levant, Pecays, Provensa, Roda, Sant Gabriel, Sant Gile, Sant Jacme, Sicilia, Tarascon, Volcan*

citoal, see *citeal*

*__citron__: pl. *citrons*, N12r14, N14v18. Lemon (Pansier 3:42, *DAO* 324, *DAOS* 230).

civada: *syvada*, N8r25. Oats (*PD* 77, Pansier 3:42, *DAO* 384, *DAOS* 299). Med. Lat. *civata* (Niermeyer), *civada* (= Occ.) (Du Cange 2:345), **civatis*; abl. *civate* (Baratier 396).

clerc, N9v20. Clerk (*PD* 79). Lat. *clericus* (Baratier 384).

Cloth, materials: see *blanquet, borrassa, brun, cohanha, coton, cuer, drap, estam, estamenha, lana, lin, pel, pelharia, pelisaria, sarja, seda, sendat, tela*

Clothing, garments: see *cota, fauda, frauc, ful, fustani, gron, mersaria, plagaria, rauba, vestir*

clovel, T7r1; *clovelh*, T13v27; **crovelh*, N14v20; **croveilh*, N12r7. Shell of an almond. *Clovel* (*PD* 80, *SW* 1:264, Pansier 3:43, *DAO* 295, *FEW* 2:445b); *croveil, crouvel, cruveil* (Pansier 3:54, *DAO* 295, *FEW* 2:445b); *cruvel, crovel* (Alibert 253). Med. Lat. **crupellum* (Mistral 1:684); abl. *crovellio*, shell of an almond (Baratier 387, Guérard 1:xciii); *crovello,* shell of a hazelnut (Guérard 1:lxxxv), both influenced by Occ. Synonym of *cortex*, abl. pl. *corticibus* in *amigdalarum cum corticibus* (Delebecque 3:54; *amigdalarum cum urticibus*, Martin-Portier 2:46).

c°., see *cent*

codon: pl. *codons*, T7r14, N12r13, N14v17. Quince (*PD* 81, *DAO* 282, *DAOS* 175). Lat. *cotoneum*; nom. pl. *condonz* (= Occ.) (Baratier 387).

cohanha, T14r18. Inferior wool from the tail of the sheep. "Comme *coaille*, laine de qualité inférieure, celle de la queue, *cauda*" (Bondurand 156n3), *coanha (SW* 1:266, Pansier 3:44). *Couaio, coualho*, "laine de la queue et des cuisses, écouailles" (Mistral 1:587). See also *Colonha*

Coins, money, currency: see *blanc, corona, denier, florin, libra, liga, mealha, moneda* (2, 3), *obol, patac, pogeza, rial, sol* (2), *tornes*. See also Payment in kind

coladier: fem. pl. *colladieras*, T6r1; *coladieras*, N11r19. Portable (*PD* 82, *SW* 1:277).

colher, see *colier*

colier, T7v17, N15r6; *colher*, N12v6. Carrier. *Colier*, "porte-faix" (*PD* 83). When a sumpter's load of glass pays its toll in kind with two pieces, the carrier adds one more piece (T7v17, N15r6). Med. Lat. *collaterius* (Baratier 377, Guérard 1:lxxxi), abl. *colleterio* (Baratier 377, 387, Guérard 1:lxxxi, lxxxii); *collerium*, abl. *collerio*, carrier (not "collar," as in Niermeyer), perhaps influenced by Occ. (Baratier 387, Guérard 1:lxxxv).

Colonha, N14r8. Cologne (Germany). *Fil de Colonha*, N14r8; cf. *fil de cohanha*, T14r18. *Colonha* looks suspiciously like a scribal error for *cohanha*; however, it may be a valid independent reading, as Cologne was noted for exporting cloth manufactured from English wool and for weaving quilts; the wool weavers organized the strongest guild in the city (Groten 1991, 1260). "Cologne (oeuvre de), ou broderie de haute lisse" (Enlart 1902-16, 3:554). Lat. *Colonia*; *Coloia*, without the expected nasal macron (Guérard 1:xcvi).

comin, T3v17, T14r28, T15r14, N7v13, N14r15. Cumin (*PD* 85), a plant resembling fennel, "cultivated in the Levant for its fruit or seed, which possesses aromatic and carminative qualities" (*OED*). Lat. *cuminum*; abl. *comino* (Baratier 385, 388, Guérard 1:lxxxiii, lxxxvi, lxxxvii).

comol, T12v28; pl. *comols*, N5r24. Heaped, describing a measure. *Comble* (*PD* 85).

companhia, T5r8; *compania*, N8v25. Partnership. "Compagnie, société" (*PD* 86), "association" (Pansier 3:45). – *de vin*, N8v25. Partnership in wine, for the purpose of trading wine.

comprar: pres. 3rd pers. pl. *compran*, N9v5; pret. 3rd pers. sg. *compret*, T9v21; past part. *conprat*, T6r18, T8r22, N11v10; fem. pl. *compradas*, T8v23. To buy (*PD* 87). Lat. *emere*; perfect 3rd pers. pl. *emerunt* (Baratier 383).

conilh, N15v12; pl. *conils*, T3v1, N7v5; *conilz*, N15v22. Rabbit (*PD* 90). *Pels de* –, N7v5, N 15v22; *pel ... de* –, N15v12. Rabbit fur. At T3v1, the word *conils* alone clearly refers in context to rabbit fur, not rabbits (the item concerns fur linings or rabbit fur, not small animals or live cargo).

conplidament, N9r2, N15v9. In full. *Complidamen* (*PD* 87).

Containers, see Furniture

contar: pres. 3rd pers. sg. *conta*, N13v2, N13v5; pres. part. *contant*, N13r20, N13v18; past part. *contat*, T5r4. To count. *Contar* (*LR* 2:464); *comtar, condar* (*PD* 87). Lat. *computare*; pres. 3rd pers. pl. passive *computantur* (Baratier 387, Guérard 1:lxxxv).

conte, N13v4. Count, reckoning. *Conte* (*LR* 2:464); *comte, conde* (*PD* 87).

contramont, N5r20, N7r10. Upstream. *Contramon* (*PD* 93).

convenir: past part. *covengut*, N13r5. To agree (*PD* 94).

copiera, T7v15, N12v5. *Load carried by a pack animal (?). "Charge d'une bête" (Bondurand 148n8), comparing *la copiera del veire*, T7v15, and *bestia carguada de veire*, T14v25, which also pay two pieces in kind. In N, *copiera* is parallel to *saumada*: *la copiera de las aisinas del veire*, N12v5; *saumada de veire*, N15r5; both pay two pieces. Cf. *cropiera, copiera,* "cropière" (*PD* 102, for croupière), Eng. crupper, "the hind-quarters or rump of a horse" (*OED*); *cropiera* (Pansier 3:54), *corpiera* (Pansier 3:50, *FEW* 16:417a). *Copiera* shows metonymy, an association of the horse's rump with the load carried on it. Levy declared Bondurand's interpretation "gewiss unrichtig" (*SW* 2.357) but proposed no other. Med. Lat. *croparium* (Niermeyer), by dissimilation **coperium, *cu-*; abl. *coperio* (Baratier 387), *cuperio* (Guérard 1:lxxxv). *De vitrio, de uno cuperio II cupas* (Baratier 387, Guérard 1:lxxxv; *coperio*), from one load (?) of glass, two cups.

Another explanation, based on *de uno coperio II cupas* (above), would derive Med. Lat. abl. *coperio* from *cupa*, cup; thus *coperium*, *a collective number of cups, a load of cups or glass. The forms are suggestive but the meanings differ in Med. Lat. *coparius*, "a *Copis* seu poculis, Gall. *Echanson*," cupbearer (Du Cange 2:552); Med. Lat. *cuparius*, barrelmaker, cooper (Du Cange 2:658, Niermeyer).

corba: pl. *corbas*, T6r9, N11v4. *Knee (*nautical*), "a piece of timber naturally bent, used to secure parts of a ship together, esp. one with an angular bend used to connect the beams and the timbers" (*OED*). "*Corba*, c'est la *Courbe*, le couple; le mot était dans le vénitien, et probablement il était usité dans les chantiers de toute l'Italie et de la Provence" (Jal 517); "*Courbe*, angl. Knee" (Jal 537). Rossiaud 2002, 2:96–8. "Pièce de bois cintrée" (Pansier 3:50). The occurrences in MSS TN are older than those reported for this meaning in *FEW* 2:1590b (sixteenth century). Fr. *courbe*, "pièce de bois coudée qui sert de contrefort" (Fennis 1:662).

A different meaning occurs in Lat. *ossa de nau seu corba*, the *orsa* (tackle, hoisting gear) of a ship, or *corba*; "L'ourse est une partie de la vergue" (Baratier 386).

corda (1), N14r20; pl. *cordas*, T3v15, T3v16, T14r24, T14r25, T15r18, T15r25, N7v14, N7v15, N8r22, N12r2; *cordes*, N12v19. Rope. "Corde" (*PD* 96); "corde, cordage" (Fourquin and Rigaud 1994, 113). – *de cassia fistula*, N7v15. Rope made of pulp from the pudding pipe tree. – *de gonc*,

N12r2; *de jonc*, N12v19. Rope made of rush. *Cordas viellas*, N8r22. Old ropes (see also *sarcia*). *Fil de corda*, N14r19; *de cordas*, T3v16, T14r25, T15r25, N7v14. Thread for ropes. Lat. *chorda*; abl. pl. *cordis*, "cordes" (Baratier 385, Guérard 1:lxxxiii).

corda (2), T4r29, N8r8. Cord, a measure of length that equalled six canes; that is, about twelve metres at about two metres per cane, according to Pegolotti, who specifies that *tele line* (linens) are sold by the *corda* (Pegolotti 1936, 225; cf. Villain-Gandossi 1969, 37). "Sorte de mesure" (*PD* 96). – *de tela*, T4r29, N8r8. Cord of linen. Lat. *chorda*; *corda canabaciorum, de x cannis mensuratis* (Guérard 1:lxxxviii).

cordovan, N7r24, N8r3, N15v21; *cordoan*, T3r19, T15v8, N14r3; *corduan*, T14r11; pl. *cordoans*, T4r30. Cordovan (*PD* 96), Eng. cordwain, "Spanish leather made originally at Cordova, of goatskins tanned and dressed, but afterwards frequently of split horsehides ... Much used for shoes, etc. by the higher classes during the Middle Ages" (*OED*). As mass noun: Cordovan leather, T3r19, T14r11, T15v8, N7r24, N14r3, N15v21. "Cuir de Cordoue ou imitation de ce cuir" (Bondurand 137n8). As count noun: (individual) hide of this leather, T4r30, N8r3. Med. Lat. *cordoanus* (Niermeyer); abl. *cordoano* (Baratier 385, 388, Guérard 1:lxxxi, lxxxiii).

corma: pl. *cormas*, N12r16. Cornel-berry (*PD* 96).

cornuda: pl. *cornudas*, T6v7, T13v36, T14v10, N11v18. Two-handled wooden jug (*PD* 97). Med. Lat. *cornuta*, "a sort of pail" (Niermeyer); abl. pl. *cornudis*, "vases de bois à deux anses (servant pour la vendange), en provençal: *cournudo*, barrils" (Baratier 388), *cornudis* (Guérard 1:lxxxvi).

coronat, masc., pl. *los coronas*, N13v8, N13v9. *Coronat*, a coin. Stressed *coronát*, pl. *coronás*; past part. of *coronar*, to adorn with a crown, describing a coin type that featured a crown. The ending in *-ás* continues the older form, *-atz*, after the simplification of the final cluster (*-tz* > *-s*). Cf. *coróna*, fem., crown (*PD* 97, *LR* 2:487).

cossa: pl. *cossas*, T13v35. Wooden bowl without handles (*PD* 98, *SW* 1:385). Med. Lat. *cossa* (Du Cange 2:592); acc. sg. *cossam* (Guérard 1:lxxv), gen. pl. *cossarum* (Martin-Portier 2:48), abl. pl. *cossis buiseis* (Guérard 1:xciii).

costa: pl. *costas*, T4r9. Bar, a measure of iron (*PD* 99).

costuma, N10r22. Custom (*PD* 99). *De costuma*, N10r22. Customary.

cota, T4r34, N8r6. Tunic (*PD* 99). "Une sorte de tunique longue, plus ou moins ajustée, sur laquelle pouvait se passer un autre vêtement, généralement court" (Bourilly 1928, 31). "Cotte, cote ou cotele (*tunica*). Vêtement porté par les deux sexes, à partir de 1200 environ, sur la chemise et sous le surcot" (Enlart 1902-16, 3:556).

coton, T4r1, T14r35, T15r26, N7v4, N7v17, N14r20, N15v15. Cotton (*PD* 100, *DAO* 450, *DAOS* 387). – *no[u],* N7v4. New cotton, with a toll of 30.5d in contrast with cotton (without modification) with a toll of 19d (N7v17). Perhaps cotton newly woven into cloth (silk had the same higher toll: *seda* immediately follows *coton no[u]*), in contrast with second-hand cotton cloth, which was used to make padding and paper (Du Cange 1:695, s.v. *bombacyna, bambax, bombacinium, bombicum*); there was "an extensive used clothing market" (French 2013, 198). An alternative view would take "new cotton" as cotton newly spun into thread, in contrast to the unprocessed substance; cf. *coton filat e non filat*, "cotton spun and not spun," in a document from the thirteenth century quoted by *LR* (2:504, s.v. *coton*). For other tolls on new products, see *nou* (1). Med. Lat. *cotonum* (Niermeyer); abl. *cotono* (Baratier 385, 388, Guérard 1:lxxxiii, lxxxvi). Synonym of *bombyx*, gen. *bonbissis* (Martin-Portier 2:41, 2:46, 2:47).

coure, T4r6, T8r12, N7v17, N12v13, N14r19. Copper. *Coire, coure* (*PD* 82, *DAO* 163, *DAOS* 71). Lat. *cuprum*; abl. *coure* (= Occ.) (Baratier 397).

covengut, see *convenir*

croveilh, *crovelh*, see *clovel*

crucol: pl. *crucols*, T6v27. Small jug (*PD* 103). Ger. "Krug?" (*SW* 1.422).

cuer, T4r32, N8r4, N8r6; pl. *cuers*, T3r18, N7r21, N7r23; *cuors*, T3r17, T14r15. Hide, skin (*PD* 103, *DAO* 547, *DAOS* 470). – *adobatz o non adobatz*, T3r17; *adobas o non adobas*, N7r23. Hides, tanned or not tanned. – *de buou*, T4r32, N7r21, N8r4. Oxhide. – *de camel*, N8r4. Camel hide. – *de chival*, N8r4. Horsehide. – *de luons*, T14r15. Lion hide. – *d'ors*, N8r6. Bear hide. Lat. *corium*, abl. pl. *coriis* (Baratier 385, Guérard 1:lxxxiii, Martin-Portier 2:40). See also *pel.*

culhier: pl. *culhiers*, N11v17; *qulhiers*, T13v34, T14v17; *qulhers*, T6v5. Spoon (*PD* 103). Lat. *coclear*; gen. pl. *coclearum* (Delebecque 3:54, 3:55; *cocleriorum* Martin-Portier 2:46, 2:48), abl. pl. *culliers* (= Occ.) (Baratier 388, Guérard 1:lxxxvi).

Currency, see Coins

datil: pl. *datils*, T3v23, N7v16, N14r17. Date (*PD* 105, *DAO* 326, *DAOS* 233). Med. Lat. *dactylus* (Niermeyer); abl. pl. *datils* (= Occ.) (Baratier 385).

davant, N10r9, N13r5, N13v9. Before. In time: N10r9, N13v9. In space: N13r5. *Davan* (*PD* 105).

declaracion, N13r10. Explanation (PD 106).

defora, N10r10. Outside. *Defor, -ora* (*PD* 108). Lat. *extra* (Baratier 385).

deisenduda, N15v2. A going downstream. See *descendre;* cf. *montada*

*__dela__, T8v23. Beyond (Pansier 5:171, Honnorat 1:658, Mistral 1:718; *FEW* 4:546b). *Las partidas dela Roze*, "des pays au-delà du Rhône, c'est-à-dire des pays de la rive droite du fleuve. Tarascon est situé sur la rive gauche" (Bondurand 150n7). Lat. *ultra Rodanum* (Baratier 388).

demandar: past part. *demandat,* N13r1. To ask (*PD* 110).

demiei, T5r[38], T5v1, etc. Half. *Demeg, -ei* (*PD* 110). Lat. *dimidius*; gen. *dimidii* (Guérard 1:lxxxii), fem. acc. *dimidiam* (Baratier 384).

denfra, T8v8, T15r12, N9v13. Within (*PD* 111). Lat. *infra* (Baratier 383).

denier (1), passim. Denier, a coin (*PD* 111). "Originally, from reign of Charlemagne till 12th c., a silver coin of about 22 Troy grains or rather less than a pennyweight; from the 13th c. to the reign of Charles IX (d. 1574), usually of billon or base silver (*denier tournois*), and weighing at different times from 10 to 14 gr." (*OED*). See also *tornes*

denier (2) (written out), N7v9; pl. *deniers* (written out), T9v15, N6v8, N13v19; abbreviated *d'*., passim; sometimes *de*., T12v8, or *de*[.], T12v18. *Denier as money of account. This is the usual sense in MSS TN, contrasted with other senses at N13r18, N13r21, N13r24.

Equivalences to the florin: 160d make a florin of Florence, N13v3, but 152d made a florin of Florence before 1330, N13v11. The rate of 160d was applied to the toll on salt, while the rate of 152d was applied to tolls on commodities, N13v14–7.

Other equivalences: 16d make a tournois, N13v4; 8d 8 grains (8.33d) make a *blanc*, N13v5; but 8d made a *blanc* before 1330, N13v19.

For *denier* (2)-(4), see Bibliothèque nationale de France 2013.

denier (3): *d'*., N13r17, N13r20, N13r23. *Denier as a measure of monetary weight (Mistral 1:724; at Mâcon, *FEW* 3:39b). The denier equalled 1/192 of the marc (the ingot from which coins were manufactured), that is, 1.27 grams.

denier (4): *d'*., N13r16, N13r22. *Denier as a measure of fineness (Fr. *titre*), or purity in silver (Honnorat 1:665). In terms of the abstract *denier de loi*, pure silver had fineness of 12 deniers; in terms of the more realistic *argent le roi*, pure silver had fineness of 11.5 deniers.

descargar: pres. 3rd pers. sg. *descargua*, N4v5, N4v16, etc.; *descarca*, T12v5; pres. subj. 3rd pers. sg. *descargue*, T12r20; pres. part. pl. *descarguans*, T12v24. To unload. Lat. *deponere*; pres. subj. 3rd pers. pl. passive *deponantur* (Baratier 385). Lat. *descargare*; pres. subj. 3rd pers. pl. passive *discargentur* (Guérard 1:lxxxiii), pres. part., abl. *descarganti* (Baratier 387).

descendre: pres. part. *descendent*, T3r3, T13r8; *deissendent*, T4v31; *dese[n]dent*, N15v8. *To go down (the Rhône). "Descendre," *PD* 114. Lat. *descendere*; gerund *decendendo* (Baratier 385), *descendendo* (Guérard 1:lxxxiii).

despens, N10r. Expense (*PD* 119).

dessus, see *sus*

dever: pres. 2nd pers. pl. *deves*, T15r2; imperfect 3rd pers. sg. *devie*, N13r2; pl. *devian*, N9v19; past subj. 3rd pers. sg. *degessa*, N13r3; pl. *deguessan*, N13r7. To owe (*PD* 123).

diaque, N9v23; *deiaque*, N9v23. Deacon, "the cleric who acts as principal assistant at a solemn celebration of the Eucharist" (*OED*). *Diague* (*PD* 128).

dire, passim; past part. masc. sg. *dich*, T8v15; *dig*, T12v23; *digz*, T12r10; *dis*, T5r6, T5r23, T11v25; *diç*, N6r24; *dit*, N4r14, N6v1, N6v24 (*en la maniera que dit es*), etc.; *dits*, N5v5; *ditz*, N13v13; etc.; pl. *ditz*, N6v18, N13v13; fem. *dicha*, N16r22; *dita*, N5r13. To tell. Lat. *dicere*; pres. 3rd pers. sg. *dicit*, pl. *dicunt* (Baratier 385).

divisament, N9r1. *As noun: separation. *En –*. Separately. Cf. the adv., *devizamen* (*PD* 124), *divisiment* (Pansier 5:173). See also *mesclament*, adv.

divisio, N1v19; *division*, N2r13. Division, apportionment. *Devezion, devi-, di-* (*PD* 123).

doas, see *dos* (3)

doga: pl. *dogas*, T14v21, N15r2. Stave (*PD* 130).

dogan, T14v20, N12r22. Set of staves. *Dogam*, "douvain" (*PD* 130). "Douvain, merrain, ensemble de douves" (Bondurand 157n3). *Dogan*, T14v20, is defined as a set of twenty-five *dogas*, staves; a *tina* or vat, N15r2, is described as made of twenty-five *dogas*. Both passages concern the Gate of Tarascon, and both call for a toll of 4d. Med. Lat. *doga* (Niermeyer); abl. *donga* (*de donga, scilicet de XXV dogis cum bugis*, Baratier 388). See also *dogat*

dogat, T6v16; *doguat*, T13v29. Drain, "égout, conduit" (*PD* 130). Levy cites *dogat* in MS T but provides no translation (*SW* 2:266).

dogena, see *dozena*

dos (1), T4r33. Fleece. "Dos, toison" (*PD* 132).

*__dos__ (2), T5r[33]. Toward. *Dos*, "sous, vers" (Pansier 3:64). *Devers, dos*, "devers, vers, du côté de" (Mistral 1:794). Mod. Occ. *dos* (*FEW* 14:313b). *A la tersa part ... dos la razis*, T5r[33], "au tiers inférieur de sa hauteur" (Bondurand 143n2).

dos (3): fem. *doas*, N6r9, N8r18. Two (*PD* 132). Lat. *duo*; fem. abl. pl. *duabus* (Baratier 383).

dozena, T4r30, T4r31; *dogena*, N8r1, N8r3; pl. *dotzenas*, T3r19, T15r1; *dozenas*, T14v32, T14v33; *dozinas*, T7v5, T7v6, T7v9; *dogenas*, N7r25, N12v1, N12v2. Dozen (*PD* 132). Med. Lat. *dozena* (Niermeyer); gen. pl. *donzenarum* (Baratier 385), abl. pl. *dozenis* (ibid.).

drap (1): pl. *draps*, T3r9, T3r11, T14r7, T14r8, T14r9, T14r10, T15v7, N7r17, N7r18, N7r19, N14r1, N14r3, N15v17, N15v18, N15v19; *drapps*, T3r7. Cloth (*PD* 132). – *d'Avinhon*, T14r9, N15v17. Cloth from Avignon. – *de Fransa*, T3r9, T14r7, N7r18, N15v18. Cloth from France. – *de Narbona*, T3r11, T14r8, N15v18. Cloth from Narbonne. Lat. *pannus*; *pannus de Aviono, Avinio, Avijono* (Baratier 385, 388, Guérard 1:lxxviii, lxxxi); *pannus de Francia, Francie* (Baratier 386, 388, Guérard 1:lxxvi, lxxxi); *pannus de Narbona, Narbone* (Baratier 386, 388, Guérard 1:lxxvi, lxxviii, lxxxi). It. *panno*, "woolen cloth"; *panno francesco*, "cloth from France (i.e., cloth purchased in France or sent through France, esp. English and Flemish cloth)" (Edler 203).

drap (2): pl. *draps*, T3r8, T3r10, T3r12, T3r13, N7r18, N7r19, N7r21, N15v17, N15v18, N15v19. *Bolt (a length of cloth). Lat. *pannus*, gen. pl. *pannorum* (Baratier 385), abl. *pannis* (Guérard 1:lxxviii).

duptar: pres. 1st pers. pl. *duptam*, T6r16. To doubt. *Doptar* (*PD* 131). *Duptam*, we (the tollkeepers) are in doubt. "Pour un navire, le péage n'est pas fixé. Il s'agit d'un navire considéré comme marchandise, sortant du chantier de construction ou acheté en vue de la vente. L'indétermination du tarif montre qu'un navire passant devant Tarascon dans ces circonstances était une rareté" (Bondurand 145n7). Lat. *dubitare*; *de nave dubitant* (Baratier 386, Guérard 1:lxxxii), *de nauno* [read *navi(g)io* (?)] *dubitat* (Guérard 1:xciii).

Dyes: see *alum, bresilh, gaida, gala, indi, roge, ros, verdet*

e, see *eser*

egalar, N13v8. To compare (*PD* 134).

egua: pl. *eguas*, T8v14. Mare. *Ega* (*PD* 134, *DAOS* 537). Lat. *equa* (Baratier 388).

***eiseptat**, T8v4; *eisseptat*, T8v5, T8v7, T9r16; *exceptat*, N16r10; fem. *eisseptada*, T8r16. Except, except for. *Esseptat, eiseptat* (Pansier 3:79). Lat. *excepto, exceptis* (Baratier 387).

Elis, ma dama –, N1v25, N2r8, N2r16, N4r20, N4v1, N4v15, N4v20. Madame Elis, a shareholder in tolls on salt by the small hogshead.

elos, N10r6, N10r7. Personal pronoun, masc. pl. They. See also *aquel*

emina: pl. *eminas*, T7r22; *minas*, T7r3. Hemina (*PD* 138), a measure of volume, one eighth of a *saumada* (which see) and one half of a setier (see *sestier*). "Mesure de capacité pour les grains valant 38,7 l[itres] à Marseille" (Fourquin and Rigaud 1994, 144). Lat. *hemina*; abl. pl. *eminis* (Baratier 387). It. *mina*, "a measure for grain (in Genoa and S. France; it varied in size in different places and for different kinds of grain)" (Edler 184).

empero, T13r14, T13r19, T13r26, T15r2. However (*PD* 139).

enap: pl. *enaps*, T14v6. Goblet (*PD* 141). Lat. *nappus*, cup (Niermeyer); gen. pl. *napporum* (Martin-Portier 2:46). Synonym of Lat. *ciphus*; abl. pl. *ciphis* (Baratier 388, Guérard 1:lxxxvi); *sciphis de fusto*, goblets made of wood (Baratier 387, Guérard 1:lxxxxv).

Engles, T9r8; *Angles*, N10r20. Englishman. Lat. *Anglicus* (Baratier 387).

enprendre: pres. 3rd pers. sg. *enpren*, N7v7. To take. *Emprendre* (*PD* 140).

ensemble, N9r1 (*PD* 151). Together.

ensens, N14r6. Incense. *Encens* (*PD* 142, *DAO* 265, *DAOS* 156). Lat. *incensum*; abl. *enses* (= Occ.) (Baratier 324, 325).

entena, see *antenna*

entendement, T15r4. Understanding (*PD* 152).

entendre, T15r2. To understand (*PD* 153). Lat. *intelligere*; pres. subj. 3rd pers. sg. passive *intelligatur* (Guérard 1:lxxxvi), fut. 3rd pers. sg. *intelliget* (Baratier 388).

entier, T5r10, N9v17. Whole (*PD* 153). *Per entier*, T5r10. For it all.

entierament, N15v6. In full. *Entieramen* (*LR* 3:564).

eruga, N14r17. Roquette. *Eruca, -ga* (*PD* 158).

esclau, N9r22, N9r margin; fem. *esclava*, N9r22. Slave (*PD* 162).

escorsa, T7r17; *scorsa*, N14v17. Shell of a chestnut (*PD* 163, *DAO* 211, *DAOS* 95). Synonymous with *pelanha* (which see): *castanhas am escorsa* at T7r17, taxed 0.5d for one *saumada*, correspond to *castanhas an la pelanha* at N12r17, taxed 0.5d for one *saumada*. Lat. *scortea*; abl. *scorcha*, influenced by Occ. (Baratier 387).

escrinh, T6v13, T13v29, T14v19; *escrin*, N15r2; pl. *escrins*, N12r21. Box. *Escrin, -inh* (*PD* 164). – *nou am pecols*, T6v13. New box with feet.

escriure, past part. *escriç*, N7r5; fem. pl. *escrichas*, N16r4; *scrichas*, T15r12. To write (*PD* 164).

escudela: pl. *escudellas,* T13v33, N11v17; *scudelas*, T6r25; *scudellas*, T14v15. Bowl (*PD* 165). Lat. *scutella*; abl. pl. *scutellis* (Baratier 387, Guérard 1:lxxxv), *scudellis* (Baratier 388, Guérard 1:lxxxvi), influenced by Occ.

eser: pres. 3rd pers. sg. *es,* passim; *e* (It.), T11v25, T13r9; pres. subj. 3rd pers. sg. *sia* (It. or Occ.), T9r16, N6v5; fut. 3rd pers. sg. *sera*, N4r15. To be (*PD* 166). *E,* T13r9. There is. *Es de*, passim. Contains. *Sia ... o*, N6v5, N8v15. Either ... or.

esgardar: past part. fem. *esgardada*, T15v2. To consider (*PD* 167).

Espanhol, N10r20; *Spanhol*, T9r8. Spaniard. Lat. *Hispanus*, Med. Lat. *Spanus* (Baratier 387).

***espiceria**, N14r5. Spice (collective). Cf. *espessia*, *especia*, "épice"; *espessiaria*, "épicerie" (Pansier 3:78). *Especiarìo*, "épicerie" (Mistral 1:1027), grocery store. *FEW* 12:154b (in Fr., not Occ.).

estam, N14r23. Fine-spun wool. "Étaim" (*PD* 175), i.e., "laine à longs brins qui provient de la partie la plus fine de la laine cardée" (*TLFi*). *Estame*, "lainage plus souple et plus élastique" (Bourilly 1928, 27). *Estam*, "laine filée dite estam d'Arles" (Pansier 3:79). It. *stame*, "long, combed wool and the worsted yarn spun from it" (Edler 280).

estamenha, N7r20, N8r7, N14r2; *stameha*, T4r28; pl. *estamenhas*, T3r14, N15v19; *stamenhas*, T14r10, T15v8. Coarse muslin cloth (*PD* 175). *Pessa d'–*, N8r7. Piece of coarse muslin cloth. Med. Lat. *staminea* (Niermeyer); abl. *stamengia* (Baratier 377, Guérard 1:lxxxi), abl. pl. *stamegiis* (Baratier 388), *stamagiis* (Baratier 386), all influenced by Occ.

estanh (1), T8r13, N7v18, N12v13, N14r21, N15v13; *stanh*, T14r33, T15r21; *stang*, T15r24; *stanhg*, T4r7. Tin (*PD* 175, *DAO* 163, *DAOS* 72). Lat. *stagnum*; gen. *stanni* (Martin-Portier 2:46), abl. *stagno* (Baratier 388), *stangno* (Guérard 1:lxxxvi, lxxxvii).

estanh (2): pl. *estanhs*, T12v27. *Salt pan, "a shallow depression near the sea into which sea-water is allowed to flow, where it evaporates, leaving a deposit of salt" (*OED*); also called a saltern. "Étang" (*PD* 175, *DAO* 115).

estanhar: past part. *stagnat*, T4r12. To tin (*PD* 175), to cover with a thin deposit of pewter. See also *piatta.*

estimasion (Fr.), N5v margin. Determination (of toll on a given quantity of salt).

estopa, N14r18; pl. *stopas*, T3v14, T15r24, N7v14. Tow (*PD* 177, *DAO* 462, *DAOS* 400), "the fibre of flax, hemp, or jute" (*OED*). Lat. *stuppa*; abl. pl. *stopis* (Baratier 385, Guérard 1:lxxxiii), influenced by Occ.

estrangier, N7r4, N7r9, N15v3. Foreigner (*PD* 178).

estrani, N6v12; *estrany*, N4v17; *strani*, T5r11, T12v1, T12v5; *estrange*, N6v21, N8v25, N9r2, N9r3, N9v6, N15r22; pl. *estranis*, T12v24; *stranis*, T5r9. Foreigner. *Estranh, -anhe* (*PD* 178). Lat. *extraneus*; abl. *extraneo* (Baratier 387).

exceptat, see *eiseptat*

fabre, T13v31. Smith (*PD* 181). Lat. *faber* (Baratier 299).

faccia, see *faire*

faire: pres. 3rd pers. sg. *fau*, T12v27, T12v28; imperf. 3rd pers. sg. *faccia* (stressed *faccía*), T5r8. To make (*PD* 182). That *faccia*, T5r8, is imperfect (stressed *faccía*, mod. It. *faceva*) and not present subjunctive (mod. It. *fáccia*), is established by the parallel usage of imperfects after *si*, if: *si avia*, T4v10, T4v24; *si venia*, T4v27, etc. Medieval It. forms were usually in *facev-*, but imperf. 1st pers. sg. *facìa*, 3rd pers. pl. *facìeno* also occur (Battaglia 5:661c; Spadafora 1709, 381); *facìeno* in a fourteenth-century text (Allaire 2002, 698). The Occ. form is *fazia* (Paden 1998, 410). Imperf. *faccía* is an Italianism in the root.

fais, T8r17, N12v16. Load (*PD* 182).

faissa, T4r35, N8r8. Strap (*PD* 182).

farina, T4v13, T4v27, T14v13, N14v11; pl. *farinas*, T13r11. Flour (*PD* 184). Lat. *farina* (Baratier 393, Guérard 1:lxxxvi).

fau, see *faire*

fauda, N12v18. Skirt or petticoat. *Faldas*, "jupes" (*PD* 182), i.e., "ensemble formé par la jupe de dessus et un ou plusieurs jupons" (*TLFi*).

fava: pl. *faves*, N8r25. Bean (*PD* 185, *DAO* 427, *DAOS* 358).

feda: pl. *fedas*, T8v17, T8v26. Ewe (*PD* 185, *LR* 3:298, *SW* 3:426).

Fees: see *arribatge, montazon, pezage, uzage*

ferre, T4r8, T8r12, T14r33, T15r22, N7v19, N12v12, N14r22, N15v13. Iron. *Fer, ferre (PD* 187, *DAO* 166, *DAOS* 75). Lat. *ferrum*; abl. *ferro* (Baratier 385, 388, Guérard 1:lxxxiii, lxxxvi).

fiera, T8r16, N12v15. Fair. *Feira (PD* 185). – *de Belcayre*, T8r16, N12v15. Fair of Beaucaire. Lat. *nundina*, market day; abl. pl. *numbdinis de Bellicadro* (Baratier 386). It. *fiera*, "a fair (market held at a given time in a given place, and attended by foreign merchants)" (Edler 120).

figa: *figua*, T3v22, T14r30; pl. *figas*, N7v13, N14r18, N14v19, N15v13; *figuas*, N12r15. Fig (*PD* 189, *DAO* 315, *DAOS* 219). Sg. as mass noun, T3v22, T14r30. Figs. Pl. as count noun: *figas frescas*, N14v19. Fresh figs. *Figuas menudas*, N12r15. Small figs. *Figas secas*, N7v13, N15v13; *figas sequas*, N14r18. Dry figs. Lat. *ficus*; abl. pl. *ficubus* (Baratier 385, 388, Guérard 1:lxxxiii, lxxxvi).

fil (1), T3v16, T14r18, T14r25, etc., N7v3, N7v14, N14r8, N15v22; *filh*, T15r25; *fill*, N14r19. Thread (*PD* 189). – *de cohanha*, T14r18. Thread of inferior wool. – *de Colonha*, N14r8. Thread from Cologne. – *de corda*, N14r19; *de cordas*, T3v16, T14r25, T15r25, N7v14. Thread for ropes. Lat. *filum*; abl. *filo* (*filo cordarum*, Baratier 385, Guérard 1:lxxxiii).

*__fil__ (2), T6r19, T6r21, N11v12, N11v15; *fill*, N11v11. Strake, "each of the several continuous lines of planking or plates, of uniform breadth, in the side of a vessel, extending from stem to stern. Hence, the breadth of a plank used as a unit of vertical measurement in a ship's side" (*OED*). "Toute rangée de planches composant la fonçure ou les bordages" (Rossiaud 2002, 2:134); Fr. *fonçure*, the planks making the keel, ibid., 2:142; Fr. *bordage*, planking, sheathing of a vessel. "Une planche, un bordage du fond du bateau" (Bondurand 145n10). Fr. *fil*, "chacune des pièces de bois qui sont endentées sur les estamenaires ou sur les lattes et qui forment plusieurs rangs de bordages placés à distances égales" (Fennis 2:921). It. "*filo di bordato*: corso di fasciame esterno" (Reale Accademia d'Italia 1937, 256).

filar: past part. *filat*, N14r23. To spin. *Estam filat*, N14r23. Fine-spun wool.

fin (1), N13r16, N16r16. Pure (*PD* 190). *Argent* –, N13r16, N16r16. Pure silver.

fin (2), N8v6. Until (*PD* 190). *Fin a*, N8v6. Up to. Lat. *usque ad* (Guérard 1:lxxxiv).

Florensa, N5v6, N5v8, N13r19, N13v11, N13v13, N13v22; *Florença*, N13v3, N16r18, N16r21. Florence (Tuscany).

florin, N13v3, N13v18; *florin de Florensa*, N5v6, N5v7, N13r18, N13v3, N13v11, N13v13, N13v18, N13v22, N16r18, N16r21; abbreviated *fl.*, N13r20. The florin, a gold coin first struck in Florence in 1252. It counted as 160d, N13r18, N13v3; as 152d before 1330, N13v11; the rate of 160d was applied to the toll on salt, while the rate of 152d was applied to tolls on commodities, N13v14–7.

Foods: see *agive, agriota, alh, amella, arsiqua, avelana, buire, castanha, caulet, citron, civada, clovel, codon, corma, datil, eruga, escorsa, farina, fava, figa, fromage, frucha, frut, glassa, graissa, lentilha, limon, liome, mel, mela, milh, nerta, nespla, noze, oli, ordi, peis, peisson, pelanha, pera, persegua, pom, poma, ponsiri, porc, raba, razis, regalisia, rest, ris, sain, seba, segla, sereira, sese, sipia, sorba, vin*. See also Spices

fora *de*, N5r14, N7r3. Out of. *Fors, fora* (*PD* 195).

forma (1), T3r1 (MS *form*, here emended), T14r1, T14r2, T15r9, T15r10, T15v2, N13v24, N16r5, N16r6. Procedure. “Forme” (*PD* 194); “règles établies, modèle sur lequel on façonne, on moule diverses choses” (Honnorat 2:265). Lat. *forma* (Guérard 1:xc); acc. *formam* (Baratier 388).

forma (2), *la, et la maniera*, T3r1, T15r9, T15v2, N13v24, N16r5. Proper and customary procedure. Compare *l'eser e la maniera* in the *ensenhamen* by Arnaut de Mareuil, translated by Eusebi as “l'essere e il modo” (Eusebi 1969, 28, vv. 65–9). Lat. *forma et modus percipiendi pedagium* (Baratier 385, 388, Guérard 1:lxxxiii, xcviii, xcix), *forma et modus pedagii* (Baratier 388, Guérard 1:lxxxvii, lxxviii, lxxix, lxxxi, lxxxvi, lxxxvii, lxxxix, xciii), *modum et formam pedagii* (Guérard 1:c), *forma et modus* (Guérard 1:xcix). See also *forma* (1), *maniera*

forma (3), N4r24, N5r3, N6v22, N12v22. Model (*PD* 194).

formage, see *fromage*

frachas, see *franher*

franc, N10r22; masc. pl. *francs*, T9r21, N10r1, N10r7, N15v10, N16r11; fem. pl. *francas*, N12v7, N12v21, N13r7, N15r14, N15r15, N15r18, N16r9; *franquas*, N16r8. Exempt (*PD* 197). Lat. *liber de pedagio*, free from toll (Baratier 387). It. *franco*, “frank, free from tax” (Edler 129).

franher: past part. *frach*, fem. pl. *frachas*, T4r4, T14r29. To break (*PD* 197). *Amellas frachas*, T14r29; *melas frachas*, T4r4 (equivalent in meaning to *amellas pessadas*, N7v25, with a standard increase from 1d to 2d at Lubières). Shelled almonds. Lat. *frangere*; past part. *fractus*, abl. pl. *fractis* as in *amigdalis fractis*, “amandes sans cosse” (Baratier 385).

Fransa, T3r9, T9r21, T14r7, N15v18; *França*, N7r19, N10r6, N14r1. France. *Rey de* –, T9r21, N10r6. King of France.

frauc, N12v17. Frock, "a long habit with large open sleeves; the outer and characteristic dress of a monk" (*OED*). *Floc, froc*, "froc" (*PD* 191), i.e., "La partie de l'habit des moines qui couvre la tête et les épaules" (*TLFi*).

fresc, T14r34, N7v11, N12v11; fem. *fresca*, N12r15; pl. *frescas*, N12r15, N14v18, N14v19; *fresquas*, T7r12. Fresh (*PD* 198, Pansier 3:88, *DAO* 189, *DAOS* 92), describing a fish, flower, fruit, or nut. *Palum* –, N12v11. *Freshwater marsh. "*Palus* désigne un écosystème aquatique très variable: marais saisonnier ... [les] variations climatiques ... le rendent doux, saumâtre ou salé" (Pécout 2010, cxlii).

fromage, N14r22; pl. *fromages*, N7v19; *formages*, T3v26, T14r30, T15r16. Cheese. *Formatge, fro-* (*PD* 194).

frucha, N14v18; *fruta*, N12r15; pl. *fruchas*, T13v18, N14v16. Fruit (*PD* 198, *DAO* 195, *DAOS* 94).

frut: pl. *frutz*, T14v5. Fruit. *Fruch, frut* (*PD* 198, *DAO* 194, *DAOS* 94). Lat. *fructus*; abl. pl. *fructibus* (Baratier 388, Guérard 1:lxxxvi).

*__ful__, N12v18. Purse (?). Cf. It. *folle*, "mantice, soffietto ...; sacco, borsa ... = Lat. follis 'borsa gonfia d'aria, mantice, sacchetto di cuoio'" (Battaglia 6:113, s.v. *folle* [2]). The *l* may be palatal, as in *fol*, variant *folh*, fool, from the same etymon (*LR* 3:348; Paden 1998, 415). Regarding the vowel, "en position tonique, *o* et *u* alternent pour noter le résultat de *o* ouvert [devant une palatale]" (Grafström 1958, 75); cf. *mog, muy*.

Furniture, utensils, containers, tools: see *arca, armari, bacon, banaston, broc, brocat, cabas, caissa, carda, cercle, cornuda, cossa, crucol, culhier, doga, dogan, dogat, enap, escrinh, escudela, faissa, grazal, grazalet, grazali(n), grazalo(n), olla, paniera, pechier, pecol, piatta, sarria, sistra, tina, torra, uleta, vaissel*

fusta, T5v18, T5v26, T13r25, N11r7, N11v19, N15r1. Timber, i.e., "wood in general as a material; esp. after it has been suitably trimmed and squared into logs, or further adapted to constructive uses" (*OED*). "Bois" (*PD* 199, *DAO* 212, *DAOS* 105); "bois de charpente ... implique un travail qualifié, ce qui n'est guère le cas des bûches ou des fagots" (Rossiaud 2002, 2:143). Med. Lat. *fusta* (Niermeyer, Baratier 386).

fustani, N7v17, N14r20, N15v15; pl. *fustanis*, T4r2, T14v1, T15r19. Fustian (*PD* 199), "formerly, a kind of coarse cloth made of cotton and flax" (*OED*). Med. Lat. *fustaneum* (Niermeyer); abl. pl. *fustanis* (Baratier 385,

388, Guérard 1:lxxxiii, lxxxvi, lxxxvii). *Fustanitae, fustani*: "un vêtement en tissu fil et coton (futaine), sans doute un vêtement de dessous" (Bourilly 1928, 29). "Futaine (*fustana*), tissu de coton ... ; vêtement, synonyme de doublet" (Enlart 1902-16, 3:568).

Gabriel, see *Sant Gabriel*

gaida, T4r21; **caida*, N8r10. Woad (*PD* 200, *DAO* 464, *DAOS* 403), "a blue dye-stuff ... now generally superseded by indigo" (*OED*). "Plante tinctoriale appelée *pastel* [woad]" (Bondurand 140n7). Reading *caida* as a variant of *gaida* is supported by the similar positions of the two forms: after the highest tolls and before cloth and leather in T, after cloth and leather in N. Med. Lat. *gaida* (*waisda, gai-*, Niermeyer 2:1463), gen. *gayde* (Martin-Portier 2:41).

gala: pl. *galas*, N12v10; *gallas*, T8r3. Gall, gallnut (*PD* 200, *DAO* 224, *DAOS* 114), "an excrescence produced on trees, especially the oak, by the action of insects ... Oak-galls are largely used in the manufacture of ink and tannin, as well as in dyeing and in medicine" (*OED*). Lat. *galla*; nom. sg. *gala* (Baratier 386, Guérard 1:lxxxii).

gargada, see *cargar*

Garments, see Clothing

gen: *gens*, N16r10; *gent*, N15v10. People. *Gen* (*PD* 205).

gentil, see *ome*

Gernegua, T15r5, T15r6, N15r12. Jarnègues (sometimes spelled without the –s), formerly an island in the Rhône at Tarascon. "Jarnègue, île du Rhône, entre Beaucaire et Tarascon, aujourd'hui réunie par atterrissement à la commune de Tarascon ... En 1298, c'était encore une île. En 1527, la porte de Tarascon du côté du Rhône s'appelait *Porte de Jarnègue*" (Germer-Durand 1868, 107). Lat. *Jernega* (Baratier 383, Guérard 1:lxxxvii, etc.). *Peage de* –, T15r5, N15r12. The tollhouse at Jarnègues. See also *Lubieras* and *pont* (1)

gingibre, T3r23, T14r12, N7v1, N14r4, N15v24. Ginger (*PD* 207). Med. Lat. *gingiber* (Niermeyer, Du Cange 4:69); abl. *gingebre* (Baratier 377, Guérard 1:lxxxi, lxxxiii, lxxxvi), *gigibre* (Baratier 388), *zinzibere* (Martin-Portier 2:40).

gioncs, see *gonc*

gip, T7v19, T13v15, N9r15, N13r10. Gypsum (*PD* 207). Lat. *gypsum*; *gipum*, "sans doute pour *gypsum*" (Baratier 238nb).

girofle, T3r24, T14r13, N7v4, N15v24; pl. *girofles*, N14r5. Clove (*PD* 207). Med. Lat. *caryophyllum* (Niermeyer); abl. *garofle*, influenced by Occ. (Baratier 388, Guérard 1:lxxxi, lxxxvi).

glassa, N12v10. Gum arabic (*PD* 208, *DAO* 261, *DAOS* 149), made of sap from the acacia tree and used in food, cosmetics, glue, and incense (*OED*).

gonc, N12r2, N12v19; pl. *gioncs*, N12r1. Rush. *Junc (LR* 3:596), *jonc* (*DAO* 533, *DAOS* 458).

graissa, N7v18, N8r14. Grease. *Graisa (*"graisse," *PD* 210, *DAO* 553, *DAOS* 475). – *de porc*, N7v18. Hog fat, lard. Late Lat. •*crassia* (*FEW* 2:1276); abl. *greza vegetum* ("tartre," tartar, Baratier 386; Guérard 1:lxxxiii), *greda* (Martin-Portier 2:41 = *greza* Delebecque 3:49).

gran (1): pl. *grans,* N7r12, N7r13, N13r21, N13r22, N13r23, N16r20. Grain (*PD* 210), the minimal unit of weight (*LR* 3:495, Honnorat 2:367, Mistral 2:81); doubted by Levy (*SW* 4:166–7). Fr. *grain*, "petit poids, qui était la soixante-douzième partie d'un gros, ou la vingt-quatrième d'un scrupule, ou gramme 0,0532" (Littré). See Bibliothèque nationale de France 2013.

gran (2): pl. *grans*, N13v5, N13v7. *As money of account, 1/24 of a denier. See Bibliothèque nationale de France 2013.

grana, N14r23; pl. *granas*, N12r16, N14r24. Seed (*PD* 210, *DAO* 173, *DAOS* 82). Lat. *granum*; abl. *grano* (Baratier 388).

grant: fem. *granda*, T4v32; fem. pl. *grans*, T6r3, T6r9; *grandes*, N11v2. Large.

grazal: pl. *grazals*, T14v16; *grasals*, N11v18. Bowl (*PD* 211, *SW* 4:178). *Grasals*, N11v18, occurs in the same context as *grasalos*, T6r27, suggesting that they might mean the same thing. *Grasal*, "baquet, auge en bois" (Pansier 3:95); "vase, vaisseau propre à boire et à servir des viandes, cratère, jatte" (Honnorat 2:375). Med. Lat. *gradale*, *gradalus* (Du Cange 4:91); *grasale* (Du Cange 4:102); *grassale*, *grassellus* (Du Cange 4:103), various kinds of bowls. Med. Lat. *gradale* also produced OFr. *graal*, whence Eng. *grail.*

grazalet: pl. *grazaletz*, T14v16; *grazallet*, T13v34. Small tub (*PD* 211, *SW* 4:178). *Grasselet* (Pansier 3:95, s.v. *grasal*). *Grazalet,* "auget, petit baquet; petit vase de terre" (Honnorat 2:375). Med. Lat. *grasaletus*, *grassaletus* (Du Cange 4:103), *graletus* (Du Cange 4:95), *grasaletis*, "jatte ou coupe sur pied" (Baratier 387, 388); gen. pl. *grasaletorum* (Guérard 1:xcvii, Martin-Portier 2:45), abl. pl. *grasaletis* (Baratier 387, Guérard 1:lxxxi, xciii), *grazaletis* (xciv).

***grazali(n)**: pl. *grazalis*, T13v35. Small bowl. Diminutive of *grazal.*

***grazalo(n)**: pl. *grasalos*, T6r27. Pan. "Terrines, jattes" (Bondurand 145n15). See also *grazal.*

greza, T4v1; *gresa*, N14v3. Tartar ("tartre?" *PD* 212), "bitartrate of potash (acid potassium tartrate), present in grape juice, deposited in a crude form in the process of fermentation, and adhering to the sides of wine-casks" (*OED*). Med. Lat. **crassia* (*OED*), *crassa* (Du Cange 2:606); *gresa vegetum*, "tartre" (Baratier 386), influenced by Occ.

***gron**, N12v17. Garment, flap of a garment (?). Variant of Occ. *giron*, "pan de robe?; flanc, côté" (*PD* 207); Ger. "Rockschoß," coat-tail (*SW* 4:123); "pan de manteau" (Honnorat 2:346). Cf. OFr. *gron*, variant of *giron,* "pan coupé en pointe, à droite et à gauche, de la robe ou de la tunique ... la tunique ou la robe elle-même; la partie antérieure du vêtement" (Godefroy 4:280). OFr. *giron, gron*, "Vorderteil des Gewandes vom Gürtel zum Knie (aus einem Stück oder geteilt ...; Mantel, Überwurf" (TL 4:329). *FEW* 16:32a.

gros (1), T4v20, T5r23, T9v5, N5r21, N5v2, N13v20; fem. sg. *grossa*, T7v4, T8v12, T14v30, T14v31, N5r21, N8v15, N9r24, N15r9; pl. *grossas*, T7v4, T8v12, T14v30, T14v31, N8v15, N9v5. Large (*PD* 213). *Bestia grossa*, N9r24, N15r9; pl. *bestias grossas*, N9v5. Large animal. *Bota ... grossa*, N8v15. Large butt. *Muey* –, N5r21, N5v2 (Table N2), N13v20. Large hogshead. *Peage* –, T4v20, T5r23, T9v5. Main (large) tollhouse. All three occurrences make explicit contrast with the tollhouse at Lubières (T4v21, T5r21, T9v14); in two of them parallel syntax underlines the contrast (*per lo pezage gros*, T4v19–20, *per Lubieras*, T4v21; *per piage gros*, T9v5, *per lo pezage de Lubieras*, T9v14). The main tollhouse must have been the one at Tarascon proper.

Bondurand (151n3) glosses *piage gros* (T9v5) as "péage total" without further explanation.

gros (2). *De* –, T5r[39], T5r[32], T13v1. Around (*PD* 213). *De gros*, T5r[32], T5r[39] = *de redon*, N10v4, N10v8.

gros (3), T9v12. *Adv. More. This occurrence cannot be the adjective, *gros* (1), as it would modify fem. *montaison*. The *FEW* (4:278b) recognizes the related meaning "very" in Fr. but not Occ.

hobrans, see *obran*

home, see *ome*

indi, T3r29, T14r11, N7r25, N14r3, N15v23. Indigo (*LR* 3:557, Alibert 446, *DAO* 467, *DAOS* 405, *FEW* 4:645a; *inde*, Pansier 3:97), a blue dye, more costly than woad. "Exported primarily from India" (Hodges 2000, 155). Lat. *indicum*; gen. *indicii* (Martin-Portier 2:46), abl. *indico* (Martin-Portier 2:40), *indi* (Guérard 1:lxxviii, lxxix, lxxxi, xcv), *indii* (Baratier 388), *inde* (Guérard 1:lxxiii), *Inde* (Baratier 385) (*indi, indii, inde* = Occ.).

Bondurand (138n6) reads *judi*, T3r29, and glosses it as "jute, substance textile"; corrected by Meyer (1891, 482).

isime, T8v1. Ape, simian. *Esimi* (*PD* 167). *Sarazin o isime dona s. ij. d. vi,* T8v1. A Saracen or an ape pays 2s 6d.

Meyer (1891, 482) averred, "Chacun voit qu'il s'agit du droit de péage exigé des Sarrazins ou Sarrazines," but MS T reads *isime*, not *sarazina.*

item (Lat.), passim. "Likewise, also. Used to introduce a new fact or statement, or, more frequently, each new article or particular in an enumeration, esp. in a formal list or document, as an inventory, household-book, will, etc." (*OED*).

jaina: pl. *jainas*, T6r1, T6r2, N11r19, N11r20. Beam (*PD* 216). Med. Lat. *jazina, jayna* (Du Cange 4:282); abl. *jazinis* (Guérard 1:lxxxii); "*Jazina* ou *jayna*, à peu près le même sens que *travata*; il y a les petites [*jazinis minutis*] et les plus grosses [*jazinis bastardis*]" (Baratier 386).

jamais: *non ... jamais*, N16r11. Never (*LR* 3:579).

Jaume, see *Sant Jacme*

Johan Alba, T3v8, T4r19, T4r23, T4v6, T4v10, T4v15, T5r17, T5r26, T5r[34], T5v8, T5v13, T5v16, T5v19, T9v6, T12r4, T12v8, T12v18; N6v4, N7v8, N7v24, N8r11, N8r16, N8r20, N8r23, N8v4, N8v11, N9r8, N10v4, N10v9, N10v13, N10v16, N10v18, N10v24, N11r2, N11r4, N11r8, N11r16, N14r12, N14v1, N14v6, N14v8, N14v9. Two men named Johan Alba, one in MS T, the other in MS N; shareholders in tolls on various commodities. Lat. *Dominus Alba*, "seigneur de Roquemartine et chevalier de Tarascon" (Baratier 1969, 384n1).

jor: *jour* (Fr. form), N12v24; pl. *jors*, N10r24. Day. *Jorn, jor* (*PD* 218). On the Fr. form cf. Ricketts 2005, where *jour, jours* occur some twenty times in narrative verse but not in lyric. *Jorn, jourt* (Pansier 3:99); *journ* (Honnorat 2:479); *jour* (Mistral 2:164).

lana, T3v12, T14r25, N7v10, N14r13. Wool (*PD* 221). Lat. *lana* (Baratier 385, Guérard 1:lxxxiii).

Laubiera, see *Lubieras*

lausa: pl. *lausas*, T6r24, T13v36, T14v6, N11v17. Roof tile. Levied in quantities of 100 (T6r24); compare *teule*, tile, levied in quantities of 1,000 (T4v9, N8r20). *Lauza* (*PD* 223). This appears to be the meaning of the Lat. word transcribed as *lanceis* (abl.) and translated as "lances" by Baratier (387n4, 388n5); also in Guérard (pp. lxxxvi, lxxxvii); correctly *lauceis*. Lat. *lausa, lauza*, "lapidis species, qua domibus cooperiendis et sternendis solariis utuntur, Gall. *dalle*" (Du Cange 5:47).

lega: pl. *legas*, T8v9, N9v13, N9v14; *leguas*, T8v10. League (*PD* 224), "an itinerary measure of distance, varying in different countries, but usually estimated roughly at about 3 miles" (*OED*).

lentilha: pl. *lentilhas*, N14v22. Lentil (*PD* 225, *DAO* 435, *DAOS* 368). Lat. *lenticula*; abl. pl. *lintilgiis*, influenced by Occ. (Baratier 397).

lentiscle, N12r19. Mastic, "an aromatic gum or resin which exudes from the bark of the lentisk or mastic tree, ... used chiefly in making varnishes and, formerly, in medicine" (*OED*). *Lentisc, -le* (*PD* 225). See also *mastec*

leon: pl. **luons*, T14r15. Lion. *Leon* (*PD* 225); cf. variant *levon* (*SW* 4:388). *Cuors de –*, T14r15. Hides of lions. The form *luons* may show influence from the variant definite article *lu* (which see). *FEW* (5:255b) mentions no form of *leon* in *lu-*.

Levant, T13r6. The Levant, "the eastern part of the Mediterranean, with its islands and the countries adjoining" (*OED*).

levar, N5r19; pres. 3rd pers. sg. *leva*, N16r16; pl. *levan*, N13r12; *levon*, N16r13; imperf. 3rd pers. sg. *levava*, N13v10; past subj. 3rd pers. sg. *levessa*, N13v15; imperative 2nd pers. sg. *leva*, N16r6. To levy (a toll). Lat. *levare*; imperf. subj. 3rd pers. pl. *levarent* (Baratier 387, Guérard 1:lxxxiv).

libra (Lat., cf. Occ. *liura*). Abbreviated *libr'*, T6r14, T8r24, T10r26, etc.; *libr.*, T5r[33]; *libr/*, N3v21, N6r13, etc.; *lib/*, N3v21, etc. Pound, the principal monetary unit; a money of account.

libre: pl. *libres*, N12v18. Book (*PD* 226).

liga, N13r16; *ligua*, N13r22, N16r17. *Fineness, purity of silver; cf. Eng. alloy. *Lia, liga*, "alliage" (*PD* 226); *liga*, "loi d'alliage de la monnaie" (Pansier 3:103, *FEW* 5:321b).

Lihon, see *Lion*

limon: pl. *limons*, N12r14. Lime (*LR* 4:76, *SW* 4:402, *DAO* 324, *DAOS* 230).

lin, N7v10, N14r8. Flax (*PD* 227, *DAO* 451, *DAOS* 388). Lat. *linum*, abl. *lino* (Baratier 344).

linh, T6r14. Oared ship, smaller than a galley. *Lenh (PD* 224); *ling* (*LR* 4:77); *lenh, linh* (*SW* 4:365). – *de Roda*, T6r14. An oared ship from Rhodes (see *Roda*). Lat. *lignum* (Guérard 1:xcv, c); abl. *ligno* (Baratier 386, Guérard 1:lxxxii, xciv, xcix).

liome, T4v12; pl. *liomes*, T13r11, T14v13, N14v12; **liolmes*, N8v1; **liormes*, N8r margin. Legume, "the fruit, or the edible portion of a leguminous plant, e.g., beans, peas, pulse ...; by extension: a vegetable used for food" (*OED*). *Legum, liome* ("légume," *PD* 224, *LR* 4:44, Alibert 463; "Gemüse," vegetables, *SW* 4:356); *liome, lieume, lieoume, lulme* (Pansier 3:104, *DAO* 395, *DAOS* 314). Fr. *lioume*, "occitanisme" (Fennis 2:1134). Lat. *legumen*; gen. *liguminis* (Baratier 377, 385, Guérard 1:lxxxi, lxxxiii), abl. *legumine* (Baratier 388, Guérard 1:lxxxvi).

Bondurand reads *home*, man: *de tot home,* T4v12, "quel qu'en soit le propriétaire" (p. 141n9); *de tot homes*, T13r11, T14v13, "qui qu'en soit le propriétaire" (p. 157n1).

Lion, N10r13; *Lihon*, T9r9. Lyon (Rhône). Lat. *Lugdunum*; abl. *Lugduno* (Baratier 387, Guérard 1:lxxxv, Martin-Portier 2:45).

lo, pl. *los*, passim; pl. *lo* before *senhors*, T4r20, T6v21, T7r5, T7v23, T12r23, T12r28. Definite article. The. Used adverbially with *carga*: *la cargua*, per load, T3v7, T4r18, T4r22, T4v5, T4v14; synonymous with *per carga*, T5r28. With *mog*: *lo muetz*, per hogshead, T9v26, T12r1; synonymous with *per mueg*, T9v8. See also *lu*

Lobieras, see *Lubieras*

Lombart, N10r16; pl. *Lombartz*, T9r1; fem. *Lombarda*, N10r16; pl. *Lombardas*, T9r1. Lombard, one from Lombardy (region in northern Italy, capital Milan). Lat. *Lombardus; fem. Lombarda* (Baratier 387).

loton, T8r13, N12v13, N14r22. Brass. *Laton, loton* (*PD* 222).

***lu**, masc. sg., T12r27, T12v2, T12v13; pl. *lu*, T10r5, T10r8, T10r10, T10r12, T10r14, T10r16, T10r18, T10r20, T10r22, T10r24, T10r26, T10r28, T10v3 = Table T1 from one hogshead to thirteen, after which the article is omitted. Variant form of the definite article. The (*LR* 4:86). See Introduction §3, Language. See also *lo*

Lubieras, T3v9, T4r20, etc. (this spelling not in N); *Lubiera*, T12r26; *Lobieras*, T4r24, T6v21, etc., N4v10, N7r14, etc.; *Laubiera*, N15r14. Lubières, an island in the Rhône that became a quarter in the southwest corner of Tarascon; downstream from the toll point at Tarascon proper, as may be inferred from N7r10–5. Still an island in 1332: *ad insulas Luperiarum et Luciani* (Pécout 2010, 8). Lat. "Luperiarum / Lupariarum, insula (*Lubières*)" (Pécout 2010, 288, s.v. Tharasco). See also *Gernegua.*

luehn, N9v18. Far. *Lonh* (*o* either open or close), "loin" (*PD* 229). *Los* –, N9v18. Those from far away.

luons, see *leon*

ma (It.), T15r5. But (Battaglia 9:343). Mistral (2:247) mentions Mod. Occ. *ma*, "mais," in Limousin and Niçois. Cf. *mais* (3)

*__mattafellon__, T4r13. Reefpoint, "each of the several short pieces of rope fixed in a line across a sail, and serving to secure it when reefed" (*OED*); T4r13 implies that a load of reefpoints (*cargua de mattafellon*) might be transported before being fixed to sails. Mod. Occ. *matafions*, "garcette, corde qui sert à attacher la voile à l'antenne" (Alibert 486); *matafion* (Fourquin and Rigaud 1994, 241); *matafioun* (Thomas 1891, 420). *FEW* 23:96a. Fr. *matafion* (Fennis 2:1211). It. *matafione*, "raban d'envergure et de tente. 'Matafioni sono funi picciole che sono cuscite alle vele et alle tende, perche si possano attaccare alle antenne et a i filari'" (Jal 990).

madiera, T6v2, T13v37. Timber; "bois de charpente? ou matériaux pour bâtir?" (*PD* 230); "madriers," pieces of timber, beams (Bondurand 146n2).

mainage, T8v6. Retinue (*PD* 231).

maior, T15r11. Greater. *Major* (*PD* 232).

mais (1), N4r14, N5v11. Adj. More. *Calque causa mais*, N5v11. Something more. *Mais de*, N4r14 (*so que y aura mais de ...*). More than.

mais (2), T5r18, T5r[41], T5v7, N5r18, N8r23, N8v21, etc. Adv. *Also (cf. conj. "und," *SW* 5:30; "plus, davantage," *LR* 4:123, *PD* 231, Pansier 3:107).

mais (3), N5r10. Conj. But. Cf. *ma*

maistre: pl. *maistres*, N10r3. Master. *Maestre (PD* 230). – *de la moneda*, N10r3. Master of the mint.

man, N5r4. Order. "Ordre, commandement" (*PD* 234).

maniera (1), T3r1, T15r9, T15v3, N5r17, N5r19, N6v24, N7r6, N8v23, N13v24, N16r5. Manner; "manière, sorte, ... conduite" (*PD* 236); "usage, coutume" (Honnorat 2:585).

maniera (2), N8v1, N14r5, N14r24, N14v18. Kind. – *de blas et de liolmes*, N8v1. Kind of grains or vegetables. – *d'espiceria*, N14r5. Kind of spice. – *de frucha*, N14v18. Kind of fruit. – *de granas*, N14r24. Kind of seeds. See also *forma* (2)

manifestar: pret. 3rd pers. sg. *manifestet*, T14r3. To declare. "Manifester" (*LR* 4:146). Lat. *manifestare*; perfect 3rd pers. sg. *manifestavit* (Baratier 388).

mantegus, see *mentaure*

mar, T4r16, N5r25, N7v11, N14r14, N15v14. Sea (*PD* 237). *Mesura de la –*, N5r25. Measure of the sea (not of Peccais). *Peis de –*, T4r16; *peyson de –*, N7v11, N14r14, N15v14. Fish from the sea, not from the Rhône or a marsh (see *palun*).

Martha, see *Sancta Martha*

mastec, N14r6. Mastic (*PD* 239, *DAO* 254, *DAOS* 140), "an aromatic gum or resin which exudes from the bark of the lentisk or mastic tree, ... used chiefly in making varnishes and, formerly, in medicine" (*OED*). See also *lentiscle*

***mastina**, N9r23. Mastiff bitch. "Chienne" (Alibert 485; mod. Occ., *FEW* 6/1:257b); cf. *mastin*, masc., "mâtin, gros chien" (*PD* 239).

Materials, see Building; Cloth

may, T8r17, N12v15. May, the fifth month. *Mai (PD* 231). Lat. *Maius*; gen. *mensis madii* (Baratier 386).

mealha: *miagla*, N2r23, N4v9, N8r5, etc.; *mi[a]gla*, N2r22 (emended from *migla*); pl. *miaglas*, N8r2; *mieaglas*, N4v9; *meallas*, T12r22. Coin worth half a denier, equal to an obole. "Maille, 1/2 denier" (*PD* 239).

Measures: see *barral, bota, cairat* (3), *cana, carga* (2), *caupolada, comol, copiera, corda* (2), *costa, emina, fais, mesura, mog, navada, naviada, palm, pes, pesa, quintal, ras, rest, saquiera, saumada, sestier, travada* (2)

Medicines, see Spices

meia, see *miech*

meins, see *mens*

mel, T3v24, T14r32, T15r15, N7v15, N14r18. Honey (*PD* 241). Lat. *mel*; abl. *melle* (Baratier 385, Guérard 1:lxxxiii).

mela: pl. *melas*, T4r4; *miellas*, N12r margin. Almond (*PD* 241, *DAO* 307, *DAOS* 206). Aphetic form of *amella*, which see.

meleze, T5v33, T6r7; *melle*, N11r17. Larch wood. *Meleze*, *melse* (*PD* 241, *SW* 5:174, *DAO* 252, *DAOS* 138); *mèle, mèlze* (Mistral 2:314).

melher, T4v9; *millier*, N8r20, N14v9. Thousand. *Milier* (*PD* 248). Lat. *milliarius*; abl. *melliario* (Guérard 1:lxxxiii), *mellierio* (Baratier 385), both influenced by Occ. It. *migliaio* (Edler 184).

melle, see *meleze*

menar: pres. subj. 3rd pers. sg. *mene*, T6r19, T8r23, N9r18, N11v10; pres. part. *menant*, T8v24. To take (*PD* 242), used here in passive sense: to be taken.

mens, T13v7; *meins*, N9r21; *meyns*, N5v3. Adv. Less (*PD* 243). Prep., N5v3. Less, minus. *Mens de*, T13v7. Less than. Lat. *minus* (Baratier 386, Guérard 1:lxxxiii).

mensa: pl. *mensas*, T8v17. Young, offspring. "Nourriture" (Bondurand 150n5, quoted by *SW* 5:200, Pansier 3:111), taken here in the sense "celui qui a été élevé, formé" (*TLFi*).

mentaure: past part., masc. pl. *mantegus*, N16r14. To mention.

menudier: fem. pl. *menudieras*, N16r3. Small, less important (*PD* 243).

menut: fem. *menuda*, N15r10; pl. *menudas*, T5v36, T7v5, T14v28, T14v32, N9v2, N9v9, N12r15. Small (*PD* 243). Modifies *bestia*, small animal, T14v28, N9v2, N9v9, N15r10; *figas*, N12r15, small figs; *perteguas*, T5v36, small poles; *sebas*, T7v5, T14v32, small onions. Lat. *minutus*; abl. pl. *minutis* (Baratier 386).

mercadaria, N13r8; pl. *mercadarias*, T15v2, N12v20, N12v22, N13v16, N15r16, N15r20. Commodity. "Marchandise" (*PD* 244).

mercandisa: pl. *mercandisas,* N7r16. Merchandise. *Mercandiza* (*PD* 244).

mersaria, T8r5, N12v10. Haberdashery, "small articles appertaining to dress, as thread, tape, ribbons, etc."; mercery (rare in Eng.), the goods sold by a mercer, "a person who deals in textile fabrics, esp. silks, velvets, and other fine materials" (*OED*). *Merceria, mersaria*, "mercerie" (*PD* 245). Med. Lat. *merceria*, "quartier de la mercerie" (Niermeyer, Baratier 272na); *mercimonia* (Baratier 386, Guérard 1:lxxxii).

mes (1), N12v25. Month (*PD* 245). Lat. *mensis* (Baratier 386, Guérard 1:lxxxiii).

mes (2), see *metre* (1)

mesclament, T5r9. Adv. Mixed together. *Mesclamen (PD* 246). Cf. *divisament*

mesura, T4v13, N2r18, etc. Measure. *Mezura (PD* 248). – *de la mar*, N5r25. Measure of the sea, in contrast to that of Peccais: 40 heaping setiers of salt by the measure of Peccais = 42 setiers by the measure of the sea. – *de Pecays,* N5r24. Measure of Peccais. – *de Tharascon,* T4v13, T13r12, N1v21, N2r18, N4r23, N4v7, N4v17, N5r1, N8v3, N8v23, N12r9, N14v13. Measure of Tarascon.

mesurar, N10v1. To measure. *Mezurar (PD* 248).

Metals, minerals, chemicals: see *acier, alum, argent, argento vivo, arzica, aur, boras, carbon, caus, cendre, coure, estanh, ferre, gip, greza, liga, loton, peira, plomb, roqua, solpre, veire, verdet, vernice*

meteis, T12v3. Same. *Mezeis, met-* (*PD* 248).

metre (1): past part. *mes*, N13v10. To set (money at an exhange rate). "Mettre, placer," etc., *PD* 247.

metre (2): pres. 3rd pers. sg. *met*, N4v25, N5r8, N7r1; pres. subj. 3rd pers. sg. *meta*, T12v1; pl. *metan*, N6r21. *To load (salt on a barge). In this usage *metre* is a synonym of *cargar*, as is seen clearly in *met* N5r8 and *carga* N5r15, N5r16, N5r17; *si metan en un navey*, N6r21, "let them be loaded in one boat."

miagla, see *mealha*

mieaglas, see *mealha*

miech, N13v22; *mieg*, T4v33; *m[ie]g*, T5r5; *miegz*, T15r31; *mieç*, N5v6, N6v14, N8r17, N10v8, N10v15, N10v21; fem. *miega*, N9r6; *meia*, T13v9; *mieia*, T5r15. Half. *Meg* (*PD* 140). *Mieç peage*, N6v14. Half toll. Lat. *medium* (Baratier 386), *medium pedagium* (388).

miellas, see *mela*

migla, see *mealha*

milh, N14v11. Millet, a cereal grass cultivated for its grain. *Melh, milh* (*PD* 241, *DAO* 388, *DAOS* 306). Lat. *milium*; gen. *milii* (Baratier 397).

millier, see *melher*

mina, see *emina*

Minerals, see Metals

mitat, T5r29, T5r[36], etc., N2r5, N4v14, etc. Half. Lat. *medietas*; acc. *medietatem* (Guérard 1:lxxxvii).

mog, T16r12; *mueg*, T5r15, etc.; *muegz*, T12r8, etc.; *muetz*, T12r27, etc.; *muey*, N1v21, N5r21; *muy*, N2r6, N5v2, etc.; pl. *mueg*, T9v9, T11v24; *muetz*, T9v12, T10r6, etc.; *muy*, N2r9, etc. Abbreviated *m*°., T9v22, T10r9, etc. (The forms *mog, mueg, muegz, muetz,* and the abbreviation *m*°. occur only in T; *muey, muy*, only in N.) Hogshead (*PD* 249), a measure of salt (passim), wine (N8v22), or tanner's bark (T5r15, T13v9, N9r6; see *ros*). "Originally signified the weight or the cubic capacity of an average-sized wagon-load" (Zupko 1978, 116).

As a measure of salt, the hogshead varied from one town to another; the hogshead of Arles, downstream from Tarascon, differed from that of Avignon upstream. The basis of variation was the *gros muid de Peccais*, equal to 60 quintals or 6.09 metric tons, but sometimes given certain *avantages* or accretions that raised it to 72 quintals or 7.3 tons, and up to a maximum of the *bon poids* at 8.1 tons (Rossiaud 2002, 2:210–1). The hogshead of Beaucaire, across the Rhône from Tarascon, was nearly identical to that of Peccais: 136 hogsheads of Peccais equalled 130 hogsheads, 43 quintals, of Beaucaire (Villain-Gandossi 1969, 39). It. *moggio*, "a dry measure ... varying greatly in size, from about 4 Florentine bushels in Caffa [Crimea] to 52 in Avignon" (Edler 187).

MS N distinguishes small and large hogsheads of salt (*muey petit*, N1v21, etc.; *muy gros*, N5r23, N5v2, etc.). The *muy gros* of Tarascon equalled 2 and 20/21 (2.952) *muy petit* (N5v2).

The hogshead of wine was less coherent because each town protected itself against importation of wine with stiff import taxes that only a poor local harvest could reduce. (Such practices contribute to the relatively slight presence of wine in TN.) At Beaucaire and Tarascon at the end of the fifteenth century, the hogshead of wine counted 24 *barrals*; the *barral* varied by town between 40 and 50 litres (Rossiaud 2002, 2:211–12). See also *bota*, *barral*. It. *moggio*, "a wine measure of 2 1/3 butts (in Avignon)" (Edler 187).

As a measure of tanner's bark, the hogshead (*lo mueg del ros)* is defined at T5r15: "Cet article fait connaître que le muid de roseaux était de 72 quintaux ou de 3 saquières et demi. La saquière valait donc environ 20 quintaux et demi (20 qx 57); et se rapprochait singulièrement de notre tonne de 1.000 kilos (20 quintaux)" (Bondurand 142n4). That is, one *saquiera* = 1,029 kilos; one *quintal* = 50.02 kilos; and one *mog* of tanner's bark = 3,601 kilos. MS A_2, speaking of tanner's bark: *Pro tribus saqueriis et dimidia, faciunt modium*, "For three *saquieras* and a half they make a hogshead" (Martin-Portier 2:48).

Lat. *modius*; gen. *modii* (Baratier 387), acc. *modium* (386).

mola, T6v17, T6v18, T13v30, T14v23, N12r23, N15r3 (twice); pl. *molas*, N12r23. Millstone (*PD* 250). – *de barbier*, T6v18, N12r23, N15r3. Grindstone, "meule à rasoirs ou à ciseaux" (Bondurand 146n12) or surgical instruments (see *barbier*). – *de molin*, T6v17, T13v30. Millstone. Lat. *mola* (Baratier 388).

molin, T6r12, T6r13, T6v17, T13v30, N11v6, N11v7, N12r23, N15r3. Mill (*PD* 250). – *d'aigua*, T6r12, N11v6. Watermill, boat mill. – *d'aura*, T6r13, N11v7. Windmill. Lat. *molendinum*; gen. *molendini* (Baratier 386, Guérard 1:lxxxii, Martin-Portier 2:42), *molendinis* (Delebecque 3:50).

moneda (1), T9r20, N10r3, N10r4, N10r8. Mint, establishment where money is coined (*PD* 251).

moneda (2), T8r15, N10r5. Coins (*PD* 251). Lat. *moneta*, "monnaies en espèces" (Baratier 386, Guérard 1:lxxxii).

moneda (3); pl. *monedas*, N13r12, N16r13. *Money of account (£ s d).

moneda (4), N13r15, N13v8, N16r13, N16r16, N16r20, N16r22, N16r margin; pl. *monedas*, N13r11. *Currency (a medium of exchange, such as tournois or florins of Florence). At N16r margin, *monede* shows the It. pl. ending *-e* (Occ. *-as*); the root is seen in sg. *moneda*, which may be Occ., but also occurs in early It. (Battaglia 10:797) beside normal It. *moneta.*

monedar: past part. *monedat*, N12v9. To coin (*PD* 251).

monede, see *moneda* (4)

monedier: pl. *monediers*, T9r19, N10r3. Coiner (*PD* 252), one who works in a mint. Lat. *monetarius*; nom. pl. *monaterii* (Baratier 389).

Money, see Coins

montada, N15v2. A going upstream. See *montar*; cf. *desidenduda*

montar, N4r21; pres. 3rd pers. sg. *monta*, N5r20, N7r10, N13v20; pl. *monton*, N5v5; pres. part. *montant*, T3r2, T4v31, T9v2, T13r7, N1v22, N1v23, N15v8, etc. *To go up (the Rhône). Lat. *ascendere*; gerund *asscendendo* (Baratier 385), *ascendendo* (Guérard 1:lxxxiii).

montazon, T9v8, T9v13, T12r5, T12r23, T12v10, T12v16, T15v12, T16r11; *montason*, T12r5, N4r19; *montaison* (Fr. suffix), N4v1, N4v19, N5r7, N6v3. *Montazon*, a fee paid by ships going up a river (*PD* 252). *La – dels cavalliers de Tharascon*, T15v12, T16r11. The *montazon* of the knights of Tarascon. *Senhors de la –*, T12r5, T12v10, T12v16, N4v19; *senhors per la –*, T12r23; *gentils homes de la –*, N4v1, N5r7. The shareholders in the *montazon*. MS T calls the shareholders *cavalliers* or *senhors*, MS N *senhors* (once) or *gentils homes*. On the form *montaison* in MS N, cf. the Fr. suffix *-aison*, "essentiellement formateur de subst[antifs] d'action" (*TLFi*).

Med. Lat. *montatio*, *montazon* (= Occ.), "droit que payaient les navires montant une rivière" (Fourquin and Rigaud 1994, 248, give citations 1140-ca. 1329; cf. Du Cange 5:512); *montazone* (It.) (Guérard 1:xciii). MS A_2

uses Lat. abl. *montaysono* (Martin-Portier 2:42), *montasono* (Delebecque 1929a, 3:51, 3:52, etc.).

mostarda, N7v16, N14r17. Mustard. *Mostalha, mostarda (PD* 254).

mouton, N7v21, N8r1, N14r23, N15v12; pl. *moutons*, T3v31, T14r26, T15r27, N9v2, N9v9. Sheep. *Molton (PD* 251). *Pels de* –, N7v21, N8r1. Sheepskin. Med. Lat. *multo* (Niermeyer); abl. *multone* (Baratier 377, Guérard 1:lxxxi). Med. Lat. *moltonus* (Du Cange 5:541); abl. pl. *multonis* (Baratier 385). Synonym of *ovis*; abl. *ove* (Baratier 377, Guérard 1:lxxxi).

moutonina: pl. *moutoninas*, T4r31. Sheepskin (*moltonina, PD* 251). Med. Lat. *multoninus*, "of or from sheep" (Latham 1975–2014, 6:1857), abl. pl. *multoninis*, "de moutons" (Baratier 388) (Guérard 1:lxxxvi, lxxxvii). It. *montonina*, "wool-fell, sheep skin with the wool on it" (Edler 189).

mueg, *muey*, see *mog*

Mujolans, *los*, T12r12; *pezage dels Mujolans*, T5v24; *pezage dels Mujulans*, T5v20; *del Mujolans*, T9v22. An unidentified tollhouse mentioned in MS T; on *Los Violans* in MS N, see below. The word survives in the sg. as *Mujolan*, a placename in Hérault and elsewhere in France; Lat. *Mediolanum*, from the Gaulish meaning "central sanctuary" (Nègre 1990–8, 1:190, item 2978), which also gives *Milano* in Lombardy.

Los Mujolans, plural in form but singular in meaning, refers to a place in *los Mujolans, que son aras del rei nostre senhor*, "Los Mujolans, which now belongs to the king our lord" (T12r12). In other passages the word may refer to either a place or people: *pezage dels Mujulans* (T5v20, spelled *Mujolans* T5v24), "the toll of of Los Mujulans [a place]" or "the toll of the Mujulans [people]." Once the word *Mujolans* is introduced by a singular article, implying that it too is singular, and that the *-s* is part of the root: *pezage que compret lo rey nostre senhor del Mujolans* (T9v22), "a toll that the king our lord bought of Lo [singular, therefore a place] Mujolans," but since this is the only case in which the *-s* is singular, it appears to be a scribal error. Bondurand interprets this passage, ignoring the singular, as referring to people: "Ces Mujulans avaient vendu leur péage au comte de Provence" (Bondurand 144n1, on T5v20).

In view of the etymology proposed by Nègre, it appears that *Los Mujolans* was originally a place name. But the word was apparently used also of the people who owned the place: Lat. *Mujulanis*, in MS A_2, refers to people who sold a certain share in the toll on salt to the king: *Pro directu empto per Curia a muiulanis percipit Curia de quolibet modio ... tres pict[as]*, "For the right bought for the court from the Mujulans, the court receives on each hogshead ... three *pites* [0.75d]" (Martin-Portier 2:42, 2:44; *Mujulanis* Delebecque 3:51, 3:53).

If *Los Mujolans* refers to people or a people, a possible albeit remote etymon is Lat. *Musulanii* or *Musolani,* a North African tribe mentioned by Pliny in the first century A.D. (Toutain 1896, 273), also called *Musulamii*. By the fourteenth century the word could have come to refer to Muslims in or near Tarascon. On commerce between Christians and Muslims in Montpellier in 1162, see Dufourcq 1975, 50; on ships owned jointly by Christians and Muslims in Spain, Dufourcq 1980, 223.

Probably identical to *los Violans* in N: *peage dels Violans*, N2r3, N2r11, N11r9, N11r12. The four places where *Mujolans* occurs in MS T (Rubrics I, wood and wood products; Rubrics II and III, salt) correspond to the four places in MS N where *Violans* occurs (Rubric II, salt; Rubric III, wood and wood products). Both are identified as belonging to the king, who is said to own the right to this toll now (*aras*, T12r12, N2r3), or simply to own it (T5v22, N11r9, N11r12); MS T says he bought it (*compret*, T9v21). See also *pezage*

Violans, with its three minims before the *o*, may be a *lectio facilior* of *mujolans*, with its six. *Violan*s, fiddler, "qui joue de la viole ... *m*. libertin, débauché" (Alibert 696). Pres. part. of *violar*. To fiddle (*PD* 385). An association of fiddlers with a tollhouse was real: a *juglar* was paid to fiddle, *violari*, at a tollhouse in Campfranch, Aragon, in 1311 (Bofarull, Bofarull, and Bofarull 1871, 166). Thus *Los Violans* may be considered a folk etymology of *Los Mujolans*.

mul, N9r25, N9v7; pl. *muls*, T8v14. Male mule (*PD* 255). Lat. *mulus* (Baratier 388), abl. *mulo* (Baratier 377, Guérard 1:lxxxi, Martin-Portier 2:45).

mula: pl. *mulas*, T8v14, T8v25. Female mule (*PD* 255). Lat. *mula* (Baratier 388).

muy, see *mog*

Narbona, T3r11, T14r8, N7r19, N14r1, N15v19. Narbonne (Aude).

natura, N9v24. Family (*PD* 256).

nau, T5r[38], T5r[32], T5v12, T6r16, T13v1, N10v3, N11r1, N11v9. Sailed ship, larger than a *navec* (which see); unlike the galley or *linh* (which see), which was driven primarily by oars. "Navire, vaisseau" (*PD* 257). Fr. *nef*, "rarement appliqué aux galères" (Fennis 2:1282). Lat. *navis*; acc. *navem* (Baratier 386), abl. *nave* (Baratier 386, Guérard 1:lxxxii), *navi* (Martin-Portier 2:46).

navada, T4v21, T5r2; *navaida*, T5r22, T7v19. Shipload, the cargo of a *nau* (*PD* 257; *SW* 5:369; Jal 1040; Fr. *navée*, Tisseur 1887, 273) or a *navec*. *Navaida de caus*, etc., T7v19; *naviada ... de caus*, etc., T13v14; and *lo navec cargat de caus*, etc., N9r15, are all used equivalently. For the suffix, compare *caupolada, naviada, barcata* (Jal 244). It. *navata* (Reale Accademia d'Italia 1937, 497). See also *naviada*

navec, N6v17, etc.; *navech*, N13r1; *navei*, T4v23, T6r18, etc.; *navey*, T4v18, T9v23, N4v4, etc. Ship of any size, including a large one; also, a convoy of ships to be towed upstream (Rossiaud 2002, 2:238–9). At T6r18, a boat smaller than a *nau*; "*navei* exprime ici un objet moins important que *nau*. C'est un bateau et non un navire" (Bondurand 145n8). *Naveg, -ei* (*PD* 257, Pansier 3:118). *Lo navec cargat*, N9r11, N9r15. Boatload (cf. *navada*). Fr. *navire*, forms *navee, navie*, from Lat. *navigium*, "bateau, vaisseau (parfois galère ou même embarcation de galère, mais aussi opposé aux galériformes)" (Fennis 2:1281–2). Lat. *navigium*, "radeau: *navigium vel lignum*" (Baratier 398, 552), but "radeau" is uncertain, as *lignum* refers to a rowed ship (see *linh*); abl. *navigio* (Baratier 387, Guérard 1:lxxxv).

***naviada**, T13r16, T13v14; cf. *navada, navaida*. Shipload, the cargo of a *navec, navei*. *Naviada*, "charge d'un bateau" (Pansier 3:118). Lat. *naviata* (Martin-Portier 2:48).

nerta, N12r19. Myrtle, "the edible fruit of a myrtle [shrub or tree] ...; a myrtle berry" (*OED*). *Mirt, nerta* (*PD* 249, *DAO* 364, *DAOS* 271). Lat. *myrta*, with assimilation of *m* to *t* (*OED*), produced Med. Lat. *nerta* (Baratier 300).

nespla: pl. *nesplas*, T7r15. Medlar (*PD* 259, Pansier 3:119, *DAO* 291, *DAOS* 186), "the fruit of the medlar [tree], which resembles a small brown-skinned apple" (*OED*). Lat. *mespilum*, Med. Lat. *mespila* (Niermeyer), *nespila* (Du Cange 5:589), *nespula* (*FEW* 6/2:47a); nom. pl. *nespole* (Baratier 387, Guérard 1:lxxxv), gen. pl. *nespularum* (Martin-Portier 2:45).

nocier, N6v10. Skipper, master (of a small vessel), pilot, riverman; "patron ... définit partout une aristocratie du travail" (Rossiaud 2002, 2:228, 230). Cf. *nauchier*, "nocher, nautonier" (*PD* 257); "nocher, responsable nautique d'un navire" (Fourquin and Rigaud 1994, 256). It. *nocchiere*, "ship's pilot" (Edler 192).

noguier, T6r8, N11v3. Walnut tree (*PD* 260, *DAO* 292, *DAOS* 186). Med. Lat. *nucarius* (Niermeyer); nom. *nugerius* (Baratier 386), gen. *nogerii* (Baratier 386, Guérard 1:lxxxii), both influenced by Occ.

non, passim. Negative adverb. Not ("non, ne," *PD* 261). Negates a noun: *non-Levant*, T13r7. Negates a verb: *non an pagat,* T15r4; *non es*, N6v10.

Negates a past part.: *non adobatz*, T3r17; *non salat*, T4r16; *salat ho non*, N15v14. Negates an adverb: *non plus*, T12r17. Negates prepositional phrase: *non de Belcayre*, N6v12. *Non ... si non*, N7r2, N8r7–8. Only.

non-Levant, T13r7. Elsewhere than the Levant.

notar: imperative 2nd pers. sg. *nota*, N12v24. To take note (*PD* 262).

nou (1), T6v13, T6v16, T13v30, T14v20; *no[u]*, N7v4, N12r22; fem. *nova*, T13v30, N12r21. New (*PD* 262).

nou (2), N7r18. Nine (*PD* 262).

novellamens, T6r18. Recently. *Novelamen* (*PD* 262).

noze: pl. *nozes*, T7r2, T7r12, T13v26; *noses*, N12r7, N14v18, N14v20. Walnut. *Nozes fresquas*, T7r12; *noses frescas*, N14v18. Fresh walnuts. Cf. *rosas frescas*, N12r14, perhaps an error for *noses frescas*. *Notz* (*PD* 262, *DAO* 294, *DAOS* 189); *nos, noze* (Pansier 3:120). Lat. *nux*; gen. pl. *nucum* (Martin-Portier 2:46), abl. pl. *nucibus* (Baratier 377, Guérard 1:lxxxi). Med. Lat. **nuca* (cf. Occ. *noga*, *DAO* 294, *FEW* 7:257a); nom. pl. *nuce* (Baratier 387, Guérard 1:lxxxv).

***obol**: abbreviated *o.*, passim. Obole, a coin worth half a denier (Pansier 3:121, Alibert 513, *FEW* 7:279a). The *obole provençale* was worth half a *tournois provençal* (see *tornes*) (Rolland 1956, 85). The counts of Provence minted oboles in the thirteenth and fourteenth centuries (Duplessy 2004–10, 2:3–13). Lat. *obolus*: acc. *obolum* (Baratier 384).

obra, T8r12. Product (*PD* 264).

obrage, N12r5, N12v12. Product (*obratge*, PD 264). – *de terra*, N12r5. Product of clay, earthenware. – *faç de ferre*, N12v12. Product made of iron.

obran: pl. *hobrans*, N10r4. Worker (pres. part. of *obrar*).

obrar: pres. 3rd pers. pl. *obran*, T9r19, N10r7. To work (*PD* 264).

***octubre**, N12v25. October. *Ochoire, octobre* (*PD* 265). The form in *-u-* is mentioned as Cat. and Sp. by *LR* 4:365.

ola, see *olla*

oli, T4r10, T14r23, T15r14, N7v20, N14r22, N15v11. Oil (*PD* 266). Lat. *oleum*; abl. *oleo* (Baratier 385, 388, Guérard 1:lxxxiii, lxxxvi, lxxxvii).

olla: pl. *ollas*, T6v24, N12r3, N15r7; *olas*, T14v27. Pot (*ola*, *PD* 266). *Olas de terras*, T14v27. Clay or earthenware pot. Lat. *olla*; Med. Lat. *olea* (Du Cange 6:41), *oletum* (ibid.); abl. pl. *ollis terre* (Baratier 388), *ollis terrae* (Guérard 1:lxxxvi), *olletis terre* (Baratier 387, 388).

ome, T8r19; *home* T12r7, N4v6, N12v16, etc.; *hom* (nominative sg., as here, before the loss of declension), T5r8; pl. *homes* T5r9, T8v6, T9v11, T9v18, T13r3, N2v3, N2v9, etc.; *homens*, N2r2, N2r8, N2r14, etc. Man, person. "Homme" (*PD* 267). *Gentils homes*, T8v5, T9v11, T9v18, etc., N1v19, N2r2, N2r13, etc. Nobles. Includes Madame Elis in Table N1 (*tos los gentils homens*, all the nobles, N2r21, etc.); does not include Madame Elis at N2r7, N4v1, etc.; Madame Elis does not appear in T. *Ome* refers to either man or woman, like its etymon, Lat. *homo* (*OLD*), and its cognate, Fr. *homme* (*TLFi*). *Homs cavalcans*, T8v10: see *cavalcador*

on, T8r22; *von*, T4v28. Where (*PD* 267); with subj., wherever. Lat. *ubi* (Baratier 387). *On que si mene*, T8r22, wherever it is taken ("quelle que soit sa destination," Bondurand 149n9). *De von que venga*, T4v28, wherever it comes from ("quelle qu'en soit la provenance," Bondurand 141n9). Lat. *ubicumque* (Guérard 1:lxxxiii), *undecumque* (Baratier 387).

ordenar: pret. 3rd pers. pl. *ordeneron*, N13v14. To order (*PD* 269).

ordi, N8r25. Barley (*PD* 270, *DAO* 386, *DAOS* 303). Lat. *hordeum*; gen. *ordei* (Baratier 392).

orri: pl. *orris*, T13r22. Hold of a ship carrying grain. "Le dérivé et l'équivalent du latin *horreum*, grenier. On dit encore aujourd'hui, d'un navire chargé de blé versé à même la cale, qu'il est chargé *en grenier*. *En orris*, comme *in horreis*, signifie donc: dans les flancs du navire, dans la cale" (Bondurand 154n5). Ger. "Kornboden, -speicher," grain floor, storehouse (*SW* 5:528); "grenier, grange" (Honnorat 2:751); "grenier à blé; réservoir ou compartiment d'un grenier; ... vivier où l'on tient du poisson" (Mistral 2:428).

ors, N8r6. Bear (*PD* 271). *Cuer d'–*, N8r6. Bearskin.

orsa: pl. *orsas*, T6r9, N11v4. Tackle by means of which the long yard supporting a lateen sail was manoeuvred (Fourquin and Rigaud 1994, 262; drawing, 265). A lateen sail is "a triangular sail suspended by a long yard at an angle of about 45 degrees to the mast" (*OED*). OFr. *ource, ours, ourse*: "quand l'artimon était une voile triangulaire enverguée sur une antenne latine ... pour manoeuvrer cette antenne ou vergue ... on établissait une estrope au Car de l'antenne, et à cette estrope on accrochait deux palans qui faisaient les fonctions de bras, un à gauche, l'autre à droite. Chacun de ces palans recevait le nom d'Orse ou d'Ourse" (Jal 1103–4, cf. Rossiaud 2002, 2:243); Fr. *palan*, "tackle, hoisting gear." Fr. *orse*, "manoeuvre du car servant de bras à l'antenne" (Fennis 2:1313). The yard might weigh more than 6 tons; "to manage such yards and the huge sails hung from them, some over 800 square metres in area, required many men and complex block and tackle systems" (Pryor 1994, 71). See also *antenna*

pagar, passim; fut. 3rd pers. pl. *pagaran*, N12v21; first conditional 3rd pers. sg. *pagaria*, T4v26, T5r9; past subj. 3rd pers. sg. *pagessa*, N13r10. To pay (*PD* 273). Lat. *solvere*: pres. 3rd pers. sg. *solvit*, pl. *solvunt* (Baratier 385). Lat. *redimere*; pres. 3rd pers. pl. *redimunt* (Baratier 387).

pais, N10r10. Region. *Paes (PD* 273).

palm, T5r[32], T13v4, etc.; pl. *palms*, T5r[38], etc.; N10v3, etc. Palm, the length of the open hand (*PD* 275). Fr. *pan*, "mesure égale à 1/4 de mètre" (Pansier 3:125); "ancienne mesure de longueur correspondant à vingt-quatre centimètres, usitée dans le Midi de la France" (*TLFi*). Lat. *palmus*; gen. pl. *palmorum* (Baratier 386).

palun, T7v30; *palum*, N12v11. Marsh (*PD* 275, *DAO* 110). *Peis de Roze o –*, T7v30. Fish from the Rhône or a marsh. *Peysson de Rose ho de – fresc*, N12v11. Fish from the Rhône or a freshwater marsh (see *fresc*), in contrast to fish from the sea (see *mar*). Lat. *palus*; acc. *paludem* (Baratier 372).

pancarte (Fr.), front cover of MS N. Schedule of tolls. "Affiche ou papier donnant le tarif de certains droits" (*TLFi*).

*__paniera__: pl. *panyeras*, N11v18. Breadbasket (Pansier 3:125, *FEW* 7:536a, Alibert 524). Cf. *panier* (*PD* 276, Alibert 524).

papier, N12v18. Paper (*PD* 277).

parelh, N11r23. Pair (*PD* 278).

parelhament, N15v6. Likewise. *Parelhamen (PD* 278). Lat. *similiter* (Baratier 385, Guérard 1:lxxxiii).

pargamins, see *pergamin*

parier: pl. *pariers*, T4v23, T13r20. Partner (*PD* 279, Pansier 3:126).

part (1), T5r[33], N5v3; *parte* (It.), T15r11. Component part of a whole. "Part, partie, portion" (*PD* 279). *La tersa –*, T5r[33]. One third. *La xxje. –*, N5v3. One twenty-first. *Per la maior parte* (It.), T15r11. For the greater part.

part (2), T9v4, N10r18, N15v4; pl. *partz*, T9r4. Region. *Autra –*, N10r18. Elsewhere.

part (3), T5v9, N2r6, N2r7, N2r8, N4r16, etc. Share. *Per aiguals pars*, N4v11. Equally.

part (4), T5r11. *A –*, T5r11. Apart, separately.

parte (It.), see *part* (1)

partida (1): sg. *partita* (It.), T9r15; pl. *partidas*, T8v13, T8v22. Region (*PD* 280). *Las partidas dela Roze*, T8v22: "des pays au-delà du Rhône, c'est-à-dire des pays de la rive droite du fleuve. Tarascon est situé sur la rive gauche" (Bondurand 150n7).

partida (2): *partita* (It.), T10r1. Share (*PD* 280). Lat. *partita*, Med. Lat. *partida* (= Occ.) ("partie," Baratier 553).

partir: pres. 3rd pers. sg. *part*, T9v13, N4r14, N4r24, N5r5, etc.; pl. *parton*, T12r9; *parten*, N4v11. To divide, share (reflexive).

partison, N13v1. Division. *Partizon (PD* 280); *partison* (Pansier 3:126).

partita (It.), see *partida* (1, 2)

Parts of ships, see Ships (1)

passar: pres. 3rd pers. sg. *passa*, T8r24, N9r19, N9r25; pres. subj. 3rd pers. sg. *passe*, N7r14; pres. part. *passant*, T8v3, T8v13, N9v12, N10r23. To cross (the Rhône). *Passant davant*, T13r8. Passing before (Lubières). Lat. *transire*; pres. 3rd pers. pl. *tranceunt* (Baratier 389).

Passengers: see *Alaman, capelan, cavalcador, cavalcan, cavalier, clerc, diaque, Engles, Espanhol, Lombart, Proensal, romieu, sotzdiaque*. See also *esclau, Sarrazin*

patac, N13r25, N13v6; pl. *patacs*, N13v6. *Patac*, a coin (*PD* 282, *LR* 4:452, *SW* 6:136), worth 1.56d according to N13r25–6; more precisely, the *patac* counted as 1.5d 4 grains (1.67d), N13v7; one fifth of a *blanc*, N13v6. Sometimes said to have been worth two deniers (Rolland 1956, 85; Alibert 531); "deux deniers environ" (Honnorat 2:769), or three (Pansier 3:127).

pauc: fem. *pauca*, T4v32. Small (*PD* 283).

Payment in kind: see *colier, copiera, pesa, rema*

pe: Foot. *A pe*, T9r5, T9r13, T9r17, N10r18, N10r20. On foot, walking (*LR* 4:470, *PD* 284). Lat. *pes*; *iverint pedes* (Baratier 387, Guérard 1:lxxxv).

peage, see *pezage*

peagier, see *pezagier*

pebre, T14r12, N7v4, N14r3, N15v24; *pibre*, T3r22. Pepper (*PD* 284). Lat. *piper*; gen. *piperis* (Baratier 385, Guérard 1:lxxxiii), abl. *pebre* (= Occ.) (Baratier 388, Guérard 1:lxxxvi).

Pecays, N5r24. The *Marais de Peccais*, a salt marsh near Aigues-Mortes (Gard). For description, see Villain-Gandossi 1969, 27–36. The measure of Peccais was established in 1248 (Wikipedia, consulted 29 April 2012).

"Peccais, hameau et chapelle ruinée, commune d'Aiguesmortes. *Salinae de Peccaysio*, 1461... *Salins de Peccays*, 1462" (Germer-Durand 1868, 160). "Peccais (Gard), 35 h., c. d'Aigues-Mortes, dans la région des Étangs, sur le Rhône-Mort. – Salines importantes" (Joanne 1890–1905, 5:3441).

pechier: pl. *pechiers*, T6v26; *pechers*, T14v6. Pitcher (*PD* 284). Lat. *urceolus*; gen. pl. *urceolorum* (Delebecque 3:54) = *urteriorum* (Martin-Portier 2:45).

pecol: pl. *pecols*, T6v13. Foot of a piece of furniture (*PD* 285). Lat. *pecollus* (Du Cange 6:236); abl. pl. *pecollis*, "pieds" (Baratier 388).

pega, N7v17, N14r20; *pegua*, T3v29, T15r20. Pitch (*PD* 285, *DAO* 257, *DAOS* 144), used in caulking. *Pege*, "poix goudron pour le calfatage" (Rossiaud 2002, 2:256). Fr. *pegue*, "poix," from the Occ. (Fennis 3:1381). Lat. *pix*; abl. pl. *pes* (= Occ. *pes*, Mistral 2:552) (Baratier 385, Guérard 1:lxxxiii).

peira, T7v20, T13v14; pl. *peyras*, N9r11 (twice). Rock (*PD* 285, *DAO* 133, *DAOS* 46). "Pierres de taille" (Bondurand 148n10), cut stone such as ashlar, "a square hewn stone for building purposes or for pavement" (*OED*). Lat. *lapis*; gen. pl. *lapidum* (Martin-Portier 2:48).

peiron: pl. *peyrons*, N11v12. *Part of a ship's hull, perhaps the sheer-rails, "the mouldings round a vessel's top sides" (*OED*). To determine the toll, the number of *fils*, "strakes" (see *fil* [2]), is counted from the *sol* (which see), "tier of goods in the hold," plus two *peyrons*. Cf. *peiron*, "perron" (*PD* 285, Pansier 3:128); "parapet" (Alibert 536). Cf. Lat. *postis*: *de duabus postibus attingentibus costatos tantum II den., quia ille computantur pro una* (Guérard 1:lxxxv, Baratier 387), "for two boards beside the ribs (?), only 2d, because they are counted as one." *De qualibet poste de sola seu fondo* (Guérard 1:lxxxv), "For each board from the bottom of the hold"; I do not agree that "sans doute s'agit-il d'un radeau descendant le Rhône et vendu en pièces à l'arrivée" (Baratier 387n5). See also *sol*

peis, T4r16, T7v30; *peys*, T14r34. Fish (*PD* 285). – *de mar, salat ho non salat*, T4r16. Fish from the sea, salted or not salted. – *de Roze o palun*, T7v30. Fish from the Rhône or a marsh. Lat. *piscis*; abl. pl. *piscibus* (Guérard 1:lxxxiii, lxxxvi, lxxxvii), *picibus* (Baratier 385, 388).

peisson, N15v14; *peyson*, N7v11, N14r13; *peysson*, N12v11. Fish (*PD* 285). – *de mar*, N7v11, N14r13, N15v14. Fish from the sea. – *de Rose ho de palum fresc*, N12v11. Fish from the Rhône or a freshwater marsh. Lat. *piscis*; gen. *piscis* (Martin-Portier 2:41), abl. pl. *piscibus*, *picibus* (see *peis*).

pel, N14r7, N15v11, N15v12, N15v20; pl. *pels*, T3v31, T3v32, T3v33, T14r26, T14r27, T15r27, T15r28, N7v5, N7v21, N8r1, N14r23, N15v22. Skin, hide. "Peau" (*PD* 286, *DAO* 547, *DAOS* 470). – *d'anels*, T14r27; – *d'aninas*, T3v33. Lambskin. – *de buou*, N14r7, N15v20. Oxhide. – *de cabret*, T3v32. Kidskin. – *de cabritz*, T15r28; *de cabris*, N7v21; *de cabrit*, N15v11. Goatskin. – *de camel*, N14r7, N15v20. Camel hide. – *de conils*, N7v5, N15v22. Rabbit skin. – *de moutons*, T3v31, T14r26, T15r27; *de mouton*, N7v21, N8r1, N14r23, N15v12. Sheepskin. Lat. *pellis*; nom. pl. *pellia* (Baratier 386), abl. pl. *pellibus* (Baratier 385, Guérard 1:lxxxi, etc.). See also *cuer*

*__pelanha__, N12r12. Shell of a chestnut; synonymous with *escorsa* (which see). Skin of a vegetable or fruit (Cantalausa 2003, 729; Fettuciari, Martin, and Pietri 2003, 369). Cf. *pelan, pelhan*, "peau, les peaux en général" (Pansier 3:128); *pelalha*, "peau de raisin" (*DAO* 196).

pelar: past part. *pelat*, fem. *pelada*, N15v13; pl. *peladas*, T4r5, T14r29, N7v12, N14r15. To peel (*PD* 286). *Castanhas peladas*, "châtaignes sèches (l'opération du blanchissage les prive de leur peau)" (Bondurand 139n13).

pelharia, T8r17; *pellaria*, T8r6. Skins used in making furs (*pelaria, pelharia, PD* 286). Exempt from toll at Tarascon (T8r6) except at the fair in Beaucaire (T8r17); must be distinct from *pelisaria* in MS N, which pays 30.5d at Tarascon (N7v3), 26.5d at the Gate of Tarascon (N14r7), 26d at Saint-Gabriel (N15v23). Med. Lat. nom. *pelliaria*, "peausserie" (Baratier 397), abl. *pellaria* (Martin-Portier 2:41).

pelisaria, N14r7; *pelliceria*, N7v3, N15v23. Skins used in making furs; peltry, "undressed skins, esp. of animals valuable for their furs; furs and skins prepared for sale; pelts collectively" (*OED*). *Pelisairia*, "pelleterie" (*PD* 286); *pelissaria*, "pelisserie" (Pansier 3:128). Distinct from *pelharia* in MS T, which see.

pena, N14r6, N15v22; pl. *pennas*, T3v1. Fur lining (*PD* 287). "Les doublures de peau, les fourrures sont désignées généralement sous le nom de *penna*, qu'il s'agisse de peaux de petits félins, de mouton ou d'agneau ... ou même de volatiles" (Bourilly 1928, 78). *Pena vayra*, N14r6; *pennas vayras*, T3v1. Varicoloured fur lining. *Pena vana*, N15v22. Irregular fur lining. Lat. *penna*; abl. pl. *pennis* (Baratier 386, Guérard 1:lxxxii).

per so car, N13r3. Because (*PD* 66).

pera, N14v16; pl. *peras*, T7r13, T13v17, N12r13. Pear (*PD* 288, *DAO* 278, *DAOS* 172). Lat. *pirum*; nom. pl. *pira* (Baratier 387, Guérard 1:lxxxv).

pergamin, T4v4; pl. *pargamins*, N8r15, N14v4. Parchment. *Pargam, -amin* (*PD* 278). Lat. *pergamentum* (Niermeyer; Baratier 386).

persegua: pl. *perseguas*, T7r9; *persegues*, N12r13; *pesseges*, N14v17. Peach. *Persegue* (*PD* 291, *DAO* 287, *DAOS* 181). Lat. *persicum*; nom. pl. *perciga* (Baratier 387), *percica* (Guérard 1:lxxxv), both influenced by Occ.

pertegua, T13v6; pl. *perteguas*, T5v36. Pole (*PD* 289). Lat. *pertica*; abl. pl. *perticis* (Baratier 386, Guérard 1:lxxxii).

pes, N13r23, N16r19. Weight (*PD* 292). It. *peso* (Edler 211).

pesa, T7v17; *pessa*, N8r7, N9v1, N11v24, N12v6, N15r6; pl. *pesas*, T7v16; *pessas*, T3r14, T14v25, N7r20, N7r21, N12v6, N15r6. Piece (*PD* 292), item of various commodities (glass, cloth, animals, baskets). The piece may serve in lieu of money as payment in kind (*dona* –, T7v16, T7v17, T14v25; *paga* –, N12v6, N15r6). It. *pezza*, "a piece of (woolen) cloth of regulation length" (Edler 212).

pesage, see *pezage*

pesar (1): pres. 3rd pers. sg. *pesa*, N5v1, N13r20. To weigh. *Pezar* (*PD* 293).

pesar (2): past part. fem. pl. *pessadas*, N7v12, N14r15. To break (almonds, *amellas*) into pieces (*PD* 292); see also *franher.*

pessas, see *pesa*

pesseges, see *persegua*

petit, masc. N1v21, N2r14, N2r15, N2r17, N2r18, N3r23, N4v7, N4v8; pl. *petit*, N6r10; *petis*, N4r12, N5v3–6r19 (throughout Table N2); fem. *petita*, N8v15; pl. *petitas*, T6r3, N12v1. Adj. Small.

peyras, see *peira*

peyrons, see *peiron*

peys, see *peis*

peyson, see *peisson*

pezage, T4v19, T4v22, T5r18, T5r30, T5v20, T5v23, T9v14, T9v20, T12v13, T13r9, T14r1, T15r11, T15r31; *pezag*, T13v18; *pesage*, T3r2, T4r20, T4r24, T6r12, T6r14, T7v9, T7v15, T9r2, T9r3, T9v1, T10r1, T13r1, T15r9, T15v3; *peage*, T5r21, T5r23, T7v27, T15r5, N1v17, N1v18, N2r3, N2r11, N2r12, N4v10, N4v14, N5r2, N5r9, N5r10, N5r19, N6v14, N6v16, N7r2, N7r5, N7r16, N7v24, N8r12, N8r18, N8r23, N8v7, N9r4, N9r13, N10r2, N11r9, N11v14, N12v8, N12v22, N13r2, N13r13, N13v1, N13v14, N13v16, N13v24, N15r12, N15r18, N15r23, N15v5, N15v9 (twice), N16r5, N16r9, N16r10, N16r12, N16r13, N16r14, N16r15, N16r20;

piage, T9v5, T15r3; *piag*, T7v23; pl. *peages*, N13r13, N16r13. Toll, fee; tollhouse. *Peatge, peza- (PD* 284). For analysis of the various forms that appear in MSS T and N, see Introduction §3, Language.

(1) Toll, payment. T5r23, T6r12, T6r14, T7v9, T7v15, T7v27, T9r2, T9r3, T9v1, T9v5, T10r1, T13r1, T13r9, T13v18, T14r31, T15r9, N1v18, N2r12, N5r19, N6v14, N7r5, N7r16, N9r4, N10r2, N12v8, N12v22, N13r2, N13r13, N13v1, N13v14, N13v16, N15r23, N15v9. – *de las mercadarias*, N12v22, N13v16. Toll on commodities. – *de las mercandisas*, N7r16. Toll on merchandise. – *de la sal*, T9v1, T10r1, N2r12, N5r19, N7r5, N13v1, N13v14. Toll on salt. *Miegz* –, T15r31; *mieç* –, N6v14. Half toll.

(2) *The association of shareholders who had the right to collect tolls at Lubières (in MS T). *Los senhors del – de Lubieras*, T3v9, T4r20, T4r24, T4v22, T5r30, T7v23. The lords of the association of Lubières.

(3) *The right to collect toll. – *que compret lo rey nostre senhor*, T9v20. Right that the king our lord bought.

(4) Tollhouse, where the toll is collected. T3r2, T4r24, T5r18, T5r21, T5v20, T5v23, T9v14, T9v22, T12r12, T13r1, T14r1, T14r4, T15r3, T15r5, T15r9, T15r11, T15v3, N2r3, N2r11, N11r9, N11r12, N13r14, N16r15; pl., N16r13. Tollhouses: *Adaul*, N6v9, N6v18, N7r14. – *de l'aigua*, N13r13, N16r14, by the Rhône. – *de Gernegua*, T15r5; *de Gernega*, N15r12, at Jarnègues. – *de Lobieras*, T4r24, T5r18, T5r21, T9v14, T12v13, T13r1, N4v10, N4v14, N5r10, N4v14, N5r2, N5r10, N6v16, N7r2, N7v24, N8r12, N8r18, N8r23, N8v7, N9r13, N11v14, N13r15, N15v5, at Lubières. *Los Mujolans*. T5v20, T5v23, T9v22, T12r12, unidentified; see also *Violans*. – *del Portal de Tarascon*, T15r11, T15v3, N13r14, N13v24, N16r5, N16r9, N16r15; – *dels portals*, T14r1, T15r3, at the Gate or Gates of Tarascon (see also *portal*). – *del rey*, N15v5, the king's toll, unidentified. – *de Sant Gabriel*, T15r9, T15v4, N13r14, N15v9, N16r7, N16r10, N16r12, N16r15, N16r20, at Saint-Gabriel. – *de Tarascon*, N1v17, N5r9, N15r18; *de Tharascon*, T3r2, unidentified. – *dels Violans*, N2r3, N2r11, N11r9, N11r12, see *Mujolans*. – *gros*, T4v19, T5r23, T9v5. Main (large) tollhouse, the one at Tarascon proper, compared to the one at Lubières; see *gros* (1).

Lat. *pedagium* (Niermeyer); gen. *pedagii* (*pedagii portalis de Tarascono*, Baratier 388; *pedagii de Sancto Gabriel*, 388); abl. *pedagio* (toll, 386; *pedagio de Portali Tarasconi*, 388). It. *pedaggio*, "transit toll (on merchandise or persons) or place where toll was collected"; also *passaggio*, with the same senses (Edler 206, 207).

pezagier, T14r3; *peagier*, T5v6, N10v23, N11v14; pl. *peagiers*, N9v18, N13v14. Tollkeeper. *Peatgier, peza-, PD* 284. Lat. *pedagiarius*

(Niermeyer), *pedegerius* (Guérard 1:lxxix, lxxxvii), *pedejarius* (Baratier 388, Guérard 1:lxxxvi); gen. *pedejarii* (Guérard 1:lxxv).

piag, see *pezage*

piatta (It.), T4r12. Plates (collective). Bondurand, reading *piacta* (cf. Textual Note), takes *piacta stagnat* "pour *Plat estagnat* ... vaisselle d'étain" (p. 140n2). Regional It. *piatta*, "recipiente nel quale si raccoglie l'olio che cola dal tinello" (Battaglia 13:314); *piatto*, "stoviglia [piece of crockery] in cui si dispongono, si portano in tavola e si consumano le vivande" (Battaglia 13:319). Cf. Occ. *plat*, "*s.m.* plat, vaisselle" (*PD* 297); *plat*, "plat, écuelle" (Pansier 3:133). Lat. *plata* (Niermeyer); *plata argenti et auri* (Baratier 344), "plaque de métal" (Baratier 553). Mod. Occ. *plata*, s.f., "prix, ce qui est proposé pour récompense ... grand plat d'étain" (Honnorat 3:900); *plato*, "grand plat d'étain qu'on décernait en prix aux vainqueurs des jeux gymniques" (Mistral 2:593).

pibre, see *pebre*

*__plagaria__: pl. *plagarias*, N12v14. Context suggests a ready-made dress (cf. *rauba*), perhaps pleated; cf. *plegar*, "faire des plis" (Alibert 552).

Plants and plant products: see *blat, bled, canape, coton, estopa, fil* (1), *gaida, gala, grana, indi, jonc, roge, ros, ruscla, rosa, sabon, seu*. See also Foods; Wood and wood products

plaser, n.m., N11v13. Discretion. *Plazer (PD* 297). *Al – del peagier*, N11v13. At the discretion of the tollkeeper. Lat. *ad arbitrium pedejarii* (Baratier 387). Cf. *albire*

plomb, N8v10; *plum*, T5r25; *plump*, T14v3; pl. *ploms*, N14v14. (In sg.) lead; (in pl.) lead weight (*PD* 298, *DAO* 165, *DAOS* 74). Lat. *plumbum*; abl. *plombo* (Guérard 1:lxxxiii), *plobo* (Baratier 385).

plum, see *plomb*

pluma, T3v3, N7v1, N7v2, N15v25. Feather (*PD* 299). See also *alum de pluma*

plump, see *plomb*

plus, N4v2, N4v10, N4v21, N8r11, etc. *Also (Fr. "plus," *PD* 299, Pansier 3:134).

pogeza, T8v18; *pogesa*, N9v4, N9v10, N13r26, etc.; pl. *pogezas*, T12r16; *pogesas*, N1v24, N2r2, N2r7, N2r10, N11r10, N13r24, etc.; abbreviated *p*°. or *p*., passim. A coin minted at Le Puy (*PD* 300, *LR* 4:586), worth one-fourth of a denier (Honnorat 3:910, Mistral 2:609). "La *pogesia*, une unité de compte équivalent à la moitié d'une obole" (Pécout 2010, cxl). Lat.

pogesa (Niermeyer); acc. pl. *pojesas* (Baratier 388). *Pites*, also worth one quarter denier, were minted by Charles II (1285–1309) and Robert (1309–43) (Duplessy 2004–10, 2:8, 10).

point, see *pont* (2)

pol, T15r20; pl. *pols*, T3v21, T14r31, N14r16. Powder. *Pols*, "poussière; poudre" (*PD* 201, Pansier 5:187). Note the sg. **pol*, T15r20. – *de sucre*, T3v21, T14r31, T15r20, N14r16. Powdered sugar. *Pols de sucre*, T3v21 (paying 21d at Tarascon), is equivalent in meaning to *polvera de sucre*, N7v14 (paying 19d at Tarascon; the change in rate is standard).

polvera, N7v14. Powder (*PD* 301). – *de sucre*, N7v14. Powdered sugar. See also *pol*

pom: pl. *poms*, T7r8, T13v17. Apple (*PD* 301, *DAO* 274, *DAOS* 167). *Poms*, T7r8 (paying 2d at Tarascon), is synonymous with *pomas*, N12r13 (paying the same).

poma, N14v16; pl. *pomas*, N12r13. Apple (*PD* 301, *DAO* 274, *DAOS* 167). Lat. *pomum*; nom. pl. *pomma* (Baratier 387), *poma* (Guérard 1:lxxxv). See also *pom*

Pons del Prat, *en*, T14r3. Sir Pons del Prat, a former tollkeeper. Lat. *Pons de Prato, antiquus pedejarius* (Baratier 388) = *Pon[cius] de Prato, antiqus pedejarius* (Guérard 1:lxxxvi). See also *pezagier*, *Prat*

ponsiri: pl. *ponsiris*, N12r14. Large lemon. "Poncire, sorte de citron" (*PD* 302, *DAO* 324, *DAOS* 230); "espèce de gros citron" (Pansier 3:135).

pont (1), N9v16, N9v19. N.m. Bridge. *Pon (PD* 302). Lat. *pons*; abl. *ponte* (Baratier 384).

pont (2), N13r6, N16r11; *point*, N12v7. Adv. Intensifies negation (Fr. point). *Non ... pont*, N12v7, N13r6. Not at all. *Non ... pont ... jamais*, N16r11. Never ever. *Ponh,* adv. "point, pas" (*PD* 302).

porc, N7v18; pl. *porcs*, T8v17, T8v26, N9v2, N9v9, N12r23. Pig (*PD* 303). *Graissa de* –, N7v18. Pig grease. *Porcs salas*, N12r23 (stressed *salás*). Salt pork. Lat. *porcus* (Baratier 394), abl. *porco* (Baratier 377, Guérard 1:lxxxi), abl. pl. *porcis* (Martin-Portier 2:45).

port: pl. *portz*, T12v22. Port (of Beaucaire or Tarascon) (*PD* 303). Lat. *portus*, abl. *portu* (Baratier 405).

portal, T15r11, T15v3, N13r14, N13v25, N15r13, N15r15, N16r5, N16r9, N16r15; pl. *portals*, T14r1, T15r3, T15r7. Gate. "Portail; porte d'une ville" (*PD* 304). The singular *Portal de Tarascon* in MSS TN seems to be a proper noun referrring to a specific gate: *Portal de Tarascon*, T15r11,

T15v3, N16r5, N16r9, Gate of Tarascon; *Portal*, N15r13, N15r15, Gate (of Tarascon); *peage (...) del Portal de Tarascon*, N13r14, N13v25, tollhouse at the Gate of Tarascon; *peage del Portal,* N16r15, tollhouse at the Gate (of Tarascon).

This gate may have been the one at the northeast corner of the town, in the sector called *Condamina*, leading toward Avignon. MSS A_1P distinguish *Portale Tarasconi* from the tollhouse on the Rhône and the one on Jarnègues: *Hec intelliget de illis qui non dederunt pedagium ad Rodonum ... Omnia supradicta donant pedagium supradictum ad portale [Portale?], si non solverint in Jernega pedagium* (Baratier 388; cf. Guérard 1:lxxxvi–lxxxvii). Similarly, MS T distinguishes the *portals* (of Tarascon) from the *peage de Gernegua*, T15r5. In 1252, two property owners associated with *Portale* were also associated with *Condamina*: *R. Barral de Portali de Condamina, pro domo; ... Joan Robaudus, de casali ad Portale de Condamina,* although another was not: *P. Gill. de Portali, pro domo sua de Mercato* (Baratier 384).

In a section heading in MSS A_1P, the phrase *Portali Tarasconi* was capitalized in the edition of A_1 by Baratier (388), though not in the edition of P by Guérard (p. lxxxvi). Bautier and Sornay capitalize Le Portal (1968–74, 1:3:1793, under Enquêtes, Provence, Tarascon; 1:3:1794, under Tarifs, Tarascon).

Lat. *portale*, "porte d'une ville" (Niermeyer; Baratier 390).

portar, N15v3, N15v7; past subj. 3rd pers. pl. *portason*, N15r24. To carry (*PD* 304). Lat. *portare*; past part. masc., abl. *portato* (Baratier 386).

potgezas, see *pogeza*

Prat, T14r3. The word, which means "meadow" as a common noun (*LR* 4:618, *SW* 6:493), is capitalized by Baratier as a proper noun referring to a specific place: people owned houses and land in *Prato* (Baratier 383, 384, 385). In 1332 there was mention of *Prata* and *Pratum Regis* (Pécout 2010, 288, Index locorum s.v. Tharasco). Not indicated on the maps of the town by Hébert (1979, 40) or Pécout (2010, ci). See also *Pons del Prat*

prelat: pl. *prelatz*, T8v7. Prelate (*LR* 2:16, *SW* 6:504).

premier: pl. *premiers*, N10r24. Adj. First. *Primier, prem-* (*PD* 307).

premierament, N1v17. Adv. First. *Primieramen* (*PD* 308).

prendre: pres. 3rd pers. sg. *pren* (Occ.), T5v8, T15r30, N4v15, N6v2, N7v24, N8r11, N8r17, N8v11, N10v13, N10v16, N10v23; *prende* (It.), T3v8, T4r19, T4r23, T4v6, T4v10, T4v15, T5r17, T5r26, T5r[34]; pl. *prendon*, T14v9; *prenon*, T15v13, T16r12; past part. *pres*, T15r10. To take (*PD* 305).

The It. form *prende* occurs in MS T between T3v8 and T5r[34], that is, within Section I: Tolls at Tarascon, from the first category (tolls of 2s 5d) to Wood. MS T uses Occ. forms at T5v8 and T15r30; MS N, from N4v15 to N10v23.

pres (1), N11v13, N12r6, N12v23. Price. *Pretz,* "prix, valeur" *(PD* 306). N13r17. Silver. "Argent" (*PD* 306).

pres (2), N12v23. Near (*PD* 306).

pres (3), see *prendre*

prim: fem. pl. *primas*, N11r18. Thin. "Fin, subtil ... délicat, léger, mince" (*PD* 307).

privat: pl. *privatz*, T12v24. Local. "Qui est du pays" (*PD* 308).

privilegiar: past part. *privilegiat*, N9v20. To privilege (*LR* 4:39). Lat. *privilegiare* (Niermeyer); past part., abl. pl. *privilegiatis* (Baratier 387, Guérard 1:lxxxv).

procan: pl. *procans*, N9v17. Nearby, neighbouring. *Los procans*. Those from nearby. *Propdan* (*PD* 310, *LR* 4.654); *propchan* (*SW* 6:588); *prochan*, "prochain" (Pansier 3:139, Honnorat 3:961).

Products of animals, see Animals (1)

Proensa, see *Provensa*

Proensal: masc. pl. *Proensals,* T9r16. Provençal.

propi: fem. *propia*, N13r8. Close (*PD* 310). *Plus propia*. Closest.

Provensa, N9r24; *Provença*, N10r11; *Proensa*, T8v13. Provence. *Pais de –*, N10r11. The region of Provence.

quairat, see *cairat* (1, 2)

qual, T14r2, N11r12. Which. *Cal* (*PD* 59). With the definite article *lo, la*: masc. *lo qual*, N2r3, N5v2, N6v14, N7v20, N11r12, N13r2, N13v23; pl. *los quals*, N13v15; *dels quals*, N13v17; fem. *la qual*, T14r2, N7r17, N7r24; pl. *las quals*, N15r16.

qualche (It. spelling), T9r15; *qualque*, T9v4, N1v22, N15v4. Some; (with subj.) whatever. Cf. the Occ. spelling *calque*, N5v10 (*PD* 60).

quatre, T14v2, T14v29, N11r20; *iiij*, passim; *iiij*^{o}., N11v22; *iiij.*^{o}, N12r6, N13v7 (It. *quattro*; Occ. *catre*, *PD* 71). Four. In MS P (Guérard 1:lxxxi), *iiii*^{or} represents Lat. *quattuor*.

que (1), rel. pron., passim. Which, that, who. *Que*, N12r8, N14v4. Of which. *Que* with possessive adj. (*que sa*), N13r16, N16r16–7; *que que* *sa*, N13r21–2. Of which. *Aquo que*, N5r21. That which. *So que*, N4r14. That which. *Per so que*, N7r14. Because. *Quant que*, T12r31, T13r16–7 (with subj.). However much. Lat. *quantumcumque* (Baratier 387, Guérard 1:lxxxiv).

que (2), subordinating conjunction, N13r2, N13r3, N13r6, N13r7, N13r9, N13v14. That. *Que*, N16r17. For, since. *Que*, N8v25–9r1 (with subj.), T13r9 (with indic.). If. *Apres que* (with subj.), N15r19. After. *De von que* (with subj.), T4v27. From wherever. *Ho ... ho ... que* (with subj.), N15r24. Whether ... or. *Mas que*, N15r18–9 (with subj.). Provided that. *Que ... que* (with subj.), N9r18–9, N9v20–1. Whether ... or. *Von que*, T4v28 (with subj.). From wherever (see *on*). *De qualque (part, luoc) que* (with subj.), T9v4, N1v22–3. From whatever (region, place).

quel, N13v4 (cf. It. *quello*; Occ. *cal*, *PD* 59). That. Unusual form of the demonstrative adj., normally Occ. *aquel* (2), that. Ricketts 2005 provides more examples: PC 461a 011 115 *et mort en quel doloros loc*; JAU 386 *que l'estorça de quel perill*, etc. In mod. Occ., Gascon *quel* contrasts with normal *aquel* (Honnorat 3:986); forms of mod. *aquéu* include *quéu* (Limousin), *quel* (Gascon), "ce, cette; celui, celle" (Mistral 1:118).

question, N13r5. Question (*PD* 312).

quintal: pl. *quintals*, T3r12, N5v1, etc. Quintal, a measure of weight, about 50 kilograms (*PD* 312). "A unit of weight equal to one hundredweight, originally 100 lb (approx. 45.4 kg; now chiefly *hist.*), later 112 lb (approx. 50.8 kg)" (*OED*). "Environ 38 kilos" (Baratier and Reynaud 1951, 902). Med. Lat. *quintale,* "unité de poids, multiple de la livre, correspond à 100, 104 ou 105 livres" (Stouff 1970, 474). It. *quintale* (Edler 233). See also *mog*

quiti: pl. *quitis*, T15r6. Exempt (*PD* 312). Lat. *quietus*, Med. Lat. *quittius* (Du Cange 6:610); nom. pl. masc. *quitii*, nom. pl. fem. *quitie*; *liber de pedagio*, nom. pl. masc. *liberi* (quitii, quitie, liberi, Baratier 387).

qulhiers, *qulhers*, see *culhier*

raba: pl. *rabas*, T7v1, T13v24, N12r18, N14v22. Rape (*PD* 312, *DAO* 405, *DAOS* 329), "the globular root of the turnip" (*OED*). Lat. *rapa*; abl. pl. *rapis* (Baratier 387, Guérard 1:lxxxvi).

radel, T5v23, T5v31, T13r26, N11r11, N11r15. Raft (*PD* 313, Bondurand 144n3). Lat. *ratis* (Baratier 394).

rais, see *razis*

rama: fem. pl. *ramas*, N11v21. *Oar (*LR* 5:37, Pansier 3:141, Honnorat 3:1003). Fr. *rame* (Jal 1257, Fennis 3:1531).

The meaning here is not "branch," as in *PD* and *SW*: fem. *rama*, "ramée, branchage" (*PD* 313); *rama*, "Gezweige, Laubwerk; Ranke, Rebe" (*SW* 7:14); masc. *ram*, "rameau" (*PD* 313), "branche" (*FEW* 10:39a). See also *rema*.

ras: fem. *raza*, T12v27. Level, filled even with the rim (*PD* 314). Lat. *radere*; past part. *rasum*, abl. pl. fem. *rasis* (Baratier 387).

rason, T5r21, T5v20, T9v20, T12r16, N4r16, N13v23. *Rate. *Per – de* T, *a – de* N, at the rate of. Cf. *razon, a –*, "à propos" (*PD* 315).

rauba: pl. *raubas*, N12v13, N12v16. Dress (*PD* 314). *Raupa, ropa*: "ce mot qui désigne d'abord d'une façon générale l'ensemble de l'habillement, finit au XVe siècle par désigner spécialement une sorte de vêtement, long, d'une seule pièce ou non, souvent lacé par derrière" (Bourilly 1928, 34). *Raubas fachas*, N12v16. Ready-made dresses. Lat. *vestis*; nom. pl. *vestes facte* (Baratier 386, Guérard 1:lxxxii).

raza, see *ras*

razis, T5r[33]; *rais*, N10v2. Root. *Razitz, rais* (*PD* 315, *DAO* 179).

realme, N15v4. Kingdom, to starboard when sailing down the Rhône; contrasted with *empire* (lacking in TN), to port, the bank of the river including Tarascon. *Reialme*, "royaume" *(PD* 321).

redon, N10v1, N10v4, N10v8, N11r1; *rodon*, T5v12, T13v5; pl. *redons*, N11r22, N11v19; fem. pl. *redonas*, T5v36, N11r18. Round (*PD* 318). *De –*, N10v4, N10v8 = *de gros*, T10v37, T10v33. Around, in girth. Lat. *rotundus*; abl. *rotondo*, influenced by Occ. (Baratier 386, Guérard 1:lxxxii).

regalisia, T8r2; *regalicia*, N12v10. Liquorice, "the rhizome ... of the plant *Glycyrrhiza glabra*. Also, a preparation (used medicinally and as a sweetmeat) made from the evaporated juice of this rhizome, and commonly sold in black cylindrical sticks" (*OED*). *Regulecia* (*LR* 5:78); *regalécia* (Alibert 593); *recalesia* (*DAO* 499, *DAOS* 430). Late Lat. *liquiritia* (*TLFi* s.v. réglisse); nom. *recaliscia* (Baratier 386), *recalicia* (Guérard 1:lxxxii), *regaliscia* (Guérard 1:xcii, xcvi), all influenced by Occ.

regardar: imperative 2nd pers. sg. *regarda*, N16r4. To look at (*PD* 320).

Regions, see Cities and regions

registre, T3r1, N1v17, N13r3. Register (*LR* 3:465, *SW* 7:180). MS N, the present document, N1v17. A document that was extant in 1325, N13r3. *Al –*, N13r3. In the register. Lat. *chartularium, cart-*; *cartularium pedagii* (Guérard 1:xcvi).

rei, T5r29, T10r5, etc.; *rey*, T5v9, etc., N1v19, etc.; *re*, T5v14, N4v14. King.

rema, T6r19, T6r22, N11v13, N11v15. Oar, as payment in kind. *Rem, rema,* "rame" (*PD* 322). Fr. *rème* (Jal 1273); Fr. *rem*, *reme*, from Occ. and/or Italian and Latin (Fennis 3:1536). Med. Lat. *rema* (Du Cange 7:115); acc. *remam* (Baratier 387, Guérard 1:lxxxv). See also *rama*

remaner: pres. subj. 3rd pers. sg. *remangua*, T15v14, T16r13. To remain (*PD* 322).

respondre: pret. 3rd pers. sg. *respondet*, N13r2. To answer (*PD* 325).

rest, T7v10, T14v9, N12v3, N14v24. Bunch of garlic bulbs or onions (*PD* 325, *DAO* 423, *DAOS* 353). Lat. *restis*; acc. *restem* (Baratier 388).

resta, N2r2. Rest, remainder (*PD* 325).

restar: pres. subj. 3rd pers. pl. *resten*, N15r19. To remain (*PD* 325).

rial: pl. *rials*, T14r21. Rial or royal, a coin bearing the inscription *Rex*; since ca. 1250 in French (*OED*, s.v. rial). *Reial, real* (*PD* 321, *LR* 5:67). A gold coin, *real d'aur* (*SW* 7:184). Med. Lat. *regalis* (Niermeyer); nom. pl. *regales* (Baratier 387), gen. pl. *regalium* (Guérard 1:lxxxv, Baratier 388), acc. pl. *regales* (Guérard 1:lxxxvi).

ribiera, N15v8. Bank, riverbank (*PD* 328, *DAO* 116).

riorta, N14v23. Withe, "a band, tie, or shackle consisting of a tough flexible twig or branch, or of several twisted together; such a twig or branch, as of willow or osier, used for binding or tying, and sometimes for plaiting" (*OED*). *Redorta, riorte*, "lien d'osier ou de bois tordu sur lui-même et servant à la confection des fagots, des radeaux, des manoeuvres [Eng. rigging, rope] courtes" (Rossiaud 2002, 2:297). *Redorta*, "hart" (*PD* 318, Alibert 591); "riorte, hart" (*LR* 5:385, *SW* 7:136); *riorta*, "lien d'un fagot, généralement en osier" (Tisseur 1887, 361).

ris, T3v25, T14r31, T15r16, N7v16, N14r19. Rice (*PD* 328, *DAO* 391, *DAOS* 310). Med. Lat. *risus* (Niermeyer); abl. *riso* (Baratier 385, Guérard 1:lxxxiii).

***roans**, T5v35. Timber from Le Royans, a region east of the Rhône between Valence (about 145 kilometres upstream from Tarascon) and Grenoble, in the modern departments of Drôme and Isère. *Royans, roans (*Rossiaud 2002, 2:308). *Roan*, "variété de pièce de bois de charpente" (Pansier 5:190; *FEW* 23:6a). *De ii quairatz de – est travada*, T5v35. Two squared timbers of *roans* is a stack. The form in *-s* is singular (*pace* Pansier), as in Lat. abl. sg. *ruans* (= Occ.): *cairan de ruans* (Guérard 1:xcii); *cairato de ruans et de saicel* (Guérard 1:xciv); *duobus cairatis de ruans* (Baratier 386); *duobus* *cairrans de ruatis* [inserted over *ruatis: ruaus,* read *ruans*] (Guérard 1:lxxxii).

Not *rouve*, oak, adduced by Bondurand, who reads *roaus*: "Je pense que *roaus* est une mauvaise orthographe de *rouve*" (p. 144n5), doubted by Baratier ("Est-ce pour rouvre, chêne?" 386).

roca, N7v2; *roqua*, N15v21, N15v25. Rock. *Roca (PD* 328). See *alum de roca*

Roda, T6r14. Rhodes, the island in the eastern Aegean Sea. According to T6r14–6, a *linh de Roda* pays £2 10s (that is, 50s); a *barca*, or small ship, pays 5s; and the toll of a *nau* is uncertain. For Bondurand (145n6), "Il s'agit ici d'un navire de Rhodes, c'est-à-dire d'une galère du Levant."[40] The syntax is transparent: "A rowing ship from Rhodes," in parallel structure with a bark and a sailed ship. This reading is confirmed by MS A_2: *De quolibet vassello facto ad rodas, libre due solidi decem*, "For a vessel made in Rhodes, £2 10s" (Martin-Portier 2:42), and by the same language in MS Avignon BM 1755 (late XVth c.), f. 11r20–1.[41] The identity of the tolls confirms the identity of this *vassello facto ad Rodas* in MSS A_1A_2 and the *linh de Roda* in MS T.

The presence of a galley from Rhodes in Tarascon should not be deemed unthinkable, considering the registers' mention of alum from Aleppo, goods from the Levant, camels' hides, lions' hides, and so on. Commerce linked Rhodes and Marseille.[42] In 1356 the city of Rhodes made an effort to attract merchants from Narbonne[43] and granted those from Montpellier the right to maintain a consul.[44] "Tous [Provençaux, Languedociens et Catalans] se rendent dans l'île de Rhodes, après sa conquête sur l'Islam par les Hospitaliers en 1309 et jusqu'à sa reprise par les Turcs en 1522; elle est un relais commode pour le commerce avec les pays musulmans d'Asie et d'Afrique, une étape vers Chypre, mais aussi vers Beyrouth et Alexandrie ... Provençaux, Languedociens et Catalans trafiquent fort

40 The French translation of the text in MS T, contained in MS Avignon AD Vaucluse 1 J 163, f. 48r34, reads: *Ung linh de rode done ... l s*, "A galley from Rhodes gives ... 50s."

41 Compare MS P on Tarascon: *De ligno facto d. [donant] L sol. De barca V sol. De nave dubitant* (Guérard 1:lxxxii). MS P on Arles: *De ligno facto rote XV sol. De nauno dubitat; De barca II sol.* (Guérard 1:xciii). I interpret this *rote* as equivalent to *de Roda* in MS T (*rote*, gen., "of Rhodes"); cf. *ad rodas* in MS A_2.

42 Baratier and Reynaud 1951, 219–21, 251.

43 Port 1854, 118–21.

44 Germain 1861, 2:11–14.

à Rhodes, tels le Montpelliérain Jacme Guilhem, le Narbonnais Jacme Olivier, la famille barcelonaise des Junyent, les Perpignanais Joan Sarda ou – au temps de Louis XI – Jaubert Seguer."[45]

Another interpretation was proposed by Baratier, who edited Latin MS A_1, f. 88v: *De ligno facto: de roda, L s.; de barca, V s.; de nave dubitant* (Baratier 386). Baratier takes *roda* as referring to an arched beam, part of the stem post ("the curved upright timber ... at the bow of a vessel," *OED*) or the stern post ("a more or less upright beam, rising from the after end of the keel of a boat and supporting the rudder," *OED*).[46] He would translate: "For prepared timber: of a *roda*, 50s; of a bark, 5s; of a sailed ship, they are in doubt." In Baratier's reading, *roda*, "arched beam," serves as a synecdoche for a type of ship, parallel to a *barca* or a *nave*. I have not found *roda* used elsewhere for a ship, although the word was used with *de* in the expression *de roda en roda*, meaning "from stem to stern" (Jal s.v. "roda," 1290; s.v. "rode," 1291; Du Cange 7:203), that is, the whole ship in all its length from stem post to stern post – not "from one ship to another." One might ask how a stem post could distinguish one type of ship from a bark or a sailed ship, both of which must have had stem posts.

A third possible interpretation would refer to *roda*, a term used at Peccais for a "small section, part of a salt pan": "Les aires salantes elles-mêmes sont mentionnés sous le nom de rode ou ruote," i.e., "zone de petite étendue, d'où, peut-être ici, bassin ou compartiment de la saline" (Villain-Gandossi 1968, 175; see also Villain-Gandossi 1969, 35n1). The *linh de roda* would then mean a "galley from a salt pan." A *caupol* was an oared barge, a sort of small galley, and a *caupolada* (the cargo of a *caupol*) could contain salt (T12v26). However, this interpretation does not accommodate *De quolibet vassello facto ad Rodas* in Latin MS A_2 (above) unless ships were constructed at salt pans, which seems unlikely.

A fourth interpretation would refer to Roda, a town in the province of Barcelona on the Ter River. Catalan pirates rowed galleys in raids on Arles and threatened Tarascon from 1395 onward. However, we have no indication that they did so earlier (Roux 2004, 1:34–7).

See also *linh*

rodon, see *redon*

45 Dufourcq 1975, 105.

46 *Roda*, "poutre en forme d'arc, pièce de l'étrave ou de l'étambot; peut-être aussi roue de moulin" (Baratier 386n19); "l'une des courbes de poupe quand celle ci est de forme ronde" (Rossiaud 2:308).

roge, N7v19; fem., *roga*, N14r22. (1) Adj. Red. *Rog, -ge (PD* 329); *roja, roga* (*DAO* 463, *DAOS* 401). (2) Used as n., N7v19, N14r22. Madder dye, the dyestuff or pigment prepared from madder, "a herbaceous scrambling plant ... formerly much cultivated, esp. in France ... for the reddish-purple dye obtained from the root" (*OED*). *Rog, roge*, "garance?" (*PD* 329; Alibert 612).

romieu, N10r13; *romiou*, N10r10, N10r16; *romio*, N10r22; pl. *romieus*, T9r1, T9r9, T9r15; fem. *romieua*, N10r23; *romia*, N10r10. Pilgrim. *Romeu (PD* 329). Lat. *romeus* (Niermeyer; Baratier 387, Guérard 1:lxxxv).

roqua, see *roca*

ros, T5r15, T13v9, N9r6. Sumach, "any of the shrubs or small trees of the genus *Rhus* ... indigenous in southern Europe, which is the chief source of the material used in tanning" (*OED*). Also the source of a yellow dye. Fr. "sumac" (*PD* 330, *SW* 7:381, Pansier 3:149, *DAO* 349, *DAOS* 256). *Lo mueg del* –, T5r15, T13v9, N9r6. A hogshead of sumach. Lat. *russus*, "red"; gen. *russi* (Guérard 1:lxxx, lxxxviii, xciv), abl. *russo* (Guérard 1:lxxxiv), abl. *ros* (= Occ.) (Guérard 1:xcii). Synonym of Lat. *rufus*; gen. *ruffi* (Martin-Portier 2:41, 2:48), abl. *ruffo* (Baratier 386).

rosa: pl. *rosas*, N12r14. Rose. *Roza (PD* 330, *DAO* 514, *DAOS* 442). *Rosas frescas*. Fresh roses. Perhaps an error for *noses frescas*; see *noze.*

Rose, see *Roze*

rossa: pl. *rossas*, T8v25, T14r16. Workmare. *Rosa (PD* 330). Lat. *equa* (Martin-Portier 2:45).

rossin: pl. *rossins*, T8v14. Workhorse. *Rocin (PD* 329, *DAOS* 525). Med. Lat. *runcinus* (Niermeyer), *ronsinus* (Baratier 388).

roure, T5v12, T5v15, T6r3, T13v5, T13v6, N11r1, N11r4, N11v1. Oak. *Roire, roure, rover (PD* 329, *DAO* 221, *DAOS* 112, 113). – *quairat*, T5v15, T13v6, N11r4. Squared oak log. – *rodon*, T5v12, T13v5. Round oak log. Lat. *robur*; abl. *robore* (Martin-Portier 2:42, 2:48), *rouvre* (Baratier 386), *roure* (*roure cairato, roure rotondo*, Baratier 386), the last two influenced by Occ.

Roze, T3r3, T4v31, T7v30, T8r24, T8v3, T8v23, T9r5, T9r13, T9v3; *Rose*, T8v13, N5r20, N7r10, N8v14, N9r19, N9v1, N9v12, N10r23, N12v11, N12v25, N13v21. The Rhône River. Lat. *Rodonium* (Baratier 383), *Rodanum* (Guérard 1:lxxxiii).

ruscla, T7r21, T13v23, N12r18, N14v22. Tanner's bark; the bark of the holm oak, used in tanning. *Rusca, ruscla*, "écorce; tan" (*PD* 331, *DAO* 211). Med. Lat. *rusca* (Niermeyer); abl. *rusca ad opus corrium* (Baratier 387n7, Guérard 1:lxxxvi).

sabon, T7v29, N12v10. Soap (*PD* 332). Lat. *sapo*; nom. sg. *sabonum* (Baratier 386), influenced by Occ.

sac: pl. *sacs*, T4v27. Sack (*PD* 332).

safran, N7v4. Saffron (*LR* 5:131, Alibert 621, *DAO* 437, *DAOS* 371), "an orange-red product consisting of the dried stigmas of Crocus sativus ... Now used chiefly for colouring confectionery, liquors, etc., and for flavouring; formerly extensively used in medicine as a cordial and sudorific" (*OED*). Synonymous with It. *çafarame* (which see). Med. Lat. *safranum* (Du Cange 7:265), *safra* (= Occ.) (Baratier 377, 393).

sagrament, T14r2. Oath. *Sagramen (PD* 332). Lat. *sacramentum*; abl. *sacramento* (Baratier 388, 389, Guérard 1:lxxxvi).

sain: *sayn,* N14r21; *saim*, T3v27, T14r32, T15r21. Lard. *Sagin, saïn* (*PD* 332, *DAO* 553, *DAOS* 476). Med. Lat. *sagimen* (Niermeyer); abl. *sagimine* (Baratier 385, Guérard 1:lxxxiii).

saisel, T5v33; *sasel*, N11r17 (*DAO* 251, *DAOS* 137). Timber from Seyssel (Haute-Savoie), on the upper Rhône (Rossiaud 2002, 2:261). "Saizel? oder saisel?" (*SW* 7.428). Lat. *saicel* (= Occ.); abl. *saycello* (Martin-Portier 242), *saicel* (*cairato de saicel*, Baratier 386; *cairant de saicel*, Guérard 1:xcii).

Not *sause* (Bondurand 144n4), perhaps a typographical error for *saule*, "willow."

sal, T9v1, N1v18, etc. Salt (*PD* 333, *DAO* 159, *DAOS* 66). Lat. *sal*; abl. *sale* (Baratier 386, 388).

salar: past part. *salat*, T4r16 (twice), T14r35, N7v11, N14r14 (twice), N15v14; pl. *salas* (stressed *salás*), N12r23. To salt (*PD* 333). *Peis ... salat*, T4r16; *peisson salat*, N14r14, N15v14. Salted fish. *Porcs salas*, N12r23. Salt pork.

salvat, N12r15, N14v19, N15r17. Except (*PD* 334).

Sancta Martha, N10r24, N10r25. The church of Sainte-Marthe in Tarascon.

Sant Gabriel, T15r9, T15r32, T15v4, N13r14, N15v9, N16r7, N16r10, N16r12, N16r15; *Sant Guabriel*, T15r9. Saint-Gabriel (Bouches-du-Rhône), about 5 kilometres southeast of Tarascon. *Pezage / peage (...) de – –*, T15r9, T15v4, N13r14, N15v9, N16r7, N16r10, N16r12, N16r15. The tollhouse at Saint-Gabriel.

Sant Gile, T9r10, N10r14. Saint-Gilles (Gard), 28 kilometres southeast of Tarascon, between Arles and Nîmes. Lat. *Sanctum Gilium* (Baratier 387).

Sant Guabriel, see *Sant Gabriel*

Sant Jacme, T9r2, T9r10; *Sant Jaume*, N10r14, N10r17. Santiago (de Compostela).

sap, T6r6. Fir (*PD* 335, *DAO* 250, *DAOS* 136). *Sap*, T6r6 (twenty boards of which make a *travada*), is synonymous with *sapin*, N11r25 (twenty boards of which make a *travada*). Pre-Latin **sappus* (*FEW* 11:214), Med. Lat. *sappus* (Du Cange 7:306), abl. *sap* = Occ.; *taulis de sap* (Baratier 386, Guérard 1:lxxxii).

sapin, N11r25. Fir (*SW* 7:470, Pansier 3:152, *DAO* 251, *DAOS* 137). See also *sap*

saquiera: pl. *saquieras*, T5r16, etc.; *sequieras*, N9r7, N9r9 (*saq-* in T, *seq-* in N). A measure of weight equal to about 1,000 kilos, a metric ton (see *mog*); "sorte de mesure" (*PD* 335). *En –*, T5r17. On the saquiera, per saquiera. Med. Lat. *sacquira* (Baratier 386), *saquira* (Guérard 1:lxxxiv); nom. pl. *saquiras* (Baratier 386), influenced by Occ.

Sarazin, see *Sarrazin*

***sarcia**, N14v7; *sarsia*, T4v2. Cordage, ropes, (nautical) gear; *sarce*, "cordaille" (Rossiaud 2002, 2:321); *sarcia*, "cordage, gréement" (Fourquin and Rigaud 1994, 334); rigging (Jal 1318); *sarsia*, "jonc servant à la sparterie," reed used in weaving (Pansier 3:152). *Sarsia vielha*, T4v2 (paying 11d on four quintals at Tarascon), is equivalent in meaning to *cordas viellas*, N8r22 (paying 9d the load at Tarascon; the change in rate is standard). Fr. *sartie, sarcie*, "agrès, ensemble des cordages" (Fennis 3:1631). It. *sartia di canape*, "hempen ropes" (Pegolotti 1936, 429); *sàrtia*, rigging (Reale Accademia d'Italia 1937, 823).

T4v2 reads *sarsia vielha*, not *sarsiamelha* ("cordages," Bondurand 141n1); cf. *sarcia vielha*, N14v7; *cordas viellas*, N8r22.

sarja, T4r27. Serge, "a woollen fabric, the nature of which has probably differed considerably at different periods. Before the 16th c. it is mentioned chiefly as material for hangings, bed-covers, and the like ... A garment made of serge" (*OED*). *Sarga* (*PD* 335). "Serge, sarge et sergeon (*sericalis pannus*), tissu de soie à côtes" [ribbed silk] (Enlart 1902–16, 3:599).

sarrazin, N9r22; *sarrasin*, N9r margin; *sarazin*, T8v1. Saracen (*SW* 7:474). *Un sarrazin, esclau o esclava*, N9r22. A Saracen slave, man or woman. Lat. *saracenus*; abl. *sarraceno vendito* (Guérard 1:lxxiii), *sarracena et sarraceno* (p. lxxx).

Not Fr. *serin*, canary (Bondurand 149n10).

sarria: pl. *sarrias*, N11v23, N12r1, N12v18. Basket. "Sorte de corbeille?" (*PD* 335). *– de gioncs*, N12r1; *de gonc*, N12v18. Basket made of rushes.

sarsia, see *sarcia*

sasel, see *saisel*

saumada, T4v19, T6v10, T7r21, N8v4, etc.; pl. *saumadas*, T4v18, N8v6, etc.; *somada*, N8v2, N12r16, N14v19. Bundle, the load that a pack animal (*PD* 336) or a man (Pansier 3:153) can carry.

The *saumada* equalled eight setiers at Tarascon proper and the Gate of Tarascon, but at Lubières either eight setiers or fifteen/sixteen, depending on the commodity. Thus at Lubières, a *saumada* of *amellas an lo croveilh*, *avelanes*, or *noses* was eight setiers "by the measure of Tarascon" (N12r9). But, still at Lubières, a *saumada* of other commodities was fifteen or sixteen setiers, even though one of the same commodity was eight setiers at the Gate of Tarascon: *blas*, N8v5 (at the Gate, "by the measure of Tarascon": N14v11, T14v12); *farinas*, T13r11 (at the Gate: T14v13, N14v11); *liolmes*, T13r11, N8v5 (at the Gate: T14v13, N14v12). For other commodities, the *saumada* was fifteen or sixteen setiers at Lubières but we have no such equivalence at other toll points: *faves, ordi, segla, seses, syvada*, "by the measure of Tarascon" (all in the same passage, N8v3). At Saint-Gabriel all measurements used the quintal.

"La *saumata* renvoie plutôt à une unité de poids, et elle est utilisée pour le vin et les raisins, et plus globalement pour toutes sortes de marchandises, avec des valeurs variables selon le moyen de transport usité" (Pécout 2010, cxli). "Mesure pour les grains qui valait de 40 à 100 litres, suivant les lieux" (Villain-Gandossi 1969, 38). Med. Lat. *saumata* (Niermeyer; Baratier 388); acc. *saumatam* (Baratier 386), abl. *saumata* (387). It. *somata*, "a load, a grain measure of 10 *mine* (in Avignon)" (Edler 273). See also *bestia cargada, carga, sestier*

sauput: fem. pl. *saupudas*, N9r3. Past part. of *saber* (to know), with the meaning of the adverbial phrase *a saubuda, à saubut*, or the adverb *sauputament* (which see): *As is commonly known, according to common knowledge. Cf. *saubuda*, "*s. f.* connaissance; *a s.* comme tout le monde sait; au su de tous, publiquement" (*PD* 336); *saubut (a)*, "*loc. adv.* publiquement, ouvertement" (ibid.; *FEW* 11:195a).

sauputament, T5r11. *With the knowledge of people generally. *Saubudamen,* "sciemment" (*PD* 336, *FEW* 11:195b); *sauputament* (Pansier 3:153, *FEW* 11:195b).

sayn, see *sain*

scorsa, see *escorsa*

scudela, see *escudela*

seba, N14v24; pl. *sebas*, T7v4, T7v5, T13v21, T14v8, T14v31; *cebas*, N12v1. Onion. *Ceba* (*PD* 74, *DAO* 422, *DAOS* 351). Lat. *caepa*, *caepe*; abl. *cepo* (Baratier 385, Guérard 1:lxxxiii), abl. pl. *cepis* (Baratier 388, Guérard 1:lxxxi, lxxxvi).

sec: fem. pl. *secas*, N7v13, N15v14; *sequas*, N14r18. Dry (*PD* 337), used here of figs.

seda, T3r25, T14r14, N7v4, N14r4. Silk (*PD* 337). Lat. *saeta, seta*; abl. *seta* (Martin-Portier 2:40), *ceda* (Baratier 386, 388, Guérard 1:lxxxi, lxxxii, lxxxvi) (= Occ.).

segla, N8r25. Rye (*PD* 338, *DAO* 380, *DAOS* 294).

segre: pres. 3rd pers. sg. *sec*, N1v17, N5r19, N7r16; pl. *segon*, N12v6, N13r11. Reflexive, cf. Fr. s'ensuivre. To follow (*PD* 338).

selce, see *cercle*

sendal, see *sendat*

sendat, T3r26, T14r14, N14r4; *cendat*, N15v24; *sendal*, N7v1. Sendal, "a thin rich silken material" (*OED*). *Cendal, cendat* (*PD* 75). "Cendal (*cendalum, cendatum*), tissu de soie souple" (Enlart 1902-16, 3:548). Med. Lat. *cendalum* (Niermeyer); abl. pl. *sandatis*, "sendal" (Baratier 386, 388) (Guérard 1:lxxxii, lxxxvi).

sendres, see *cendre*

senhor, T9r20, T9v7, etc., N13r4; sg. *senhors*, T5v9; pl. *senhors*, T3v9, T4v24, etc., N4v19; *senors*, T4v7, T4v16. Lord (*PD* 340). Owner, T4v24. *Lo rey nostre senhor*, T9v7, etc.; *nostre senhor lo rey*, N13r4. Our lord, the king; "le roi de Naples, comte de Provence" (Bondurand 154n1). See also *montazon (senhors de la), pezage (senhors del)*

sent, see *cent*

sequieras, see *saquiera*

sera, see *cera*

sereira: pl. *sereyras*, T7r16, *seriesas*, N12r14, N14v17. Cherry. *Cereia, -reira, -rieza* (*PD* 75, *DAO* 284, *DAOS* 177). Lat. *cerasus* fem., Med. Lat. *cereria* (Du Cange 2:271); abl. pl. *cereiriis* (Baratier 387, Guérard 1:lxxxv).

sese: pl. *seses*, N8r25. Chickpea. *Ceze* (*PD* 76, *DAO* 432, *DAOS* 365).

sestier: pl. *sestiers*, T4v13, N5r24, etc. Setier (*PD* 343), a measure of volume; one-fourth of a *saumada* (which see). One *saumée grosse d'Avignon* = five setiers of Avignon = eight setiers of Tarascon = four setiers of Arles

(Rossiaud 2002, 2:213). "Mesure de grains, celui d'Arles, mesure de référence, valait environ 57 l[itres]" (Fourquin and Rigaud 1994, 342). Lat. *sextarius*; acc. pl. *cestarios* (Baratier 382), abl. pl. *cestariis* (*fit saumata de viii cestariis*, a bundle is made of eight setiers, Guérard 1:lxxxvi). It. *sestiere*, "a dry measure (in S. France ...)" (Edler 270).

seton: pl. *setons*, T6v4, T13v33. *Strut, ship's rib that covers the caulking. Rib, "any of the curved transverse struts of a vessel, originally made of timber ... which extend up from the keel and form the framework of the hull" (*OED*). "Les cetons: sortes de costes" (Rossiaud 2002, 2:206); Fr. *costes*, "minces baguettes de genévrier servant à couvrir le calfatage" (Rossiaud 2002, 2:99). Mod. Occ. *setoú*, "chevron servant à composer le plancher d'un séchoir à châtaignes" (*FEW* 11:404b).

Not Eng. seton, "a thread, piece of tape, or the like, drawn through a fold of skin so as to maintain an issue or opening for discharges," etc. (*OED*, *PD* 338); and not snare ("lacet," Bondurand 146n3, *SW* 7:637).

seu, T3v28, T14r32, T15r22, N12v19, N14r21; *sieu*, N7v18. Tallow (*PD* 343, *DAO* 553, *DAOS* 476). Lat. *sebum*; abl. *cepo* (Baratier 385).

seucles, see *cercle*

Ships (1), parts of: see *antenna, arbre, biga, cairat* (2), *corba, fil* (2), *mattafellon, orri, orsa, pega, peiron, rama, rema, sarcia, seton, sol* (1), *timon*

Ships (2), types of: see *barca, caupolada, linh, molin, nau, navec, radel*

sia, see *eser*

Sicilia, N10r5. Sicily. *Rey de –*, N10r5. King of Sicily.

sicrum, *sitrum*, see *alum sicrum*

siera, see *cera*

sieu, see *seu*

sipia: pl. *sipias*, T8r1, N12v11. Cuttlefish. *Sepcha* (*PD* 341).

***sistra**: pl. *sistras*, N11v18. Basket. "*Cistria* (ou *cistra*?) ... corbeille" (*PD* 77), "*Cistria*, cor. *cistra*?" (*SW* 1:255), *cistria* (Pansier 5:168). Cf. *cistra*, "sorte d'arbrisseau" (*LR* 2:398); "esp. de plante" (*FEW* 11:660a); *citra*, "cistre, fenouil des Alpes" (*DAO* 397).

sobreplus, T11v25, N6r24. Excess (*PD* 347).

sol (1), N11v12. *Tier of goods in a vessel's hold. Cf. Occ. *sol*, Fr. *sol*, floor (*PD* 349). OCat. *sol*, "plan d'arrimage des marchandises dans un navire de commerce" (Jal 1366); cf. ground-tier, "the lowest tier of goods in a vessel's hold" (*OED*). Cf. Fr. *sole*, "planche qui couvre certaines pièces de bois; plat-bord," gunwale (Fennis 3:1670). Med. Lat. *sola*: *de qualibet poste de sola seu fondo* (Guérard 1:lxxxv, Baratier 387n5), "on each board in the bottom of the hold." *Sola*, "planus navis fundus, Gall. sole" (Du Cange 7:510), flat bottom of a ship; "sole, la partie plate du fond du navire, le fond de la cale" (Jal 1366; Rossiaud 2002, 2:324–5). *Fondo*, "le fond du navire" (Jal 709). See also *peiron*

sol (2), not written out in TN but abbreviated *s/*, passim. *Sol*, Fr. sou, corresponding to the English shilling. One *sol* was worth 12 deniers; twenty *sols* made a pound (*libra*). A money of account that might be paid in *rials* (as at T14r21). Lat. *solidus*. *Solt*, "sou" (*PD* 350); *sol*, "lat. solidum, sou" (*LR* 5:249); *soou, sol*, "sou, monnaie de compte, qui faisait la vingtième partie de la livre tournois, valant douze deniers, et aujourd'hui cinq centimes" (Honnorat 3:1192).

solpre, T8r8, N12v11. Sulfur; *solfre, solpre* (*PD* 350, *DAO* 156, *DAOS* 62). Lat. *sulphur*; abl. *solpre* (Baratier 399).

soma, N2r6; *somma*, T9v25. Total (*PD* 350). Lat. *summa* (Baratier 383). Adv., N2r6. In sum.

somada, see *saumada*

somma, see *soma*

sorba: pl. *sorbas*, T7r10, N12r13. Sorb apple (*PD* 352, Pansier 3:159, *DAO* 245, *DAOS* 131). Lat. *sorbum*, Med. Lat. **sorba*; nom. pl. *sorbe* (Baratier 387, Guérard 1:lxxxv).

sotterran, N10v1. Lower. *Soteiran*, "inférieur, bas" (*PD* 353).

sotzdiaque, T8v8; *subdiaque*, N9v21. Subdeacon (*PD* 353), "a member of the clerical order next below that of deacon" (Dictionary.com, consulted 16 March 2014).

Spanhol, see *Espanhol*

Spices and medicines: see *anis, çafarame, canela, cassia fistula, citeal, comin, ensens, espiceria, gala, gingibre, girofle, lentiscle, mastec, mostarda, pebre, pol, polvera, safran, sal, sucre*. See also Foods

stagnat, see *estanhar*

stameha, *stamenhas*, see *estamenha*

stang, *stanh, stanhg*, see *estanh* (1)

stopas, see *estopa*

strani, stranis, see *estrani*

subdiaque, see *sotzdiaque*

sucre, T3v20, T3v21, T14r31 (twice), T15r18, T15r20, N7v13, N7v14, N14r16 (twice). Sugar (*PD* 355). *Pols de –*, T3v21, T14r31, T15r20, N14r16; *polvera de –*, N7v14. Powdered sugar. Med. Lat. *sucrum* (Du Cange 7:646); abl. *sucre* (= Occ.) (Baratier 385, Guérard 1:lxxxiii).

sus, T5r2, N4r12, etc. *De sus, en sus*, passim. Up, over, above. "En sus, en haut, de plus" (*LR* 5:289). *Dessus*, N6v25, N12v25. Above. *In sus* (*in* Lat., *sus* Occ.), T4v17, T4v19, T4v25. *De ... en sus*, N9v23, N10r13. From ... up. Lat. *supra* (Guérard 1:lxxxiii).

syvada, see *civada*

tafarame (Bondurand), see *çafarame*

talhador: pl. *talhadors*, T13v34, T14v16, N11v17; *talhador[s]*, T6r26. Trencher, a plate or platter (*PD* 357); trencher, a knife (Bondurand 145n14). Lat. *talliator* (Niermeyer); abl. pl. *talliadors* (= Occ.) (Baratier 387, 388, Guérard 1:lxxxv).

tant quant, T9r19. As long as. Lat. *tamdiu quamdiu* (Baratier 389).

tant solament, T5r12, T13r17, T15r32, N9r4, N9r13, N9r21; *tant* [*solament*], T13v12; *tant solamens*, T5v24, T12r1, T13r27. Only. *Solamen, tan s. (PD* 349). Lat. *tantum* (Baratier 387), *tantummodo* (Baratier 388, Guérard 1:lxxxvii), *solummodo* (Guérard 1:lxxxiv).

Tarascon, N1v17, etc.; *Tharascon*, T3r2, T4v14, T14r2, etc., N1v22, N4r23, N4v6, etc. Tarascon (Bouches-du-Rhône).

taula: pl. *taulas*, T6r3, T6r6, T6r7, T6r8, N11r25, N11v1, N11v3. Board (*PD* 359; Rossiaud 2002, 2:327), a piece of timber sawed thin. – *de meleze*, T6r7. Larch-wood board. – *de noguier*, T6r8, N11v3. Walnut board. – *de roure*, T6r3, N11v1. Oak board. – *de sap*, T6r6. Fir board. – *de sapin*, N11r25. Fir board. Lat. *tabula* (Guérard 1:lxxiv); abl. pl. *taulis nogerii ... de rouvre ... de sap* (Baratier 386).

tela, T4r29, N8r8, N14r2, N15v21; pl. *telas*, T3r16, T14r9, T15v7, N7r25. Linen cloth (*PD* 359). Sg. *tela*, linen, in quantities of one cord (*corda*), paid 0.5d (T4r29, N8r8). Pl. *telas*, linen cloths, in quantities of four quintals, paid 29.5d (T3r16) or 30.5d (N7r25). Lat. *tela*; abl. pl. *telis* (Baratier 377, 386, 388, Guérard 1:lxxxi, lxxxiv, lxxxvi).

tener: past part. *tengut*, N9r4. To oblige (*PD* 361). Lat. *tenere*; pres. 3rd pers. pl. passive *tenentur* (Baratier 382).

termine, N7r15. Border. *Termeni, -ini* (*PD* 362).

terra (1), T6v28, N12r3, N12r4, N12r5, N15r7; pl. *terras*, T14v27. Clay (*PD* 362, *DAO* 139), used to make earthenware.

terra (2), N15r24, N15v4. Land (*PD* 362, *DAO* 129). *Per* –, N15r24, N15v4. By land.

terratori, N15r17. Territory, jurisdiction of Tarascon. *Terrador, territori* (*PD* 362).

ters, N10v1, N13r22; fem. *tersa,* T5r[33]. Third (*PD* 363). *La – part*, one third. Lat. *tertius*; abl. *tertio* (Baratier 387), fem. *tertia* (384).

teule, masc.: pl. *teules*, T4v9, N8r20, N14v9. Tile (*PD* 363). Levied in quantities of 1,000 (T4v9, N8r20); compare *lausa,* roof tile, levied in quantities of 100 (T6r24). Lat. *tegula*; gen. pl. *tegularum* (Baratier 385, Guérard 1:lxxxiii).

timon, T5v12, T13v5, N11r1. Tiller or rudder. "Timon" (*PD* 364), "gouvernail" (Bondurand 143n4; Rossiaud 2002, 2:330–5; Fourquin and Rigaud 1994, 361). "D'abord la Barre du gouvernail [tiller], puis, par extension, le Gouvernail lui-même [rudder]" (Jal 1451). Fr. *timon*, "gouvernail (d'abord latéral, ensuite central)" (Fennis 3:1746). Lat. *temo,* Med. Lat. *timonus* (Niermeyer); abl. *timono* (Guérard 1:lxxxii), "gouvernail" (Baratier 386).

tina, T6v14, T13v29, T14v19, N15r2; pl. *tinas*, N12r22. Vat (*PD* 364). A *tina* made of twenty-five staves, N15r2; cf. *dogan*. Lat. *tina*; abl. *tina* (Baratier 388, Guérard 1:lxxxvi). It. *tino*, "dyer's vat" (Edler 297).

tirar: pres. 3rd pers. sg. *tira*, N5r14, N7r3; pl. *tiran*, N11r23; past part., masc. pl. *tiratz*, T6r5. To haul (*PD* 364), as oxen haul timber (T6r5, N11r23) or as men and animals haul a ship upstream (N5r14, N7r3). Lat. *trahere*; pres. 3rd pers. pl. passive *trahuntur* (Guérard 1:lxxxii), *trauntur* (Baratier 386).

Tollhouses, see *pezage* (4)

Tollkeeper, see *Pons del Prat*

Tools, see Furniture

tornes, N13r17, N13v4, N16r19; pl. *tornes*, N5v4, N13r15, N13r18, N13r20, N13v4, N13v9, N13v16, N13v21, N13v24, N16r17; *torneses*, N5v5, N5v6, N5v7; **tornesos* (Cat. or Sp.), N16r16. Tournois, a coin (*LR* 5:382, Pansier 3:167) minted in Tours, or resembling coins minted there (Blancard 1868, 3). Counted as 16d (N13r18, N13v4, N13v16). A distinction between large tournois, ten to the florin of Florence, versus small ones, 12.5 to the florin, is made at N13r17–20; the small tornois is counted at 15.21d (N13r21). – *d'argent*, N5v4, N13r15, N13v21, N16r16. Silver tournois.

On Cat. *tornesos* see Bernat Desclot, *Crònica* (second half 13th c.), chapter 146 (Bernat Desclot 1982, 296; Alcover 10:371): *per mil sous de tornesos que hom li havia promesos*, "for a thousand sous tournois that had been promised him." On Sp. *tornesos*, cf. fem. *libras tornesas* (Corominas 5:558).

Lat. *Turonensis*, of Tours; gen. pl. *turonensium* (*denarios turonensium*, Baratier 387, 388; *obolos turonensium*, 388).

torra: pl. **torras*, N7v18. Pot. *Tora*, "Übers. 'pot'. Haltbar? Oder zu ändern und wie? Etwa *topinas*?" (*SW* 8:277), quoting Forestié (1901, 216, line 23): *toras plenas de gomas ho de sulpre vio e de estopas e ceu mesclat que hom jete sobre lor,* "des pots pleins de résine, de soufre vif, d'étoupes et de suif mêlés pour les jeter dessus" (trans. Forestié).

tot, passim; **tout* (Fr.), N5r8, N10v1. All, every. *Tot* (*PD* 367, *LR* 5:389–91, *SW* 8:330); *tot, tout* (1411) (Pansier 3:168). Lat. *omnis*; abl. pl. *omnibus* (Baratier 386).

totas fes, N15r11, N15r19. However. "Toutefois" (*SW* 8:716). Cf. OFr. *totes foiz* (TL 3:1996). *Fes* shows influence from OFr. *fois* (Godefroy 4:45, 9:633), *foiz* (TL 3:1994–7); cf. Occ. *vetz*, "fois" (*PD* 382, *LR* 5:530, *SW* 8:714).

totas vegadas, N7r3, N9r2, N12r1, N12r4, N12v14, N13v13; *totas vegades*, N9v22. However. "Toutes fois" (*LR* 5:531, *SW* 8:603).

tout, see *tot*

tractar: pres. 3rd pers. sg. reflexive *tracta*, N1v18, N2r12. To deal with, set forth. *Trachar, tractar* (*PD* 368).

traire: past subj. 3rd pers. pl. *traguessan*, N15r21. To take out (*PD* 368).

travada (1), T5v18, T5v21, T5v26, T13r25, N11r7, N11r13, etc.; pl. *travadas*, T13r26, N11r2, N11r5, N11r10, N11r14, etc. Log, "an unhewn portion of a felled tree" (*OED*). "Poutre?" (*PD* 370); "poutre," referring to Bondurand 1890 (Pansier 3:169). – *de fusta*, T5v18, T5v26, T13r25. Wooden log. Lat. *trabata, trav-* (Niermeyer); *travata de fusta*, "poutre" (Baratier 386). *Pace* Rossiaud: "*Travada* n'a jamais signifié poutre ... mais travée, ou si l'on préfère portée d'une poutre, poutrée" (2002, 2:345).

travada (2), T5v33, T5v34, T5v35, etc., N11r17, N11r18, etc.; *travata* (It., Battaglia 21:276), T6r4. Not a single log, but a *collective measure for various numbers of wooden items that are treated as equivalent to one log for the purpose of the toll; translated here as "stack." "Unité de taxation des fustes aux péages de Beaucaire et Tarascon (ADV [Archives départementales Vaucluse] 1 J 163); les tarifs qui font état de la *travade* – équivalant à l'aise – sont des copies tardives (XIVe–1446) de très anciennes pancartes. Le mot ne devait plus être employé passé 1400" (Rossiaud 2002, 2:345); *aise*, "unité de mesure du bois d'oeuvre ... Originellement, l'aise est un ais, une poutre, une grosse pièce de fuste" (Rossiaud 2002, 2:12). Med. Lat. *trabata* (Niermeyer), *travata* (Niermeyer; Baratier 386).

travata, see *travada* (2)

trobar: past part. *trobat*, N13r3. To find (*PD* 373).

Types of animals, see Animals (2)

Types of ships, see Ships (2)

*__uleta__, T8r11. Funnel. *Uleta*, "comme *ulheto*, entonnoir pour les futailles," funnel for casks or tuns (Bondurand 149n5, Pansier 3:172). *Ulheta*, "entonnoir de bois" (Alibert 685). Cf. OOcc. *oelhet*, "trou"; *ulhat*, "percé de trous" (*FEW* 7:319a).

un, T10r4, N4r13, etc.; *uno* (It.), T9v2, T13r14, T16r19; fem. *una*, T4r27, N3v20, etc.; usually written *.i.* or *.j.* One (*PD* 375).

uno (It.), see *un*

Utensils, see Furniture

uzage, T12r21, T12r30; *usage*, N4v7, N4v15, N5r2. *Uzage*, a user's fee. "Usage, habitude; sorte de droit" (*PD* 376). Med. Lat. *usaticus, usagium* (Niermeyer); acc. *usagium* (Guérard 1:lxxxiv), abl. *usagio*, a tax on salt (Baratier 387, Guérard 1:lxxxiv).

vair (1): n., pl. *vars*, N15v22. Vair (*PD* 376), "a fur obtained from a variety of squirrel with grey back and white belly, much used in the 13th and 14th centuries as a trimming or lining for garments" (*OED*). "Mosaïque de ventres blancs et de dos gris d'écureuil" (Bourilly 1928, 80).

vair (2): adj., fem. *vayra*, N14r6; pl. *vayras*, T3v1. Varicolored (*PD* 376). *Pennas vayras*, T3v1. "Poils vairs (mêlées de gris et de blanc) de lapin ou d'animaux semblables" (Bondurand 138n7).

vaissel, T6v15, T13v29, T14v19; *vaysel*, N15r2; pl. *vaisels*, T5r11; *vayssels*, N12r22. Cask (Bondurand 146n10); *vaisel*, "vaisseau, vase," receptacle (*PD* 377); *vaisseau*, "tonneau" (Rossiaud 2002, 2:347). Lat. *vas* with diminutive suffix produced Med. Lat. *vaissella* (Niermeyer), *vaissellum* (Du Cange 8:233); abl. *vaicello* (Baratier 388, Guérard 1:lxxxvi), abl. pl. *vaicellis*, "petit tonneau" (Baratier 386).

valer: pres. 3rd pers. sg. *val*, N9r19, N9r20, N13r17, etc.; pl. *valon*, N13r18, N13v12, N13v18, etc.; *valen*, N5v7, N16r17; imperf. 3rd pers. sg. *valia*, T8r23. To be worth (*PD* 377).

van: fem. *vana*, N15v23. Irregular. *Van*, "faible, épuisé, irrégulier" (*PD* 377).

vars, see *vair* (1)

vayra, *vayras*, see *vair* (2)

vaysel, see *vaissel*

veire, T7v15, T14v25, N12v5, N15r5 (twice). Glass (*PD* 378). Lat. *vitrum, vitreum*; abl. *vitrio* (*de vitrio, de uno coperio*, from one load (?) of glass, Baratier 387) (Guérard 1:lxxxv); *veire* (= Occ.) (Baratier 386, 388, Guérard 1:lxxxi, xciv, xcvii), *verre* (= Fr.) (Guérard 1:lxxxvi); *vitri* (Martin-Portier 2:46); *bestia cargata de veire*, an animal loaded with glass (Baratier 388).

vel: pl. *vels*, N14r8. Fleece (*PD* 378, *DAO* 548).

vendre, T6r19, T8v25, N9r19, N11v11; *vendere* (It.), T8r23; pres. 3rd pers. pl. *vendon*, N15r16; pres. subj. 3rd pers. pl. *vendan*, T12v21; past part. *vendut*, T8r22, N9r18, N11v10; fem. pl. *vendudas*, T8v24, T14v28, N15r20. To sell (*PD* 379). *Per vendre*. For sale, "acheté nouvellement en vue de la vente" (Bondurand 145n9). Lat. *vendere*; gerund *vendendo* (Baratier 386, Guérard 1:lxxxiii).

venir: pres. 3rd pers. sg. *ven*, T9r13, T12v26, N7r11, N8v14, N8v22, etc.; pl. *venon*, N9v6; pres. subj. 3rd pers. sg. *venga*, T4v28; imperf. 3rd pers. sg. *venia*, T13r15, N8v24; pret. 3rd pers. sg. *venc*, N13r5; pres. part. *venent*, N10r23; pl. *venens*, T8v22. To come (*PD* 379).

verdet, T8r4, N12v9. Verdigris (*PD* 380, *DAO* 170, *DAOS* 79), "a green or greenish blue substance obtained artificially by the action of dilute acetic acid on thin plates of copper (or a green rust naturally forming on copper and brass), and much used as a pigment, in dyeing, the arts, and medicine" (*OED*). Med. Lat. *verdetum* (Du Cange 8:278); abl. *verdeto* (Guérard 1:xcii), *verdent* (= Occ.? *SW* 8:660 does not record the variant with *-n-*) (Baratier 385, 386, Guérard 1:lxxxii, lxxxiii).

vergan: pl. *vergans*, N11v23. Twig (*PD* 380).

vernice (It.), T4r14. Varnish. *Vernis* (*LR* 5:511, Pansier 3:175, *DAOS* 153).

vestir, n.m., N10r1. *Clothes, clothing given by a lord to people in his service; Fr. *livrée* since ca. 1290 ("habits donnés par un seigneur aux personnes qui étaient attachées à son service," *TLFi*). Not demonstrably extended to the sense of Eng. livery, "the characteristic uniform or insignia worn by a household's retainers or servants ... typically distinguished by colour and design; the dress, uniform, or insignia ... by which a family, etc., may be identified" (since 1399, *OED*). The former sense recurs in the *Vida* of Gausbert de Poicibot: *il li det arnes de joglar, vestirs e cavals*, "he gave him equipment of a jongleur, clothes and horses" (Boutière and Schutz 1973, 229.4), and in a *partimen* by Albertet de Sestaro and Monge: *ricx vestirs* *amples e gens arnes*, "rich, ample clothes and noble equipment" (*Monges, cauzetz*, PC 16.17 = PC 303.1, ed. Appel 1930, 136, no. 97 v. 11). "Vêtement" (*LR* 5:528, *PD* 382, Pansier 3:176), "Kleidung" (*SW* 8:710).

veul: pl. *veuls*, N15v23. Calf. *Vedel* (*PD* 378, Alibert 689).

vezer: pres. part. *vesent*, N13r6. To see (*PD* 383).

vielh: fem. *vielha*, T4v2, N14v7. Old. *Velh* (*PD* 378). *Sarsia vielha*, T4v2; *sarcia vielha*, N14v7. Old ropes.

vila, N5r14, N7r9. Town, city ("ferme; ville," *PD* 384). *Vila de Tarascon*, N5r14. *Vila*, N7r9, i.e., Tarascon. Lat. *villa*, "résidence royale ... agglomération à l'extérieur d'un castrum ... château ... *ville* dans le sens juridique, douée de droits et de privilèges" (Niermeyer 2:1436); abl. *in villa Tarasconi* (Baratier 382), gen. *ville de Tarascono* (Baratier 383). Cf. *civitas*, "diocèse, territoire spirituel d'un évêché ... siège d'un évêché" (Niermeyer 1:241); abl. *in civitate A[vinioni]* (Baratier 389), *civitas Aralatensis* (395).

vin, T4v31, T4v33, T5r1, T5r3, T5r4, T5r9, T5r10, N8v17, N8v18, N8v20, N8v22, N9r1, N9r3. Wine (*PD* 384). Lat. *vinum*; abl. *vino* (Baratier 386, Guérard 1:lxxxiv).

Violans, see *Mujolans*

visitar: pres. part. *visitant*, T9r2, T9r9. To visit (*LR* 5:554, Pansier 3:177).

vivono, see *argento vivo*

Volcan, T4v3; *Bolcam*, N14v3; *Boulcan*, N8r14. Vulcano, a small island north of Sicily. See *alum de Volcan*

von, see *on*

Wood and wood products: see *bresilh, buguet, cairat* (2), *fusta, jaina, madiera, meleze, noguier, papier, pega, roans, ros, roure, ruscla, saisel, sap, sapin, taula, travada* (1), *vergan*

zozita (Bondurand), see *arzita*

English Names of Commodities in the Glossary

Parenthetical numerals, as in "*cairat* (3)," refer to entries in the Glossary.

Aleppo, alum from: *alum d'Alap*
alloy: *liga*
almond: *amella, mela.* almond shell: *clovel*
alum: *alum*
animal: *bestia*
anise: *anis*
ape: *isime*
apple: *pom, poma*
armoire: *armari*
ash: *cendre*
ass: *aze*

bar (measure of iron): *costa*
bark (of a tree), tanner's: *ros, ruscla*
bark (small ship): *barca*
barley: *ordi*
barrel: *bota*
basket: *sarria, sistra.* breadbasket: *paniera.* plaited shopping basket: *cabas*
beam: *jaina*
bean: *fava*
bear: *ors*
blanc (coin): *blanc*
board: *taula*
book: *libre*
borax: *boras*
bowl: *escudela, grazal.* small bowl: *grazali(n).* wooden bowl without handles: *cossa*
box: *escrinh*
brass: *loton*
Brazil wood: *bresilh*
breadbasket: *paniera*
bunch (of garlic bulbs or onions): *rest*
bundle: *saumada*
butter: *buire*

cabbage: *caulet*
calf: *veul*
camel: *camel*
cane (measure of oil): *cana*
carat: *cairat* (3)
card (implement for raising a nap on cloth): *carda*
cargo of a *caupol*: *caupolada.* cargo of a *nau: navada.* cargo of a *navec: naviada.* See also load
carrier: *colier*

cask: *vaissel*
cassia fistula: *cassia fistula* (Lat.) See pudding pipe tree
chaplain: *capelan*
charcoal: *carbon*
cheese: *fromage*
cherry: *sereira*. sour cherry: *agriota*
chest: *arca*, *caissa*
chestnut: *castanha*. chestnut shell: *escorsa*
chickpea: *sese*
cinnamon: *canela*
clay: *terra* (1)
cloth: *drap*. brown cloth: *brun*. coarse muslin cloth: *estamenha*. coarse woollen cloth: *borrassa*. linen cloth: *tela*. white cloth: *blanquet*
clove: *girofle*
coin: *moneda* (2). See also money of account
coiner: *monedier*
coins. see *blanc, coronat, denier, florin, mealha, obol, patac, pogeza, rial, tornes*
commodity: *mercadaria*
copper: *coure*
cordage, ropes: *sarcia*
cordovan: *cordoan*
cornel berry: *corma*
coronat (coin): *coronat*
cotton: *coton*
cumin: *comin*
cuttlefish: *sipia*

date: *datil*
deacon: *diaque*
denier: *denier*
drain: *dogat*
dress: *rauba*. dress, pleated (?): *plagaria*

Englishman: *Engles*
ewe: *feda*

feather: *pluma*. feather alum: *alum de pluma*
fig: *figa*
fir: *sap, sapin*
fish: *peis, peisson*
flap (of a garment): *gron*
flax: *lin*
fleece: *vel*
florin (coin): *florin*
flour: *farina*
foot (of a piece of furniture): *pecol*
foreigner: *estrangier*, *estrani*
frock: *frauc*
fruit: *frucha, frut*
funnel: *uleta*
fur: *pelharia, pelisaria, pena, vair* (1)
fur lining: *pena*
furniture, foot of: *pecol*
fustian: *fustani*

gallnut: *gala*
garlic bulb: *alh*. garlic or onions, bunch: *rest*
garment, flap of a: *gron*
German: *Alaman*
ginger: *gingibre*
glass: *veire*
goat, male: *boc*. female goat: *cabra*
goblet: *enap*
gold: *aur*
goods: *aver*
grain: *blat* (Occ.), *bled* (Fr.)
grease: *graissa*
gum arabic: *glassa*
gypsum: *gip*

haberdashery: *mersaria*
half denier: *obol, mealha*
hamper: *banaston*
hazelnut: *avelana*
hemina: *emina*
hemp: *canape*
hide, skin: *cuer, pel*
hogshead: *mog*
honey: *mel*
hoop: *cercle*
horse: *caval*. workhorse: *rossin*
incense: *ensens*
indigo: *indi*
iron: *ferre*

jug: *brocat*. small jug: *crucol*. two-handled wooden jug: *cornuda*

keg: *barral*
kid: *cabret, cabrit*
knee (nautical): *corba*
knife or plate, trencher: *talhador*
knight: *cavalier*

lamb: *anhel*. lambskin: *anina*. lambswool: *anhis*
larch wood: *meleze*
lard: *sain*
lead: *plomb*
lemon: *citron*. large lemon: *ponsiri*
lentil: *lentilha*
lime (alkaline earth): *caus*
lime (fruit): *limon*
lining, fur: *pena*
lion: *leon*
liquorice: *regalisia*
livery: *vestir*
load: *carga, fais*. load carried by a pack animal (?): *copiera*. loaded animal: *bestia cargada*. See also cargo
log: *travada* (1)
Lombard: *Lombart*

madder dye: *roge*
mare: *egua*. workmare: *rossa*
mast: *albre*
master: *maistre*
mastic: *lentiscle*, *mastec*
mastiff bitch: *mastina*
meat: *carn*
medlar: *nespla*
merchandise: *mercandisa*
mill: *molin*
millet: *milh*
millstone: *mola*
money of account: *libra, sol* (2). See also coins
mount: *cavalcadura*
mule, male: *mul*. female mule: *mula*
mustard: *mostarda*
myrtle: *nerta*

oak: *roure*
oar: *rama, rema*
oats: *civada*
ochre: *arzica*
oil: *oli*
onion: *seba*. onions or garlic, bunch: *rest*
ox: *buou*

pan: *grazalo(n)*
paper: *papier*
parchment: *pergamin*
patac (coin): *patac*
peach: *persegua*
pear: *pera*
peltry, fur skins: *pelisaria*
pepper: *pebre*
piece: *pesa*
pig: *porc*

pilgrim: *romieu*
pitch: *pega*
pitcher: *broc, pechier*
planking in the gunwale, row of (?): *peiron*. planking on hull, course of: *fil* (2)
plate or knife, trencher: *talhador*
plates: *piatta*
pogeza (coin): *pogeza*
pole: *pertegua*. long, thin pole: *biga*
pot: *olla, torra*
pound: *libra* (Lat.)
powder: *pol, polvera*
prelate: *prelat*
product: *obra, obrage*
Provençal: *Proensal*
pudding pipe tree: *cassia fistula* (Lat.)
purse (?): *ful*

quicksilver: *argento vivo* (It.)
quince: *codon*
quintal (about 50 kilograms): *quintal*

rabbit: *conil*
raisin: *agibe*
rape, turnip: *raba*
reefpoint: *mattafellon*
retinue: *mainage*
Rhodes: *Roda*
rial (gold coin): *rial*
rice: *ris*
rider: *cavalcador, cavalcan*
rock: *peira, roqua*. rock alum: *alum de roca*
roof tile: *lausa*; cf. *teule*
root: *razis*
rope: *corda*. ropes, cordage: *sarcia*
roquette: *eruga*
rose: *rosa*
Royans, Le, timber from: *roans*
rudder or tiller: *timon*
rush: *jonc*
rye: *segla*

sack: *sac*
saffron: *çafarame, safran*
salt: *sal*
saquiera (about 1,000 kilograms): *saquiera*
Saracen: *Sarrazin*
seed: *grana*
sendal: *sendat*
serge: *sarja*
setier: *sestier*
Seyssel, timber from: *saisel*
sheep: *mouton*. sheepsbelly: *arsiqua*. sheepskin: *aluda, moutonina*
shell of an almond: *clovel*. shell of a chestnut: *escorsa*
shilling: *sol* (2)
ship, sailed: *nau, navec*. ship, oared: *linh*
silk: *seda*
silver: *argent*
skin (animal), hide: *pel*. skins used in making furs: *pelharia, pelisaria*
skin (vegetable or fruit): *pelanha*
skirt: *fauda*
slave: *esclau*
smith: *fabre*
soap: *sabon*
sorb apple: *sorba*
Spaniard: *Espanhol*
spice: *espiceria*
spoon: *culhier*
stack of timber: *travada* (2)
stave: *doga*. set of staves: *dogan*
steel: *acier*
stem post (for Baratier): *roda*
stone, quarry: *cairon*
strap: *faissa*

strut: *seton*
subdeacon: *sotzdiaque*
sugar: *sucre*. sugar alum: *alum sicrum*
sulfur: *solpre*
sumach: *ros*

tackle for manoeuvring a lateen sail: *orsa*
tallow: *seu*
tanner's bark: *ruscla*
tartar: *greza*
thread: *fil* (1)
tile: *teule*; cf. *lausa*
tiller or rudder: *timon*
timber: *fusta, madiera*. timber from Le Royans: *roans*. timber from Seyssel: *saisel*. large squared timber: *cairat* (2)
tin: *estanh* (1)
tournois (coin): *tornes*
tow: *estopa*
tree: *albre*
trencher, plate or knife: *talhador*
tub, small: *grazalet*
tunic: *cota*
turnip, rape: *raba*
twig: *vergan*

utensil: *aizina*

vair: *vair* (1)
varnish: *vernice*
vat: *tina*
vegetable: *liome*
verdigris: *verdet*
Vulcano, alum from: *alum de Volcan*

walnut: *noze*. walnut tree: *noguier*
washbasin: *bacon*
water: *aigua*
wax: *cera*
wedge (?): *buguet*
weight: *pes*
wine: *vin*
withe: *riorta*
woad: *gaida*
wool: *lana*. fine-spun wool: *estam*. inferior wool from the tail: *cohanha*
worker: *obran*

yard supporting a lateen sail: *antenna*
young (of an animal): *mensa*

zedoary: *citeal*

APPENDICES

Appendix 1

Analysis of Table T1

Salt in Hogsheads: Tolls and Shares

MS T, f. 10r–11v

Legend
Units: Hogsheads.
Toll: As in MS T.
Corr.: Editorial correction to the preceding column.
Incr.: Increment of this figure over the preceding one.
Rate: Toll or share divided by units.
King: Share to the king.
Knights: Share to the knights.
Bal.: Balance (Toll minus King and Knights, as corrected).
Om.: Omitted.
All values are given in deniers.

Units	Toll	Corr.	Incr.	Rate	King	Corr.	Incr.	Rate	Knights	Corr.	Incr.	Rate	Bal.
1	29.25	29.75		29.75	22.75			22.75	7.00			7.00	0.00
2	59.50		29.75	29.75	45.50		22.75	22.75	14.00		7.00	7.00	0.00
3	89.25		29.75	29.75	68.25		22.75	22.75	21.00		7.00	7.00	0.00

Units	Toll	Corr.	Incr.	Rate	King	Corr.	Incr.	Rate	Knights	Corr.	Incr.	Rate	Bal.
4	119.00		29.75	29.75	91.00		22.75	22.75	28.00		7.00	7.00	0.00
5	148.75		29.75	29.75	113.75		22.75	22.75	35.00		7.00	7.00	0.00
6	178.50		29.75	29.75	136.50		22.75	22.75	42.00		7.00	7.00	0.00
7	205.25		26.75	29.32	157.75		21.25	22.54	47.50		5.50	6.79	0.00
8	232.00		26.75	29.00	179.00		21.25	22.38	53.00		5.50	6.63	0.00
9	284.00		52.00	31.56	206.00		27.00	22.89	78.00		25.00	8.67	0.00
10	310.00		26.00	31.00	226.50		20.50	22.65	83.50		5.50	8.35	0.00
11	336.00		26.00	30.55	247.00		20.50	22.45	89.00		5.50	8.09	0.00
12	368.00		32.00	30.67	269.00		22.00	22.42	99.00		10.00	8.25	0.00
13	394.00		26.00	30.31	289.50		20.50	22.27	104.50		5.50	8.04	0.00
14	421.00	420.00	26.00	30.07	310.00		20.50	22.14	110.00		5.50	7.86	0.00
15	446.00		26.00	29.73	330.50		20.50	22.03	115.50		5.50	7.70	0.00
16	472.00		26.00	29.50	351.00		20.50	21.94	121.00		5.50	7.56	0.00
17	498.00		26.00	29.29	371.00	371.50	20.50	21.82	126.50		5.50	7.44	0.00
18	529.00		31.00	29.39	393.25		22.25	21.85	135.75		9.25	7.54	0.00
19	555.00		26.00	29.21	413.75		20.50	21.78	141.25		5.50	7.43	0.00
20	581.00		26.00	29.05	434.25		20.50	21.71	146.75		5.50	7.34	0.00
21	607.00		26.00	28.90	454.75		20.50	21.65	152.25		5.50	7.25	0.00
22	633.00		26.00	28.77	475.25		20.50	21.60	157.75		5.50	7.17	0.00
23	659.00		26.00	28.65	495.75		20.50	21.55	163.25		5.50	7.10	0.00
24	685.00		26.00	28.54	516.25		20.50	21.51	169.75	168.75	5.50	7.07	0.00
25	723.00		38.00	28.92	539.75		23.50	21.59	183.25		14.50	7.33	0.00
26	749.00		26.00	28.81	559.25	560.25	20.50	21.51	194.25	188.75	5.50	7.47	0.00
27	Om.	775.00	26.00	28.70	Om.	580.75	20.50	21.51	Om.	194.25	5.50	7.19	0.00
28	801.00		26.00	28.61	601.25		20.50	21.47	199.75		5.50	7.13	0.00
29	827.00		26.00	28.52	621.75		20.50	21.44	205.25		5.50	7.08	0.00
30	853.00		26.00	28.43	642.25		20.50	21.41	210.25	210.75	5.50	7.01	0.00
31	879.00		26.00	28.35	662.75		20.50	21.38	216.25		5.50	6.98	0.00
32	905.00		26.00	28.28	683.25		20.50	21.35	221.75		5.50	6.93	0.00

33	931.00		26.00	28.21	703.75		20.50	21.33	227.25		5.50	6.89	0.00
34	957.00		26.00	28.15	724.25		20.50	21.30	232.75		5.50	6.85	0.00
35	983.00		26.00	28.09	744.75		20.50	21.28	238.25		5.50	6.81	0.00
36	1009.00		26.00	28.03	765.25		20.50	21.26	243.75		5.50	6.77	0.00
37	1045.00		36.00	28.24	788.25		23.00	21.30	256.25	256.75	13.00	6.93	0.00
38	1071.00		26.00	28.18	808.75		20.50	21.28	262.75	262.25	5.50	6.91	0.00
39	1097.00		26.00	28.13	829.25		20.50	21.26	267.75		5.50	6.87	0.00
40	1126.00		29.00	28.15	850.00		20.75	21.25	276.00		8.25	6.90	0.00

Notes

Unit 1, Toll. Scribal error at T10r4: *po.* (*pogeza*) for *o. po.* (1 obol, 1 *pogeza*). Corr. adds 0.5d, confirmed at T9v26 (*o. po.*); consistent with the shares for 1 unit, the increments in Toll for 2–6 units, and Table N1.

Units 14, Toll. Corr. subtracts 1d, consistent with shares for 14 units, increment for units 13–17, and Table N1.

Units 17, King. Corr. adds 0.5d, consistent with the total of toll plus shares for 17 units, the increment for King for 13–16 units, and Table N1.

Units 24, Knights. Corr. subtracts 1d, consistent with the total of toll minus shares for 24 units and the increment for Knights at 19–23 units and elsewhere. Not consistent with Table N1.

Units 26, King and Knights. Corrs. add 1d for King, subtract 5.5d for Knights, consistent with the total of toll minus shares for 26 units and the shares for King and Knights at 28 units, assuming increments at 27–8 units for King of 20.6d and for Knights of 5.5d; also consistent with Table N1.

Units 27, Toll, King, Knights. MS T omits line entirely.

Units 30, Knights. Corr. adds 0.5d, consisent with the total of toll minus shares for 30 units and the increment for Knights at 26–36 units; not consistent with Table N1.

Units 37, Knights. Corr. adds 0.5d, consistent with the total of toll minus shares for 37 units and the share for Kngiths at 38 units (as corrected) and 39 units. Consistent with Table N1 as corrected.

Units 38, Knights. Corr. subtracts 0.5d, consistent with the total of toll minus shares for 38 units, the increments for Knights at 39 units and elsewhere, and Table N1 as corrected.

Appendix 2

Comparison of Tables T2 and T3

The *Montazon* on Salt at Tarascon, Versions 1 and 2

MS T, f. 15v–16r and 16r–17r

Legend
Units: Hogsheads.
T2: *Montazon* in Table T2.
Corr.: Editorial correction to the preceding column.
Incr.: Increment of this figure over the preceding one.
Rate: *Montazon* divided by units.
T3: *Montazon* in Table T3.
All values are given in deniers.

Units	Table T2	Corr.	Incr.	Rate	Table T3	Incr.	Rate	T3 - T2
1	4.50			4.50	4.50		4.50	0.00
2	9.00		4.50	4.50	9.00	4.50	4.50	0.00
3	13.50		4.50	4.50	13.50	4.50	4.50	0.00
4	18.00		4.50	4.50	18.00	4.50	4.50	0.00
5	22.50		4.50	4.50	22.50	4.50	4.50	0.00

6	27.00		4.50	4.50	27.00	4.50	4.50	0.00
7	31.50		4.50	4.50	31.50	4.50	4.50	0.00
8	36.00		4.50	4.50	36.00	4.50	4.50	0.00
9	60.00		24.00	6.67	60.00	24.00	6.67	0.00
10	64.50		4.50	6.45	64.50	4.50	6.45	0.00
11	69.00		4.50	6.27	69.00	4.50	6.27	0.00
12	78.00		9.00	6.50	80.00	11.00	6.67	2.00
13	82.50		4.50	6.35	82.50	2.50	6.35	0.00
14	87.00		4.50	6.21	87.00	4.50	6.21	0.00
15	91.50		4.50	6.10	91.50	4.50	6.10	0.00
16	96.00		4.50	6.00	96.00	4.50	6.00	0.00
17	100.50		4.50	5.91	100.50	4.50	5.91	0.00
18	108.75		8.25	6.04	108.00	7.50	6.00	–0.75
19	113.25		4.50	5.96	113.25	5.25	5.96	0.00
20	106.75	117.75	4.50	5.89	117.75	4.50	5.89	0.00
21	122.25		4.50	5.82	122.25	4.50	5.82	0.00
22	126.75		4.50	5.76	126.75	4.50	5.76	0.00
23	131.25		4.50	5.71	131.25	4.50	5.71	0.00
24	135.75		4.50	5.66	135.75	4.50	5.66	0.00
25	149.25		13.50	5.97	149.25	13.50	5.97	0.00
26	153.75		4.50	5.91	153.75	4.50	5.91	0.00
27	159.25		5.50	5.90	158.25	4.50	5.86	–1.00
28	162.75		3.50	5.81	162.75	4.50	5.81	0.00
29	167.25		4.50	5.77	167.25	4.50	5.77	0.00
30	171.75		4.50	5.73	172.75	5.50	5.76	1.00
31	176.25		4.50	5.69	176.25	3.50	5.69	0.00
32	181.75		5.50	5.68	180.75	4.50	5.65	–1.00
33	185.25		3.50	5.61	185.25	4.50	5.61	0.00
34	189.75		4.50	5.58	189.75	4.50	5.58	0.00
35	194.75		5.00	5.56	194.75	5.00	5.56	0.00

Units	Table T2	Corr.	Incr.	Rate	Table T3	Incr.	Rate	T3 - T2
36	198.75		4.00	5.52	198.75	4.00	5.52	0.00
37	210.75		12.00	5.70	210.75	12.00	5.70	0.00
38	215.25		4.50	5.66	215.25	4.50	5.66	0.00
39	219.75		4.50	5.63	219.75	4.50	5.63	0.00
40	227.00		7.25	5.68	227.00	7.25	5.68	0.00

Note

Units 20. Toll in T2 is a reduction from preceding; this reduction creates an anomalous increment for following units. Corr. consistent with standard increment from 19 tc 24 units in MS T and with increment for this unit in T3.

Appendix 3

Analysis of Table N1

Salt in Small Hogsheads: Tolls and Shares

MS N, f. 2r18–4r11

Legend
Units: Small hogsheads.
Toll: As in MS N.
Corr.: Editorial correction to the preceding column.
Incr.: Increment of this figure over the preceding one.
Rate: Toll or share divided by units.
King: Share to the king as in MS.
Nobles: Share to the nobles as in MS.
Bal.: Balance (Toll minus King and Nobles, as corrected).
Om.: Omitted.
All values are given in deniers.

Units	Toll	Corr.	Incr.	Rate	King	Corr.	Incr.	Rate	Nobles	Corr.	Incr.	Rate	Bal.
1	29.75			29.75	22.75			22.75	7.00			7.00	0.00
2	59.50		29.75	29.75	45.50		22.75	22.75	14.00		7.00	7.00	0.00
3	101.25	89.25	29.75	29.75	68.25		22.75	22.75	21.00		7.00	7.00	0.00

Units	Toll	Corr.	Incr.	Rate	King	Corr.	Incr.	Rate	Nobles	Corr.	Incr.	Rate	Bal.
4	119.00		29.75	29.75	91.00		22.75	22.75	28.00		7.00	7.00	0.00
5	148.75		29.75	29.75	113.75		22.75	22.75	36.00	35.00	7.00	7.00	0.00
6	178.50		29.75	29.75	om.	136.50	22.75	22.75	54.00	42.00	7.00	7.00	0.00
7	205.25		26.75	29.32	157.75		21.25	22.54	47.50		5.50	6.79	0.00
8	232.00		26.75	29.00	179.00		21.25	22.38	53.00		5.50	6.63	0.00
9	284.00		52.00	31.56	206.00		27.00	22.89	78.00		25.00	8.67	0.00
10	310.00		26.00	31.00	226.50		20.50	22.65	om.	83.50	5.50	8.35	0.00
11	346.00	336.00	26.00	31.45	247.00		20.50	22.45	89.00			8.09	0.00
12	368.00		32.00	30.67	269.00		22.00	22.42	99.00		10.00	8.25	0.00
13	394.00		26.00	30.31	289.50		20.50	22.27	om.	104.50	5.50	8.04	0.00
14	420.00		26.00	30.00	310.00		20.50	22.14	110.00			7.86	0.00
15	446.00		26.00	29.73	330.50		20.50	22.03	103.50	115.50	5.50	6.90	0.00
16	472.00		26.00	29.50	351.00		20.50	21.94	121.00		17.50	7.56	0.00
17	498.00		26.00	29.29	371.50		20.50	21.85	126.50		5.50	7.44	0.00
18	529.00		31.00	29.39	393.25		21.75	21.85	135.25	135.75	9.25	7.51	0.00
19	556.00	555.00	26.00	29.26	413.75		20.50	21.78	141.25		6.00	7.43	0.00
20	581.00		25.00	29.05	434.25		20.50	21.71	146.75		5.50	7.34	0.00
21	607.00		26.00	28.90	454.75		20.50	21.65	152.25		5.50	7.25	0.00
22	633.00		26.00	28.77	476.25	475.25	20.50	21.65	157.75		5.50	7.17	0.00
23	659.00		26.00	28.65	495.75		19.50	21.55	163.25		5.50	7.10	0.00
24	685.00		26.00	28.54	516.25		20.50	21.51	171.00	168.75	5.50	7.13	0.00
25	723.00		38.00	28.92	527.75	539.75	23.50	21.11	183.25		12.25	7.33	0.00
26	749.00		26.00	28.81	560.25		32.50	21.55	188.75		5.50	7.26	0.00
27	775.00		26.00	28.70	580.75		20.50	21.51	194.25		5.50	7.19	0.00
28	801.00		26.00	28.61	601.25		20.50	21.47	199.75		5.50	7.13	0.00
29	827.00		26.00	28.52	621.75		20.50	21.44	205.25		5.50	7.08	0.00
30	853.00		26.00	28.43	642.25		20.50	21.41	210.75		5.50	7.03	0.00
31	879.00		26.00	28.35	662.75		20.50	21.38	216.25		5.50	6.98	0.00
32	905.00		26.00	28.28	683.25		20.50	21.35	221.75		5.50	6.93	0.00

33	931.00		26.00	28.21	703.25	703.75	20.50	21.31	227.25		5.50	6.89	0.00
34	959.00	957.00	26.00	28.21	724.00	724.25	21.00	21.29	232.25	232.75	5.50	6.83	0.00
35	993.00	983.00	24.00	28.37	744.75		20.75	21.28	238.25		6.00	6.81	0.00
36	1009.00		16.00	28.03	765.25		20.50	21.26	255.75	243.75	5.50	7.10	0.00
37	1045.00		36.00	28.24	788.25		23.00	21.30	255.75	256.75	1.00	6.91	0.00
38	1071.00		26.00	28.18	688.75	808.75	20.50	18.13	262.25		6.50	6.90	0.00
39	1097.00		26.00	28.13	829.25		140.50	21.26	267.75		5.50	6.87	0.00
40	1126.00		29.00	28.15	850.00		20.75	21.25	276.00		8.25	6.90	0.00

Notes
Units 3, Toll. Corr. consistent with Incr. for 1–6 units and Table T1.
Units 5, Nobles. Corr. consistent with Table T1 and Balance.
Units 6, King, om. in MS. Corr. consistent with Table T1 and Balance. Nobles, Corr. consistent with Table T1 and Balance.
Units 10, Nobles, om. in MS. Corr. consistent with Table T1 and Balance.
Units 11, Toll. Corr. consistent with Table T1 and Balance.
Units 13, Knights, om. in MS. Corr. consistent with Table T1 and Balance.
Units 15, Nobles. Corr. consistent with Table T1 and Balance.
Units 18, Nobles. Corr. consistent with Table T1 and Balance.
Units 19, Toll. Corr. consistent with Table T1 and Balance.
Units 24, Nobles. Corr. consistent with Table T1 and Balance.
Units 25, King. Corr. consistent with Table T1 and Balance.
Units 33, King. Corr. consistent with Table T1 and Balance.
Units 34, Toll, King, Nobles. Corr. consistent with Table T1 and Balance.
Units 35, Toll. Corr. consistent with Table T1 and Balance.
Units 36, Nobles. Corr. consistent with Table T1 and Balance.
Units 37, Nobles. Corr. consistent with total of Toll plus Shares for 37 units and Table T1.
Units 38, King. Corr. consistent with Table T1 and Balance.
Total: 17 corrections required to produce balance consistent with Table T1.

Appendix 4

Analysis of Table N2

Salt in Large Hogsheads: Tolls and Shares

MS N, f. 5v2–6r20

Legend
L.h.: Large hogsheads.
S.h.: Small hogsheads.
Corr.: Editorial correction to the preceding column.
L./S.: L.h. divided by S.h. as corrected.
Toll: As in MS N.
Incr.: Increment of this figure over the preceding one.
Rate: Toll or share divided by units.
King: Share to the king as in MS.
Nobles: Share to the nobles as in MS.
Bal.: Balance (Toll minus King and Nobles, as corrected).
All values are given in deniers.

L.h.	S.h.	Corr.	L./S.	Toll	Incr.	Rate	King	Incr.	Rate	Nobles	Incr.	Rate	Bal.
1	2+20/21		0.34	80.00		80.00	61.50		61.50	18.50		18.50	0.00
2	5+		0.41	160.00	80.00	80.00	122.25	60.75	61.13	37.75	19.25	18.88	0.00

3	8		0.38	240.00	80.00	80.00	185.00	62.75	61.67	54.00	28.25	18.00	1.00
4	10		0.40	320.00	80.00	80.00	234.00	49.00	58.50	86.00	32.00	21.50	0.00
5	13		0.38	400.00	80.00	80.00	294.00	60.00	58.80	106.00	20.00	21.20	0.00
6	16		0.38	480.00	80.00	80.00	348.00	54.00	58.00	123.00	17.00	20.50	9.00
7	19		0.37	560.00	80.00	80.00	405.50	57.50	57.93	142.50	19.50	20.36	12.00
8	22		0.36	640.00	80.00	80.00	480.50	75.00	60.06	159.50	17.00	19.94	0.00
9	25		0.36	720.00	80.00	80.00	537.50	57.00	59.72	182.50	23.00	20.28	0.00
10	25	28	0.36	720.00	0.00	72.00	537.50	0.00	53.75	199.50	17.00	19.95	–17.00
11	31		0.35	760.00	40.00	69.09	663.50	126.00	60.32	216.50	17.00	19.68	–120.00
12	34		0.35	960.00	200.00	80.00	784.50	121.00	65.38	233.50	17.00	19.46	–58.00
13	37		0.35	1040.00	80.00	80.00	784.50	0.00	60.35	256.50	23.00	19.73	–1.00
14	40		0.35	1120.00	80.00	80.00	844.00	59.50	60.29	276.00	19.50	19.71	0.00

Notes

Toll.: Incr. regular except for error (?) at 10 units and compensation for error at 11–12 units.

King: Incr. irregular throughout; zero at L.h. 10, 13.

Nobles: Incr. mostly irregular, with repetition of 17.00 at L.h. 6, 8, 10–12.

No corrections to Toll, King, or Nobles.

Bal. fails in seven of fourteen lines (50%), by large margins at L.h. 10, 11, 12; elsewhere by 1d, 9d, or 1s.

Appendix 5

Evolution of Tolls at Tarascon

Legend
MSS
A_1: Latin MS A_1, Aix-en-Provence, A.D. B.d.R., B 169; *enquête* 1252, MS second half of thirteenth century.
P: Latin MS P, Paris, B.n.F., lat. 10125; *enquête* 1252, MS end of the thirteenth century.
A_2: Latin MS A_2, Aix-en-Provence, A.D. B.d.R., B 1019; *enquête* 1298.
T: Occitan MS T, Tarascon, Archives municipales, AA9, f. 3r–17r; early fourteenth century.
N: Occitan MS N, Newberry Library (Chicago)/Northwestern University (Evanston) MS 1; Newberry Library, Vault Case MS 220; early fifteenth century.
Aggregates are given in deniers.

MS or MSS	A1	A1 & P	P	P & A2	A2	A2 & T	T	T & N	N
Toll-House									
Tarascon									
Total items	160		156		144		235		262
% of A1	100%		98%		90%		147%		164%
Aggregate	4,589.00		4,547.25		4,510.25		5,341.50		4,893.75
% of A1	100%		99%		98%		116%		107%
Items in Both		155		100		104		169	
In Only One		5 1		56 44		40 131		66 93	

Gate(s) of T.																	
Total items	57				57				52				79				115
% of A1	100%				100%				91%				139%				202%
Aggregate	688.75				688.75				626.25				1126.5				1541
% of A1	100%				100%				91%				164%				224%
Items in Both			57				48				48				60		
In Only One		0		0		9		4		4		31		19		55	
Saint-Gabriel																	
Total items	68				68				57				31				42
% of A1	100%				100%				84%				46%				62%
Aggregate	674.50				629.50				530.25				455.00				871.00
% of A1	100%				93%				79%				67%				129%
Items in Both			68				34				16				13		
In Only One		0		0		34		23		41		15		18		29	
Bridge																	
Total items	25				25												
% of A1	100%				100%												
Aggregate	24.25				24.25												
% of A1	100%				100%												
Items in Both			25														
In Only One		0		0													
Lubières																	
Total items									43				136				138
% of A2									100%				316%				321%
Aggregate									360.50				519.50				574.50
% of A2									100%				144%				159%
Items in Both											32				100		
In Only One										11		104		36		38	
All Five Toll-Houses																	
Total Items	310				306				296				481				557
% of A1	100%				99%				95%				155%				180%

MS or MSS	A1	A1 & P	P	P & A2	A2	A2 & T	T	T & N	N
Total Aggregate	5,976.50		5,889.75		5,666.75		6,923.00		7,305.75
% of A1	100%		99%		95%		116%		122%
Pezage on Salt							Table T1		Table N1
Hogsheads (Small)							40		40
Total Aggregate							22,798.50		23,605.00
% of Table T1							100%		104%
Large Hogsheads									14
Total Aggregate									8,200.00
Montazon on Salt						Table T2		Table T3	
Hogsheads (Small)					40	40		40	
Total Aggregate					6,285.00	4,703.50		4,700.25	
% of A2					100%	75%		75%	

Concordance of Items, as numbered by Bondurand, with folio and line in MS T

B. n. = Bondurand number

B. n. 1: T3r7
B. n. 2: T3r9
B. n. 3: T3r11
B. n. 4: T3r13
B. n. 5: T3r14
B. n. 6: T3r16
B. n. 7: T3r17
B. n. 8: T3r19
B. n. 9: T3r21
B. n. 10: T3r22
B. n. 11: T3r23
B. n. 12: T3r24
B. n. 13: T3r25
B. n. 14: T3r26
B. n. 15: T3r27
B. n. 16: T3r28
B. n. 17: T3r29
B. n. 18: T3v1
B. n. 19: T3v2
B. n. 20: T3v3
B. n. 21: T3v12
B. n. 22: T3v13
B. n. 23: T3v14
B. n. 24: T3v15
B. n. 25: T3v16
B. n. 26: T3v17
B. n. 27: T3v18
B. n. 28: T3v19
B. n. 29: T3v20
B. n. 30: T3v21
B. n. 31: T3v22
B. n. 32: T3v23
B. n. 33: T3v24
B. n. 34: T3v25
B. n. 35: T3v26
B. n. 36: T3v27
B. n. 37: T3v28
B. n. 38: T3v29
B. n. 39: T3v30
B. n. 40: T3v31
B. n. 41: T3v32
B. n. 42: T3v33
B. n. 43: T4r1
B. n. 44: T4r2
B. n. 45: T4r3
B. n. 46: T4r4
B. n. 47: T4r5
B. n. 48: T4r6
B. n. 49: T4r7
B. n. 50: T4r8

B. n. 51: T4r10
B. n. 52: T4r12
B. n. 53: T4r13
B. n. 54: T4r14
B. n. 55: T4r15
B. n. 56: T4r16
B. n. 57: T4r21
B. n. 58: T4r27
B. n. 59: T4r28
B. n. 60: T4r29
B. n. 61: T4r30
B. n. 62: T4r31
B. n. 63: T4r32
B. n. 64: T4r33
B. n. 65: T4r34
B. n. 66: T4r35
B. n. 67: T4v1
B. n. 68: T4v2
B. n. 69: T4v3
B. n. 70: T4v4
B. n. 71: T4v9
B. n. 72: T4v12
B. n. 73: T4v17
B. n. 74: T4v23
B. n. 75: T4v27
B. n. 76: T4v31
B. n. 77: T4v33
B. n. 78: T5r1
B. n. 79: T5r2
B. n. 80: T5r4
B. n. 81: T5r15
B. n. 82: T5r20
B. n. 83: T5r25
B. n. 84: T5r[38]
B. n. 85: T5r[42]
B. n. 86: T5r[32]
B. n. 87: T5v1
B. n. 88: T5v2
B. n. 89: T5v3
B. n. 90: T5v4
B. n. 91: T5v5
B. n. 92: T5v12
B. n. 93: T5v15
B. n. 94: T5v17
B. n. 95: T5v20
B. n. 96: T5v26
B. n. 97: T5v30
B. n. 98: T5v33
B. n. 99: T5v35
B. n. 100: T5v36
B. n. 101: T6r1
B. n. 102: T6r2
B. n. 103: T6r3
B. n. 104: T6r5
B. n. 105: T6r6
B. n. 106: T6r7
B. n. 107: T6r8
B. n. 108: T6r9
B. n. 109: T6r12
B. n. 110: T6r13
B. n. 111: T6r14
B. n. 112: T6r15
B. n. 113: T6r16
B. n. 114: T6r18
B. n. 115: T6r24
B. n. 116: T6r25
B. n. 117: T6r26
B. n. 118: T6r27
B. n. 119: T6v1
B. n. 120: T6v2
B. n. 121: T6v3
B. n. 122: T6v4
B. n. 123: T6v5
B. n. 124: T6v6
B. n. 125: T6v7
B. n. 126: T6v12
B. n. 127: T6v13
B. n. 128: T6v14
B. n. 129: T6v15
B. n. 130: T6v16

B. n. 131: T6v17
B. n. 132: T6v18
B. n. 133: T6v19
B. n. 134: T6v24
B. n. 135: T6v25
B. n. 136: T6v26
B. n. 137: T6v27
B. n. 138: T6v28
B. n. 139: T7r1
B. n. 140: T7r2
B. n. 141: T7r3
B. n. 142: T7r8
B. n. 143: T7r9
B. n. 144: T7r10
B. n. 145: T7r11
B. n. 146: T7r12
B. n. 147: T7r13
B. n. 148: T7r14
B. n. 149: T7r15
B. n. 150: T7r16
B. n. 151: T7r17
B. n. 152: T7r21
B. n. 153: T7r24
B. n. 154: T7v1
B. n. 155: T7v4
B. n. 156: T7v8
B. n. 157: T7v15
B. n. 158: T7v17
B. n. 159: T7v19
B. n. 160: T7v29
B. n. 161: T7v30
B. n. 162: T8r1
B. n. 163: T8r2
B. n. 164: T8r3
B. n. 165: T8r4
B. n. 166: T8r5
B. n. 167: T8r6
B. n. 168: T8r7
B. n. 169: T8r8
B. n. 170: T8r9
B. n. 171: T8r10
B. n. 172: T8r11
B. n. 173: T8r12
B. n. 174: T8r14
B. n. 175: T8r15
B. n. 176: T8r16
B. n. 177: T8r19
B. n. 178: T8r22
B. n. 179: T8v1
B. n. 180: T8v3
B. n. 181: T8v10
B. n. 182: T8v12
B. n. 183: T8v16
B. n. 184: T8v17
B. n. 185: T8v22
B. n. 186: T8v26
B. n. 187: T9r1
B. n. 188: T9r4
B. n. 189: T9r5
B. n. 190: T9r8
B. n. 191: T9r13
B. n. 192: T9r15
B. n. 193: T9r19
B. n. 194: T9v2
B. n. 195: T9v8
B. n. 196: T9v12
B. n. 197: T9v14
B. n. 198: T9v16
B. n. 199: T9v20
B. n. 200: T9v23
B. n. 201: T9v25
B. n. 202: T10r2
om. B: Table T1
B. n. 203: T11v22
B. n. 204: T12r7
B. n. 205: T12r11
B. n. 206: T12r15
B. n. 207: T12r19
B. n. 208: T12r26
B. n. 209: T12v1

B. n. 210: T12v5
B. n. 211: T12v12
B. n. 212: T12v21
B. n. 213: T12v26
B. n. 214: T13r6
B. n. 215: T13r10
B. n. 216: T13r14
B. n. 217: T13r19
B. n. 218: T13r25
B. n. 219: T13r26
B. n. 220: T13v1
B. n. 221: T13v4
B. n. 222: T13v5
B. n. 223: T13v6
B. n. 224: T13v 9
B. n. 225: T13v11
B. n. 226: T13v14
B. n. 227: T13v17
B. n. 228: T13v21
B. n. 229: T13v23
B. n. 230: T13v26
B. n. 231: T13v29
B. n. 232: T13v33
B. n. 233: T14r7
B. n. 234: T14r8
B. n. 235: T14r9
B. n. 236: T14r9
B. n. 237: T14r10
B. n. 238: T14r11
B. n. 239: T14r12
B. n. 240: T14r13
B. n. 241: T14r14
B. n. 242: T14r15
B. n. 243: T14r15
B. n. 244: T14r18
B. n. 245: T14r23
B. n. 246: T14r24
B. n. 247: T14r25
B. n. 248: T14r26
B. n. 249: T14r27
B. n. 250: T14r28
B. n. 251: T14r29
B. n. 252: T14r30
B. n. 253: T14r31
B. n. 254: T14r32
B. n. 255: T14r33
B. n. 256: T14r34
B. n. 257: T14r35
B. n. 258: T14v1
B. n. 259: T14v3
B. n. 260: T14v4
B. n. 261: T14v5
B. n. 262: T14v6
B. n. 263: T14v7
B. n. 264: T14v8
B. n. 265: T14v10
B. n. 266: T14v12
B. n. 267: T14v15
B. n. 268: T14v19
B. n. 269: T14v23
B. n. 270: T14v25
B. n. 271: T14v27
B. n. 272: T14v28
B. n. 273: T14v30
B. n. 274: T14v31
B. n. 275: T15r1
B. n. 276: T15r2
B. n. 277: T15r14
B. n. 278: T15r15
B. n. 279: T15r16
B. n. 280: T15r17
B. n. 281: T15r18
B. n. 282: T15r20
B. n. 283: T15r21
B. n. 284: T15r22
B. n. 285: T15r23
B. n. 286: T15r24
B. n. 287: T15r25
B. n. 288: T15r26
B. n. 289: T15r27

B. n. 290: T15r28
B. n. 291: T15v1
B. n. 292: T15v7
B. n. 293: T15r10
B. n. 294: T15v17
om. B: Table T2
B. n. 295: T16r18
om. B: Table T3

Works Cited

Abu-Lughod, Janet L. 1989. *Before European Hegemony: The World System A.D. 1250–1350.* New York: Oxford University Press.

Akehurst, F.R.P. 2005. "Adultery in Gascony." In *De sens rassis: Essays in Honor of Rupert T. Pickens.* edited by Keith Busby, Bernard Guidot, and Logan E. Whalen, 1–15. Faux Titre 259. Amsterdam: Rodopi.

Alcover, Antoni Maria. 1968–9. *Diccionari català-valencià-balear.* 2nd ed. 10 vols. Palma de Mallorca: Alcover.

Alibert, Louis. 1966. *Dictionnaire occitan-français selon les parlers languedociens.* Toulouse: Institut d'Études Occitanes.

Allaire, Gloria. 2002. *Il tristano panciatichiano. Arthurian Archives 8*, vol. 1. Italian Literature. Woodbridge: Boydell & Brewer.

Appel, Carl. 1930. *Provenzalische Chrestomathie mit Abriss der Formenlehre und Glossar.* 6th ed. Leipzig: Reisland. Reprint Olms: Hildesheim, 1971.

Arlinghaus, Franz. 2004. "Bookkeeping, Double-entry." In *Medieval Italy: An Encyclopedia*, edited by Christopher Kleinhenz, 1:147–50. 2 vols. New York: Routledge.

Asperti, Stefano. 1995. *Carlo I d'Angiò e i trovatori: componenti "provenzali" e angioini nella tradizione manoscritta della lirica trobadorica.* Ravenna: Longo.

Aurell, Martin. 1986. *Une famille de la noblesse provençale au Moyen Âge: Les Porcelet.* [Avignon:] Aubanel.

Aurell, Martin. 1989. *La vielle et l'épée: troubadours et politique en Provence au XIIIe siècle.* Paris: Aubier.

Aurell, Martin, Jean-Paul Boyer, and Noël Coulet. 2005. *La Provence au Moyen Âge.* Aix-en-Provence: Publications de l'Université de Provence.

Balard, Michel, Jean-Philippe Genet, and Michel Rouche. 2003. *Le Moyen Âge en Occident.* New ed. Paris: Hachette.

Baldinger, Kurt, and Inge Popelar. 1975–. *Dictionnaire onomasiologique de l'ancien occitan: DAO*. Tübingen: M. Niemeyer. *Supplément*, 1980–.

Baratier, Édouard. 1961. *La démographie provençale du XIIIe au XVIe siècle*. [Paris:] S.E.V.P.E.N.

Baratier, Édouard. 1969. *Enquêtes sur les droits et revenus de Charles Ier d'Anjou en Provence (1252 et 1278)*. Paris: Bibliothèque nationale.

Baratier, Édouard, Georges Duby, and Ernest Hildesheimer. [1969.] *Atlas historique: Provence, Comtat Venaissin, principauté d'Orange, comté de Nice, principauté de Monaco*. Paris: Colin.

Baratier, Édouard, and Félix Reynaud. 1951. *Histoire du commerce de Marseille*. Edited by Gaston Rambert. Vol. 2: *De 1291 à 1480*. Paris: Plon.

Battaglia, Salvatore. 1961–2002. *Grande dizionario della lingua italiana*. 21 vols. Turin: Unione tipografico-editrice torinese.

Bautier, Robert-Henri. 1989. "La circulation fluviale dans la France médiévale." *Recherches sur l'économie de la France médiévale. Les voies fluviales–La draperie. Actes du 112e Congrès national des Sociétés savantes (Lyon, 1987). Section d'histoire médiévale*. Paris. Reprinted in Bautier, *Sur l'histoire économique de la France médiévale. La route, le fleuve, la foire*. Hampshire: Variorum, 1991. Article V.

Bautier, Robert-Henri, and Janine Sornay. 1968–74. *Les sources de l'histoire économique et sociale du Moyen Âge. Part I: Provence, Comtat Venaissin, Dauphiné, États de la maison de Savoie*. 3 vols. Paris: C.N.R.S.

Bec, Pierre. 1984. *Burlesque et obscénité chez les troubadours: pour une approche du contre-texte médiéval*. Paris: Stock.

Bennett, Judith M., and Ruth Mazo Karras, eds. 2013. *Oxford Handbook of Women and Gender in Medieval Europe*. Oxford: Oxford University Press. http://dx.doi.org/10.1093/oxfordhb/9780199582174.001.0001. Consulted 12 August 2015.

Benoit, Fernand. 1925. *Recueil des actes des comtes de Provence appartenant à la maison de Barcelone: Alphonse II et Raimond-Bérenger V (1196–1245)*. 2 vols. Paris and Monaco: Imprimerie de Monaco.

Bertran Boysset. 1893. "Die Chronik des Garoscus de Ulmoisca Veteri und Bertrand Boysset (1365–1415)." Edited by Franz Ehrle. *Archiv für Literatur- und Kirchengeschichte des Mittelalters* 7:311–420.

Bibliothèque nationale de France. Dossier pédagogique: Le franc. Repères: cours, poids, titre. Online. http://classes.bnf.fr/franc/nav/droite/dte_cour.htm. Consulted 27 October 2013.

Biraben, Jean-Noël. 1975–6. *Les hommes et la peste en France et dans les pays européens et méditerranéens*. 2 vols. Paris: Mouton.

Blancard, Louis. 1868. *Essai sur les monnaies de Charles Ier comte de Provence*. Paris: Dumoulin.

Bloch, Marc. 1931. *Les caractères originaux de l'histoire rurale française.* Oslo: H. Aschehoug.

Blois, Guy. 1976. "Noblesse et crise des revenus seigneuriaux en France aux XIVe et XVe siècles: essai d'interprétation." In *La noblesse au Moyen Âge,* edited by Philippe Contamine, 219–33. Paris: Presses Universitaires de France.

Bloomfield, Morton W. 1955. "The Magic of In Principio." *Modern Language Notes* 70, no. 8: 559–65. http://dx.doi.org/10.2307/3040442. Consulted 12 August 2015.

Bofarull y Mascaró, Próspero de, Manuel de Bofarull y de Sartorio, and Francisco de Asís de Bofarull y Sans. 1871. *Archivo General de la Corona de Aragón.* Colección de documentos inéditos del Archivo General de la Corona de Aragón 39. [Barcelona:] J.E. Montfort.

B[oislisle], A. [de]. 1872. "Variétés: Projet de croisade du premier Duc de Bourbon (1316–1333) (Suite)." *Annuaire-Bulletin de la Société de l'histoire de France* 9:246–55, 272.

Bondurand, Édouard. 1890. "Les Péages de Tarascon, texte provençal." *Mémoires de l'Académie de Nîmes.* Ser. 7. 13:135–59.

Bondurand, Édouard. 1891a. "Les coutumes de Tarascon." *Mémoires de l'Académie de Nîmes.* Ser 7. 14:27–160.

Bondurand, Édouard. 1891b. *Les Péages de Tarascon, texte provençal. Extrait des Mémoires de l'Académie de Nîmes, 1890.* Nîmes: F. Chastanier.

Bonnassie, Pierre. 1999. "Liberté et servitude." In *Dictionnaire raisonné de l'Occident médiéval*, edited by Jacques Le Goff and Jean-Claude Schmitt, 595–609. [Paris:] Fayard.

Boström, Ingemar. [1985.] *Anonimo meridionale: Due libri di cucina.* Stockholm: Almqvist & Wiksell International.

Bourilly, Joseph. 1928. *Le costume en Provence au Moyen Age.* With drawings by Étienne Laget. Marseille: Institut historique de Provence.

Boutière, Jean, and A.H. Schutz. 1973. *Biographies des troubadours: textes provençaux des XIIIe et XIVe siècles.* 2nd ed., with Irénée-Marcel Cluzel and M. Woronoff. Paris: Nizet.

Boyer, Marjorie Nice. 1976. *Medieval French Bridges: A History.* Cambridge, Mass.: Mediaeval Academy of America.

Cantalausa, Joan de. 2003. *Diccionari general occitan: a partir dels parlars lengadocians.* Lo monastèri (Rodés): Cultura d'óc.

Carbasse, Jean-Marie. 1987. "*Currant nudi*; la répression de l'adultère dans le Midi médiéval." In *Droit, histoire et sexualité*, edited by Jacques Poumarède and Jean-Pierre Royer, 83–102. [Villeneuve-d'Ascq:] Publications de l'Espace juridique.

Castellani, Arrigo. 1952. *Nuovi testi fiorentini del dugento.* 2 vols. Florence: Sansoni.

Chambers, Frank M. 1971. *Proper Names in the Lyrics of the Troubadours.* Chapel Hill: University of North Carolina Press.

Charlet, Jean-Louis. 1976. "Les ateliers monétaires des comtes de Provence." *Provence numismatique [Annales du Groupe numismatique de Provence]* no. 2, 3rd trimester. No pagination.

Charlet, Jean-Louis. 2004. "Les monnaies des comtes de Provence." *Annales du Groupe Numismatique de Provence* 17:31–47.

Corominas, Joan, with José A. Pascual. 1980–91. *Diccionário crítico etimológico castellano e hispánico.* 6 vols. Madrid: Gredos.

Coulet, Noël. 1988. *Aix en Provence: espace et relations d'une capitale (milieu XIVe s.–milieu XVe s.).* 2 vols. Aix-en-Provence: Université de Provence.

Coulet, Noël. 1991. "Un dragon nommé Tarascon." *Provence historique* 41:574–8.

Courcelles, Jean Baptiste Pierre Jullien de. 1820–2. *Dictionnaire universel de la noblesse de France.* 5 vols. Paris: Au Bureau général de la noblesse de France.

Cropp, Glynnis M. 1975. *Le vocabulaire courtois des troubadours de l'époque classique.* Genève: Droz.

Davidsohn, Robert. 1896–1908. *Forschungen zur älteren Geschichte von Florenz.* 4 vols. Berlin: Mittler.

De Roover, Raymond. 1956. "The Development of Accounting Prior to Luca Pacioli According to the Account-books of Medieval Merchants." In *Studies in the History of Accounting*, edited by A.C. Littleton and B.S. Yamey, 114–74. Homewood, IL: Irwin.

Delebecque, Catherine. 1929a. "Histoire de la ville de Tarascon depuis les origines jusqu'à l'avènement de la reine Jeanne (1343)." 3 vols. Dissertation, École nationale des Chartes, Paris. Manuscript preserved at the Bibliothèque des Archives municipales, Marseille, call number 24ii18, 19, 20.

Delebecque, Catherine. 1929b. "Histoire de la ville de Tarascon depuis les origines jusqu'à l'avènement de la reine Jeanne (1343)." *Positions des thèses* (École nationale des chartes, Paris). 57–67.

Denel, F. 1970. "La navigation sur le Rhône au XVe siècle d'après les registres de péage de Baix." *Annales du Midi* 82, no. 98: 287–99. http://dx.doi.org/10.3406/anami.1970.4685. Consulted 12 August 2015.

Derrer, Felix. 1974. *Lo Codi: eine Summa codicis in provenzalischer Sprache aus dem XII. Jahrhundert. Die provenzalische Fassung der Handschrift A (Sorbonne 632). Vorarbeiten zu einer kritischen Textausgabe.* Dissertation Universität Zürich. Zürich: Juris Verlag.

Desclot, Bernat. 1982. *Crònica.* Edited by Miquel Coll i Alentorn. Barcelona: Edicions 62.

Drouard, Alain. 1973. "Les juifs à Tarascon au Moyen Age." *Archives juives: Cahiers de la Commission française des archives juives* 10, no. 4: 53–60.

Du Cange, Charles du Fresne. 1883–7. *Glossarium mediæ et infimæ latinitatis.* 10 vols. Niort: L. Favre.

Dufourcq, Charles-Emmanuel. 1975. *La vie quotidienne dans les ports méditerranéens au Moyen Age: Provence-Languedoc-Catalogne*. Paris: Hachette.

Dufourcq, Charles-Emmanuel. 1980. "Chrétiens et musulmans durant les derniers siècles du Moyen Âge." *Anuario de Estudios Medievales* 10:207–25.

Duplessy, Jean. 1988–9. *Les monnaies françaises royales: de Hugues Capet à Louis XVI (987–1793)*. 2 vols. Paris: Maison Platt; Maastricht: A.G. van der Dussen.

Duplessy, Jean. 2004–10. *Les monnaies féodales françaises*. 2 vols. to date. Paris: Platt.

Du Roure, [Scipion]. 1906. *Généalogie de la maison d'Albe, marquis de Roquemartine. Les anciennes familles de Provence*. Paris: Champion,

Edler, Florence. 1934. *Glossary of Mediaeval Terms of Business, Italian Series, 1200–1600*. Cambridge, MA: The Mediaeval Academy of America.

Elbl, Martin Malcolm. 2000. "Economics and Trade." Friedman and Figg 2000:162–71.

Enlart, Camille. 1902–16. *Manuel d'archéologie française depuis les temps mérovingiens jusqu'à la renaissance*. 3 vols. Paris: A. Picard.

Enluminures, Les. [2011.] *Register of Toll Charges for Tarascon*. Lo registre del peage de Tarascon. Internet resource. http://www.textmanuscripts.com/descriptions_manuscripts/TM_275_Tarascon%20Peage.pdf. Consulted 4 November 2013.

Esquieu, Yves. 1979. "L'église Sainte-Marthe de Tarascon." *Congrès archéologique de France* 134:126–51.

Eusebi, Mario. 1969. "L'*ensenhamen* di Arnaut de Mareuil." *Romania* 90:14–30.

Faraudo de Saint-Germain, Lluís. Under construction. *Vocabulari de la llengua catalana medieval*. On line at www.iec.cat/faraudo. Consulted 20 August 2013.

Fauris de Saint-Vincens, Jules François Paul. 1778–80. *Mémoires sur les monnaies de Provence*. Reprint Nice: Serre Éditeur, 1977.

Feniello, Amedeo. 2011. *Sotto il segno del leone: storia dell'Italia musulmana*. Rome: Laterza.

Fennis, Jan. 1995. *Trésor du langage des galères: dictionnaire exhaustif*. 3 vols. Tübingen: Niemeyer.

Fettuciari, Jòrgi, Guiu Martin, and Jaume Pietri. 2003. *Dictionnaire provençal-français = diccionari provençau-francés*. Aix-en-Provence: Edisud.

Février, Paul-Albert. 1964. *Le développement urbain en Provence de l'époque romaine à la fin du XIVe siècle*. Paris: Boccard.

Fitting, Hermann, ed. 1906. *Lo Codi in der lateinischen Übersetzung des Ricardus Pisanus*. Halle: Niemeyer. Reprint Aalen: Scientia Verlag, 1968.

Forestié, Édouard. 1901. "Hugues de Cardaillac et la poudre à canon (XIVe siècle) (Suite)." *Bulletin archéologique et historique de la Société archéologique de Tarn-&-Garonne* 29:185–222.

Fourquin, Noël. 1990. "Navires marseillais du Moyen Age." In *Navigation et migrations en Méditerranée de la préhistoire à nos jours*, edited by Jean-Louis Miège, 181–250. Paris: Éditions du Centre National de la Recherche Scientifique.

Fourquin, Noël, and Philippe Rigaud. 1994. *De la nave au pointu: Glossaire nautique de la langue d'oc (Provence, Languedoc) des origines à nos jours*. Saint-Tropez-Toulon: Objectif Mer et Capian Méditerranée.

Frank, István. 1957. "Tomier et Palaizi, troubadours Tarasconnais (1199–1226)." *Romania* 78:46–85.

French, Katherine L. "Genders and Material Culture." Bennett and Karras 2013, 197–212.

Friedman, John Block, and Kristen Mossler Figg, eds. 2000. *Trade, Travel, and Exploration in the Middle Ages: An Encyclopedia*. New York: Garland.

Gasparri, Françoise. 1979. "Les Italiens à Orange au XIVe siècle." *Provence historique* 28:47–67.

Gasparri, Françoise. 1980. "La population d'Orange au XIVe siècle." *Provence historique* 30:215–18.

Gaudemet, Jean. 1987. *Le mariage en occident: les moeurs et le droit*. Paris: Cerf.

Germain, A. 1861. *Histoire du commerce de Montpellier*. 2 vols. Montpellier: Jean Martel aîné.

Germer-Durand, Eugène. 1868. *Dictionnaire topographique du département du Gard*. Paris: Imprimerie Impériale.

Godefroy, Frédéric. 1881–1969. *Dictionnaire de l'ancienne langue française et de tous ses dialectes du IXe au XVe siècle*. 10 vols. Paris: F. Vieweg.

Grafström, Åke. 1958. *Étude sur la graphie des plus anciennes chartes languedociennes*. Uppsala: Almqvist & Wiksells.

Groten, M. 1991. "Köln, 4. Wirtschaft." *Lexikon des Mittelalters* 5:1259–61.

Guérard, Benjamin, with Natalis de Wailly (pseud. Marion) and Léopold Delisle. 1857. *Cartulaire de l'abbaye de Saint-Victor de Marseille*. 2 vols. Paris: Lahure.

Guida, Saverio. 1979. "Nuovi documenti su alcuni trovatori del XIII secolo." *Cultura Neolatina* 39:81–105.

Guida, Saverio. 1987. "La tenzone fra Ricau de Tarascon e 'Cabrit.'." *Cultura Neolatina* 47:197–221.

Guida, Saverio. 2009. "Pour l'identification du troubadour Cabrit." *Cahiers de Civilisation Médiévale* 52:21–36.

Guida, Saverio, and Gerardo Larghi. 2014. *Dizionario biografico dei trovatori*. Modena: Mucchi.

Harvey, Ruth, and Linda Paterson. 2010. *The Troubadour Tensos and Partimens: A Critical Edition*. 3 vols. Cambridge: Brewer.

Hasenohr, Geneviève, and Michel Zink. 1992. *Dictionnaire des lettres françaises: Le Moyen Âge*. 2nd ed. Paris: Fayard.

Hébert, Michel. 1979. *Tarascon au XIVe siècle: histoire d'une communauté urbaine provençale*. Aix-en-Provence: Edisud.

Heers, Jacques. 1973. *L'Occident aux XIVe et XVe siècles: aspects économiques et sociaux*. 4th ed. Paris: Presses Universitaires de France.

Hodges, Laura F. 2000. "Dyes and Pigments." Friedman and Figg 2000:154–6.

Honnorat, Simon Jude. 1846–7. *Dictionnaire provençal-français*. Digne. Reprint Marseille: Lafitte Reprints, 1971.

Horden, Peregrine, and Sharon Kinoshita, eds. 2014. *A Companion to Mediterranean History*. West Sussex, England: John Wiley and Sons. http://dx.doi.org/10.1002/9781118519356. Consulted 12 August 2015.

Jal, A. (Augustin). 1848. *Glossaire nautique: répertoire polyglotte de termes de marine anciens et modernes*. Paris: Didot frères.

Janson, H.W. 1952. *Apes and Ape Lore in the Middle Ages and the Renaissance*. London: Warburg Institute, University of London.

Joanne, Paul. 1890–1905. *Dictionnaire géographique et administratif de la France*. 7 vols. Paris: Hachette.

Kahn, Salomon. 1899. "Les Juifs de Tarascon au moyen âge." *Revue des Etudes Juives* 39:95–112, 261–98.

Kelly, Kathleen Coyne. 2000. "Animals, Exotic." Friedman and Figg 2000:23–5.

Labande, Léon-Honoré. 1894–5. *Catalogue général des manuscrits des bibliothèques publiques de France. Départements*. Vols. 27–8: *Avignon*, vols. I–II. Paris: Plon.

Labande, Léon-Honoré. 1909. "Guide archéologique du Congrès d'Avignon." *Congrès archéologique de France, 76e session, Avignon, 1909* (published 1910). Paris: Picard. 1:2–314.

Lacroix, Paul. 1864. "Les graffiti du château de Tarascon." *Revue des sociétés savantes des départements*. 3rd ser. 4:330–3.

Lalou, E. "Péage." 1993. *Lexikon des Mittelalters* 6:1841–2.

Lane, Frederic C. 1964. "Tonnages, Medieval and Modern." *Economic History Review* 17, no. 2: 213–33.

Langdon, John L. 2000. "Transportation, Inland (European)." Friedman and Figg 2000:607–13.

Latham, R.E. 1975–2014. *Dictionary of Medieval Latin from British Sources*. London: Published for the British Academy by Oxford University Press.

Lecoy de la Marche, Albert. 1875. *Le Roi René: sa vie, son administration, ses travaux artistiques et littéraires*. 2 vols. Paris: Firmin-Didot Frères, Fils.

Lee, Geoffrey A. 1977. "The Coming of Age of Double Entry: The Giovanni Farolfi Ledger of 1299–1300." *Accounting Historians Journal* 4, no. 2: 79–95.

Leone, Alfonso. 2003. "Sul commercio degli schiavi a Napoli nel secolo XV." In *Il commercio a Napoli e nell'Italia meridionale nel XV secolo: fonti e problemi*, edited by Alfonso Leone, 115–20. Naples: Athena.

Levy, Emil. 1894–1924. *Provenzalisches Supplement-Wörterbuch: Berichtigungen und Ergänzungen zu Raynouards Lexique roman*. 8 vols. Leipzig: O.R. Reisland.

Levy, Emil. 1909. *Petit dictionnaire provençal-français*. 5th ed. Heidelberg: C. Winter, 1973.

Lewis, P.S. 1968. *Later Medieval France: The Polity*. London: Macmillan.

Lexikon des Mittelalters. 1977–99. 10 vols. Stuttgart: Metzler.

Lieftinck, G.I. 1954. "Pour une nomenclature de l'écriture livresque de la période dite gothique: Essai s'appliquant spécialement aux manuscrits originaires des Pays-Bas médiévaux." *Nomenclature des écritures livresques du IXe au XVIe siècle*. Paris: Centre national de la recherche scientifique. 15–34.

Littré, Émile. 2010. *Dictionnaire de la langue française*. Internet resource. http://littre.reverso.net/dictionnaire-francais/. Consulted 12 August 2015.

Lopez, Robert S. 1976. *The Commercial Revolution of the Middle Ages, 950–1350*. Cambridge: Cambridge University Press. http://dx.doi.org/10.1017/CBO9780511583933. Consulted 12 August 2015.

Maiden, Martin, and Mair Parry, eds. 1997. *The Dialects of Italy*. London: Routledge.

Malacarne, Giancarlo. 2000. *Sulla mensa del principe: alimentazione e banchetti alla corte dei Gonzaga*. Modena: Il Bulino.

Martin-Portier, Christine. 2006. "Les enquêtes domaniales des comtes de Provence Charles Ier (1250–52), Charles II (1296–99) et Robert Ier d'Anjou (1331–33): vigueries de Tarascon et d'Avignon. Édition et commentaire." 2 vols. Thèse de doctorat, Université d'Aix-en-Provence.

McGowan, Alan. 1981. *The Ship: Tiller and Whipstaff, the Development of the Sailing Ship, 1400–1700*. London: Her Majesty's Stationery Office.

McKee, Sally. 2013. "Slavery." Bennett and Karras 2013:281–94.

Meliga, Walter. 2008. "Ricau de Tarascon, Cabrit: *Cabrit, al meu veiaire* (BdT 422.2 = 105.1)." *Lecturae Tropatorum* 1. http://www.lt.unina.it/Meliga–2008.pdf. Consulted 17 November 2014.

Melville, Gert, and Martial Staub. 2008. *Enzyklopädie des Mittelalters*. 2 vols. Darmstadt: Primus.

Mesqui, Jean. 1986. *Le pont en France avant le temps des ingénieurs*. Paris: Picard.

Meyer, Paul. 1865. "Observations sur la publication de l'inventaire des archives de Tarascon-sur-Rhône." *Bibliothèque de l'École des Chartes* 26, no. 1: 65–70. http://dx.doi.org/10.3406/bec.1865.445991. Consulted 12 August 2015.

Meyer, Paul. 1865–7. *Collection des inventaires-sommaires des archives communales antérieures à 1790. Ville de Tarascon*. [Tarascon: s.d.].

Meyer, Paul. 1871. *Les derniers troubadours de la Provence*. Paris: Franck. Reprint Genève: Slatkine, 1973.

Meyer, Paul. 1891. Review of Bondurand 1891b. *Romania* 20:381–2.

Meyer, Paul. 1893. "Rapport de M. Paul Meyer sur une communication de M.E. Bondurand relative au *Livre rouge* de Tarascon-sur-Rhône." *Bulletin historique et du Comité des travaux historiques et scientifiques*. 503.

Miskimin, Harry A. 1969. *The Economy of Early Renaissance Europe, 1300–1460*. Englewood Cliffs: Prentice-Hall.

Mistral, Frédéric. 1879–87. *Lou trésor dóu Felibrige*. 2 vols. Aix-en-Provence: Veuve Remondet-Aubin.

Molin, Jean-Baptiste, and Protais Mutembe. 1974. *Le rituel du mariage en France du XIIe au XVIe siècle*. Paris: Beauchesne.

Monfrin, Jacques. 1996. "Discours de M. Jacques Monfrin, Président de la Société de l'histoire de France en 1996." *Annuaire-bulletin de la Société de l'histoire de France* 3–20. https://books.google.ca/books?id=hpcaSLyohIoC&pg=PA10&dq=meyer+inventaire+tarascon&hl=en&sa=X&ei=6Eb5Uee_BeeuyQHn9IGwDQ#v=onepage&q=meyer%20inventaire%20tarascon&f=false . Consulted 23 September 2014.

Nègre, Ernest. 1990–8. *Toponymie générale de la France*. 3 vols. Genève: Droz.

Niermeyer, Jan Fredrik, and C. van de Kieft. 2002. *Mediae Latinitatis lexicon minus*. 2nd ed. Revised by J.W.J. Burgers. 2 vols. Leiden: Brill.

Origo, Iris. 1955. "The Domestic Enemy: The Eastern Slaves in Tuscany in the Fourteenth and Fifteenth Centuries." *Speculum* 30, no. 3: 321–66. http://dx.doi.org/10.2307/2848074. Consulted 13 August 2015]

Oxford English Dictionary [electronic resource]. 1992, http://www.oed.com.turing.library.northwestern.edu. 2nd ed. Oxford: Oxford University Press.

Oxford Latin Dictionary. 2013. 2nd ed., 2 vols. Edited by P.G.W. Glare. Oxford: Oxford University Press.

Paden, William D. 1998. *An Introduction to Old Occitan*. New York: MLA.

Paden, William D. 2009. "La poésie des troubadours et le mariage: Deux pratiques sociales sans élément commun?" In *L'occitan, une langue du travail et de la vie quotidienne du XIIe au XXIe siècle: Les traductions et les termes techniques en langue d'oc. Actes du colloque de Limoges les 23 et 24 mai 2008*, edited by Jean-Loup Lemaître et Françoise Vielliard, 17–41. Ussel: Musée du Pays d'Ussel-Centre Trobar.

Pansier, P. (Pierre). 1924–32. *Histoire de la langue provençale à Avignon du XIIme au XIXme siècle*. 5 vols. Avignon: Aubanel frères.

Pasero, Nicolò. 1973. *Guiglielmo IX d'Aquitania: poesie*. Modena: STEM Mucchi.

Pécout, Thierry, and Germain Butaud. 2008. *L'enquête générale de Leopardo da Foligno en Provence orientale (avril–juin 1333)*. Paris: Éditions du Comité des travaux historiques et scientifiques.

Pécout, Thierry, with Christine Portier-Martin and others. 2010. *L'enquête générale de Leopardo da Foligno dans la viguerie de Tarascon: janvier-février 1332*. Paris: Éditions du Comité des travaux historiques et scientifiques.

Pegolotti, Francesco Balducci. 1936. *La pratica della mercatura*. Edited by Allen Evans. Cambridge, MA: The Mediaeval Academy of America.

Pfister, Max. 1980. *Einführung in die romanische Etymologie*. Darmstadt: Wissenschaftliche Buchgesellschaft.

Pillet, Alfred, and Henry Carstens. 1933. *Bibliographie der Troubadours*. Halle (Saale): M. Niemeyer.

Port, Célestin. 1854. *Histoire du commerce maritime de Narbonne*. Paris: Durand et Dumoulin.

Pressouyre, Sylvia. 1963. "Le château de Tarascon." *Congrès archéologique de France, CXXIe session, 1963, Avignon et Comtat Venaissin*. Paris: Société française d'archéologie. 221–43.

Pryor, John H. 1994. "The Mediterranean Round Ship." In *Cogs, Caravels and Galleons: The Sailing Ship 1000–1650*, edited by Robert Gardiner, 59–76. Conway's History of the Ship. London: Conway Maritime Press.

Pulsoni, Carlo. 1994. "'Lo senher que formet lo tro' (BdT 323,22) ed alcune considerazioni sul corpus poetico di Pons de Capduelh." *Studi provenzali e galeghi 89/94*. L'Aquila: Japadre. 81–119.

Raynouard, François-Just-Marie. 1844. *Lexique roman*. 6 vols. Paris: Silvestre.

Reale Accademia d'Italia. 1937. *Dizionario di marina medievale e moderno*. Rome: Reale Accademia d'Italia.

Renouard, Yves. 1941. *Les relations des papes d'Avignon et des compagnies commerciales et bancaires de 1316 à 1378*. Paris: Boccard.

Ricketts, Peter T. 2003. "La *chanso* de Ricau de Tarascon (PC 422,1): édition critique, traduction et notes." *Romance Philology* 57:65–70.

Ricketts, Peter T. 2005. *Concordance de l'occitan médiéval. COM2. Les troubadours, les textes narratifs en vers*. Turnhout: Brepols.

Riquer, Martín de. 1975. *Los trovadores: historia literaria y textos*. 3 vols. Barcelona: Planeta.

Rolland, Henri. 1956. *Monnaies des comtes de Provence, XIIe–XVe siècles*. Paris: Picard.

Ronjat, Jules. 1930–41. *Grammaire istorique des parlers provençaux modernes*. 4 vols. Montpellier: Société des langues romanes.

Rossiaud, Jacques. 2002. *Dictionnaire du Rhône médiéval: identités et langages, savoirs et techniques des hommes du fleuve (1300–1550)*. 2 vols. Grenoble: Centre Alpin et Rhodanien d'Ethnologie.

Rotman, Youval. 2014. "Forms of Slavery." Horden and Kinoshita 2014:263–78.

Roucaute, Emeline. 2009. *Ville de Tarascon, Direction des Archives et du Patrimoine. Actes constitutifs et politiques de la commune: Correspondance générale, Série AA. Inventaire*. Internet resource. http://www.tarascon.org/tarascon-en-provence/habiter-a-tarascon/mairie-services-administratifs/archives-municipales/141.html. Consulted 4 November 2013.

Roux, Claude. 2004. "Tarascon au XVe siècle: espace et société au temps des derniers comtes angevins de Provence (1400–1481)." Thèse de doctorat, Université Aix-Marseille 1.

Rouyer, Jules, and Eugène Hucher. 1858. *Histoire du jeton au Moyen Âge*. Paris: Chez Rollin.

Singer, Charles. 1948. *The Earliest Chemical Industry: An Essay in the Historical Relations of Economics and Technology, Illustrated from the Alum Trade*. London: Folio Society.

Smith, Cyril Stanley, and John G. Hawthorne. 1974. *Mappae clavicula: A Little Key to the World of Medieval Techniques*. Transactions of the American Philosophical Society, new ser., vol. 64, pt. 4. Philadelphia: American Philosophical Society.

Spadafora, Placido. 1709. *Prosodia italiana, óvero l'arte con l'uso degli accenti nella volgar favella d'Italia*. Palermo: Per Francesco Cichè.

Spufford, Peter. 1986. *Handbook of Medieval Exchange*. London: Royal Historical Society.

Spufford, Peter. 2002. *Power and Profit: The Merchant in Medieval Europe*. London: Thames & Hudson.

Stein, Henri. 1907. *Bibliographie générale des cartulaires français ou relatifs a l'histoire de France*. Paris: Picard. Nendeln, Liechtenstein: Kraus Reprint, 1967.

Stempel, Wolf-Dieter. 1996–. *Dictionnaire de l'occitan médiéval: DOM*. Tübingen: Niemeyer.

Stouff, Louis. 1970. *Ravitallement et alimentation en Provence aux XIVe et XVe siècles*. Paris-La Haye: Mouton.

Stouff, Louis. 1986. *Arles à la fin du Moyen-Age*. 2 vols. Aix-en-Provence: Publications Université de Provence.

[Thomas, Antoine.] 1891. "Chronique" [review of Bondurand 1891b]. *Annales du Midi* 3:419–20.

Tisseur, Claire. 1887. *Dictionnaire étymologique du patois lyonnais*. Lyon: H. Georg.

Tobler, Adolf, and Erhard Lommatzsch. 1925–. *Tobler-Lommatzsch Altfranzösisches Wörterbuch*. 12 vols. to date. Berlin: Weidmann.

Toutain, J. 1896. "Le territoire des Musulamii." *Mémoires de la Société nationale des antiquaires de France* 57:271–94.

Trésor de la langue française informatisé. No date. Internet resource. http://atilf.atilf.fr. ATILF: Analyse et traitement informatique de la langue française. CNRS. Université de Lorraine.

Unger, Richard W. 2000. "Ships and Shipbuilding." Friedman and Figg 2000:553–8.

Valérian, Dominique. 2014. "The Medieval Mediterranean." Horden and Kinoshita 2014:77–90.

Venturini, Alain. 2008. "Les monnaies en Provence orientale au moment de l'enquête de Leopardo da Foligno." Pécout and Butaud 2008:clxiv–clxxi.

Verlinden, Charles. 1955–77. *L'Esclavage dans l'Europe médiévale*. 2 vols. I: *Péninsule ibérique, France*. Brugge: De Tempel. II: *Italie, Colonies italiennes du Levant, Levant latin, Empire byzantin*. Gent: Rijksuniversiteit te Gent.

Vignal, Robert. 1989. "Le passage du Rhône à Tarascon." *Provence historique* 39, 157:385–9.

Villain-Gandossi, Christiane. 1968. "Le tirage du sel de Peccais à la fin du XIVe siècle d'après les livres de compte de Francesco Datini (1368–1379)." In *Le rôle du sel dans l'histoire*, edited by Michel Mollat, 173–81. Paris: Presses universitaires de France.

Villain-Gandossi, Christiane. 1969. *Comptes du sel* (Libro di ragione e conto di salle) *de Francesco di Marco Datini pour sa compagnie d'Avignon, 1376–1379*. Paris: Bibliothèque nationale.

Wailly, Natalis de. 1865. "Note relative à l'inventaire des archives de Tarascon-sur-Rhone." *Bibliothèque de l'École des Chartes* 26, no. 1: 171. http://dx.doi.org/10.3406/bec.1865.445996. Consulted 12 August 2015.

Wartburg, Walther von. 1928–. *Französisches etymologisches Wörterbuch*. 25 vols. to date. Bonn: Klopp.

Weiß, Stefan. 2002. *Die Versorgung des päpstlichen Hofes in Avignon mit Lebensmitteln (1316–1378): Studien zur Social- und Wirtschaftsgeschichte eines mittelalterlichen Hofes*. Berlin: Akademie Verlag.

Widmayer, Jeffrey Scott. 2004. "A Critical Edition of Montpellier H119: A Thirteenth-Century Old Occitan Coutumier." Dissertation, University of North Carolina at Chapel Hill.

Xhayet, Geneviève. 1990. "Partisans et adversaires de Louis d'Anjou pendant la guerre de l'Union d'Aix." *Provence historique* 40:403–27.

Zupko, Ronald Edward. 1978. *French Weights and Measures before the Revolution: A Dictionary of Provincial and Local Units*. Bloomington: Indiana University Press.

www.ingramcontent.com/pod-product-compliance
Lightning Source LLC
LaVergne TN
LVHW040151080826
844660LV00014B/922/J
* 9 7 8 1 4 4 2 6 2 9 3 4 9 *